I Wrote the Script, but I Want to Change the Ending

DALE PERRIN

iUniverse, Inc.
Bloomington

I Wrote the Script, but I Want to Change the Ending

iUniverse books may be ordered through booksellers or by contacting:

iUniverse
1663 Liberty Drive
Bloomington, IN 47403
www.iuniverse.com
1-800-Authors (1-800-288-4677)

Because of the dynamic nature of the Internet, any Web addresses or links contained in this book may have changed since publication and may no longer be valid. The views expressed in this work are solely those of the author and do not necessarily reflect the views of the publisher, and the publisher hereby disclaims any responsibility for them.

Any people depicted in stock imagery provided by Thinkstock are models, and such images are being used for illustrative purposes only.

Certain stock imagery © Thinkstock.

ISBN: 978-1-4502-6891-2 (sc)
ISBN: 978-1-4502-6892-9 (ebook)
ISBN: 978-1-4502-6893-6 (dj)

Library of Congress Control Number: 2010916049

Printed in the United States of America

iUniverse rev. date: 3/30/2011

for Irma,
the one person in the world who *knows* me
and loves me

"Now I don't know if it actually happened this way, but I know it's true."

—a Native-American storyteller whose name I do not know

ACKNOWLEDGEMENTS

I am immensely grateful to Kim McCarthy, Jodi Steele and Ira Henderson for their ongoing support and encouragement. I so appreciate their generous gift of time: hours upon hours of reading and editing. I extend a thank you and my appreciation to Lucy Freedman and Vince Gilpin. To Lindsey Mills, Linda Gerger, Pat Webster, Inge Neilson, Noreen Lachapelle, Terry Patterson and Margaret Black, a thank you for reading and validating several stories and helping me "remember." I thank Janet Saunders, Tessa Law, Janice Hatt, Mary Beer and Chris Jagt for their suggestions and editorial recommendations. I thank the iUniverse editorial staff for their expertise and support.

I extend a special thank you to Irma for her constant encouragement, insightful questions and suggestions. She has been, and continues to be, my inspiration, my model of strength and courage, a living affirmation that anything is possible.

And with deep affection and gratitude, I thank the men, women and children who have opened themselves to me during a time in their lives when they were most vulnerable. I am honoured and humbled to have walked with them during those challenging times.

Contents

AUTHOR'S STATEMENT

Memory is a complex phenomenon. I doubt whether any of the people mentioned in the stories you are about to read remember the incidents or events as happening in the exact same way that I do. And, I suspect, I may have forgotten significant statements or events relevant to the stories that may alter their "factual truths." Nonetheless, with notes and recordings written immediately or shortly after the reported experiences, with newspaper clippings and other documents and with the dust blown off the long-filed-away material stored in the memories of those who also lived through these scenes, I have given you "me."

In order to live the experiences, to present here-and-now moments in real time, I have taken liberties with dialogue and with the chronology of events.

With some examples of "therapy work," I have combined different experiences to better illustrate the significance of the work. And certainly with the story of my parents' romance, I allowed my fiction-writing spirit free rein.

I do hope your experience of reading is pleasurable and elicits many "aha" awarenesses that illuminate your own journey. If so, we may both celebrate success.

SPIRITUAL BIRTH:
FOR HEAVEN'S SAKE

After eons of deliberation, a radiant soul beamed with excitement. A decision! I can't stay here in this glorious garden, this oasis of comfort, just experimenting with the Creator's palette, painting with colours more brilliant than imaginable in any of the solar systems. No, I've got to explore the unknown. I need to know. I need ... well, I don't know what. Something! I know I can get closer to the Source, the Energy, the Light, if only ... Whatever it is, I know it will enrich my understanding and enhance my brilliance.

And so the radiant soul called forth the Council of Wisdom from the chambers in the mansions that surround the Source and made this special request.

"Wise guardians and nurturers of radiance, I would like to be sent to the planet Xpanex in the galaxy of Uratise. The life-form in existence there is so evolved, so pure of heart, so compassionate and in harmony with its surroundings. I just know my radiance would extend so much further with the experience of sharing a life span with these wonderful beings. May I have your permission to go?"

"Radiant one, what is it you feel you need to learn?" asked the senior guardian soul, cloaked in the traditional ruby-red garment of the council members.

"I want to expand my capacity for compassion and joy. I want to contribute, to comfort, to reflect courage. That's it! That's what I want."

The guardians and nurturers of radiance, glancing quickly at each other, smiled that knowing smile, that smile one has for youth and innocence. "Dear radiant one," said the eldest guardian, "Xpanex's not the place to develop what you want. If you're serious, we'll empower you to exit to the planet Earth, the planet with just one moon, in the galaxy that is still expanding."

"But wise guardians and nurturers, humans, the most evolved life-form on the planet Earth as I understand them, are filled with fear. Aren't they the race of beings that reject differences and strike out with anger and rage, creating havoc around their own globe? Aren't they the ones who destroy their own environment? Aren't they the ones on the path of inevitable self-destruction? I see such little brilliance emanating from that planet. How do I learn compassion and joy with Earthlings?"

The councillors had not evolved into white-haired, tall, straight, eternally brilliant beings without having developed their capacity to mask their amusement and delight at the exuberance and curiosity of souls like this one, virtually dancing in front of them.

"Radiant soul," said the senior guardian, "where better to develop compassion? Anyone can love in an environment of peace and telepathic understanding. You'll be surprised to discover other radiant souls on the planet Earth, other souls on missions as great and as challenging as the one you propose. Earthlings, those of the human race, all began their journeys on Earth as radiant souls just like you."

"Oh dear, oh dear, does that mean I risk losing my radiance if I go to the planet Earth as a human?"

"What it means is that you'll be provided with the experiences you need to learn your lessons and evolve the way you've identified. The lessons are in the experiences, and what happens will be up to you."

"But will I be able to meet the challenges and learn the lessons? What if I stumble? Will my light be extinguished?" asked the radiant soul, beginning to experience fear—that most human of all emotions.

"We'll be available to guide you. You won't be alone."

"Ah, that must mean you'll give me a partner for this journey, someone on Earth to guide me through the labyrinth of experience," the radiant soul said, with obvious relief.

The councillors struggled to keep their wise demeanor. They knew this soul, transparent and so sincere, would be a challenge for the world in which it found itself.

"We believe you'll learn best traveling on your own and being available, vulnerable and open to the meaning of humanness. You've got to trust our wisdom. Take whatever time you need, dear soul, to decide if this is important to you. You're radiant and perfect here just as you are. It's up to you."

With a fading of pink-purple colour, not unlike the setting of the Earth's sun as experienced by humans, the councillors disappeared, returning to their chambers the same mysterious way they had come. The radiant soul, conscious again of the garden, decided to meditate. *Do I really need to evolve? Do I really need to take the risk of having my radiance extinguished?*

Like the rising of the Earth's sun, the answer slowly surfaced, yellow-gold brilliant and certain.

On Earth on the ides of March—according to calculations on the time chart called a calendar—in the Earth year 1938, a little girl was born to Don and Louise Perrin, a beautiful, radiant light that beamed good health and innocence. With big brown eyes as yet unfocused, she looked up at these humans who would be called "parents" and experienced an enveloping welcome.

BOOK ONE

BOOK ONE

ALL THE WORLD'S A STAGE

In some respects my life as a psychotherapist paralleled that of a police detective. Given fragments of information, hidden or obscured data related to me by the person seeking therapy—data frequently given without awareness of its significance—we teamed together to weave a tapestry highlighting the patterns so that the information-giver could see and recognize their own drama. We did this through the intensive investigation of emotional scenes, gathering clues and having them processed through the laboratory of the person's adult awareness.

In some ways we (the storyteller and I) were artists, not just detecting and weaving together remarkable threads but sculpting from the person's story, chiseling away irrelevant material to manifest the beautiful heart and soul of the storyteller. Then the task was to skillfully nurture that soul to reflect the authentic self. The storytellers frequently undervalued the uniqueness of their own stories. Not I. I was captivated and awed from the beginning of my professional practice, and especially so after I entered my own private practice, by the human drama shared with me in such intimate, graphic, emotionally intense detail. I was privileged to be welcomed into the lives of the storytellers and to bear witness to both their suffering and their healing.

I recognized early in my training as a psychotherapist—working with transactional analysis and gestalt theory and techniques—the concept of "script": how the child in the formative years makes decisions of critical significance, often of lifelong significance, based on his or her perception of reality. Those key decisions influence sexuality, career choices, marriage (or not), choice of spouse (or not), success (or not) and sometimes health, disease or even premature death. That is not to say that early life decisions are not modified by maturity or altered by other significant events; they are. But I learned through my experiences and training that if we could piece together the child's early life decisions, we could make sense of the adult's current pain or confusion and facilitate the healing process. I learned, too, that some scripts are tragic and some are not. The significant difference between the two patterns of scripts often is determined by the circumstances of conception, birth and the bonding and attachment of infant and parental figures. The more successful and complete the bonding, the less likelihood that the life will end with suicide, homicide, imprisonment or mental illness.

This is *my* story, the unfolding of *my* script. Can I weave my own tapestry? My own drama? My own mystery? And can I share these fragments of information, threads of events that shaped my life and being, in a way that allows you to bear witness to my evolution, to the healing into the me that I am today?

What were the circumstances of my conception and birth? What were my parents thinking and feeling as they prepared to bring me into this world? Was I to live a tragic script?

As my story unfolds, as I share the vignettes of my life, it is my hope that you will review those experiences in life that you hold sacred in the treasure box of your memory. And that you too will experience the "aha's" of awareness as script patterns emerge and the underlying decisions that may hold you "in script" surface. To assist you with your reflections, I have listed a set of questions after each story.

Will you journey along with me?

WHAT'S IN A NAME?

"Well, what did he say?" Don asked before Louise had even closed the apartment door.

"I'm pregnant," Louise said, approaching Don in the kitchen.

"Oh dear, we've got some decisions to make, Louise. I can tell by the look in your eyes that you're delighted—and that's great—but what are we going to do now?"

"We're going to have a baby. That's what we're going to do," Louise said, dropping her purse on the kitchen counter.

"I'll make us some coffee. We've got some talking to do," Don said, getting up from the table in the tiny yellow kitchen.

"Let me just go and check on the boys, honey. Then we can talk."

Louise opened the screen door leading to the flat roof of the back verandah, which served as a balcony for their second-floor apartment, and bent over the railing. From here she had a clear view of the backyard—the flower beds, the vegetable gardens and the play area, fenced in by the owners of the house, who were living on the main floor.

"How are you doing, sweetie?" she yelled down to Bayne, who was playing in the sandbox. Bayne, their three-year-old, looked up at his mom.

"Come see what I've made, Mommy. The cars go under this tunnel. See, Mommy? Is Daddy coming back down, Mommy? Can Kenny play with me now?"

Louise smiled—*he's so beautiful, this curly-headed, blue-eyed, little boy of ours.* "Kenny is still napping, Bayne. You go ahead and play. Daddy and I are right here in the kitchen if you want us."

Louise stepped back into the apartment and went to the small bedroom to check that Kenny was indeed sleeping. He was. Louise, smiling at their younger son, his blanket kicked off exposing a diapered bum and a small brown teddy bear, leaned over the crib and gently replaced the blanket. She picked up a dozen plastic soldiers, two unmatched socks, two storybooks and some crayons from the floor, tossing them all onto the blue-fringed bedspread on Bayne's bed, pushed up against the wall. She frowned at the blue of the bedspread, which didn't quite match the blue wallpaper with its white "kites and cars" design, and told herself for the hundredth time, "Kids don't care about such things."

Don had two cups of coffee on the table when Louise came back into the kitchen. He had tidied up the lunch dishes and had done the dusting and mopping while Louise had been at Dr. Gillespie's. He didn't much like this two-bedroom apartment. It was sparsely furnished with secondhand furnishings; it was cramped and in need of a major paint job. It certainly didn't feel like "home." Louise had done her best to make it attractive with prints, handmade throws and fresh bouquets of flowers when they were available. Granted, it was better than living with the Riehms and Elthea, Louise's older sister, on the corner of Alma and Cedar Street, and 7 Dekay Street was a whole lot closer to the Dominion Tire Factory.

"Honey, you know what I'm concerned about," Don said, getting up to get the sugar he had forgotten. "You're the most important person in my life. I love you—more every day! Weesa, I don't want to lose you …," Don said, choking back tears.

"Don, listen. I'll be fine. In my heart I just know that this baby is a girl. This is the daughter you and I talked about—and I want a little girl. I'm not going to die," Louise said firmly.

"But sweetheart, Dr. Gillespie told us after Kenny was born that you … well, that you … that is, that your heart couldn't take another pregnancy. He said … well, you know." Don, getting up, turned his back to Louise, not wanting her to see the tears in his eyes. He opened first one cupboard door, then another.

"What are you looking for, honey?"

"The cookies," Don said, without turning around.

"They're up above, honey, out of reach of the children."

Don, cookies in hand, returned to the table, composed.

"Did Dr. Gillespie mention the possibility of a D and C?"

"There will be no D and C, Don."

"Well, let's go and talk to him together. We still have time to think about this. I'm concerned about a second C-section. It's not that I don't want you to have the daughter you want or that I don't want another child; but we have no assurance that this will be a girl, and what's worse, Dr. Gillespie said there's a good probability ..."

"Don, we can go and talk to Dr. Gillespie together, but I'm telling you, there'll be no surgery." Louise got up and disappeared into the boys' bedroom. Don could hear her talking to Kenny.

Louise can be irritating, he thought. He knew from early experience that when Louise decided on something, she became an immovable object.

"I'm going downstairs to check on Bayne, Louise," he said, taking the coffee mugs to the sink as he headed for the stairs. *My God, my God, what's going to happen now? What if ...? How could I ...?*

"What? Yeah, I can see that, Bayne. That's terrific," he said in response to Bayne's comment. Smiling, he picked up the black toy Ford and began moving the car into the tunnel. *This is the same model that Louise bought,* he thought, and recalled the day that Lois, the eldest of his four sisters, introduced him to Louise. *You're wrong, Lois,* he thought. *She's anything but a "pussycat."*

"Donny, you've got to help my friend out," Lois had said, charging into the den where Don was reading. "You won't believe what Louise has done. You remember Louise. I've mentioned her before. She's the receptionist at the office, that sweet pussycat of a woman who mothers everyone who comes into the welfare office. I can't believe she'd do such a thing!"

"What?" Don asked, setting his book aside. "What are you talking about?"

"Louise! She told us that she was going to buy a car, but we didn't believe her. She can't drive."

"And?"

"She did. She just went out and bought a car. She paid a small fortune for it, Donny. I'm sure the salesman took advantage of her. She's so naive and trusting. She believes everybody!"

"What do you want me to do, Lois?" Don couldn't believe that anyone, especially a woman, would go and buy a car without first doing some research and getting comparative prices. Perhaps Louise had taken someone with her who knew about cars. *Lois probably doesn't have all the facts. She can be emotional and impulsive, this sister of mine.*

"Will you just come and check out the car and see if it's worth what Louise paid for it?"

"Okay, but I don't know what I can do about it now."

Reluctantly, Don had accompanied Lois to the office to meet Louise and arrange to look at the car, still at the dealership.

Don smiled to himself, remembering that occasion. He knew: he knew immediately that Louise was the woman he would marry. She was a slim, trim, neat young woman, with short, brownish-red hair closely framing her face on one side, a stylish flip on the other. She had big brown eyes framed in skin so white and clear. She seemed shy, vulnerable, transparent.

Yes, he did in fact check out the car and he did negotiate with the manager of the dealership to have $500 worth of repairs done to it immediately. The manager agreed to do the work free of charge and pleaded innocent of any fraudulent intent. Don agreed not to pursue court action. Louise was appreciative.

When they left the dealership, Don said, "My friends are having a party at the sergeants' mess hall on Saturday. Would you like to come with me?"

Louise said yes. After making the arrangements, Don left the dealership and Louise and headed back home, a bounce to his step, a smile on his face, whistling a nondescript tune. Louise, late for dinner, almost knocked Elthea over in her haste to greet her parents already sitting at the kitchen table.

"You look upset. What's happened, Louise? Are you okay?" Elthea asked.

"Oh, nothing," Louise said, attempting to be casual. "I just met Lois's brother, Don, at the dealership. I'm sorry I'm so late. I should've called."

"Is that why you're blushing? You like him, don't you?" Elthea asked, smiling and enjoying her sister's embarrassment.

"Oh, Elthea, he's so handsome. He was wearing this really stylish suit and a classy tie. And he has this unruly mop of hair, he wears glasses, he was smoking a pipe and he was so serious. He got the dealership to do repairs to the car, and you know what else? He asked me to go out to a party Saturday night. I think he likes me."

He did. She did—and the romance began.

Don, a soldier in the reserve army, was especially handsome dressed in the scarlet, blue and khaki regalia of the full-dress uniforms of the Scots Fusiliers of Canada. Neither he nor his friends were prepared for what was to come several years later. The Japanese had invaded Manchuria. Daily news reports indicated an escalation of their aggression. But that seemed far away. No one could really envision a second major conflict in Europe. Hitler was named Chancellor and shortly thereafter he dissolved Parliament. Over the next many months, he became dictator, started expelling Jews from the country and was rearming beyond the limitations imposed by the Treaty of Versailles. But those issues seemed remote and Don and Louise had a new and budding relationship underway.

After a few white-knuckle experiences with Louise behind the wheel of the car—including an accident in which Louise drove straight off the road into a ditch just inches away from a hydro pole—Don did what any noble suitor would have done: he offered to drive *all the time, everywhere*. And Louise accepted. Together with Lois and her suitor Frank, a tall, dark, handsome fellow with a dark, neatly trimmed mustache, a booming voice and a boisterous laugh, Don and Louise courted.

Sleigh riding in the bush behind the old farm where the neighbours kept "old Lady," the horse that the Riehms owned when they farmed; hiking experiences with Frank and Lois—and the winter of '33 just blew itself away. To Don, the spring meant tennis. After a noble but futile attempt at teaching Louise how to hit the ball, they both agreed that, well, Louise would just enjoy watching and applauding Don from the sidelines.

Lois and Frank married first, and before long Don and Louise were godparents. Don was deeply touched by the way Louise responded to the baby.

"Oh, you sweet little boy," Louise said, crinkling her nose and holding little Donny up so she could nuzzle his belly. "Such a cutie, such a wee precious soul. There, there, little one, that's it, you just burp," she said, gently rubbing his back as the baby chortled and made those sounds unique to infants.

In August Don told his family of his intentions to marry Louise. Sitting at the dining-room table in Lois's newly decorated apartment with Lois, Frank and his other three sisters, Fran, Inez and Eunice, Don announced, "Louise and I are going to get married on my birthday."

"Oh no, Donny," Fran said. "I thought you were going to marry Dorcas."

"Whatever gave you that idea?"

"Well, you and Dorcas have been friends all throughout high school. You always played tennis together. I thought—we all thought—well, we just assumed you would marry her."

"You two have a lot in common, Donny. Her family goes to the same church as we do, and her dad's been a friend of Dad's for years," Eunice said.

"What do you really know about Louise's family, Donny? They're from Germany and farmers! Now I've nothing against German people, or farmers, but you know it's better to marry someone from your own background. What could you possibly have in common with German farmers? And isn't Louise older than you, Donny?" Inez asked.

"Louise is a lovely woman with a heart of gold," Lois said, getting up to prepare the dessert. "You'll love her when you get to know her."

"Hold on!" Don said, visibly angry. "I'm not asking permission— just telling you. Louise and I will be getting married on my birthday!"

"We don't mean to be hurtful, Donny. We're just concerned about you; that's all. Of course we'll love her," Inez said.

His family's response had been the least of his concerns. What worried Don most was the issue of money—he didn't have any. He had started work at sixteen and finished his grade thirteen on a part-time basis. Several of his older siblings had gone to teachers' college, and Don had hoped to go to university. He knew that wasn't an option for him since the family could no longer afford such a luxury. His dad had abandoned the family the previous year and had gone off with a young widow who had a child. He had left his wife of many years and his own eight children, of which Don was the fifth. He knew that financially he was on his own. He began work at the Dominion Tire Factory—a good job, but not one that paid him a wage to support a wife and, later, children. He knew he couldn't really afford to marry, but life would certainly not be worth the struggle without Louise.

At the following Sunday dinner—the Riehms, Louise's parents, liked having the family together for Sunday dinners—Don talked about their plans. He enjoyed the warmth, the coziness, the unpretentiousness of the Riehm home, with its piano in the dining area; the big stuffed, flowered furniture, covered with hand woven afghans, in the living room; the wooden floor covered with handmade rag rugs; the big square kitchen with its iron gas-burning stove, always alive with boiling pots. The smells of fresh-baked breads and pies, endive salad, pot roast with onions and other delicious aromas made him feel welcome.

Sometime before the coffee and pie were served—he hadn't eaten much of that meal; it's hard to swallow when you're chewing on the most important words you're ever likely to say in your whole life—Louise and Elthea excused themselves as prearranged. "Mr. and Mrs. Riehm," Don said, "I would like permission to marry your daughter."

Don couldn't tell from outward appearances if the Riehms liked him. Unlike his family, the Riehms weren't demonstrative. Mr. Riehm was not a well man—Don wondered if he would live another two years—and Mrs. Riehm was inscrutable. She had a stern face, though not unkind, wore no makeup and had her grey-streaked hair pulled tightly into a bun at the back of her head.

William, Louise's dad, clean-shaven, moustache trimmed, simply dressed in clean work clothes, said, "Yes, Don, by all means. If you love our Louise, we'll be happy to have you in the family." There was no handshake, no congratulations, but no objections.

Pauline, Louise's mom, had more to say. "Don, you should know that Louise is a frail woman. She had scarlet fever as a child. We didn't think she would live. It left her with a weak heart. She gets tired easily and always seems to have a cold. The doctor said that we couldn't expect to see Louise reach her thirtieth birthday."

Don was shaken by the bluntness of Mrs. Riehm's statement. Louise mentioned having scarlet fever, but not the doctor's prediction. Maybe they hadn't told her. *It doesn't matter,* he thought. *I'd rather have a few years with Louise than a lifetime with anyone else.*

Louise had to confront a scary issue too. She knew when she married Don that she would have to give up her job at the welfare office. Government legislation required that married women not be employed. Supposedly that would make more jobs available for men. She loved her work at the relief department. It was the best job she had ever had and she had been working since the age of fifteen. She talked a lot about her work experiences with Don.

"Miss Jackson said the fire at the furniture factory last night was probably arson. She says that several hundred more people are now out of jobs and our welfare rolls are bound to go up again—not that they've ever stopped since I've been here. I don't know how on earth we're going to manage more people on relief. Miss Jackson believes there's no end in sight as far as she can predict and the city council has been insisting that she cut back the number of recipients on the rolls."

"Yeah, she's probably right. The editorial last night was talking about that. And you know who's going to pay the price—as if we're not already overtaxed! You know I don't mind paying my share of taxes, but it's the fraud that really gets me angry."

"Oh Don, you can't believe that stuff about fraud. I see people every day, people just like you and me, who're really scared and looking for work. They're good people, Don, not crooks. We're just lucky that we've got jobs. This depression has hurt everybody."

"Well, Louise, the city council and the police are looking into welfare fraud. They've set up a task force to examine the welfare records. Did you know that recently they've found businessmen's wives masquerading as single and penniless to claim welfare? And the paper reported 122 cases of people getting free clothing from the relief department while receiving steady incomes."

"I can't believe that. Sometimes I think the papers make things up just to make the politicians look good. I read that the mayor cut his salary this year by 50 percent. Do you believe that? The people I see don't have incomes to cut. Honestly, Don, these people are hurting. There are no jobs out there."

"Well, I don't think it helps when we have to deal with beggars knocking on the door asking for handouts. I'll bet many of those people are on relief and still asking for more."

"Oh honey, it's not like that, really. Remember the Schmids? I told you about them before. A couple of weeks ago, Mr. Schmid cried in Miss Jackson's office because he couldn't get his little girl a dress for confirmation. Little Martha—she's only seven years old—sat in the waiting room with me and she cried. She told me the other little girls were making fun of her because her daddy needed welfare. She was so cute, Don. She curled up her lip and said, 'I don't wanna go to no silly old confirmation thing anyway.' Honestly, Don, it broke my heart."

"I know, Louise. Lois told me what you did. She told me it cost you a week's salary to go and buy that little girl a dress."

It might just be a good thing that Louise will have to give up her job after we're married, Don thought. *She's such a soft touch. She doesn't seem cut out for the tough realities of poverty.*

Before the couple married, they talked many hours about values, about the family they wanted and about what they expected from family life.

"When we have children, honey, I want them to be loved and to love each other. I don't want to have our kids fighting and backbiting, competing with each other, being mean and nasty."

"I couldn't agree more. You know when we were young, Elthea could be really mean. She'd go off with the Swartz kids and leave me behind. I felt that she never wanted to play with me, that I was a bother. Were your brothers and sisters mean?"

"Well, the girls certainly could be gossipy. I tried to stay away from that kind of thing. And Mac, well, I looked up to him, but he was really competitive. He was sometimes mean."

"What matters most to me, Don, is that our kids *know* they're wanted and loved and that they *feel* loved. I believe that Mom and

Dad loved me, but you know, it was so hard to tell. I don't think I ever heard either of them say, 'I love you.'"

"The worst thing for me was the gossip and shame when my parents divorced. I hated it! Everyone knew that my dad had committed adultery. I could handle it, but the younger girls, I felt so bad for them. The kids at school teased them. I never want our kids to experience that kind of humiliation."

"We won't let that happen, Don. We just won't."

Don and Louise planned their wedding. Don didn't want to be a financial burden to the Riehms. They'd been generous enough to offer accommodation for the two of them until they were able to finance an apartment on their own. He felt they'd be hard-pressed with two daughters to finance weddings, and he and Louise agreed that they didn't want to start their marriage in debt. So they decided to elope. The Riehms were informed beforehand and didn't object, or if they did, they certainly didn't say so.

Frank suggested that Don and Louise marry in Coldwater, a beautiful, small community near Orillia, north of Kitchener. Frank grew up in Orillia and knew the area well. He arranged for them to be married by Reverend Madden in the United Church, September 9, 1933, exactly one year after their first date, on Don's twenty-first birthday. Frank stood up for Don, and Lois for Louise. Mrs. Madden acted as witness. Don had a bouquet of special roses for his new bride, roses that came from the Dale Estates in Brampton. Each rose had a little tag on the stem, a tag with the name "Dale" imprinted on it. And beautiful they were. And happy *they* were. Don felt he couldn't possibly love anyone any more than he loved his Louise, that all the love he was capable of experiencing was invested in his new and beautiful bride.

On November 13, 1933, Louise's twenty-sixth birthday, the first since their marriage, Don had the Dale Estates deliver a half-dozen red roses for Louise, each rose neatly labeled with the distinguished Dale tag, with a note that read, "To Weesa, the most beautiful rose of them all," the first of many such birthday thoughts and sentiments. On their first anniversary, Louise received a white box wrapped with a red ribbon, one Dale rose neatly attached. In the box—a midnight-blue negligee. Louise was touched, though she could think of a hundred and one other ways to spend their limited resources, especially since she was no longer a wage earner.

When Bayne was conceived, they were both excited and scared. Could they make their dreams come true? And could they do this on Don's very limited income?

"You know what worries me most, Louise? What if I can't give Bayne all the love he needs? I don't think I have the capacity to love any more than I do now. I don't think I can love anyone as much as I love you!"

Louise, cuddling their newborn, just looked at Don and smiled. "You will, Don, you will," she said gently.

And she was right, Don reflected. He found out much to his relief that not only could his heart open up to this new little soul, but his feelings for Louise had not been diminished. Indeed, he loved Louise even more.

He experienced the same worries when Kenny was born. How could he possibly love *more* than he already loved? And he discovered, again to his great relief, that not only could he love Bayne, but his heart opened even more to include Kenny and his love for Bayne and Louise had not been diminished. Again he discovered that his feelings for Louise were even more intense. *Could this miracle happen yet a third time? And could he love his little boys if ...* well, he wasn't even going to think about that.

"Supper's ready, Don," Louise said, looking over the railing at her husband playing with Bayne and Kenny, who had joined them after his nap.

"Okay, sweetie, we're on our way," Don said, bringing his full attention back to the present.

"The doctor said everything's normal," Louise said, entering the apartment after returning from her evening visit in this, her eighth month.

"Wonderful, honey; did he say anything about your fatigue?" Don asked before Louise even had her coat off.

"He said I needn't worry about that. It's to be expected. After all, I'm not as young as I used to be. But my heart's managing the extra work, Don. He said as long as I don't have any pain, I'm okay." Louise picked up a colouring book from the floor on her way into the kitchen. Don got up from the chair to greet Louise with a hug and a kiss.

"I laughed when he told me that I should just take it easy from now on. How does anyone with a three-year-old and a two-year-old 'take it easy'? Oh, and Don, he wants to do a full hysterectomy. He doesn't want to wait and have me go through surgery again later. You remember; we discussed this in his office."

Louise didn't share with Don how difficult it was for her to keep up. She tried to keep decent meals on the table, but she couldn't manage that and the housework and the kids. Even though Don agreed with her priorities and encouraged her to use her energy to play with the boys and attend to their needs, it really bothered her to see Don pick up the broom and dust mop after helping with the evening meal and then do the dishes.

Louise so enjoyed the boys. They were her sweethearts. Bayne was at the stage where exploring, taking things apart, creating amazing new structures with his tinker toys and colouring fabulous pictures for the icebox required constant monitoring and participation. Kenny was getting into everything. He adored his big brother and wanted to do whatever Bayne did, a want that demanded a great deal of ingenuity on Louise's part. Noon hours were a relief. Don, home for dinner, attended to the boys and their stories until Kenny was ready for his nap. When Don returned to work, Bayne sat quietly on the floor in front of the radio, thumb in his mouth, while Louise tidied up. Together they listened to *The Happy Gang, John's Other Wife* and if Kenny didn't wake up early, *Ma Perkins. Uncle Bob* came on at five o'clock with his stories for little people, and that gave Louise the time she needed to get supper started.

"Bayne, did you tell Daddy what Uncle Bob said today?" Louise asked.

"Oh Daddy," Bayne said, his face animated. "Uncle Bob saw me, Daddy, he really did."

"What do you mean, Bayne? How could Uncle Bob see you, honey?"

"Well, he did, Daddy. He said, 'and you there, Bayne, sitting on the floor with your thumb in your mouth,' and something else I forget—didn't he, Mommy?"

"He did," laughed Louise. "And you should have seen the thumb pop out of Bayne's mouth."

Don laughed too. "Uncle Bob sure is amazing, honey. He must have magic powers." He winked at Louise, amazed that she would take the time and energy to organize such a trick when she was so visibly tired.

Don tidied up and prepared coffee. After the children had their baths and stories and were tucked into bed, Louise and Don sat down at the kitchen table.

"I'm fine, Don, really," Louise said, knowing full well that Don didn't believe her. "I just have to rest more; and I will, I really will."

"Do you think we should have your mom come?"

"No, no, Don. I prefer to do things my own way. You'll just have to put up with the untidiness. What about you?" Louise asked, changing the subject. "Any more layoffs at work?"

"No, we've been told that we won't be getting any raises again this year, but there'll be no more layoffs. What really concerns me, sweetheart, is what's going on in Europe and the Far East. Did you see the headlines tonight?" Don asked, picking up the newspaper he'd been reading.

"Hitler now in command of the armed forces," Don read out. "And this, 'Religious freedom put on trial.' I don't like what's happening. Chamberlain says the League of Nations is inadequate and totally incapable of dealing with any of the stuff that's going on. He says the League's 'a sham and delusion.' I think Europe's in for big trouble, honey."

"Yeah, I heard that on the radio. And with Britain and France rearming, do you think something's going to happen? Do you think this will involve you, Don?"

"It won't come to that, honey, as long as Germany doesn't move into Poland. Britain and France have to defend that country. Hitler isn't that stupid. Don't worry, Louise, I don't think Canada will be involved." He glanced at Louise, hoping to see by her expression that she believed him.

"Besides," Don said, "we have our own crisis to worry about. Did you ask Dr. Gillespie if you should be staying in bed until the baby's due?"

Louise looked anxiously at Don. Tension had edged fine lines around his eyes and he was developing dark circles. His face was drawn and his mouth tight. She dearly wished that he'd stop worrying. *War? Job? Money? Whatever! We'll deal with it.* She reached across the table and took Don's hand in her own.

"Honey, Dr. Gillespie says that everything looks 'normal.' I don't need to stay in bed. I'll be fine. Let me show you what I sewed this afternoon." Louise went into the dining area, where the treadle sewing machine had taken up permanent residence beside the table. She picked up some outfits that had been left on a pile of fabrics, scattered patterns—some for children's outfits, some for maternity clothes—packages of needles, spools of thread and scissors. Don was right behind her.

"They're beautiful," Don said. "We'll have to get pictures of the boys in their velvet pants and coloured shirts. Are the red ones for Kenny or Bayne? And what's this?"

Louise looked at the magazine Don had picked up, a magazine with a French Impressionist painting on the cover. "I didn't know you were interested in art, Louise."

"Well, you know, if you look at beautiful things when you're pregnant, you'll have a beautiful baby," Louise said. She had told that to Dr. Gillespie, and he had dismissed it as an old wives' tale. She hoped Don wouldn't do the same.

"Sweetheart, you couldn't have anything but beautiful babies," he said, putting his arms around Louise and kissing her.

In early March the Nazis invaded Romania. Hitler and his army marched victoriously through Vienna. Mussolini announced a treaty with Germany. Italy would not be defending Austrians. And the Japanese were continuing their assault on China. Don hoped Louise was too preoccupied and busy to listen to the news, and he no longer commented on world events.

Louise *was* preoccupied. She nurtured such hopes and dreams about this baby. She had spent a lonely childhood on the farm and she so looked forward to the companionship of a daughter. Her stoic, hardworking parents talked about work and getting things done but never about feelings and dreams. It never occurred to Louise to share with Don the depth of her longing for a daughter. This little girl would be dressed in the prettiest clothes that Louise could make. This little girl would *know* what it was like to have a close and affectionate relationship with *her* mother. Louise imagined fussing over her hair and teaching her to knit, crochet, cook, sew, keep house. She pictured the two of them playing dolls. She could see her daughter all grown up, moving into the world a confident, self-assured young person, a person who attracted lots of friends. How could Don possibly understand that she wanted this little girl to have all the things in life that she had missed?

And then the time came.

Pauline came to the apartment to mind the boys. All the arrangements had been made. Don called a taxi, and off he and Louise went to the K-W Hospital, just a city block away. Louise was settled in that evening. Surgery was scheduled for the next day. Don, preparing to leave the room, gave Louise a final kiss. As he turned his back to walk out the door, tears welled up in his eyes, threatening to unmask his "be strong" composure. Would he ever see his Weesa alive again?

The C-section was performed at 10:30 the following evening, the evening of the ides of March.

Don paced and paced. The pipe in his mouth occasionally issued a sweet, wood-scented aroma, but failed to soothe. He wasn't allowed to be in the delivery room. He wasn't allowed to see Louise or talk to her. The only information forthcoming when he inquired at the nursing station was a noncommittal, "Your wife's doing fine." The bouquet of roses Don brought with him was surviving the stress far better than he since a thoughtful nurse had brought a container of water for them. And yes, each rose had been carefully labeled.

Damn, he thought. *What's the delay?* Don had taken the day off work and had been in the waiting room since early afternoon. He had settled the boys and walked over to the hospital expecting that the surgery would be underway, only to learn that the schedule was changed. Dr. Gillespie had an emergency to deal with before he could undertake the operation, though Louise had been in the delivery room now for hours. He had the waiting area all to himself. That pleased him. He certainly didn't want to make small talk; and the little ten-by-twelve alcove, with its coffee table scattered with tattered and outdated magazines, was too small to ignore the presence of someone else. The half-dozen green, stained, hard-backed chairs did not encourage lounging; and besides, he couldn't sit down for more than a few minutes at a time anyway. The drabness of the room matched the greyness of this cold March day and the blackness of his mood.

What the hell's the matter? Why isn't she out of surgery? I bet her heart's stopped. I bet she couldn't take the anesthetic. What if the anemia was worse than Dr. Gillespie had told them? I knew the strain would be too much. I should have insisted on a D and C. I should have insisted she have a hysterectomy after Kenny. I bet they're not telling me the truth. If anything happens to Louise, I swear I'll sue Dr. Gillespie and this whole damn hospital. She's probably dying and nobody's telling me. Don fumed and paced. It was close to midnight before Dr. Gillespie finally put in an appearance.

"Congratulations, Mr. Perrin. You've a beautiful little girl," Dr. Gillespie said as he walked into this now much-cluttered waiting room, heavy with the unpleasant stink of stale pipe smoke, his mask pulled casually off his face, fatigue showing in his eyes and the drooping of his shoulders. His rumpled outfit and messy hair seemed ominous to Don.

"Yeah, that's fine, but Louise. How's my Weesa?" Don asked, not daring to breathe.

"Oh, she's done remarkably well. She's heavily sedated and we're giving her a transfusion to get her blood count up in order to fend off infections, but you can go in and see her. There's no point in staying though, Mr. Perrin. Louise won't be awake for several hours yet.

She'll be much better tomorrow after a good night's rest. You can visit then."

"But can I see her now?" asked Don.

"Oh yes, yes. Nurse Donnelly will take you in."

Don hadn't noticed Nurse Donnelly standing by. He responded immediately to her smile, her warmth, as she took his arm and guided him to Louise's room.

"Weesa, I love you," Don whispered as he bent over to kiss a very still, pale figure.

In spite of Nurse Donnelly's encouragement, Don wouldn't go home. He sat beside the bed all night in another green, worn, straight-backed chair, convinced that the moment he left the room—with its dim light, drab yellow walls, medical paraphernalia and the antiseptic smell that seemed to invade every inch of hospital landscape—Louise would die. She looked so very white, just inches from death, and the IV she was receiving looked so threatening. After a brief call to Mrs. Riehm (he still couldn't call her Pauline), he sat and he looked and he stroked Louise's face, her hair, her hand, and gradually drifted into a shallow sleep, lulled by the monotonous humming of the intercom, disturbed occasionally by the presence of Nurse Donnelly. He awoke immediately when he became aware of movement. Louise was stirring.

"I'm here, Weesa. I love you," he whispered, leaning forward again to kiss her.

"I told you it'd be a girl," Louise said, smiling, though only half-conscious. In a voice scarcely audible, she said, "We'll name her Dale."

NOTES AND QUESTIONS FOR REFLECTION

As you go through the questions, you may want to record your responses in a journal for further reflection at a later point.

The first two stories in Book One illustrate the early life messages and how we, as children, arrive at the conclusions and decisions that form the basic structure of our scripts. The following stories in Book One illustrate how the script evolves and how we play out our "roles" in the real world.

Book Two begins the process of unraveling the mystery of the reoccurring dramas that unfold when we live "in script." The questions and suggestions relevant to these stories are designed to help us connect the significance of those script decisions and how we might go about changing the thoughts, feelings and behaviours that keep us from being all that we are capable of being.

Book Three illustrates how life can be lived "beyond script."

WHAT'S IN A NAME

Do you know stories about how your parents met?

Do you have information about your grandparents and how your parents and grandparents got along?

Do you have photographs that give you an idea of how your parents looked as young people? How they dressed? What they enjoyed doing?

Have you heard stories about your birth? Any special circumstances associated with your birth?

Were you named after anyone? Does your name have a particular significance?

From all the stories you have heard and what you are aware of now, do you think or feel that your life has been impacted or influenced by this information? If so, in what way has this been helpful or hurtful to you?

THE WEAVING OF A TAPESTRY

I'm looking through the lens of a time warp: looking at photographs of the little girl that my mother wanted so dearly, the little girl who might have cost her her life. I see a nine-month-old child, huge smile, sparkling deep brown eyes, in front of a Christmas tree, beside a stuffed yellow dog as big as she is. She's wearing a pink dress with a round collar edged in lace, pink socks and white soft leather shoes. She's thrilled. As I look at her, I am too, for I know that I almost didn't make it. Mom wrote a story for me for my fortieth birthday celebration. In it she gives my time of birth, 10:20 p.m., and my birth weight, six pounds nine ounces and describes me as "a little pink bundle of joy." In her autobiography, written for me when she was in her seventies, Mom described me as "a little soft bundle of happiness, and the pride and joy of her father."

Mom said that when Dad carried me into the apartment, he was terrified, heart-poundingly scared that he might drop this precious bundle and I would break into pieces. Bayne and Ken were allowed to peek into the room to greet their new sister but were not to disturb me. Mom related that she had a difficult time finding the right formula and in the meantime I'd lost considerable weight. By sheer accident, she added too much water to the formula—and voilà. I wonder now, *was that a mistake? An accident? Intuition? Or a radiant angel whispering in Mom's heart?* Shortly after that, in the summer of 1938, I won first prize and a big red ribbon in a local baby contest for being the smallest baby in the competition. Mom was delighted—it was the first of many trophies.

I'm looking at another photograph. Ken and I are standing in the backyard. Ken is holding a black-and-white cat, and I'm staring intently at this little creature. Now I have curly hair and I'm dressed in a simple, short-sleeved cotton dress, with tiny purple flowers, a round purple collar and white socks and shoes. Ken is dressed in brown short pants, knee-length brown socks, one neatly pulled up the leg, the other buckling at the ankle and scruffy leather brown shoes. He is cradling the kitten in a very nurturing way, a demonstration as to how you should hold a cat. The kitten's name is Winnie, named after Winston Churchill, one of Mom's heroes.

Two other specific photographs that predate my actual memories: me standing tall, my hair neatly combed, with a black plastic barrette holding the bangs off my forehead, one arm straight at my side, the other wrapped awkwardly around a doll. I'm dressed in a pale-blue dress with a lace collar and smocking, white socks and shoes. I have a gold chain with a locket on it around my neck. I'm looking up at whoever is taking the picture and smiling, no doubt as instructed.

A second picture taken at the same time—and I now conclude that Ken and I were celebrating our birthdays, me three and Ken five—shows Ken dressed in a khaki soldier's outfit, the sleeves of the shirt almost hiding his hands, the cuffs of the pants covering his shoes, and he looks delighted. He has his arm around me and there's a big toy drum behind. I wonder: *who is that little person?*

In other photos up to and including this age, she's being held by a proud mother, by a smiling grandmother, by an aunt. She's sitting in a little yellow child's chair, in a patterned living-room chair, or on the floor. She's standing alone, with Ken, or with Ken and Bayne together. And she's dressed in pretty dresses, lovingly sewn by her mom. In some of the photos she's holding a doll. In others—and these are by far the most animated—a stuffed animal, Winnie the cat, or a black-and-white Springer spaniel named Dolly. And when she has hair, always neatly brushed, she frequently has a big ribbon. She is pretty and very feminine—not at all the little girl I experienced as me.

After a brief stay in an apartment at 4 Mount Hope Street, my parents moved the family to 25 Gruhn Street, a semidetached six-room rental house within a few blocks of Dad's work at the Dominion Tire Factory, the schools and the church. This was the first home I knew: the place of my earliest memories and, I believe, the first place that Mom and Dad actually felt was truly a home. Let me describe it from my child perspective.

If I come up the verandah into the house, I get to walk on the red and purple carpet with its fancy border—Mommy calls it a Persian rug—but I can't play with the stuff on the mantel over the fireplace 'cause Mommy has special things there. And I can't jump on the wine-coloured chesterfield 'cause it's really a bed-in-hiding and Bayne told me Daddy keeps special magazines in there that sometimes have bare-naked ladies, which we're not supposed to see. I can sit on the carpet in front of the console radio to listen to the hockey game on Saturday night and I can fall asleep there if I want.

I just run through the dining room 'cause I only get to eat at the big table when Auntie and Gramma come or maybe some other important people. Then Mommy gets the dishes out of the buffet, which is pushed against the wall.

I have to be careful not to spill food on the linoleum floor and I'm never supposed to touch the grandfather clock, which came from Daddy's house. Kenny sometimes is allowed to pull the chains on it when Daddy helps.

I can play at the little yellow children's table and chair set if I want to crayon or something. Mommy and Daddy play cards with us at that table instead of the big one. Mostly I eat in the kitchen at the table that drops its leaf and I sit beside Kenny. Mommy doesn't have to go so far because this table is close to the stove and the sink and the cupboards. On Good Fridays—it always rains on Good Fridays—me and Kenny and Bayne help Mommy clean those cupboards and get to know everything that is in them.

If I come in the back way, I have to go through the pantry first. I can see big and small cans and bottles of stuff and a really big tub of peanut butter. Daddy sometimes hangs fancy dead ducks there. Mommy doesn't allow me to go into the pantry then because she says I will cry.

Mostly I play upstairs in the big room that Bayne and Kenny share. Bayne has a Meccano set and tinker toys and he makes bridges and houses and cars, and sometimes he lets me help.

I have to wear shoes or slippers when I play upstairs, or I'll get slivers in my feet from the barn-wood floor. Coming down the stairs,

I can play bumpety-bumpety-bump as much as I want without getting slivers.

The most fun place in the house is the basement, but I don't get to play there much. Daddy made a darkroom and built a big box for making pictures. He has a funny sink made of rubber and he puts something in it I am never, never to drink. Daddy told all of us never to touch anything there. The windows are covered with funny-looking red paper, which makes it hard to see without the lights on.

Mommy has a washing machine down there. It has a wood hand-wringer, which is very dangerous. I can watch her and watch the wet clothes drop into the tin tub, but I am not to play with that machine when she isn't here. Nor am I supposed to go into the coal bins—four of them. One has very fine black dust, like sand, and this is the most dangerous. Another bin just has black lumps, and I get really dirty from touching them. And one has big, big chunks of coal with red or blue streaks in them, and Daddy puts these into the furnace last. And one has coke in it—not the stuff you drink though. Daddy says this crinkly, crusty stuff that isn't really shiny like the other coal has the gas pulled out of it. I don't know how they do that.

During these early years, before precious memories are collected and stored away in my childhood treasure box, other important events and influences that colour and shape the fabric of my story are unfolding. Dad brought with him into his marriage, and into my life, the influences of his family of origin. His relationship with his father, whom I have never experienced as "grandfather," was estranged. Dad blamed his father for his mother's early death.

As I understood it, when he was a boy of sixteen, Dad's father separated from his mother and the children and moved in with a much younger woman and her little girl. Imagine the scandal. The Perrins were a prominent family with English-Scottish-Welsh and French ancestry and discernable Christian beliefs; Grandfather was a professional photographer, and Grandmother was a teacher, a path followed by one of her sons and two of her daughters. I know the visibility and shame of his father's behaviour; this perceived betrayal weighed heavily on Dad's heart and spirit, the soul of a vulnerable young man who cherished a close attachment to his mother.

In his early years Dad suffered chronic ear infections. I can just imagine this young boy, stuck in bed for weeks and sometimes months, while his sisters and brothers were having a great time at school playing with friends, feeding and petting his rabbits, and sure enough, the next school year, same old earaches. I imagine that as a kid he didn't appreciate his mother insisting that he do lessons at home in order to keep up, even though his mom was a dynamic teacher. On the upside this did provide the opportunity for Dad to develop a close and affectionate relationship with his mother and I know he adored her.

When his mother was dying—dying of a broken heart, Dad believed—Dad decided to kill his father. He retrieved his father's shotgun from its storage place and loaded the gun. He went into his mother's bedroom to see her face once more before he set out on his journey of filial revenge. His mother, who had not been conscious for some time, sat bolt upright when he entered the room and uttered a prayer: "God bless Donny." Dad broke into sobs and returned the gun.

Although I didn't hear this story until many years later, I felt the impact of that estrangement. Dad was uncomfortable in the presence of his father and we seldom entertained him in our home. It was the influence of "the sisters," though, that most disturbed my spirit.

"Bayne, why is Mommy crying?" I ask as I enter the kitchen. I notice tears sliding silently down Mommy's cheeks as she talks on the telephone, which is mounted on the dining-room wall, just outside the kitchen doorway.

"Shush, Dale, Mommy's okay. She'll be okay. Just don't bother her," he answers, continuing to slab peanut butter on his toast. "She's just talking to Aunt Inez."

Somehow I knew I wasn't to ask Mom why she was crying. I noticed. I was frightened. I felt sad. Her tears soaked into my soul like monsoon rains on desert clay and threatened my sense of safety. It seemed to me, in the early years, that Mom was *always* crying and that it was *always* Aunt Inez, Aunt Eunice or Aunt Lois that triggered her tears. I must have intuited that these aunts were hurting Mom's feelings, criticizing her for who knows what.

I can't understand why Daddy doesn't fix it for Mommy. He can fix anything. Please, please make it better, Daddy. Mommy's sad and I can't fix it. If Mommy is happy then I'll feel okay too. I don't know how to make Mommy happy.

I couldn't understand why my parents entertained "the sisters" and their husbands, why my parents insisted (at least until I was nine or ten) that we, as a family, attend the infrequent extended-family events, since clearly neither Dad nor Mom enjoyed them. And on occasion, my parents even invited the couples to our home to play bridge. I could see and feel the discomfort Mom experienced in their presence. And, very early in life, I determined that *when I get big I will fix it for Mommy. I will make her better and protect her from those mean old people.*

The early formative years, these childhood years—rich threads of gold and silver, interwoven with all the primary colours available to the Creator—woven brilliantly into patterns, in time form a whole, a unique expression of beauty. My early memories surface as threads of that tapestry. Why these fragments of experience? Why these threads of memory remain fixed on my fabric, only the weaver knows. I'll let the child in me tell her stories.

What was that? I sit up in bed with a start. Crash! Lightning blitzing everywhere and the booms are right on top of the house. I'm scared. I pull the blanket over my head. Oh, oh! It won't stop. Gotta wake up Mommy. Not supposed to wake up Mommy when Mommy and Daddy are sleeping, but I gotta. I'm so scared.

Mommy? Mommy? Where's Mommy? I'm in my parents' bedroom. No one's here. The bed is still made and the house is all dark. Where's my Mommy? I stand in front of the bedroom window looking out onto Gruhn Street, watching the lightning, jumping at the crashes that I'm sure are going to hit the house and bust right into the room. I'm crying quietly, doubly scared now because Mommy isn't here. And Kenny comes into the room.

"Don't cry, Dale, Mommy's just over visiting Mrs. Pierce next door. Don't cry, Dale. She'll be back soon. I'll take care of you."

Kenny puts his arms around me and holds me. I'm really glad Kenny's here but I'm still scared.

I don't recall the rest of that scene, my very earliest memory. I recall most vividly the feelings and the struggle as to whether or not to go and get the nurturing I needed. Curious, why would a three-year-old hesitate to approach her parents for comforting when she needed it?

Mrs. Pierce and her husband Bob lived on the other side of the duplex. A delightful woman, probably in her early fifties, Mrs. Pierce was Mom's confidant and dearest friend. And she never complained about the inevitable noises that three little children make. Only once do I remember hearing noises from Mrs. Pierce's side.

The sun has changed colours and the sky is crayoned pink and purple. Bayne and Kenny and me are drawing pictures at the little yellow table and Mommy is putting the supper dishes away. I'm going to colour my picture pink like the sky and—suddenly we hear a scream from next door. I jump. Mommy runs outside. We wait. I'm shaking, scared. I think I'm going to cry. Bayne says, "It's okay, Dale, Mommy will take care of it." I don't know how he knows that.

Mommy comes back in a very few minutes "Everything's fine now," she says. "Mrs. Pierce was just frightened by some snakes that were in her pantry. She's no idea where they came from. We shooed them away and she's okay now."

Bayne and Kenny look at each other. Bayne has a funny smile. Mommy looks at Bayne and I think she's going to say something but she doesn't. Bayne says, "I gotta go to the bathroom," and disappears.

Kenny whispers in my ear. "We caught eight green snakes in the 'third bush.' Bayne hid them under the pantry."

Sometimes Kenny takes me with him to the third bush and sometimes down Glasgow Street to Bauer's Bush. I love it. The woods always smell like grass after it rains. I can hear sounds of little furry creatures but mostly I can't see them. If I listen really carefully and don't talk, I can hear twigs breaking and leaves singing, though they only do that if the wind is blowing. Pretty water-coloured birds fly up into the sky like paper airplanes, and I can hear them twitter and caw. Kenny says the chirps and croaks are sounds that the frogs and toads make, not the birds.

When I turn over the green fuzzy rocks and rotting branches, I find salamanders—beautiful brown-spotted-with-red-dots salamanders. They scurry up my arm thinking I'm a branch, but they end up in a jar with holes in the lid. Sometimes when we are very quiet we find adults in the woods, sometimes without all their clothes on. When we yell they get mad so we run.

Sometimes I play by the tracks behind the Granite Club, that place at the end of the street where grownups go to skate and play with rocks. There is lots and lots of room behind there to play. It's just a big field of weeds and a pond with scummy, green-blue stuff on the top and big brown weeds that die in the water and bulrushes that sometimes sprout white feathers. Me and some of the neighbourhood boys make a raft from some wood we borrow from the stacks of lumber on the other side of the tracks and we pretend we're driving boats. We make a fort that has a roof you can sit on, and we can bring our raft right up to the boards we put in the mud to get into the fort.

I don't play near the big willow pond that is farther up the tracks on the other side of the big sand pile, 'cause Mommy told me that some children drowned there. You can't drown in this little pond. I fell in once and it isn't very deep. Ralphie doesn't like playing on the pond.

"Ralphie, wait for me," I yell. I run to catch up with my neighbour, a boy just a year older than me. "Where yuh going?"

"I'm going to play in the big sand pile," Ralphie answers, swinging a blue bucket that has yellow stars on it.

"Me too," I say, eyeing that bucket, hoping he'll let me play with it for some of the time.

We skip down Gruhn Street, cross Agnes Street and trip along the narrow path through the trees. Running and skipping along, we reach the edge of the world where the field disappears, swallowed up no doubt by an earth-eating monster. We come to a sandy slope that drops to the very edge of the cinders bordering the tracks. On the weedy area, just before the world drops, a tall pine tree that is forever old stands like a soldier guarding the outhouse. Gurgling tummies interrupt our play, so Ralphie and me zigzag our way back, leaving our sandy cowboy ranches to fate. Maybe they'll still be here when we get back.

"Did you take Ralphie's pants down?" Mommy asks, coming into my bedroom shortly after my return.

"Yes, Ralphie had to pee and he couldn't get his pants down, Mommy. I helped him," I say. I wonder how Mommy knows that and why it's important.

"Did you pee too, Dale?"

"Yes, that outhouse has two holes, and boy does it stink, Mommy."

"Well, I don't want you to play there. That's not a good place for you to be. And if you have to go to the bathroom, you come home, okay?"

"Okay, Mommy," I say—and true to my word, I never peed there again.

"Now I want you to take a bath," Mommy says and heads for the bathroom. I can hear the water running. Now this is puzzling. This isn't even bedtime. A bath? And I'm not even dirty. Not only do I get a bath, but Mommy dresses me up in a Sunday-best yellow dress, not just an ordinary play dress. I figure I've done something pretty bad, but I'm not sure just what.

Not many years ago when I mentioned this to Bayne, he informed me that Ralphie had a rash on his behind. When Mom undressed me, I too had a behind covered with ugly red welts. I wonder why Mom never explained that to me. I associated this bath and dressing up as somehow connected with sexuality. As a teenager I repeated this ritual cleansing. Such a simple thing: questions not asked, questions not answered and conclusions with far-reaching consequences.

At four years of age I was allowed to ride the red tricycle that originally was given to Bayne. Another image surfaces:

Gramma, Auntie and Mommy are chatting and clearing away the dinner dishes. Daddy moves into the living room to watch Bayne and Kenny play but soon falls asleep on the chesterfield. I zoom around the living room, into the dining room, into the kitchen and track back the same way on the tricycle.

"Beep, beep, beep," I say to Gramma and Auntie. Gramma smiles at me and moves out of the way.

"Beep, beep," I say, whipping through the dining room again. Gramma doesn't move this time. She's frowning. Auntie's smiling. She moves.

Boom! I'm right up against Kenny blocking the entranceway to the kitchen; Bayne's nowhere in sight.

"Beep, beep," I say. Kenny doesn't move.

"Beep, beep," I say again. Kenny still doesn't move. I burst into tears and shout at Daddy.

"I said, 'beep, beep' and Kenny wouldn't beep."

Startled, an angry frown on his face, Daddy says, "Kenny, let her through. She's only playing."

"But I ..."

"Let her through, Kenny!"

Vroom, vroom, off I go into the kitchen. I can hear Auntie say, "Lord, love us! She's a headstrong little soul." I think she means me. But I know that when you say "beep," the other person is supposed to "beep." It's a rule. Daddy makes most of the rules, and a rule's a rule.

Ken would say now that as a child I could get away with just about anything where Dad was concerned. He experienced that he was held accountable for a lot of my mischief and misdeeds, although for the life of me, I can't think of any misdeeds on my part. If I was favoured, as Ken perceived it, I was oblivious of this special status, but it wouldn't surprise me, knowing as I know now that Dad believed it was his job to raise their sons to be *men* and Mom's job to raise me to be—*what*?

Male chauvinism, this all-pervasive attitude that infringed on my choices throughout much of my life, was a double-edged sword. Bayne and Ken experienced an aspect of Dad unknown to me. Bayne recalls an incident of playing with matches with Larry Musselman, in the Musselman garage, the car still in the garage. Mr. Musselman, very upset with this discovery, told Dad. Generally, and on this occasion, Dad's way of exercising discipline was to sit down with Bayne or Ken and explain what was wrong and the danger of such an activity. The punishment, to reinforce the lesson, was a spanking on the bum with a leather belt, occasionally on a bare bum. Dad "lost it," really lost his temper, on two occasions that Bayne recalls. These spankings caused welts and bruises. Ken also experienced some severe spankings. His memory is that he was "thrashed all the time." Me? I just got a verbal lecture from Dad—if that. According to Mom, Dad spanked me once, although I don't remember this, and it frightened him. I think Dad over idealized women on the one hand and discounted them on the other. He had a saying, often repeated, usually with a shake of his head and a warm smile on his face, "Women are stranger than people." My discipline was left to Mom—I being one of those strange people—and she was much gentler, just the occasional swat on the bum. But she rarely discovered my transgressions and really didn't look very hard; in retrospect, I wonder why. And did she have any idea of the dangerous play activities I engaged in?

The neighbourhood was populated by kids—kids everywhere, always ready to play hide-and-go-seek, kick the can, tricks with yo-yos, swinging on the school-yard swings. Some of us, usually little Bobby and me, would sneak off to the back of the Granite Club, play beside the railway tracks, in the ponds, climb through the lumber piles and make forts, all highly dangerous activities. I would be gone hours at a time. I don't recall Mom ever asking me where I was or what I was doing.

Parents didn't supervise children's play like they do today. Occasionally the moms played street games with the children, but rarely ever did a parent come to the school fields or Kaufman's park to supervise. Safety didn't seem to be an issue. I didn't know anything about child molestations, nor did I interpret my world as dangerous. When I listen to the concerns of parents today and the time commitment involved in taking children to a multitude of structured activities, I wonder, *have we progressed? Or ...?* In Kitchener, the world of my childhood, crime was almost nonexistent. No one locked doors. I wasn't warned about strangers; there was no such thing as a neighbourhood watch. My concerns centered on the accidents and mischief of childhood. Only later in life did I question my safety as a child. Only then did I ask, "Mom, where were you? Why didn't you check up or ask me what I was doing?" And then I conclude, someone must have been looking out for me; those angels, again? Fortunately, only two incidents resulted in physical injury.

"Mommy, Mommy," I say, slamming open the backdoor as I run into the kitchen, tears rolling down my frosty, red cheeks, tears mixed with red blood, oozing from a gash in my forehead. "Gary Becker hurt me."

"Oh my goodness," Mommy says, immediate alarm registering in the look on her face. Wetting a handkerchief to wipe my forehead, she asks, "What happened?"

"He threw ice at me, Mommy. He was mad that I wanted to play hockey too. He said girls weren't supposed to play hockey."

That accident took six stitches. The next took thirteen.

"Where yuh going, Kenny?" I ask, chasing down Gruhn Street to catch up with him.

"Nowhere," Kenny says, as he continues down past the Granite Club, heading onto Park Street.

"Can I come?" I say, already marching right along beside him.

"Sure, but I'm not going anywhere, just down the street."

And way down the street we go, right down to Victoria Park. We cross over a wooden bridge, planks of barn board with a wood handrail, arched over the twenty-foot-wide river to what appears to be an island in the park. This area has wooden picnic tables, chain-link swings and a big wooden slide. Nearby I can see flower beds with big red geraniums that smell a bit like Mommy's cleaning stuff. The grass smells alive with fish worms, like after a big rain.

We head back to the bridge. The clear water flows slowly and ever so gently, and I can see pebbles and the occasional minnow. I stop to see if I can grab a minnow in my fist but they are swimming too quickly.

"I bet you're afraid to walk through this water," says Kenny, a smile on his face.

"I'm not," I say, frowning at Kenny for thinking I'm afraid.

"Are so."

"Am not." And I begin to take off my socks and shoes. Kenny also takes off his socks and shoes and together, hand in hand, we carefully step into the water. It's cool and feels ticklish. The green and blue pebbles are slippery.

"Ouch! Something cut me."

Kenny looks around and sees a tin can with a jagged edge on the river bottom.

"You musta stepped on that can," he says, pointing at a can partly hidden in the mud, between pebbles.

I start to cry. We now move quickly to the other side, still carrying socks and shoes, and head up Park Street. My foot is bleeding heavily. Kenny now starts to cry. We continue to walk, hand in hand, both crying, leaving a trail of blood. Several ladies along Park Street come from their porches and ask if we will let them help. We shake our heads "no" and continue walking and crying. I want Mommy and I wanna go home.

Daddy comes running down Gruhn just after we turn onto the street. He grabs me up in his arms and carries me the rest of the way.

"Phone Dr. Gillespie," he says to Mommy, who is already on the phone when Daddy brings me in.

Dr. Gillespie tells me I'm very brave 'cause I don't yell when he pours a whole bottle of orange liquid on my foot and sews me up with a needle like Mommy uses, only bigger.

Just natural events of childhood, no apparent cause for alarm or much supervision; but I wonder, now that I know about the frequency and ravages of childhood sexual abuse, should my parents have alerted me about the potential dangers of strange men, or for that matter, any man who wanted to touch inappropriately?

Stewart Park, the caretaker at the Granite Club, was the source for hammer, nails and paint for making forts and rafts for the pond behind the club. He might very easily have been a perpetrator. Stew, as we called him, lived in a back room of the Granite Club year-round and maintained the building and rinks. Between the ages of seven and eleven, I would go and visit him and help him with a variety of activities. Stew liked to have me (and other children?) around. I would help him remove storm windows and clean them with Bon Ami. He let me drive the tractor that was used to clear ice in the winter and clean up debris under the refrigeration pipes beneath the rink's surface in the summer. He let me run the tuck shop during skating season (and eat all the chocolate bars I wanted) and arranged for me to play the music for the adult skate sessions. He paid me nickels, dimes and then quarters. And he hugged me and called me his friend.

Stew never touched me inappropriately, though I did have a sense that some of the hugs were "too long." When I was eleven Stew gave me my first badminton racquet—probably taken from the pro's office in the badminton section of the Granite Club. When I was twelve, he paid for my first year of membership as a junior player.

Now I think, *Mom, didn't you ever wonder about Stew? Question what I was doing spending time alone with this middle-aged man? Didn't it seem inappropriate to you?*

Ken and I experienced an incident one Saturday when we went off to the cowboy movies. A man sat beside me—and this was in the second row of the theatre with no other children around us—and rubbed his hands along my thighs. I nudged Ken and whispered in a voice that this man could hear that I had to go to the bathroom. We headed for the lobby and I told him what the man was doing. We then went to another section of the theatre. The man came looking for us. We spotted him in time to slip down on the floor out of view.

On another occasion, a man at a carnival offered me free passes for rides if I sat in the cab of his truck with him. *Hey, this is great. Free tickets! I climb into the cab. He begins to touch my thighs. I ask him, "What are yuh doin'?" He says, "This is what you do to make babies." I sense something is very wrong with this. "I gotta go and meet my brother," I say, and he doesn't attempt to stop me.*

But for sheer good fortune—or was it the angels?—I might have been one of those children deeply traumatized and psychologically damaged for life. I wasn't. I have a much keener wisdom now as to the pervasiveness of these experiences. I can't help but wonder, *didn't anyone know about such exploitation in the forties?*

As I moved out into the world of school, new opportunities to weave experiences into the fabric of my emerging script, opportunities to crystallize my perception of self, others and the world, the foundation upon which I would build my life drama, inundated me. The child in me delighted in the sensual experiences and the new challenges—and shared them with no one.

The hollyhocks in our backyard are the most special. Yellows, pinks and occasional whites open their hearts to the sun. I delight in picking off first the blossom—really the skirt of a ballet dancer—and then the green sheaths—really the heads of the dancers—and stage imaginary arabesques.

I skip along the grassy pathways, through the back gardens, to get to Bobby's house—Bobby's my best friend, outside of Kenny and Bayne, that is. I like Bobby. He's quiet, fun to play with—and he doesn't stab frogs. He and his sister Gloria live on Park Street, and his mom and dad are Russian. I call for him to come and play—never Gloria, she just wants to play dolls or other girls' games—just Bobby.

"Bobby, Bobby, you ready to go to school?" I call out.

We start kindergarten together, Bobby and me. I have to sit at a separate table except for cutout times. Then I get to sit with Bobby.

I am helping Bobby with his strips of coloured paper for use in making mats. The teacher comes over and makes me sit at the table with the children who have a lot of difficulties. I don't know why she does this. Miss Heath makes no sense at all. I thought being helpful was a good thing, but she's mad.

One afternoon Miss Heath invites mommies to attend school; this must be a very important occasion. Miss Heath is dressed in her Sunday-best clothes, I think, because she looks a lot different than she did yesterday. She has pink lipstick and red patches on her cheeks. I think she did that herself, or maybe she's just cold. I don't know.

"Okay, children, get into the circle; and when the music starts, you may skip and sing along just like we did yesterday," Miss Heath says, waving her hand, her glasses sliding down her narrow nose.

I enter the circle, start to skip and I feel fat, ugly and awkward; tears well up in my eyes. I think I'm gonna cry. I feel bad—really bad. I wish Mommy wasn't here. I don't feel good when Mommy watches me. I think she wishes I would like girl games, that I would like being dressed up pretty, like getting my hair brushed and combed.

I think this is my first awareness that I'm not the little girl Mom wanted: I don't play the games girls like; I don't like being dressed up so pretty; I don't like getting my hair brushed and combed; I don't like what my Mom likes, the crafts, the sewing, the "feminine" things. And I'm overwhelmed with feelings of shame and embarrassment. I feel fat, ugly and awkward. Just being me doesn't seem to please Mom.

I go to Sunday School. Bayne and Kenny are in with big kids but I'm not. The church is up the street, on Park Street. This Sunday morning Mommy and Daddy are coming with us. Mostly they don't. The lady is taking us small kids into the big room where the older children are sitting on chairs, and I think that maybe I'm big enough now to be where Bayne and Kenny are. She takes us to the front of this room onto a stage, and I can see the kids and parents sitting out front. I see Mommy and Daddy smiling at me. I see doors to lots of other rooms all around this big room. The doors are closed. All the other children must be here, but I don't see Bayne and Kenny. I see pictures of Jesus and lambs and Christmas stars on the walls and doors. I don't know what I'm doing here.

The lady says we are to sing "Jesus Loves Me" and someone starts to play the piano. I can sing this song but I don't feel so good. I have little butterflies flip-flopping in my stomach, like I do when there's a thunderstorm. I begin to cry. I also begin to pee. I feel the rush of warm pee down my legs and I cry more. I don't know what to do. I hope that Mommy and Daddy will come and get me. They don't. I'm afraid to look at them 'cause maybe they're mad at me. So I look at the picture of the lamb. It's hard to see it though 'cause my tears are making it all wet and streaky. Finally, the lady comes and takes me off the stage. She takes my hand and leads me to the bathroom and tells me that I can go in there. I think this is a silly thing to say because I've already peed. She turns to go back to the big room. I don't want to be here anymore. I gallop up the basement stairs, leave the church and go home.

"Oh, there you are, Dale. I'd like you to come back to the church with me. I want to take your picture, okay, sweetheart? It'll only take a few minutes."

I still have on my wet pants, though by now I think they're dry. I don't want to go back with Daddy, but I go. Maybe he'll be really mad if I don't, even though he doesn't look mad.

"Okay, Daddy," I say, and back we go, down the stairs into the Sunday School, right up to the stage. A gate with big white ribbons is in front of the stage. Daddy puts me in front of the gate, hands me a piece of white paper, all rolled up and tied with a red ribbon. He takes my picture. I feel real bad inside and I want to cry again.

I don't understand why Mommy and Daddy aren't talking to me about peeing my pants. Why don't they say that accidents happen? Why don't they tell me they're not mad at me? They say nothing. I think that I've done something so bad that it's too hard to talk about. When I go home, only Dolly acts normally. She greets me in the house, wagging her tail, asking to be petted and I bury my face in her fur.

This experience, etched deeply in my psyche, is the origin of crippling stage fright, a key element of my script. Frightened of being onstage centre front, a place meant for the men in the world, I develop many tricks to avoid such threatening scenes.

Other significant caretakers influence us in formulating our dramas. My grandmother and my aunt, Mom's sister Elthea, were for me "nuclear family members" and the only relatives that ever mattered. Again, I'll let the child in me tell her stories.

Most Sundays we dress up in our very good clothes and walk up the Agnes Street hill. In the warm weather, we walk across town, along King Street to Cedar Street. We walk along Cedar the one block to Alma Street and Gramma's house. The first house on the other side of the street is 101 Alma. In the winter we take the streetcar along King Street to Cedar, but Daddy says we don't have the money to do that in good weather.

I try to beat Bayne and Kenny into the house, but I never can. Bayne usually gets there first and runs up the front stairs onto Gramma's verandah with its big swing couch. He bursts open the front door, with Kenny and me and Mommy and Daddy right behind. I smell dinner—endive salad with fried onion sauce, pot roast of beef simmering with carrots, whole onions and potatoes; and I spot the Dutch apple pie, cooling on the counter. This is my favourite. Daddy always gets a special apple dumpling, which no one else is allowed to eat.

"We're here, Gramma," I announce, though she already knows. *"Hi, Auntie."*

"Just in time," Gramma says, a warm smile on her face. *"Everything's ready. I just have to make the gravy."*

"I'll do that, Mom," Mom says.

"And I'll get the table ready," Auntie says.

Auntie pulls the big, square table out from the corner wall, and Kenny and I slip in behind one part and Bayne and Daddy the other. The gas-burning iron stove, with all the good smelling stuff, is over there and the sink and countertops are under the big window. Gramma used to have a water pump at the sink to pump well water from outside, but it's not there anymore. A brown cookie jar, always filled to the brim with oatmeal and peanut butter cookies, sits on the countertop.

After dinner, sometimes, especially when Homer is here—Homer comes to visit his daddy, Angus, who lives in Gramma's upstairs bedroom—we go into the dining room and living room to play. Homer has carrot-red hair like I've never seen before and lots of freckles. We push the dining-room table, its wings down, as close to the wall as possible and then from way up in the living room, right up against the big white chesterfield, which is covered with little purple and green tiny flowers—or maybe they are just dots—we roll Gramma's special big pennies, which she keeps in a little wooden barrel, down the hardwood floor, trying to hit special spots on the wood. You aren't supposed to lose the pennies under the piano. But mostly we can crawl on our bellies and reach the pennies that go too far.

When Homer isn't here, sometimes Angus takes me for a bus ride—he drives the big buses that go back and forth to Waterloo— and sometimes he lets me turn the big wheel. Gramma and Auntie like having Angus here; he laughs a lot.

I love coming to Gramma's. This house is full of surprises and I always feel so good here. Lots of different things to do. We can play different games and explore different rooms. The side door on the landing to the basement often hides Limburger cheese, in the process of being cured—that's what Gramma says. You can tell it's sick because of the horrible smell of the brownish-yellow-looking, stinking blob. That's enough to keep me from going out that door *and from eating cheeses of all kinds—at least cheeses in Gramma's house.*

At the bottom of the basement stairs is a big, brown crock with a lid on it. Bayne or Kenny lifts the lid to let me smell the sauerkraut. It smells almost as bad as the Limburger cheese, but it never smells so bad when Gramma makes it on the stove. Other crock jars have pickles pickling, Gramma says. And in the fruit cellar part of the basement I see lots of glass jars, all neatly labeled: peach, strawberry, raspberry and cherry jams and marmalades, sweet pickles, dill pickles, pickled corn, pickled onions, tomato sauce, chili sauce and canned beets. Homer hates beets worse than Limburger cheese.

After dinner Gramma says, "You children go and play now while your mom, Elthea and I clear up the kitchen."

Gramma, Auntie and Mommy play Chinese checkers after dinner—always after the dishes are done, 'cause Gramma believes you must do your work before you play. I hear bits and pieces of conversation as I move in and out of the kitchen.

"Sometimes I wonder why I even bother," Auntie says, after losing three games in a row, two to Mommy and one to Gramma. "Louise always wins. You can't beat her."

"Now come on, Elthea, you sometimes win too," Gramma says.

"Would you like to play Parcheesi or rummy?" Mommy asks.

"Okay," Elthea says. "But not if you're going to win all the time."

Sometimes I think Auntie is mad. Sometimes I think Mommy and Auntie aren't having fun. Why do they play these games if they're not having fun?

Daddy disappears into the living room, and having eaten not just the dinner but two pieces of bread, smothered in gravy, and the special dumpling, smothered in milk and sugar, falls asleep on the chesterfield. We know we can't play there when Daddy is sleeping.

"Can we go to the attic, Gramma?"

Kenny and I run past Auntie's bedroom at the top of the stairs. Her room is at the front and has a big window that looks onto Alma Street. We never play there. Auntie has a big, white spindle bed with a colourful, hand-stitched quilt made from squares cut out of Gramma's rag collection and a something that will break if it's dropped. She hides earrings and necklaces in it. I peeked once but didn't break anything.

Gramma's room is on one side of the attic stairs and Angus's room is on the other. Gramma's bed has four posts and is dark brown, like her dresser. And she has stiff, white doilies on her dresser top too and a gold brush and comb. Her quilt is pretty, like Auntie's, with little rectangles, mostly whites and a big starlike design in blue patches in the middle. She said the ladies at the church helped her make it.

The attic stairs are very steep and you have no railing to hang on to.

"Look at this, Kenny," I say.

"Whatcha got?" Kenny says.

"I think they're called bloomers," I say, pulling my head out of a cedar-lined chest, proudly displaying a pair of long-legged, white woolen underpants. "I betcha Gramma wears these in the wintertime."

"And look what else. I found a box of white stones," I say, showing off one of the little rectangular white, carved objects.

"Those aren't stones. Those are Gramma's Sprengerle cookies," Kenny says, temporarily distracted from his pursuit, his voice coming from the darkest corner of the attic. "You get to eat those at Christmas. And look what I found. I think this must be Grandpa."

I skip over the spike of sunlight extending from the little window at the front of the attic, braving the dust particles caught and suspended, like struggling flies in a cobweb, living creatures, ready to eat unsuspecting children, to where Kenny is inspecting a photograph album. I smell mothballs, probably hidden behind the stack of newspapers and magazines way behind the rack of albums.

"That's Grampa? I didn't know we had a Grampa," I say, looking at a photograph of a sober, middle-aged man, dark eyes, a Hitler mustache, short flat hair brushed to one side.

"I don't know but I think so. I think he died a long time ago," Kenny says. "Let's go down to the verandah and ask Bayne."

The three of us rock wildly back and forth on Gramma's rocker couch while Bayne explains that Mom told him that Grampa died when he was a baby. Then Daddy appears at the front door.

"Come on, kids, time to go home."

On the way out the door Auntie calls out, "Knock, knock." Bayne or Kenny answers, "Who's there?"

"Elthea."

"Elthea who?"

"El thee yuh tomorrow," Auntie responds, breaking into her familiar aha-ha-ha-ha laugh, echoing the sounds of tommy guns.

Going home isn't so much fun. From Cedar Street right to Agnes seems to be uphill all the way. Daddy carries me on his shoulders when I get tired, but Bayne and Kenny have to walk. They sometimes grumble about that.

I especially love Gramma. She's so strong and can do almost anything. She never cries and I never hear her complain or say bad things. She walks very tall and straight and looks like a movie star—like Katherine Hepburn, Mom says. She never says, "I love you," nor does she ever give me a hug. But I know she loves me. Mrs. McCardle, the next-door neighbour, always tells me, "Your grandmother really loves you. She was excited about you coming to visit." And I get to stay overnight with Gramma by myself sometimes, on a weekend.

Gramma's house on a Saturday morning is exciting. By the time I tumble out of bed and come down to the kitchen, Gramma has returned from her third trip to the Kitchener market and I smell dandelion salad, sauerkraut and pork starting to cook for dinner. I smell cooked cheese, fresh bread, coffee cake and apple-butter on the table for my breakfast.

And sleeping with Gramma is—well, Gramma always smells good. I snuggle under the downy quilt and watch Gramma in her long, white, flannelette nightgown remove the hairpins that fasten the bun at the back of her head and then her long, silky white hair falls down her back, well below the waist. She brushes and brushes while I watch silently, fascinated with this miraculous change.

Auntie's different from Gramma and Mommy. She goes out to work, like Daddy. Mommy says she works at Mutual Life, helping people save money for when they get old and die. I don't want Gramma to die. Auntie has to take the streetcar every day. Maybe that's why she's always in Sunday-best clothes.

Auntie likes school. She asks us lots of questions about school, especially Bayne, 'cause he's way ahead of Kenny and me. And she likes to read books to us. Often they're books about Jesus because she likes Jesus. And she plays the piano and likes to sing about Jesus. Bayne's learning to play the piano but I'm too young, Auntie says, and besides, I don't want to practice like Bayne does.

I wonder how Auntie can read the page so far away. She has thick glasses, which make her look like an owl sometimes. Mommy says Auntie is very good with the piano, but Mommy doesn't like her songs much.

Well, there you have it! Threads of memory woven into the fabric of that unique tapestry, memories that I cannot associate with the little girl in the photographs, with her pretty dresses and lace collars, pink and purple bows, barrettes in neatly brushed hair. The elements of script are definitely in place. These first seven years are the most significant, and patterns are becoming defined. Later childhood experiences enrich the patterns and give added depth to the drama that will unfold as surely as night follows day.

THE WEAVING OF A TAPESTRY

Who are the significant adults in your early life experience? How would you describe each one of them, their unique personalities?

How did they relate to each other?

From observing these interactions, what did you learn about the role of men, of women?

What was your relationship with each parent or parent substitute?

What early memories stand out for you, especially the earliest memory you have? What were your feelings, thoughts and behaviours as you experienced those events?

Do you experience those same thoughts, feelings and behaviours, or modifications of them, presently?

Can you identify any decisions you made as a result of those experiences? Or any conclusions about yourself (your "lovability"), others, or what you can expect in the world?

Are you carrying some (or all) of those decisions, perceptions, conclusions with you today?

When you were disciplined, what was mild and what was severe? How did that affect you? What decisions did you make regarding what was "good behaviour" and what was "bad behavior"?

Were these messages helpful or hurtful?

TEACHERS, TRAUMAS
AND TREACHERY

It's late summer, 1945. I am now age seven, and my world expands. The family moves just a block away, to 301 Park Street. The home that my parents live in until age and infirmity force them out in their early eighties is a two-story, red-brick house with five cement steps leading up to a small porch with a wrought-iron rail, a porch just big enough for two lawn chairs and two flower boxes or pots of red geraniums. The neighbourhood doesn't change; the school—the same. The family stabilizes; routines and responsibilities evolve as I mature. And new adventures in play and in school set the stage for further decisions that impact the script I will take into my adult world.

Our Saturday chores completed—linens changed, floor mopped, furniture dusted, clothes put away, bathroom cleaned—I ask, "Wanna play cowboys?"

Kenny and I play for what seems like hours in the big bedroom he shares with Bayne. We put folded grey army blankets over the foot rails of the two steel beds—saddles over our horses, sometimes red stallions, sometimes the Clydesdales that Dad likes, sometimes palominos, like Trigger, or wild horses that have to be broken. With the force of our reins—ties borrowed from the boys' closet—we ride the western ranges fighting bad cowboys or wild Indians. Today I have a red polka-dot handkerchief around my neck and I'm Dale Evans; and Kenny, with a blue handkerchief tied at his neck, is Roy Rogers. He gets to ride Trigger. Kenny always gets to play the good parts—Roy, Gene Autry, Tom Mix, Hopalong Cassidy, the Lone Ranger, while I only get to be the sidekick.

47

Kenny tires of this game and suggests we go out and inspect our territory, the territory that he has mapped out on a piece of paper, the territory of the Blue-Masked Gang. Off we go to play behind Kaufman's field and the Granite Club—Kenny, the captain of the gang, and me, his trusty lieutenant. Two boys, about my age I think, one overweight, the other younger and much thinner, are playing in the sand hill that slopes to the tracks.

"What are you doing in our territory?" Kenny asks, hands on his hips, rope slung over the shoulder, his blue handkerchief tied around his neck backwards, white short-sleeved shirt tucked into blue jeans—every bit a mean cowboy.

"What do you mean? We're just making sand castles," the older boy answers, looking up from his activity with a questioning look on his round face.

"You're in the territory of the Blue-Masked Gang and you'll have to be hanged. What do you think, Lieutenant? Should we string 'em up?"

"You betcha, they're enemies in our territory," I say, no rope around my shoulders, just a red polka-dot handkerchief, not even a blue mask.

Kenny lets the rope slung over his shoulder fall to the ground, makes a lasso and grabs the skinny kid. He slips the lasso under his armpits and tosses the other end of the rope over the lower branch of the sentry, that tall pine tree that guards the outhouse.

"Don't do it," the big kid says, his big brown eyes filling with tears, which begin rolling down his cheeks in earnest. "Here, I'll give you my daddy's knife—it's … it's from the war. Please, don't hurt my brother."

He wouldn't, would he? Kenny? Is he really going to hang the little kid?

"Okay," Kenny says, much to my relief. I didn't believe he would do it. Kenny? No way. Honestly, I didn't really think he would.

The big kid hands over the knife. Kenny takes the rope off the younger boy and the two of them, still crying, run. Kenny and I look at each other. This game doesn't feel good. We decide to go home.

There are girls living on Park and Agnes Streets. Donna Weese, whose mom owns and operates Mabe's Lunch just down on the corner of Agnes and Park Street, Carol Frank, Rosemary Bush, Irva McGinnis and Gloria Deorksen, Bobby's sister, all play together. On occasions I join them but I'm not really interested in skipping, playing dolls, jacks, school, or other girls' games. I do have dolls, but rarely play with them. Mom makes rag dolls for me but now she gives them to my cousins.

I have a sense that the activities I enjoy are not "feminine." Mom suggests I play with the girls across the street but they're not much fun. I think she wants to show me how to sew. I know she likes to make things. Maybe I'll do that when I get old. Although I don't think Mom much likes me going to Kaufman's park and watching adult men play baseball—they often let me be the bat girl—she never actually says "don't." She never says "don't" much at all. Mom says that she didn't have many friends to play with and show her how to do things when she was a kid growing up on the farm. Maybe she likes that I'm happy and having lots of fun even if it's not with girl things—and well, I am.

We do play stuff with Mom and Dad, too—lots of card games, checkers, Romoli, puzzles. Dad teaches us to play poker—for toothpicks, not money—and I sometimes win. Blackjack is my favourite. It's sometimes hard to lose though even if it's only toothpicks. Saturday night is "Hockey Night in Canada," and we get to stay up late and listen to the game. All of us cheer for the Toronto Maple Leafs. Sometimes Dad will pretend to cheer for Montreal but we know he's only kidding. On Sundays we listen to Just Mary and her stories of Maggie Muggins. Throughout the week we get to hear the *Amos 'n' Andy Show*, *The Shadow*, *Inner Sanctum*, with its squeaky door introduction, *The Thin Man*, *The Fat Man*, *Fibber McGee and Molly*, *The Jack Benny Program* with his buddy Rochester and lots of other exciting radio programs.

As I get older Mom and Dad teach me to play bridge. I hate this game but I have to play when they need a fourth person. Dad says, "There is only one possible card you can play." I hate it when he says this and I have eight cards in my hand. I like playing outdoors the most, better than cards.

"Well, Dalia," Mr. Deorksen says, his Russian accent no longer noticeable to me. "What do you want with Bobby?" Mr. Deorksen, a tall, heavyset, gruff-looking man, always calls me Dalia. He likes to tease me though I don't quite know why. Or perhaps he thinks my name is Dalia. I'm never certain.

"Can Bobby come and play with me?"

"Sure, Dalia," he says, turning to hide the smile on his face. I can hear him call out to Bobby somewhere in the house that his girlfriend wants him to come and play.

"Wanna play on the lumber piles, Bobby?"

"Oh yeah, let's see if our hideout is still there. I bet no one's found it yet."

Off we skip, running across the park where we play tippie on that little triangle of space in front of the Granite Club, dash around the asphalt tennis courts, through the trees to Kaufman's park and slide our way down the sand hill to the tracks. No people around. No train coming down the tracks. Over we scoot to the sheltered lumber piles belonging to the Honsberger Lumber Company. Crawling up a section of piled lumber, we place a plank over the six feet of space leading to a higher stacked pile. We crawl over the plank just as fast as you can say "Billie-be-damned." By pushing some wood aside, maneuvering other planks, we crawl down into a space blocked from view. Spaces in the woodpile create tiny windows for us to see out onto the path leading to the building.

"Bobby, look," I say in a hushed tone. Bobby looks. The two of us hold our breath. Within six feet of us an old hobo has come from nowhere. He's dressed in sagging grey pants held up by black suspenders, a green soiled shirt, with black running shoes on his feet and no socks. He stops at the edge of the opposite lumber pile, pulls out his penis and starts to pee. He pees forever. Then he shakes his penis and shakes his penis until he squirts more pee. Only reluctantly it seems, he finally puts it back in his pants with one hand while leaning against the lumber with his other. We're too scared to giggle. When he continues walking down the path, moving away from us, Bobby and I make a hasty retreat. Scrambling back to the right side of the tracks seems like a good idea.

"Do yuh see him, Bobby?" I say, peeking around the pile of lumber on our side of the tracks, close to the pond.

Before he can answer, the hobo comes around the other corner of the pile and confronts us—a spooky figure straight from any child's nightmare, unshaven, hair dirty and uncombed.

"I know what you're doing," he says, a wicked curl to his lip. I know what he's implying.

"Do yuh see them, Bobby?" I say, and then turn directly to face the man. "We're playing hide-and-go-seek. There's lots of kids around here. Come on, Bobby, let's go find them."

Bobby takes his cue and we make a fast exit. We jump off the lumber onto the ground, our feet hitting cinder with a crunch, and take off up to the hill, heading for the safety of Kaufman's park. I hear the old man say, "Yeah sure, I know what you're up to. I did that too when I was young."

That doesn't stop us, or me on my own, from going back to the track, or the pond, or lumber piles adjacent to the tracks, but soon I get bored with this play. My attention shifts to group activity in the school field or on Gruhn Street, especially in the evenings. When it's time to come home, usually after dark, Dad blows his whistle at a pitch that would cause any dog to shriek. He blows little dots and dashes, which he calls Morse code, and when those sounds are in a certain pattern I know that he wants me. When he calls, you gotta run home fast.

One day Kenny and I hear that the midway is in town, over on Belmont Boulevard. I'm eight years old and we have bikes now and can easily ride over and see what's happening. Kenny notices an arcade, which has big glass jars with prizes in them. If you put a nickel in the slot, a big claw moves out over the stack of prizes, grabs onto one and drops it in a bin. The prize shoots out of a tube and it's yours. That's exciting. The jar has lots of highly desirable stuff in it—little whistles, plastic frames to put a picture in, chocolate bars, bubble gum, miniature pistols, key chains and toy trucks, from what I can see. Our problem is that we don't have any nickels to put in, but that's easy to fix. On the floor of the arcade you can see several grey slugs about the size of a nickel. I don't know where they came from, but both of us figure they're as good as nickels any day.

Kenny puts a slug in the slot and shoves the slot in. It sticks. No amount of juggling loosens it. So Kenny brings out the brand-new ivory-covered pocketknife, the knife that Dad brought him from Detroit just yesterday, and uses the blade to see if he can get the slug out and release the pushing mechanism.

"What do you think you're doing?"

Startled, we turn to see one of the carnival men hovering over us. He has a grizzly, bearded face, grey hair and mean-looking blue eyes. He's not smiling.

"My nickel got stuck. I'm just trying to get it out," Kenny says.

"You're a liar," the man says and reaching over, grabs the knife out of Kenny's hand. We run for our bikes and take off home.

"What am I going to tell Dad?" Kenny asks. I don't have an answer for him.

Kenny goes into the house, tells Dad the story—only altering it ever so slightly—and comes out to tell me that Dad's calling the police. We run across the street and hide under Michael Slaunwhite's verandah, even though the smells of dead leaves and animal droppings are not inviting. The latticework provides camouflage and the opportunity to spy. Sure enough, a police car drives up and an officer goes into the house. A moment later the officer comes out with Dad and both get into the car. What seems like hours later the car arrives back and Dad gets out and goes into the house. Oh God, now what?

I wait outside while Kenny goes in to face the consequences. I wait. I wait. I sit on the verandah, looking at the popcorn clouds in the powder-blue sky, look for an omen, a sign from God or the angels that Kenny is not being killed, dead.

"Well, what'd he say?" I ask the moment Kenny pops his head out the front door.

"Nothing," Kenny says. "He just said, 'Here's your knife.'"

"Nothing! Nothing! Do you think he believed us, Kenny?" I didn't think for a moment that we had fooled Dad.

"I don't think so."

Sometimes adults behave in ways that are puzzling and unpredictable. Take, for example, Uncle Frank.

Uncle Frank can get really mad. Sometimes I visit my cousins at their house. A couple of times I even stayed for a sleepover. But all the time I'm there I'm very uncomfortable, my stomach's on guard, ready to toss up undigested terror at a moment's notice. Uncle Frank yells, screams, swears at the children and he's mean to Aunt Lois, too. I'll bet he's even meaner when the kids don't have visitors. Kenny tells me that Uncle Frank's an alcoholic, but I'm not sure what that means. I don't think Kenny knows either. Is this how come Jenny, Bonny, Patsy and Sandy all run away at one time or another? They pop up at our house like unexpected prizes in boxes of crackerjacks.

I don't understand this family. I know I don't want to stay overnight at their house anymore. Mom sews dresses and special clothes for these cousins. She's always doing things for them and for Aunt Lois. I don't know why.

Uncle Mac, Dad's oldest brother, is like Uncle Frank in many ways. These cousins live in Hamilton, so I don't get to see them often. On one occasion Uncle Mac asks Mom and Dad if I could spend a week at his cottage in order to be company for Claire. She's Bayne's age and I feel shy with her. She seems so much older than me. Mom's especially pleased and helps me pack my clothes. I don't want to go but I go.

"Now, Dale, I have to talk to you about your manners. Last week you were a bad influence on Claire and I don't want that to happen this week. I simply will not tolerate it."

I don't respond. *Was there something wrong with my manners?* I'd been on my best behaviour, but this week for sure, I figure I'll have to be increasingly alert. I'll watch Aunt Eva and Claire all the time and do everything they do.

One evening Uncle Mac insists that Claire and I go fishing with him. *Gee, this'll be fun.* It isn't! What Uncle Mac means by us going fishing: Claire and I sit in the boat without talking, without moving, for an hour or more, while Uncle Mac fishes. And his mood is ugly; his rowing is angry; even the water, black and shimmering in the early evening, quivers at his touch. I'll bet that's why no fish come anywhere close to his fishing line. When we arrive back on shore, Claire runs away crying and I'm left to make my way back to the cottage. It's clear to me that Claire's terrified of her dad. I think Aunt Eva is, too. She tries awfully hard to please him.

I don't understand this anger and the silences that scream in my ears. I've never heard my parents speak in angry voices, and Gramma and Auntie sure don't yell. I know I can't ask Dad, and Mom doesn't seem to want to know either. *Maybe just men are like this? Then why isn't Dad like Uncle Frank, Uncle Mac?*

"Merry Christmas, Gramma. Merry Christmas, Auntie," we call out, all at once, our excitement spilling over like milk on puffed wheat in a tiny cereal bowl. The smells of breakfast are accentuated by the chill in the air and the lateness of the hour—it's already 9:30 and Bayne, Kenny and I have been up since 6:30. We plead with Dad to let us open one gift before going to Gramma's, but only Mom's asking makes it happen.

"Look, Gramma, I got this thing. What do you call it again, Mom?"

"A kaleidoscope, sweetie," Mom says, while taking off her coat. "You play with the boys until breakfast is on the table."

As we play in the living room, smells of scrambled eggs, sausages, coffee and freshly baked coffee cake are pushed out of our minds when the phone rings. I soon determine that Aunt Eunice is on the other end. Before long I see tears on Mom's cheeks. That's it! I'm gonna go up the street—Aunt Eunice and Uncle Howard live six houses up from Gramma's on Alma Street—and I'm gonna kill her. I slip on my coat, explain that I just want to swing on the front porch for a while and off I go, anger firing my spirit, to avenge Mom and protect her from that mean, mean, mean person! I walk right up to the house, well, to the sidewalk in front of the house, stand and stand and stand, unaware of the cold, unaware of the time, swallowing feelings, a breakfast of rage and … and, well, I blaze a thunderbolt of hate … and … wish Auntie Eunice dead. Impotent to do anything, I turn in frustration, overcome with feelings of helplessness, explode into tears and walk back down the street. I vow that I will never call Eunice "Aunt" again. In fact, if I'm given a choice, I'm going to stop visiting Dad's brothers and sisters and never ever call any of them Aunt and Uncle again.

I'm nine years old now and Mom enrolls me in a dancing class at the YWCA—tap dancing. Every week I go to class with my tap-dancing shoes and hate it. I don't understand why this experience is so painful. I know that Mom is thrilled and likes sewing my dancing costume for the recital. I'm a bear at *The Little Bear's Picnic*, and Mom thinks I look great. I don't know about that, but I do know about the feelings. Oh yes, the feelings—I feel fat, ugly, awkward. And the tears are hard to hold back.

For the next three years, Mom enrolls me in the Elsie V. Ewald School of Dancing and I practice ballet dancing. Every year the same—Mom excited about sewing the dancing costumes, helping others, if need be, prepare for the recital; Mom and Dad attending the recitals—and me, feeling fat, ugly, awkward and humiliated. A summer's worth of figure skating—Mom sewing the costume—produces the same emotional result.

It's winter now. Bayne and Kenny make a skating rink out the back and Bayne's giving it another hosing to make it smooth again after the snowfall. Bayne's yelling at Kenny, who just threw a snowball at him. Uh-oh, now they're fighting, and Bayne jumps on Kenny and pushes him into the snow bank. He's pushing snow in Kenny's mouth.

"Daddy, Daddy, come quick. Bayne's killing Kenny," I yell, slamming the kitchen door as I blast into the room.

"Hold on, hold on, Dale. Don't get so excited," Dad says as he enters the kitchen.

"But Daddy, he's stuffing snow down Kenny's throat. He's killing him! Come, now!" I say, choking out my words between near-hysterical sobs.

I remain rooted to the kitchen floor gulping for breath as Dad runs for the backdoor. I'm still rooted to the spot when Dad finally reappears, shaken, ashen in colour, minutes—or was it hours?—later, no boys in tow. *Where were they? What happened?*

Dad turns to me. "And don't you be a tattletale!"

Stunned by his remark, I watch as Dad leans against the refrigerator, his head back, struggling to catch his breath. Slowly—

like the super-slow motion of a televised hockey replay—he slinks down the fridge door and collapses on the floor.

Still frozen, I don't notice Dad crawl from the kitchen to the bedroom just across the hall. Propelled by a need outside of my conscious awareness, I move to the bedroom doorway and see Dad lying on his bed, motionless, hands folded over his chest, as still as death in a coffin.

I stare, unable to comprehend what's happening. "Please, God," I pray, "please, God, don't let him be dead. I promise I will never ask anyone for anything again."

No one explains to me what's wrong with Daddy. He goes away for a couple of weeks, and then he comes home and that's that. Maybe now I won't ever be frightened again.

I think being ten years old is much easier than being nine—at least, it seems this way until September. School starts again and I can't begin grade four with the rest of the kids.

I sit at the front window of the house, watching the kids coming and going from school. My throat feels better now but the stitches in my belly are still bandaged and they itch something awful. I didn't want to get my tonsils out. I didn't want to get my appendix out. Dr. Gillespie said that I had to. Now that I'm home from the hospital, Mom allows me to sit, wrapped in a blanket, in the front chair. Staying in bed with no one to talk to is boring. Kenny tells me that I will go into Miss Godfrey's class when I return to school. That scares me. Kenny and Bayne both had Miss Godfrey for grade four and they say she's a witch. Even Dad had her as a teacher, so she's really old.

My first day back at school, Miss Godfrey explains that she thought I was a boy. This doesn't surprise me. Every first day of school since grade one, when the names of the girls were called out in front of the school stairs, my name was always omitted. I would end up in the principal's office to find out which class I was to attend. I knew after the first year that my name was called out on the boys' side because Clare Williams, a boy, always had his name called out on the girls' side. Miss Godfrey tells me that I will have to sit at the back with the boys because that is the desk she designated for me. The sharpness in her voice, the irritation in her body movements—she clucks and wobbles her neck just like a chicken—clearly imply that I'm not to object. She needn't worry. I'm much too scared to talk back. I know I'm not supposed to do that.

I like sitting with the boys. I like Grant. After a few weeks Grant sends me a note. I answer him. He writes another.

"Give me that note," demands Miss Godfrey, in a thunderous voice, trained to intimidate little children. "I saw you put that note from Grant in your desk. Now give it to me or I'll retrieve it myself and you'll wish I hadn't."

Immobilized by fear, I don't move a muscle.

Oh boy, oh boy, where did she come from anyway? Just a moment ago Miss Godfrey was at the far blackboard pointing to a map of the world with her long wooden pointer, nattering on about Samuel D. Champlain. I look up, reluctantly, at this four feet eleven inches of towering, glowering, old lady, strategically tapping the palm of her hand with the pointer held in her other hand. *She's going to hit me—she is!* The other day she whacked Judy Weber across the legs with that pointer just because Judy wasn't sitting up straight in her chair with her hands folded on the desk and her feet placed neatly together under the seat. That's the truth. Honest. Cross my heart and hope to die if it's a lie.

Her chicken-like face is bending ever closer to mine, close enough for me to smell the garlic from her noon-hour lunch—I didn't know chickens ate garlic. Even with her granny-like glasses, grey hair tightly pulled back into a bun, I know that Miss Godfrey is not your average gramma.

I reach into my desk, fingers trembling, exploring both of the hidden notes, hoping that by their crumpled landscape I will know which of the two is the least incriminating. *Please, God, please, God, let it be the right one.* That moment of stillness—everyone around me holding their breath—rows of desks, rows of children, and yet no tittering, no shuffling, no scraping of restless feet on the old wooden floor, not a sneeze, not a cough; anticipation suspended in the air, smelling very much like sweat, waiting, waiting.

I hold my breath, pull out one of the crumpled notes and hand it to Miss Godfrey.

"I think the class might be interested in knowing what you and Grant have to say to one another," Miss Godfrey says. Clearly enjoying my discomfort and embarrassment, she turns to the class and reads, "Will you kiss me?" "Yes."

I feel my face flush, feel tears of humiliation and utter a silent "Thank you, God!"

After serving my detention in the classroom—I don't know where Grant served his time—I find Grant Bernhardt, loitering, waiting for the opportunity to talk to me about the contents of the second note.

"Do yuh still want to fuck?" he asks.

"Okay," I answer, anxious to explore what this word means and see if Kenny was telling me the truth when he told me this summer how this is done and that moms and dads do this to bring children into the world. He told me that ministers and their wives do it too, and that makes the whole idea very suspect.

"But where're we gonna go to do this?"

"Ken Ruby lives just across King Street. He's waiting for us. We can go under his verandah. No one will see us there."

"Oh, is he coming too?"

The crawl space under the verandah smells musky, like damp, rotting stuff. Through the latticework I can see a woman walking down the street. I notice, too, clouds are beginning to form in the sky and wonder momentarily if rain will come through the latticework and soak the ground I'm sitting on. Grant and Ken are whispering.

"You go first."

"No, you go first."

"No, I can't. I'm not ready. You do it."

"Well, okay."

"I'm going first," Grant says. "Take your pants off."

I comply, wondering what will happen next. Strange sensations in my belly signal—what? Excitement? Fear?

"I think you should lie down."

Where's he going to put it? I wonder, again responding without hesitation.

That's it? That's what fucking is? I realize that Grant has touched my vagina with his penis or I assume that was what happened. I experienced a light touch, a brushing sensation. *Where is the hole? There must be a hole. No?*

Amidst all these questions a voice from somewhere inside says, "*You're doing something bad!*" Startled, I move suddenly to push Grant off my body.

"I don't wanna do this anymore."

"Okay," Grant says. "Ken, it's your turn."

More whispers. I think I hear Ken mumble, "I can't. It won't stay up."

"Are we gonna kiss?" I ask.

"Sure," Grant says, leaning forward to touch lips ever so gently. Ken makes no such overture. *Maybe he can't keep it up,* I think.

Panties intact, I notice that it is starting to rain. "I've gotta go home," I say, relief masked by a clap of thunder. Now, starting to run, I experience a sense of alarm. The sky looks ominous: the storm threatening to hail God's vengeance on this newest of sinners.

The storm doesn't, nor does Mom, who meets me halfway home on Agnes hill, with an umbrella in one hand and the other free to give me a whack on the behind—the smack I know more from scare than anger.

With this experience my childhood innocence gradually fades, just dims into oblivion like the afterimage on a TV screen but with a time warp. Several days later, the boy who sits behind me leans over and says, "Is it true? Did you fuck Grant?" A year later, even my friend Bobby asks me that question.

That was mean. None of the children in my neighbourhood ever told anyone when we played doctor or any of our other exploring games. *How could they tell? Was that such a bad thing to do? Is everyone going to know now? Why would they tell? Are Mom and Dad going to find out? Will the teachers know? What about the girls? They're really mean. I'm not ever going to talk to those boys again, maybe not even any boys.*

Shortly after this experience, still at the age of ten, on a rainy school day, the girls are all directed to play in the dank, poorly illuminated basement of the school for recess. During recess a girl whom I know only as one of the McAllister kids comes into the area where we're playing. One of my classmates points her out and says,

"Do yuh see that kid? She just came out of reform school. She had to go there because she was bad. She fucked a boy. Yuh gotta stay away from her." My heart drops. *Uh-oh, I hope the girls don't find out about me. What will I do if they don't like me? Will I go to reform school?*

I'd better make sure the boys never tell any of the girls. If I can be a good friend to the boys, a good buddy, and help them and listen to their secrets, maybe they won't tell. I become highly skilled at intuiting what the boys need by way of compliments and which boys like which girls so that I can encourage the relationships. And it works. As far as I know, the girls don't find out.

To be safe with the girls, I'd better be skilled at all the things that matter—primarily sports. If I'm number one, then I get to be the captain of teams. I get to do the choosing and will never be left out or rejected. That's it. The thing to do is to be number one. Fortunately I'm gifted with athletic abilities and think sports are fun. I think I can do this—anything to ward off the possibility of hearing that evil question, "Did you fuck Grant?"

My athletic skills, especially as a badminton player, provide me with opportunities to express my sense of fun and in a way, dance—a natural and graceful way for me to flow with my body. I like the rhythm of my body, the running, the throwing, the stretching. Mom and Dad never see me play these games. Without the weightiness of having to be something to please Mom, I'm so much freer with myself and my body. I feel like a girl—I'm becoming a girl, at least in my own mind—much less interested now in playing with the boys and much keener on being "somebody" with the girls.

I'm absolutely delighted the day my first period arrives. Just a week before, the girls in the class were whispering about something and teasing me because I didn't seem to know what they meant. I feigned knowing, not wanting to be found naive or uninformed. Just a few days after that, Mom comes into my bedroom with a box of Kotex. She tells me what the pads are for and she seems excited about what she believes is about to happen. And it does—just one week later.

"Oh Dale, it's really wonderful to be a female and be able to have babies. Having you three children has been a real miracle. Someday you'll be grown up and you'll discover the same joy I know."

She doesn't tell me exactly how this happens but I already know that part. I wonder how she knew that my period was going to start. I'm glad it's happening when I'm still twelve. I'm sure this is what the girls were giggling about.

With a sense of smugness I announce shortly thereafter, "I can't play badminton today because I have my period." Now the girls know that I know. See, I'm not so dumb. And with that, and coincidentally the purchase of my very first bra, I have my picture taken—me sitting on my bike with a see-through T-shirt, evidence of my mature status in life showing through like a girl guide badge of honour.

"Guess what, Mom? One of the grade eight girls, Marguerite is her name, invited me to a party Saturday night. Can I go?" I say. I wasn't sure that I really wanted to go. I don't think any of the other kids in my grade seven class were invited.

"Sure, if you want to," Mom says. "I'll sew you a new blouse to wear with the skirt we just got you. You'll look real nice, you'll see." And I did. It was pink, Mom's favourite colour, and had a scalloped neckline.

I go to the party with mixed feelings. *What do they do at grade eight parties? Will I know anybody?* I wish she hadn't invited me. *Why me, anyway? If I don't go, maybe the boys will talk about me. Maybe Marguerite knows about me and Grant.*

I arrive at the house but I don't see any lights on. Marguerite lets me in and I hear the music blasting. I'm led into the living room. It's dark. I can make out some girls sitting on boys' laps. Lots of laughter. Although this is new to me, I soon figure out that the idea is to match up with one boy and kiss, then go to the washroom, return and match up with another boy and do the same. I spot Dougie Pfaff. He asks me to sit down. We kiss. Some kids start dancing. I know some boys, maybe girls too, are in the kitchen. I smell cigarette smoke and I recognize the sounds of glasses clinking and bags of chips or pretzels being opened. I excuse myself and go to the washroom. I don't like this. *What am I doing here?*

When I return to the dark room, bodies are spread out in chairs and chesterfields and on the floor. I recognize Dennis Huth, one of Grant's closest friends. He gestures for me to come over. Dennis leads me to a room off the kitchen, a bedroom I discover, and indicates that I should lie down with him. I do. We kiss and I taste potato chips. He slips his hand down the neckline of my pretty pink blouse and begins to fondle my breast. I excuse myself and head for the bathroom quickly. Near panic; *has Grant told Dennis? Is this why I was invited to this party? Are all the boys going to take liberties?* I can't bear the thought of another "Did you fuck Grant?" experience.

When I return everyone is gathered in the kitchen to play spin the bottle. Whoever is lucky enough to have the bottle point at her has to kiss one of the boys. I'm lucky. The bottle *doesn't* point to me. I fake having fun but I can hardly wait until it's time to go. I'm mad at Mom for making such a stupid blouse, with such a stupid neckline. I don't want to be here.

I make it through the evening and through another party before I have the courage to say no. At the party I don't go to, one of the girls gets pregnant. I wonder if she fucked Grant.

I pray for high school, for a reprieve. At the Kitchener-Waterloo Collegiate and Vocational Institute, a school of twenty-five hundred children, surely I will escape. Surely I will get a fresh start. I will begin a new life—I will be safe. I can just be me, no? Please, God, make it so.

TEACHERS, TRAUMAS AND TREACHERY

As we approach puberty, the thoughts, feelings and behaviours we have integrated in the younger years are coloured now by sexuality. We take this programming into our tentative experiments with our peers. How did your parent(s) or parent substitutes prepare you (or didn't prepare you) for the physical/body changes as you moved into and through puberty?

Were those messages helpful or hurtful in helping you with your self-image?

Do you recognize how the messages you received from your parents prepared you (or didn't prepare you) for coping with peers and authorities?

When you had a problem or an event that caused you to feel hurt or sad, what did you do? And why?

Can you see similarities in the way you learned to cope with relationships then and how you manage relationships today?

Are you carrying any of those early decisions and coping strategies into today's world?

TROPHIES AND TRIUMPHS

"Did you fuck Grant?"—that's what he's going to ask! Shit! Terror pierces my heart and grabs at my stomach like wolves on a fallen deer. Four more years of hell; I thought I was safe. I knew it, knew when I saw Grant and Ron talking in the school corridor the other day, that my life would be unbearable. Grant would tell. And obviously he has, *and where on earth has he come from anyway?*

I'd looked forward to this hayride. Ron was proof, proof that my strategy was working. I decided last September, when I walked up the twenty-five stairs leading to the entrance of the Kitchener-Waterloo Collegiate and Vocational Institute (KCI), that I would win every award the school had to offer. I would be number one. Then I would be safe. Now, here I am, a new grade ten student, with Ron Shane, a grade eleven boy, a member of the senior basketball team—who has an athletic letter sewn on his yellow basketball jacket—snuggling in the hay, his date for the senior class hayride.

All the work I did to establish myself as a somebody wasted? Elected as class representative to the Girls' Athletic Association, winning a position on the junior girls' volleyball team, the junior girls' basketball team, the school badminton team, even winning the Western Ontario Secondary School Association's singles championship—wasted? I thought my strategy had worked. Sylvia Clemmens, Bobby Deorksen and Esther Hermosa were the only people in my class from public school, and I hadn't crossed paths with anyone else from past. I was so sure that I was safe, that I could soon establish myself as a leader, a top athlete, an achiever. No one would ever know my shame. Now all of this was threatened by this one stupid question—"Did you fuck Grant?" Damn you to hell, Grant Bernhardt!

Ron is waiting; ignoring the sounds of laughter, singing, threats of jumping, mock fights and male horseplay, typical of young tomcats strutting their stuff, waiting for my response to his question.

I stiffen in Ron's arms, no longer aware of the smell of the freshly cut hay, gently prickling my skin through my blue jeans and long-sleeved white cable-knit sweater; no longer aware of the crispness of the evening breeze. I revisited that day that I have relived a hundred times a year since grade four. If only I hadn't missed the first month of school; if only I had a different name, a name that wasn't sexually ambivalent; if only Miss Godfrey had found the other note; if only, if only.

"You're awfully quiet," says Ron. "Did you hear me? Do you mind if I ask you a personal question?"

Ron, dear Ron, this six-foot-tall, blond, blue-eyed, gentle boy who dances awkwardly—a young giraffe on wobbly, unsure legs—will toss me out of his life like a used Kleenex. I might as well get it over with.

"Go ahead, Ron. Ask your question," I say with a shrug, resignation clearly audible in my voice.

"Will you go steady with me?"

Did I hear right? Tears of joy begin to trickle down my cheeks. *He didn't tell. He didn't tell. Oh thank you, Grant. Thank you.*

"Yes, yes, Ron," I say, relaxing into his body, planting a big kiss squarely on his thin lips.

Fourteen months of going steady with Ron, an innocent romance, gives me time to secure a place for myself in the social life of a very active high school: the Christmas formal dance, Friday night sports activities and dances in the boys' gym. I'm spared that horrible experience of standing against the wall hoping that some boy will find me attractive and ask me to dance. I enjoy being in love. Trevor Bennett, a recent graduate of the school, comes for the Friday dances with his band, and romance flourishes, nurtured by the big-band sounds of the forties and the music of the early fifties: "Autumn Leaves," "C'est Si Bon," "Dear Hearts and Gentle People," "Harbour Lights," Nat King Cole with his hit "Too Young," which I know he is singing just for me. As the bewitching hour approaches, the playing of "Good Night, Irene" telegraphs the pending return to reality; gradually the fantasies of the evening gently evaporate, the romantic mist clears.

Reality—the girls' gymnasium, with its unique perfume of sweat embedded in every inch of the painted and repainted, now faded, yellow walls, with its smell of waxed and polished wooden floors. Insignificant in size compared to the immensity of the school, the gym is my universe, the classroom of my personal growth.

The gym is just big enough for a basketball court, with players' benches pushed tightly against the inner wall. Tumbling mats and gymnastic equipment are squashed against the far wall near the door that accesses the boys' gym, built just a year or two before my arrival at the school. Maggie Doyle and Verna Schweigert, the primary educators for my six-year experience, have a small office to the left of the gym.

I don't have gym class the afternoon that Dad, now home for lunch, looks at my grade ten Christmas report card and almost refuses to sign it.

"A 'C' for effort in phys ed, Dale? How can you possibly get a 'C' for effort with all your abilities? I won't tolerate this," Dad says, frowning and beginning what I know will be another "anything worth doing is worth doing well" lecture.

"It isn't my fault," I say, getting up from the table, taking dishes to the counter. "Miss Schweigert was my coach all last year and she knows I do my best. It isn't fair. She's a stupid marker."

"Miss Schweigert isn't the one who got a 'C' for effort, Dale. She isn't the one who's being graded."

"Well, I don't think she likes me. It's not my fault. I haven't done anything to her," I say, attempting to justify my poor mark and avoid the lecture, diligently preparing to do the dishes, not even waiting for Kenny's help.

Mom slips into the kitchen after Dad leaves for work. "Go easy on your dad, Dale. He's only interested in your well being."

"Well, he's being unfair," I say, muttering under my breath the obscenities I would never dare say out loud.

"You know he gets upset when you argue. Why not just let him say his piece and be quiet?"

"You always protect him," I say, pleased though that Mom has picked up a tea towel to dry the dishes. I just want to get out of here and get back to school.

Right after classes I go down to the gym. Bursting into the office without knocking, I confront a startled Verna Schweigert.

"It's your fault I got in trouble with my dad this noon," I say, surprised to experience tears on my cheeks.

"What's the matter, Dale? What are you so angry about?" she asks, jumping up from her desk as if I had struck her. I could have belted her right in the nose. Her short blue jumper and white blouse, soiled from her day's activities, the white socks and white running shoes showing signs of chronic use, did little to hide spindly knees, which I'm sure trembled even more than her lips. If she's shocked by this display of righteous indignation, I'm even more startled. Me? Angry? Mouthing off?

"My dad's really mad at me for getting a 'C' for effort. Why did you do that? That's not fair," I say, surprised that I can talk and cry at the same time.

"Well, you were fooling around all the time. You know, you're the best student in the class in phys ed and when you fool around everyone else does too."

Maggie Doyle enters the office just as Verna Schweigert is edging her way into the inner-office washroom. Maggie is my coach this year for both the senior girls' volleyball team and the senior girls' basketball team.

"Dale," she says, "you have no right to talk to Miss Schweigert that way."

"Well, she got me in trouble," I say, sniffling and wiping my nose on a balled-up Kleenex extracted from the dusty pocket of my blue blazer.

"No, Dale, *you* got you in trouble. I heard what Miss Schweigert said to you and it's true. You're a natural leader and very talented. When you fool around the others follow your example. You have to take responsibility for your behaviour. Now apologize to Miss Schweigert."

Taken aback by this comment, especially coming from Miss Doyle, my very favourite phys ed person, and experiencing the queasiness of my explosion—a censoring voice from within saying, *"My God, what are you doing?"*—I mumble, "I'm sorry, Miss Schweigert. I'm just upset," as she reenters the office area, feeling safe now, I guess, that Miss Doyle is present.

"Okay, Dale, I'm sure you'll do better next term."

Both stand looking at me as I back my way out of the office feeling sheepish, heading to the girls' change area to hide until I recover from the shock of my behaviour.

I do check it out in the very next phys ed class, and you know what? It's true. The others do indeed follow my lead. That awareness puts a very different spin on my behaviour from that point on—the responsibility of leadership.

Unlike the sports culture of the boys' world—competitiveness and winning, at least from what I can observe—the most pervasive value stressed in girls' sports is "relationships." Winning is secondary to caring about teammates, enjoying the game, having fun and the satisfaction of putting forth our collective best effort—echoes of Dad. Win or lose, the bus trips to and from competitive games reflect what is right about the experience of high school team sports for me.

From my grade eleven year on, I captain most of the teams and move into greater leadership roles on the Girls' Athletic Association, moving from vice-president to president in my grade twelve year. The summer in between, I represent my high school at the Ontario Athletic Leadership Training Camp at Lake Couchiching. There I'm chosen to be the leader of my cabin group. The camp focuses on developing leadership skills, providing opportunities for participants to learn to teach skills and referee sports activities, as well as improve individual competencies.

And no one knows, not even my closest buddies, Judy Weber, Elaine Voelzing and Dot Howse, especially not Elaine, Miss K-W Press Club, because she's so beautiful and knows all about clothes and makeup. No one knows that behind the kibitzing, behind the applause from my teammates and my performance on the sports floor, is a scared little girl. Not surprisingly, it doesn't occur to me to talk about my insecurities: my growing awareness of stage fright—

my fear of talking in front of groups, which I discover when Mr. Roebuck, my grade eleven English teacher, puts me in front of the class reading the part of Riana in *Arms and the Man,* and my body shakes like an autumn leaf in a windstorm and I almost pee my pants. Still lurking beneath a calm exterior, I harbour that fear of being found out and rejected. As my interest in the world of boys increases, so too does my growing sense of discomfort about my feminine attractiveness. No one knows—not my teammates, not my teachers, definitely not my parents—that I feel socially inadequate, unattractive, unsophisticated.

I recognize that I'm not significantly different from any other young girl: I wear the appropriate saddle shoes; I have the grey skirt, the plaid skirt, the neckerchiefs and artificial collars that all the other girls are wearing. I have the penny loafers with real pennies, the felt skirt and crinoline, the cincher belt. Although always slightly overweight—Joanne Rennie and I compete for the biggest team uniforms—I'm not obese, not unattractive, and yet the familiar early childhood feelings continue to surface—fat, ugly, awkward. Will they ever go away?

I continue to thrive in my Granite Club activities. The Granite Club, the sports facility that houses two major sections on the ground level, one with six badminton courts, another with six curling rinks, is my second home throughout the winter season. Badminton is my passion. The trophies that started coming from the time of my first competitive singles tournament at age fourteen continue to come. I'm chosen to be on a team of Canadian junior players in competition against an American team, an event sponsored by the Granite Club in Toronto. That same year I earn top seeding for the Ontario Singles Championship—alas to be defeated by the flu bug. And I'm given the privilege of playing in senior tournaments and with the seniors at my own Granite Club, including partnering with many of the teachers from my high school who also enjoyed membership at the club.

The phys ed teachers, or perhaps the culture of girls' sports, teaches me how to be a gracious loser, how to acknowledge superior skills and maintain a comfortable sense of self, but it's Dad who teaches me to be a gracious winner.

"How'd it go, Dale?" Dad asks as I come in the front door, lugging the blue Samsonite makeup case that contains my soiled badminton outfit and a blue twelve-inch-square box containing my first prize, a cut-glass fruit bowl.

"Oh, I won," I answer with a shrug of the shoulders and a so-what-else-is-new attitude. I continue on, heading towards the stairs to go on up to my bedroom.

"Just a minute, Dale, tell me about the game." Dad puts down the book he's reading—a bad sign for sure—and Mom, sitting on the chesterfield opposite Dad's chair, stops her crossword puzzle and looks at me, expectantly.

"Well, there's not much to say. The other finalist wasn't very good, so it wasn't a very competitive game."

"Dale." I always know a lecture is coming when he begins with my name. "Since you're doing a lot of winning, you'd better learn how to be gracious about it."

"What do yuh mean?"

"I'm sure your opponent had some skills or she wouldn't have made the finals. Surely you can acknowledge that and give credit where credit is due."

"Uh, well, uh, she had a terrific drop shot from backcourt," I say, inching my way closer to the stairs.

"That's better. And did you have fun?"

"Uh, yeah, I had a great time."

"Then say so," he says, picking up his book, freeing me to bolt the stairs two at a time. I hate it when he's disapproving. Embarrassment flushes my cheeks and I fume, fuss and dump my case unceremoniously on the floor. I do recover. And by the next day I do forgive him. But I hate it when he's right.

I learn a work ethic in a very different way. When I am fifteen, Mrs. McCullough, a neighbour who works at the K-W Hospital, asks my mom if I want a summer job. Mom sends me over to her house the next day to inquire about it. For the next six summers, Christmas holidays and whenever else I can, I work at the hospital, first in the kitchen and then the cafeteria. It just takes one summer's experience as a kitchen aide for the dieticians to recognize the hopelessness of having me prepare food, even under direction. However, I work very diligently at trucking food to the pavilion or washing trays when they come down the chute from the upper floors and earn the opportunity to work in the cafeteria. Now this is fun—and educational.

Tina, a German woman with a wiry, muscular body, thick, dark hair, no makeup, a spirited soul who takes no nonsense from anyone, always has the 6:30 a.m. shift, and I'm her partner this morning. As we do the cleanup after the lunch hour—the cafeteria now closed— me washing down the tables and Tina doing the sweeping, in the large, brightly lit cafeteria area, she tells me how she snuck out the back window last night after her husband went to bed.

"Weren't you scared?" I say, slopping soapy, Javex-diluted water from my basin onto the four-by-four wooden tabletop.

"Nah, he doesn't scare me. He was so drunk, I knew he wasn't going to wake up till morning."

I wonder about her bravado because Dora, her very timid sister who works the cash register, told me that Tina's husband beats her up.

"You think he's the only guy I've ever had in my life? No way. I do what I want and he never knows," Tina says, swinging the chairs up onto the table after I dry them off.

"Why don't you leave him if he's drunk all the time?"

"Why would I do that? He pays the bills. We have a nice house and I do what I want," she says, looking at me as if I am an innocent sixteen-year-old kid—which I am.

We're interrupted by Mrs. Gies grouching about whoever was on her section last night leaving the fruit juice cans open and the lower fridge area soiled with spilt milk. Mrs. Gies, now in her late sixties, grey, tightly-permed, curly hair framing her very wrinkled, scowling face, could get away with her petulance, since that was considered to be her normal state, justified by the fact that she continued to live with a grouchy old man whom she hated and whom she kicked out of her bed at least a hundred years ago. I can't figure this one out either. Why does someone stay in a marriage when they hate their partner? I don't find the answer to that, but I learn very quickly from Mrs. Gies that you *never,* repeat *never,* leave your shift without having everything sparkling clean and all the stock replenished. I hear about "these young kids who come in for the summer, pick up a pay cheque and don't give a damn about how things should be done. They never pull their weight." I determine not to be one of them. I make sure things are Windex-perfect whenever I work the salad section with her.

I hear Mildred giggling in her girlish way by the steamer trays that Louise is cleaning. Mildred, with a white, netted, Mennonite bonnet atop her straight, pulled-back-into-a-bun, thin, dark hair, is a woman in her early forties. She just became engaged and Louise, a seasoned German woman with a gruff voice and equally gruff manner, loves to tease her about sex—not really using that term, mind you, but I know it's about sex. They all talk about sex. Mildred blushes beet red and responds with that giggle.

I like Louise. If it weren't for her I would probably still be referring to myself as "stupid." One very rushed noon hour I am the server and getting quite flustered. The hot section of the line serves the soup of the day, a hot meat, gravy, potatoes and two vegetables. The server dishes out the plates as ordered when the nurses and doctors and others come down the line. Louise, working the ice cream and dessert section right beside me, hears me apologize to someone for serving them carrots instead of peas and mumbling something about "I'm so stupid." Quite sternly and loud enough for everyone in the cafeteria to hear, she says, "If you call yourself stupid one more time, I'm going to believe you." I decide that moment never to refer to myself as stupid again! It occurs to me that my dad calls himself stupid whenever he makes the most insignificant of mistakes. Guess that's where I learned it.

I'm concentrating on Tina's story when I feel a very cold, wet sensation down the back of my uniform. "Ahhhhh," I scream out and turn to face Nina, who snuck up behind me and put a handful of ice cubes down the back of my uniform. Tina colluded and laughs with Nina at catching me unaware. Nina, her sensual, lusty laugh befitting her voluptuous body, the only Russian woman working the cafeteria, could get away with anything. You had to love her. I couldn't believe that she was married to a man twenty years her senior whom she described as an old fuddy-duddy who would hardly ever do "it." You knew when he did "it," because she would come on shift laughing and happy and one of the women would say, "She did 'it' last night."

Tina and I finish our shift and are about to leave, me dead tired—I could never adjust to getting up at 5:30 a.m.—when a donut fight breaks out. Iris and Nina have come on shift. Iris, with her Mary, Mother-of-God, innocence, Irish red hair, freckled face and the mischief of the devil who makes her do things, tosses a fresh-from-the-kitchen chocolate donut at Nina, who fortunately ducks. Nina pinches a leftover honey-glazed donut from the tray and throws a strike, bang on Iris's white collar—such a contrast to working with the very serious Tina. Enough already, I'm going home.

The money I earn these first three summers of employment provides me with the opportunity of going shopping for my school clothes. Mom has a friend, Rose Pickles, who lives in Detroit, and that's where we go to shop. I'm excited to be traveling alone with my mom to the United States, my first experience out of the country.

"Get ready to run," Mom says as we stand on the curb of the double-lane highway just back of Rose's house in the Dearborn suburb of Detroit. The light changes to green and off we run, hand in hand, laughing, not quite making it to the other side before the light turns red.

The bus that takes us to the downtown shopping area of Detroit comes as quickly as the red traffic light, transporting us to a new world—big city sophistication: Montgomery Ward, Hudson's, Kaufmann's Department Store, Sears, JCPenney, we shop at all of them; theaters, restaurants, tall office buildings, big hotels and streets filled with people, some of them black-skinned. Never before have I encountered someone with black skin—Mom calls them "chocolate drops," a term that creates discomfort for me, although I don't quite know why.

We're seated at a cocktail table, and I listen as Mom and Marguerite Boland chat—Marguerite drinking a Gin Fizz cocktail, Mom a Pink Lady and me some orange concoction with a Maraschino cherry and a little yellow umbrella.

"Did you know you were named after Marguerite?" Mom asks, her eyes dancing, delighted I'm sure that she has saved this announcement for just the right moment.

"No, I didn't know that," I say, noticing Marguerite's radiant smile, a smile that transforms her gentle face into an expression of affection that surprises me and tugs at my soul.

"Marguerite and I worked together at the welfare department," Mom says, and the two of them are off again, chatting about people and events unknown to me. I wonder if being named after someone is the same as having a godmother, but I don't want to interrupt to ask. I look around the cocktail lounge—I have never before been in a hotel—and watch the men and women, all dressed in suits, ties and fashionable clothes, the likes of which I haven't noticed in downtown Kitchener. A busy humming, a droning of voices occasionally interrupted by laughter, bluish smoke circling around heads, dark coffee-coloured or transparent liquids, some with olives, with or without ice cubes, and brown bottles of beer, all fascinating.

Marguerite suggests we move into the dining room quickly or we'll be late for the eight o'clock movie. I listen and watch, too excited to eat much of the smoked salmon dinner that Mom has ordered for both of us. Dad hates fish and the smell of it, which he says makes him sick. So Mom regards fish of any kind as a treat. Mom is excited too, flushed cheeks, giggles, animated conversation. I've never experienced her like this—alone, without Dad's authoritative presence.

The Red Shoes is a sad movie. Mom sheds quiet tears. I wish we'd seen a happier movie. I enjoy the animated, giggling Mom that I experienced in the restaurant.

"Did you meet Rose Pickles at the welfare office too, Mom?" I ask on the bus trip back.

"Oh no, Rose grew up with Elthea and me. She lived on a neighbouring farm, and we all went to school together. We had great times. In the winters the field between our farms and the school was covered with ice and snow. In some parts we could just walk across the fences. We took our sleighs to school and could slide all the way down as far as the lower swamp. Rose just lived across the swamp."

"I thought the Hergotts were your neighbours."

"Yeah, they were, too. They had the farm closer to New Dundee. I think I was at their place more often than my own. Bertha and Elsie were like sisters. We all played together—Rose too."

"Do you remember lots about your childhood, Mom?"

"Oh sure, I have memories back as far as age two."

"No! How can you remember back that far?" Mom never shared anything like this before.

"I remember waking from an afternoon nap in the reed carriage that had a parasol for shade. I was in the middle of the potato field. I could hear sounds of Mom hoeing—right in the field between the barn and the Wilhelm lane, along the main road to Strasburg—and a cat came along and jumped into the carriage. I got real excited, and when the cat jumped out, I tried to follow, not realizing that I couldn't walk."

"What happened?"

"Well, I hit the ground with a plop and a howl. Mom came running."

The bus arrives at the stop much too soon. Our conversation ends as we, hand in hand and giggling, try to beat the red light back to the other side of the highway and lose.

Mom calls Dad before going to bed—every night. Not surprising. Dad calls Mom every night when he's out of town on business. Kenny tells me after we arrive home that Dad was gloomy and depressed all the time we were away. His job was to entertain Dad, but no matter what he did he couldn't lift Dad's spirits. Nothing could—except Mom arriving back home.

Gramma and Auntie now come to our house for Sunday dinners, served in the dining room with Mom's best china and silverware. The kitchen, always a mess, is my job to clear up, but who can complain after a roast beef dinner, roasted onions, potatoes, gravy, green beans, carrots and a pie of some sort—Mom's pies were even better than Gramma's, at least Dad always said so. Her crusts were melt-in-your-mouth, like no one else could ever duplicate, according to Dad. Auntie comes and helps, though sometimes I wish she wouldn't. Still Mom's protector, I find it difficult to listen to Auntie criticize Mom.

"When's Louise ever going to get new tea towels? These are worn to threads," Auntie says and, "My goodness, this garbage disposal is filthy. Doesn't your Mom ever clean it?

"I do, Auntie. That's my job," I say. "I just haven't had time yet."

And it works both ways. I listen to Mom grouse about Auntie as well.

Dad has a friend at work who occasionally lends him the use of her car. On these occasions Dad takes Mom, Auntie, Gramma and sometimes me for a Sunday afternoon drive, usually to tour the farm area where they grew up. Auntie, who suffers a mild form of narcolepsy, falls asleep in the backseat of the car and misses most of the outing. This infuriates Mom.

"Why does she have to come with us? She always falls asleep. But she won't let us go anywhere without her. She's so afraid she'll miss something," Mom says when Auntie and Gramma are out of earshot.

"Now Louise, you know she can't help it. She has a problem. Don't let it get you."

"Well, she makes me so mad. If she isn't sleeping she's bitching, and if she isn't bitching she's humming those stupid hymns."

"Louise, she's your only sister. We've got to accommodate her habits."

I stay discreetly out of the conversation. I wonder though why Mom and Auntie are so competitive. And why doesn't Dad do something about Auntie's put-downs? Mind you, I'm not sure Dad has ever heard Auntie criticize Mom.

My attention though is not primarily on my family. I meet Paul and my worldview changes.

Paul, one of Bayne's close friends, has been to the house many times. I didn't pay much attention to Bayne's friends since they were older and so much more sophisticated than me. But it was Bayne who suggested that I ask Paul to take me to the Christmas formal dance. Paul had "run away from home" and joined the navy and was coming back for Christmas leave.

Do I feel like Cinderella at the ball? I'm dressed in a pale blue formal dress—the same formal gown, I must admit, that I wore to my grade ten dance—long, full layered skirt, a netted shawl around my shoulders and the purple orchid that Paul has given me—a purple orchid, would you believe? Paul, five feet eight inches tall, slim and trim in his midshipman's uniform, light brown hair, stylish brush cut, his blue-grey eyes mirroring my excitement, looks like the Prince Charming of any young woman's fantasy. I hardly notice Ed Koenig and Judy Weber—my good buddy, who's just got me a part-time job at Schnarr's Florist, across from the school—the friends who are at the dance with us.

And can he dance. We swirl, swinging forwards, backwards, the Fred Astaire and Ginger Rogers of the young set, the waltz champions of the school, in the glorious ballroom of the gym, transformed by Christmas decorations. Trevor Bennet and his band play all the hits of the mid-fifties as well as the big band music of the forties. I sing them all: "Till I Waltz Again With You," "Blue Gardenia," "Hey There," "Mr. Sandman," "Shaboom Shaboom," "Sincerely," "Unchained Melody," "Secret Love" and "Fly Me to the Moon." He does, and I'm in love—no longer a secret, I'm sure.

I don't see Paul again until the fall, the fall of 1955. He resigned from the navy and started work with Waterloo Manufacturing as a cost accountant. Now the romance blossoms: another experience at the Christmas formal dance, another night of sheer joy. I can't believe that this handsome, bright, witty, fun-loving man, this man who treats me as if I'm a special being, can be in love with me. But he says he is and his blue-grey eyes fog over, fill up with emotion, and I know he means what he says. Some of the girls at school, and Bayne, warn me that Paul is "fast" and that I should watch out for myself. Secretly I'm hoping that this is true and that now I will have a chance to explore my sexuality.

No one has money for dating. No one has cars. Paul and I catch a few movies, play badminton at the Granite Club—he never can beat me—and spend many evenings playing bridge with Mom and Dad. Paul reads novels when I do my homework and study for exams. He prefers being anywhere but at his home, a home with a high-school teacher father, a high-school teacher stepmother and an unwelcoming basement bedroom. Often, late in an evening, Dad makes up the greatest hamburgers, a combination of beef and pork,

which Paul dearly loves, and the four of us end the evening together
quite comfortably. And at least on one occasion, Paul takes me to
dinner at his aunts' home, a large grey house close to the road, out
in the farming community of Bloomingdale. These three adorable
and adoring aunts care about Paul and lavish him with special foods
and wonderful country meals. To be taken to meet the aunts is an
auspicious occasion, one not to be taken lightly.

We do party occasionally. Bayne, attending Royal Roads
Military College in Victoria, British Columbia, comes home for
Christmas leave, accompanied by Barbara Saville, an attractive,
blond, ditzy young woman, a woman who almost becomes his wife,
but doesn't, thank goodness. He organizes a New Year's Eve party
at the Highlands; Kenny and his current friend, Charlotte, Paul and I
dance, drink—never mind that the legal age for drinking is twenty-
one—and then adjourn to a motel for a post-party party. The party is
abruptly ended when I discover, to my horror, that my neck is covered
with hickies. My God, how do I hide this from Mom and Dad? They
would never sanction such a party. Bayne lied, saying that we were
going to a party at Jackie Boehmer's house.

Do I care what my parents think? Yes, but with ambivalence.
By this time they are getting apprehensive about the intensity of my
relationship with Paul. Mom, who has been talking in general for a
few years about my getting married, now is not enamored with the
idea of me marrying Paul. I'm not sure why—emotional immaturity?
His outward arrogance—which I know masks a vulnerable, sensitive
little boy? Or is it just his worldliness and my lack thereof? For
certain, the only thing that really matters to Mom is marriage. That
message is abundantly clear.

Saturday night, the Saturday before Easter Sunday, March 1956,
just after my eighteenth birthday, Paul and I decide to marry. Paul
is to accompany my parents and me to church the next day, have
dinner with us and then ask Dad for permission for us to marry.
We are quietly necking and petting on the living-room chesterfield,
lights down low. Suddenly, with a burst of profanity, Dad emerges
from the bedroom, no glasses, blue nightshirt swinging in the breeze,
and confronts a startled Paul—who has fallen off the couch onto the
floor—and me, hastily covering an exposed torso.

"You," he yells, pointing at me, "get up to your room immediately." I don't move. "Get upstairs immediately before I do something I might regret." I move.

"And you," pointing at Paul, "get out."

"But, Mr. Perrin, we just ..." Paul says, stammering, picking himself off the floor.

"Now! Out!" Dad says, pointing to the door. "We'll talk tomorrow."

I sit at my bedroom window looking into the black night, the streetlight profiling the big maple tree on the boulevard in front of our neighbour's house. I hate him. I really do. How could he humiliate me this way? I hate him. I continue to stare out the window, not noticing the moon crossing high in the sky, not noticing the tears spilling down my cheeks, dampening the windowsill. I refuse to undress, refuse to go to bed. He can send me to my room but he can't make me go to bed. Somehow this do-nothing behaviour helps still the agitation in my gut and the furious dialogue in my head. Hours later, or maybe it was only minutes, I yield to my fatigue. Tomorrow I'll tell him, so help me.

Paul arrives. Mom and Dad and the two of us walk up Park Street to Calvary Church. Once, maybe twice a year, my parents attend church. And this Easter Sunday has to be that time. I twitch, shuffle in the pew and pluck a few dog hairs and lint from my skirt. Paul clears his throat, shifts position. He crosses his legs, uncrosses his legs. The sermon is the longest, most boring sermon I have ever not quite heard. Mom and Dad look blessedly relaxed, though Mom shuffles and shifts, not unusual behaviour for her in this context. She always has difficulty sitting in the hard, uncomfortable, unpadded, wooden pews. It's over and finally we go back home.

After dinner Paul and Dad adjourn to the living room and Mom and I set about to clear the table and begin dishes. I can hear the two of them talking but I'm unable to make out their words. Mom insists on chatting about trivialities but finds a way to mention again—how many times have I heard this?—"go easy on your Dad." Finally Paul and I are free. We leave the house going nowhere in particular. As soon as the door closes behind us, I ask Paul, "Well, what did he say?"

"He apologized," Paul says.

"What?"

"Yeah, really, he said he thought it was one o'clock and not midnight and he was tired and resented being woken up. And then we talked about our relationship. I said, 'Mr. Perrin, I want to marry your daughter,' and he said that he appreciated me being straight with him and encouraged us to give ourselves lots of time."

"He wasn't angry?"

"No, he was quite calm."

When Paul brings me back home, Dad asks to speak to me.

"I'm sorry for my outburst last night, Dale. I really thought it was much later than it was. I know you and Paul are very serious about each other, but I do have one request. I feel that you are still quite young for an intense sexual relationship. But what you do with your body and how you chose to express yourself in your relationship is entirely up to you. I just ask that you not be sexual in this house, that you honour our values here. It's a request. It's entirely up to you. I would like you to think about it, okay? Just because I'm your dad doesn't mean that I'm automatically wrong."

Well, how do you rebel against that? I'm well aware that my parents do not want me to have intercourse before marriage but the way he said it, I don't even get to tell him to go to hell, though I'm not sure I could have done that anyway. He's damn lucky though. If he had said "don't" to anything in reference to my sexual behaviour, I intended to "do" just that. I'd marry Paul tomorrow if he so much as said, "You can't." So there! Thank goodness the angels whispered in his ear and gave Dad the wisdom to say and do the right thing. I'm no more ready to marry than I am to move into the work world with absolutely no skills and limited confidence.

They needn't have worried. My own sexuality, still a mystery, still overwhelming for me to manage, and my fear of pregnancy—no guaranteed safe contraceptive method—and intense ambivalence, wanting to explore sexually and being frightened by my own desires, brought the relationship to an end. Paul, now working in the Bank of Nova Scotia, has bought himself a green pickup truck and this provides more opportunities for exploring than I can safely handle.

But the decisive moment occurs on a Sunday afternoon in the house, with the parents and Kenny out for the day.

"We're going to be alone all afternoon," I say to Paul as we kiss and settle into snuggling on the living-room couch.

"No parents?"

"Yeah, they won't be home till early evening," I say, my face aglow, my eyes sparkling, smiling that can-we-be-evil smile, a clear invitation to fool around with impunity. And we do. Paul suggests that we'll be more comfortable on the living-room carpet, and we are. Paul suggests we'll be freer with fewer clothes on. And that too is true.

The feel of Paul's lean, strong body against mine, his hands exploring more freely than ever before, that part of my womaness as yet uninvestigated by me, let alone anyone else (if you don't count Grant), creates in me increasingly explosive sensations that erupt in bursts of orgasmic shatterings that rocket my body into an all-consuming oneness. When I land, and I don't know how long that took, I'm overwhelmed with—I don't know what. Peacefulness? No. Fear? No. Guilt? No. Oh God, a desire for more!

"Paul," I say, overwhelmed with shyness. "Did we do it? Did you, uh, did you ... Was that your penis?"

"No," Paul answers, now stroking my hair and gently kissing my neck and shoulders. "That was my finger."

"Oh God, Paul, we gotta stop."

And with that pronouncement I get myself off the floor, gather up my clothing in a flash and ascend the stairs as quickly as if I was being chased by demons. I run a warm bath and wonder what I am doing. *Is this what girls meant when they said they didn't know what was happening? Did it feel this way for other young women?*

Paul makes no attempt to intrude nor does he question me when I return to the living room dressed in Sunday clothes, suggesting we go out somewhere, anywhere. Somewhere, lurking just outside of my awareness, is a sense that taking a bath and dressing up is somehow connected with sexual behaviour. I'm not sure how, but I do feel better.

I end my relationship with Paul just weeks later before the end of my grade twelve school year. It is hard to admit that I'm scared—not just of the sexual tensions, though I know there is no going back. I wanted more. No, the scare is something else. I'm not quite sure what. I just hear this inner voice saying, *"Who are you kidding? You can't get married. You haven't a clue about life."*

I suppose I owe my typing skills to Paul. Because we planned to marry, I've switched from the academic program leading to grade thirteen and university to what is referred to as special commercial, a crash course in shorthand, typing and other useful skills to enable me to enter the work world. I bury myself in school activities, adding assistant editor of the school yearbook (for the athletic news) and senior girls' choir to my already heavy agenda of sports. I've been asked to run for Student's Council president but my fear of public speaking renders that opportunity prohibitive—I do wish that the attempts of two of my English teachers to help me through this problem had succeeded. At the graduation ceremony I receive my senior athletic letter (I already had the junior letter) and a citizenship pin for nonathletic achievement and I'm named Outstanding Girl Athlete—I did it! I won every award this school has to offer—just as I told myself I would the first day I climbed the twenty-five steps up to the front entrance of the school.

My experience in the work world as a clerk-typist is short-lived. After several interviews I accept a position at the Dominion Tire Factory, in the same office where Dad works. I type eight hours a day, type up numbers and data relative to quality control of tires—I presume that's what the figures are about. Every time I go into the lab to run off copies on the ditto machine, Fred Gies, a dear friend of Dad's, whom I have long called Uncle Fred, shakes his head and says, "You shouldn't be here." And he's right. By mid-September I know that I have to go back to school, complete grade thirteen and go on to university. Bayne, now home on leave from the Royal Military College in Kingston (the Military College in Victoria does not offer the second two years of undergraduate study), helps me do it.

"How am I going to get back to school, Bayne?" I say, sitting on the front step of the verandah on this cool, fall-smelling, orange and yellow day. Bayne always seems to be available when I need to talk about something that really matters.

"Just tell Dad you've changed your mind. You know how much he values education."

"Yeah, but I hinted at it the other day and he said something about the fact that Kenny was thinking of going back to school. He made it clear that if Kenny wants to go back, he goes back. He said that men need an education more than women. You know how he is about things like that."

"Kenny won't go back. He's always hated school. Just tell him what you want to do. What do you want to do?"

"I'd like to write, get a job as a journalist. Ryerson has a good program in journalism but I know I can never go anywhere but Waterloo College. I can't afford to live away from home. I'm in debt already from buying that dumb Rena Ware set. I still owe a couple of hundred dollars."

"I'll give you that money, Dale. Do it. Tell Dad whatever he wants to hear to get into university and then you can study what you want."

And I do. And he does.

"Dad, I want to be a phys ed teacher. I need the university degree. Please let me go back to school. I've got to get into grade thirteen right away before I get too far behind."

"Well, okay, Dale. You'd make an excellent phys ed teacher, but I don't want you wasting time studying to be a do-gooder like my sister. As long as you're doing something practical; but I need to check with Ken first. If he's decided to go back to school his needs come first and we can only support one of you at school."

The school year goes quickly. What do I do when I've run out of awards? Live sports, especially badminton, shake with Elvis Presley, twist with Bill Haley, study and win a bursary from the Waterloo Lions Club to attend Waterloo College, an affiliate of the University of Western Ontario. I ask Hubert Guy, another of Bayne's buddies, to teach me how to drive—because Kenny bought himself a beautiful, turquoise Ford and he'll let me practice on it, and maybe forgive me for putting a dent in the driver's side door just when he's ready to trade it for a super MGA white sports car. And go with Auntie to Toronto to help organize the Ontario Chapter of the International Grapho-Analysis Society and start calling Auntie "Elthea." You can't expect me to call Auntie "Auntie" in front of a whole bunch of adults, me now being one of them—twenty years old and a smoker—very mature for my age, as Mom relishes telling her friends.

So far the plan is working. Will the pattern change when I hit the university world? Or ...?

TROPHIES AND TRIUMPHS

What messages did you get around sexuality and what was appropriate sexual behaviour from your parents (or parent substitutes), your peers? From your neighbourhood/city/country/culture?

As you began to develop romantic relationships, what type of person attracted your attention? What were his/her characteristics?

Quite often we tend to gravitate to the person who has similar characteristics to a parent figure; sometimes to the opposite. I had two very "opposite" male role models: my father, who was gentle, loving, definitely the patriarch/gentleman and the uncles who were controlling misogynists—but charming and extroverted. I recognize how this influenced my choices. Do you recognize similarities?

Did your educational experiences prepare you for the work world? Or further academic pursuits?

What messages were you given about how to be successful in the world?

Did your mother and/or father (or substitute parent figures) have favourite sayings about life that impacted on your choices?

Were these messages helpful or hurtful?

ARTEMIS AND ARROWS

Straight ahead, on target—just like Artemis, the Greek virgin goddess, who roamed the forests with her sister nymphs, hunting with her bow and arrows, always hitting the mark. Gloria Deorksen and I journey together into the unexplored forest of university, Gloria in a stylish dark brown suit and me in my light blue suit, both in heels, purse and matching gloves. You had to look smart; registration is a serious affair. You'd think we were going to a wedding, or heaven forbid, a tea. Whatever, we are going to impress.

Caught up in a whirlwind of activity, I soon forget my first-day jitters and rush through the first term like an Olympic sprinter focused only on the finish line. Gone were the party days with high school friends and the first round of showers and wedding activities. The frosh float parade grabs my immediate attention and I'm at it again—organizing, planning, involved. I move into an executive position on the women's undergraduate association, then called Phi Delta Pi, become chair of the decorating committee for the freshman dance that is to be held in February and become involved in track and field and other sports activities. I'm on a familiar path. I stop only long enough to confront death.

Gramma received her first chemotherapy treatments for cancer of the esophagus prior to the family celebration at Tony's Inn early in September 1958—Mom and Dad's twenty-fifth wedding anniversary. This is such a significant celebration. Bayne introduced his fiancée, Bette Sharpe, to us, along with her little, four-year-old son, Michael, just weekends before; and this is Bette's first Perrin family activity. Gramma, now eighty-five, seemed to be responding well to her treatments, though with Gramma you could never really tell. But before the celebration, she goes back to the hospital in Hamilton for a second course of treatments.

"Hey, Marilyn, do you want to come over to the house after curling and have a coffee?" I say, furiously brushing the ice with a straw broom, coaxing that solid round rock to move just another inch forward. It's February 17, 1959, just a few short weeks after we'd celebrated Gramma's eighty-sixth birthday.

Marilyn McNeill, a tall, blond, bubbly, extroverted young woman, who seems so confident in any situation, shares many of my classes, and we are rapidly becoming close friends. Marilyn, from Aylmer, Ontario, and her roommate Betty Lyn Boyle, from Tillsonburg, share accommodation with two sophomore students in an apartment on Albert Street, just up from the college. As one of the few local students I am pleased to develop friendships with resident students, to share part of the college culture and intimacy unique to those whose daily lives are enriched by the sharing of meals, late-night discussions and playfulness.

"Can't," Marilyn says, puffing icy breath, her face flushed with radiant health—that exercise stuff will do it to you. "Gotta get to the library to work on that psych assignment. I thought you were playing badminton at Seagram's gym tonight."

"Yes, but the tournament doesn't begin until seven. Mom and Dad have gone to Hamilton to visit Gramma. I'm just going to get a sandwich and head on up to the school."

I get in the door just as the phone rings.

"Hello, may I speak with Mr. or Mrs. Perrin, please?" an unfamiliar, deep, melodious, male voice says.

"I'm sorry but they're not home. May I take a message?"

"Yes, just tell them it's Mr. Bechtel, from Ratz and Bechtel Funeral Home calling back. I'll wait here for their call."

"Yes, I will," I say and hang up the phone. I don't collapse, don't dissolve into histrionics. I just sit down right there on the living-room carpet. *My God, my God, she died.* Tears well up and flow quietly down my cheeks. *Oh Gramma, Gramma, you're gone. And I didn't get to say good-bye. And I didn't get to tell you I love you. And I won't see you anymore.*

Mom, Auntie and Dad arrive shortly after the call, Dad driving the big two-tone, grey-and-pink Plymouth they purchased a year ago, before Gramma's second hospitalization. I'm ready now, ready to be brave, to help Mom, to make things easier. Mom and Auntie are red-eyed and quiet. We sit at the kitchen table while Dad returns Mr. Bechtel's call. They seem to have everything under control. Mom makes coffee and sandwiches. They hardly notice me, don't really need me at all.

I go to the university to play in the tournament. Between games I sit in the women's changeroom, just sit and stare at unpainted cement walls decorated with rows of lockers on two sides and a shower room just beyond the wooden benches. A few young women ask me if I'm okay and I say yes as if I always sit staring into space, dressed in my white badminton outfit. How can I tell them I'm talking to Gramma, asking her if she can now tell me what it's all about? *Is there really a heaven? Were you greeted by angels? Are you watching me and do you know what I'm thinking? Will you ever visit me in my dreams?*

Visitation, an open casket and people coming to see Gramma lying dead, looking peaceful in her navy blue dress, a white corsage pinned to her shoulder, her round, silver-rimmed glasses in place, white hair neatly pulled back in a bun as she always wore it. And her hands folded together over her stomach, the hands, smooth, covered in freckles, nails neatly trimmed, not the hands of Gramma playing Chinese checkers or taking fresh, hot, sweet-smelling bread out of that old gas-burning oven. I watch. I'm sure she'll move her hands, those very active hands. She doesn't.

Perhaps at twenty years of age, almost twenty-one, I should be more mature. I choke back tears during the funeral ceremony. They cascade out in the limo, a torrent of emotion that could no longer be restrained. Kenny and Bayne, the only other passengers in this car, put their arms around me and I notice that they also have tears in their eyes.

"Only once in my whole life did Gramma criticize me," I say through my tears. "And that was because I ate too many cookies out of the cookie jar. I always thought that Gramma made those cookies just for us. I was so surprised when Mom told me to go easy on the cookies."

"Yeah," Bayne says. "She was a remarkable woman. I always felt loved. I'm just so sorry she won't be here to see Bette and me get married. I know she would have loved Bette. We planned the wedding to take place at Calvary, just so she could attend."

The reception follows. Expressions of admiration and condolences—an empty spot in my heart—and life goes on.

I have to get on with my studies and the arrangements for the dance, which I hear later was a great success. I didn't get there. No date. I did get to complete my assignments and begin the rush to study for final exams, amidst a flurry of weddings and a new romance.

"Is Kenny Perrin there?" I ask Rick, who answers the phone at his family's restaurant on Lancaster Street in Bridgeport.

"Just a minute," he says. I can hear him shout out Kenny's name.

"Kenny, I'm going bananas. Will you come and get me and take me to the restaurant for a break?" I knew where Kenny would be. It is Thursday night and Kenny and his buddies meet at the golf course right across from Rick's restaurant to play and do guy things. Then they adjourn and go over to Rick's to feast on lasagna, spaghetti and other Italian delights that Mama and Papa Vettraino lavished on Rick's friends, along with worldly advice seasoned with a liberal dose of love and affection.

"Yeah, sure, be there in about half an hour."

I pop out the door as soon as I see a car pull into the driveway. It isn't Kenny.

"Hi, I'm Tommy Wunder, a friend of Kenny's. He asked me to come and pick you up," he says and opens the door for me to get into the car. Hmm, I think. *Who's this friend that opens car doors?* I've never met him before. Kenny, unlike Bayne, rarely brings his friends to the house, preferring to maintain his friendships apart from the family. Tommy continues to "pick me up" for another eighteen months. He's a quiet, gentle man, whose smiles contrast with his could-have-been-a-college-football-linebacker body type. If you didn't know that he was softer than a Boston cream donut, you could easily be intimidated. Our relationship continues to grow quietly without much introspection, without much communication about feelings.

I don't know how I manage to find time for classes, assignments or final exams. During March and April my high school friends get married. Elaine marries on the twenty-eighth of March and Dot and I are bridesmaids, the one and only time I agreed to do such a thing. Dot marries a week later—hadn't told a soul—another friend a week after that, and Bayne and Bette on the twenty-fifth of April, the afternoon of my first year-end exam.

The beginning of second year, I'm on target—it's straight ahead, holding back nothing. I select psychology as my major course of study, English literature as my minor, never for a moment sharing with Mom or Dad that I've chosen a different career path. It is Vicki Graf, a deeply reflective, attractive, honours English major, who influences the shift. After an intense conversation during which Vicki shares some of her poetry and her pain, she suggests that I would be a good social worker. I don't know what prompted her remark, nor do I have any knowledge about what a social worker actually does, but I'm attracted to human drama and I don't want to be a teacher, nurse or secretary. No one tells me that the business world is open to women and that certainly doesn't cross my mind. So, this is it; I'll be a social worker.

I can handle the welcoming tea for the new women students to the college. No problem—they'll never know I've never been to a tea before. As president of the newly designated Women's Undergraduate Association, a name change that I'm instrumental in facilitating, I don the hat and gloves to play hostess, along with other members of the association, to the fifty-five new women students, nearly twice the enrolment of my first year. The initiation week activities, held in Conrad Hall, the women's residence, are also fun and manageable. It's the first-ever pinning ceremony that challenges me and causes me near paralysis.

"I can't do it," I say to Joan McGill, Dean of Women.

"Yes you can, Dale, and you must," Joan answers in an encouraging, though authoritative, tone as we sit in her crowded office, papers already stacked on her desk, her certificate hanging just slightly off angle on the far wall above her bookshelves. "This is your idea and a good one, and you have to carry through."

I explain about my terror of public speaking.

"You have to confront this fear, Dale. If you don't, you'll seriously impede your success in the future. I tell you what. The Y sponsors a Dale Carnegie course designed to help people develop their speaking skills. I'd be happy to have the university sponsor you to attend the course. What do you say?" I feel an immediate adrenalin zap throughout my body. "I'll personally drive you there and pick you up."

I'm touched by Joan McGill's obvious sincerity and generosity of spirit. Easy for her to say. She's a striking brunette, smartly dressed in a maroon-coloured suit, cream-coloured blouse, two strings of pearls around her neck, the epitome of sophistication and confidence. I can't imagine her ever experiencing the terror that threatens to overwhelm me. I agree to make a "short" speech at the ceremony and exit the office just as quickly as I can. Boy that was close.

Right on cue, the lights in the dining hall are turned off. The candles held by the new students, all dressed in choir gowns, glow, creating an aura of mysticism. I step up to the podium—well, the music stand that doubles as a podium when required—and I pause, struggle valiantly to catch my breath. Looking out at that very moving sight, catching the look of concern and anticipation on the faces of the women who had helped organize and orchestrate this event, all of whom were aware of my terror, I manage the first few sentences. I even make it through half the page, right to the point where I'm to identify the significance of the candles, and—I can't read my notes: the fold in the page and the limited lighting from the candles in the six-candle holder placed on the table right beside me—my God, what is the symbolism? A voice from within: *Just make it up,* and that's what I do. I don't remember what I say but I do get through it and move on, calling up each new student to be pinned with the university pin by her appointed "big sister." I introduce Peggy Nairn, the CBC producer who is the speaker for the evening, and then experience an inner glow of satisfaction. I did it!

They lie, and I'm grateful. They say I did a great job and that the evening is a huge success. The new students appreciate the ceremony. They say that they feel a connection that I certainly hadn't experienced the preceding year. The float parade comes and goes without my participation. The Purple and Gold Show, *Don't Tip the Canoe*, the college production that always brings forth the community in droves, is highly successful. I contribute behind the scenes as assistant makeup director. Behind the scenes is where I feel most comfortable, just like Mom—the "woman behind." *Doesn't everyone know that men are the important, out-front people?*

Although the women's movement raised consciousness about role stereotypes, glass ceilings, patriarchy and institutional and systemic prejudice, body and self-esteem issues are resurfacing in literature and the media, and some university traditions remain "traditional." One of those issues—beauty contests—has to be addressed early in my term as president. By some process of voting, a campus queen is chosen annually at the Christmas formal. Exactly how this comes about I don't know. I do know that I don't like the whole idea of honouring someone just because they're attractive. Although I'm not successful in ending the process, I do manage to shift the emphasis and procedure for the selection of the queen. The women themselves will be asked to nominate ten candidates. The nominees must be contributing to the life of the college, women who demonstrate leadership and citizenship. From this group the college at large will vote on the selection for queen. A small victory but a step forward in consciousness raising and a wee victory for me—women are not just pretty faces and bodies.

Sometime during the busyness of activities and studies, it does occur to me that since I'm going to be a social worker, it might be useful to find out what that means. Joan McGill, in one of our discussions, informs me that the Department of Reform Institutions takes summer students. She gives me the information necessary to apply for a summer position. I apply and am accepted, a fact that both excites and frightens me. I'm going to find out. Can I handle being a social worker, whatever that is?

Shelley Finson, a resident in the house on Albert Street on the corner of the college property used primarily by senior women students, approaches me shortly after my application has been approved.

"I hear you're going to work in the Galt Training School," Shelley says as we pick up our coffee from Nora, the woman who runs the snack bar, and head for the women's lounge to escape the hubbub and din of heated conversations in the already crowded coffee/lunchroom. Shelley, a tall woman with short dark hair, piercing eyes the colour of Columbian coffee, a thick English accent that immediately identifies her country of origin, is a relative stranger to me.

"Yes, I start the beginning of May. Why? Are you interested?"

"Yes, I just submitted my application. I can't start though until mid-May because I'm committed to attend a retreat at Five Oaks, in Paris. Would you be interested in sharing an apartment with me for the summer?"

I'm delighted. I don't have to face this challenge alone. Now I've just one major activity before exams and year-end. The Women's Undergraduate Association organizes a spring tea, a fundraiser that we decide is to be used for a bursary/award to be given to a deserving woman student next school year. On March 26, 1960, the coffee/lunchroom is transformed into a spring garden complete with cherry blossoms—Kleenex flowers tied to cherry tree branches cut from the tree in our back garden. A long table covered with a frilly, lace tablecloth, two silver candelabra with yellow tapers flanking a bouquet of yellow daffodils and borrowed silver tea services, a display table, white tablecloth with elegant chinaware and a similar table with articles for the white elephant sale complete the metamorphosis. And me? Here I am again in dress, heels, hat and gloves, greeting the women in the community, definitely not a role that I'm comfortable with. I wonder as I watch Mom and Elthea out of the corner of my eye, the only two women from the community that really matter to me, and the very first occasion when Mom witnesses me *performing* in any capacity since my dancing days, *Am I doing it right? Is this the daughter you wanted?*

That night Tommy and I, Kenny and his new girlfriend, Charlotte, and the gang from the restaurant go out to Leisure Lodge, a nightclub that provides an opportunity for romance: corsages, drinks from little brown bags containing forbidden little bottles of rye whiskey, vodka, or rum, which the gentlemen bring in and hide under the table, and dancing to the music popularized by *American Bandstand.* Images of Kleenex cherry blossoms, hats and gloves fade as "Mack the Knife," "Poor Little Fool," "Dream Lover," "Canadian Sunset," "Autumn Leaves," the wonderful calypso music introduced by Harry Belafonte, "Smoke Gets in Your Eyes"—and it certainly does, as most of us are smokers—and the perennial big band favourites carry me into a world that only Tommy and I share, the world of his body and mine, touching, moving rhythmically, sharing thoughts, good feelings, just about us.

And then—the summer.

Shelley and I find a little basement apartment in the home of Betty and Fred McPherson and their two-year-old son, Robert. It's located just off Highway Eight, the main highway leading from Kitchener to Galt, near the hospital—a good thing, as it happens, because at the hospital cigarettes are available through vending machines all night, for those occasions when we talk until the moon gives up and yields to the nudging of the pending sunrise. The street dead-ends at a protective rise of ground, cinder and train tracks. A hill rising up from the far side of the tracks leads to the grounds of the Ontario Training School for Girls. Shelley and I are just minutes away from work.

I don't know why I face new situations with such a scare in the pit of my stomach, but I do. I always do. My first morning—I walk up the incline, aware of the morning dew still on the hillside, sparrows chirping reassurances, a touch of pine fragrance in the air, the smell of a fresh spring day promising sunshine and warmth. I check my green suede heels to be sure I haven't collected inches of dewed pathway. I straighten my flowered green cotton skirt. Check that my dark green blouse is tucked in. *Am I dressed appropriately for the first day at the Ontario Training School for Girls? Do I look mature? Sophisticated? More important—do I look like I know what*

I'm doing? Oh God, what am I doing? I don't know a thing about delinquency or children in trouble.

The administration building, a red-brick, two-story building, has a big white round-framed entranceway, with solid wood doors and a massive wrought-iron latch and key. My hand shakes as I open that door and enter a spacious hallway. The reception and office area to the right has a sign that reads, "All visitors must register." I enter the office and am greeted by a clerk/secretary who informs me that Reverend Wilson will be with me as soon as the morning assembly is finished. A sudden burst of sound, like the start-up of Formula One engines, informs me that assembly is over. Within moments Leonard Wilson approaches. What a handsome man: tall, grey-haired, elegant, in his late forties. "Good morning, Miss Perrin," he says, extending his hand. His handshake is very gentle, soft. I have a hunch that he is, too. He certainly doesn't fit my stereotype of an administrator of a training school, though where the stereotype comes from, I don't really know. I hope he doesn't notice that my hand is slightly moist.

After the welcoming niceties, he telephones Mrs. Kozak, a senior supervisor who is to provide a brief orientation to the school and take me to the house I have been assigned to work in for the summer. Mrs. Kozak arrives. She does indeed fit the stereotype: a big, burly woman, solid flesh masking layers of toughness—shaped a bit like a pork barrel on stilts—an English accent and a demeanor that suggests "don't fool with me." Her appearance fills me with dread. *What am I doing here?*

"As you can see, the four residences face the parade square," Mrs. Kozak says. "The building to the left of the square is Beatty House. The building beyond—that's reception. That's where the girls go when they first arrive directly from the courts before they are processed and assigned to one of these houses."

"What does 'processed' mean?" I ask, hoping that isn't something I should already know.

"Well, all the girls undergo psychological and academic testing when they arrive. Any social histories, court records or other community agency evaluations are kept on record at reception. The clinical team determines a suitable program for the girls and placement in one of these four houses.

"To the right of the square, where we are now headed, is Drake House. That's where you will work. Nelson House is connected to the other residence, though the connecting doors are always locked. The farthest residence is Collingwood House. The dining area is in that building."

All the buildings, two story, red brick, with white window frames and panes, look the same to me as the administration building. Constructed in 1942, this setting served as a military base for the Women's Royal Canadian Naval Service and was called the HMCS *Conestoga*. Each residence was named after a well-known British admiral and had the capacity to house thirty women. I wonder what "training" these young girls, who range in age from twelve to eighteen, are getting and what battles they will be fighting or have already fought.

"Quiet," Mrs. Graham, head supervisor, Drake House, says in an authoritative voice, not menacing, but certainly commanding attention, a voice that I doubt I can ever duplicate. "This is Miss Perrin, a university student who will be working with us for the summer."

"Why?" asks a tall, blond, athletic-looking, young girl with flashing, angry, steel-grey eyes that look right into my soul, her mouth twisted in a mocking, defiant smirk.

"Shut up, Gloria," Ronnie says. "Knock it off."

"I'm here because I've decided that I want to be a social worker and work with young people and I haven't a clue how to do that. So I'm here to learn and contribute whatever I can," I say, hoping that to state the obvious might save me the risk of being found out.

Ronnie laughs, a delightful trilling, lilting scale, and says, "You've come to the right place. We'll teach you a few things all right." A chorus of laughter and "You got that right, chickie," and the moment passes.

"Is it time?" one girl asks, standing up, tugging at her cardigan, looking directly at Mrs. Graham.

And the girls, giggling, hitting and pushing each other, with a rush of energy like caged experimental mice released from confinement, some chatting, some swearing, scramble into organized rows to march over to the dining room at Collingwood House. Georgie, a short, dishevelled girl with tousled brownish-blond hair and mocking brown eyes, pushes by me to get into line, making a point of brushing against my breast. In a deep, gravelly voice, startling coming from such a small frame, she says, "Oh, excuse me," her eyes and body language daring me to object. I note an inked tattoo on her arm, a heart with an arrow through and the name Patsy inscribed in the center. Mrs. Graham explains later how the girls carve their bodies with pins, pens and whatever sharp objects they can get their hands on, frequently tattooing the names of their "lovelite," the girl for whom they feel a sexual attraction, though from what I can see, these attractions have little opportunity to be acted out.

I supervise the smoking circle after lunch and listen and respond to the girls' chatter and questions. They want to know my first name. I have already been informed that I am *never* to give that information, though the reason for this is unclear. This becomes a game that lasts all summer—the girls trying to trick me into giving my name, or identifying Shelley's name after she arrives to begin her summer employment.

And she does arrive—Shelley Finson that is.

"Well, what's it like?" Shelley says after she's unpacked her belongings and settled into our tiny residence. We sit on the couch, which later unfolds into a double bed, steaming coffee in hand, cigarettes, ashtrays on the side tables, the newspaper I'd been reading on the floor, the entire apartment still reeking of chili and garlic, one of the very few meals I know how to make, and talk into the wee hours of the morning, a pattern of behaviour that we repeat throughout the summer.

I tell Shelley all I have experienced in the two weeks. My original feelings of intimidation have subsided now that I've become familiar with routines and many of the girls. I express my observations and the questions that are beginning to surface in my mind. Why are these young girls here? Is the militaristic regime necessary? Is it really important to control where the girls sit? Is it really necessary to dole out only five pieces of toilet paper to each girl? To control when the girls can talk and when they have to be silent? To be secretive and formal about names?

Shelley listens and asks questions. She doesn't appear to be the least bit apprehensive about beginning this new experience. Boy, I couldn't have picked anyone more diametrically opposed to me in personality and life experience than Shelley. Cool, emotionally self-contained, confident—where does she get this strength? As a child Shelley was one of the children evacuated to South Wales during the World War II bombings. Shortly thereafter, her mother ran off with a Canadian soldier, leaving Shelley to be raised by a great aunt, and Shelley's only sibling, Brian, to be raised by a grandmother. Her father moved to Jamaica, abandoning all responsibilities, to start a new life and a new family. Several years later, Shelley moved in with the Jamaican family. At the age of seventeen she joined the air force, then left that experience less than two years later to keep house for her brother, who had contracted tuberculosis and needed help. In 1956 at age twenty Shelley immigrated to Canada on her own to take up a position as office manager of a small manufacturing company in Toronto.

Although she didn't talk much about it, I knew that underpinning her courage was a deep commitment to a belief system that somehow was connected to the Five Oaks Centre in Paris, Ontario. With the encouragement of the people at the Centre and after several years of working in Toronto, Shelley decided to get her university degree. And here we are, me with my scares, my feelings, I believe, transparent, still intimidated by a world outside of the Kitchener-Waterloo area and securely nestled in the bosom of a caring, if imperfect, family—and Shelley, just two years older and worldly sophisticated.

The following week my work experience changes dramatically.

"Miss Perrin, you are to spend the day in the second-floor corridor on the back wing of Drake House. There are five girls there and you are to be their supervisor full-time. Here are the keys. You can take the girls to lunch at 12:15 out the back exit. You can also use the first-floor room at the base of the stairs for activities if you want. Mrs. Kozak will be over later in the day to explain."

Mrs. Graham doesn't know what's happening. She's unable to answer any questions. So off I go—to do what? I don't know. For how long? I don't know. With whom? I don't know. And what am I to do if one of the girls runs away while moving to or from Collingwood House for lunch? I don't know.

"Good morning," I say as I let myself into the narrow corridor that houses six small bedrooms, each with bunk beds, grey wool army blankets on top, a wooden dresser with four drawers and a small built-in closet. The window, with its white frame and individual panes of glass, has wrought iron vertical bars on the lower half—for safety, I presume. The faded yellow corridor, with its marblelike, grey-green dotted flooring, houses a bathroom at one end and stairs leading down the back way to an exit with a locked door at the other. At the base of the stairs another locked door opens into a classroom-sized room, also faded yellow in colour.

"What the fuck am I doing here?" Sharon asks, her lip curled up in a snarl, the tone of her voice unmistakably hostile and near hysteria.

"I don't know," I say, anxiety flooding my stomach, threatening to toss up the breakfast so recently consumed and shipwreck my precarious appearance of composure. "All I know is that we're to be together and Mrs. Kozak will be here later to tell us what's going on."

In my earlier two-week period I learned that this type of language warranted a "blue sheet," a negative behaviour report, the consequences of which were determined by Mrs. Graham, Mrs. Kozak or Miss Durham, another British bulldog of a woman, next in command to Mrs. Kozak. No way was I about to confront "language" when clearly all the girls and I are distressed by this unexplained move.

I don't know Sharon, a young fourteen-year-old, very small for her age, built like a miniature tank armed with heavy verbal artillery; nor do I know Jane, Monica nor Danielle. I do know Ronnie. *What on earth is she doing here?* I wonder. She has been warm and friendly and not a behaviour problem in Drake. I must admit I'm glad to see her. She and I struck up a relationship immediately and chatted on several occasions during those times when chatting was permitted and on a few occasions at bedtime when chatting wasn't permitted. She too is upset to be locked in this corridor, taken from her usual school activities.

Jane frightens me—spooks me out. She is crying quietly. A tall, thin, sixteen-year-old, with mousy brown hair and whitewashed brown eyes covered with a glaze "where am I and who are you," she doesn't respond to my questions and concerns for her, nor does she acknowledge my presence. I'm not sure she actually hears me or even knows I exist.

Now Monica, she knows I'm here. She's carving the back of her left hand with a pin she's pilfered, no doubt, from her sewing class, droplets of blood obvious on the skirt of her pink uniform. She makes no attempt to conceal what she's doing.

"Monica, will you give me that pin?"

Monica looks directly at me, her big, robin's-egg-blue eyes challenging. She smiles sweetly and continues to carve. From what I can see Monica has already carved the word "Mom" on her upper arm and has scratches of arrowlike marks on her forehead and right cheek. *God, how can such an attractive, young fifteen-year-old mess up her body that way?* Her response is crystal clear. I'm not about to get her pin and I'm not about to insist or threaten a "blue sheet."

"Are you okay, Danielle?" I say, when Ronnie tells me the young girl's name.

"Am I being punished?"

"Gee, I don't think so. I don't know why any of you are here and we won't find out until Mrs. Kozak comes by. Let's go downstairs to the big room, where we can just sit and talk until we can figure out what we're going to do since we're going to be together all day."

I move to the back stairs. No one moves. Finally Ronnie says, "Come on, it's better than standing here." Slowly, the girls begin to move and I let out my breath, releasing the tightness in my chest. My stomach continues to be on alert, ready to heave at the first sign of physical aggression. *Shit, they don't teach you how to deal with situations like this in introductory psychology.*

Mrs. Kozak comes by just before lunch and explains that this unit is to be called Counsellor's Hall. I will be in charge every day, to be relieved by another staff member when my shift is finished. She explains that the girls chosen to be here are thought to be in need of a break from the usual routines and rowdiness of everyday activities, and here, after the usual cleanup activities, the girls and I can do whatever we decide. She doesn't know yet how long this will go on or when each girl will go back to her own house. And that's that. No explanation given to me as to what these girls need, what I'm to do with them or what to do in the event of a runaway.

No one runs away today, much to my immense relief, and life in Counsellor's Hall settles into a very comfortable routine with only the occasional disaster. Word circulates amongst the larger community of girls that this is a status thing and everyone wants to get in to the hall. This helps the girls adjust.

"Hi everyone, I'm here," I say, now in the second week of Counsellor's Hall.

"Miss Perrin," Ronnie whispers. "Sharon has a note for you hidden under her mattress. You're not supposed to find it until we go for lunch."

"Okay, thanks, Ronnie. I'll take care of it."

The note reads, "dear Miss Paren. I hate this fucking place. I'm scared shitless all the time. I had a bad nitemaer and it makes me sick. I can't talk to you." And it is unsigned. Wow, a real breakthrough. Sharon has only spoken to me in snarly monotones since our original meeting. I thought she hated me and I was actually frightened to turn my back on her. The next morning, Ronnie tells me another note is hidden, and in fact, I get a note every morning until the end of Counsellor's Hall, a day or two before I quit to return to school.

"Sharon," I say the next morning as she rests on her bed, fully dressed, her room tidied up. "I found your note. Do you want to talk about it?"

"Get real," Sharon snarls, grunting an ugly, guttural sound that substitutes for a laugh.

"Well then, I'll talk to you. I'm really sorry about your nightmare. If it'll help a bit, just write it out and maybe I can help you sort it out. I know you're scared, Sharon, all 'tough shits' are scared on the inside. If you want to tell me about it, I'll listen or read notes, okay?" No response.

We agree that afternoon to go walking around the perimeter of the grounds for some exercise and then stop off in the playground area before coming back to the hall. Jane, who still hasn't spoken much, states that she doesn't want to go out. Unfortunately, that means that she has to be locked in her bedroom.

Mrs. Spak, head supervisor of Collingwood House, has her girls out in the play area so we wait, sitting on the grass, until that group moves on. The girls giggle as they hear Sylvia, one of the residents of Collingwood, trying to explain to Mrs. Spak that swinging makes her sick. Mrs. Spak scowls, her tight body rigid with authority, her glasses sliding down the bridge of her very sharp nose. Through clenched teeth, she says, "We're out here to have fun. So you will swing."

"But, Mrs. Spak, the swing makes me feel sick," Sylvia says, pleading again for understanding.

"Swing."

"But ..."

"Swing!"

"Yes, Mrs. Spak," and swing she does, with one hand over her mouth.

When we arrive back in our hall, I unlock Jane's door. Blood and feces everywhere!

Jane is not seriously injured. But she is removed from Counsellor's Hall later that day and taken to sick bay to be observed and attended to by the medical staff.

"I wish I knew more about the girls," I say to Shelley later that evening after she finishes her shift.

"I think the permanent staff ought to be more informed too," Shelley says. "Even the head supervisors aren't given any personal history about the girls. They only know what the girls themselves tell them." Shelley works with the youngest children on the premises, in Beatty House.

Shelley and I work different shifts, and on my days off I go to Kitchener to catch some "parenting time" for myself. Shelley, whose schedule works around a summer course she's taking at the college, stays over at my parents' home to attend the classes. Mom and Dad soon take her under their wing—Dad helps her with geography, a subject of little interest and virtually incomprehensible to Shelley; Mom provides encouragement, food for the belly—relief for the stressed-out grey cells—and does laundry. Throughout the summer when they are available Mom and Dad come to Galt, pick us both up and take us out to a restaurant along the highway to fill us with hamburgers and other nutritious junk. Knowing my lack of culinary skills, Mom's concerned that both of us will die if we have to depend on me for meals. The pies she brings help ward off starvation.

Early in the summer Shelley teases me about "going home to Mommy and Daddy" and hints that my relationship with my parents is one of dependency and immaturity. I don't know if she actually believes that or is just teasing. Midway through the summer the teasing stops. By the end of the summer, Shelley's calling my parents Mom and Dad and blessed be—I think I have myself a sister.

Several days before my summer employment comes to an end, Mrs. Kozak dismantles Counsellor's Hall the same way she started it. I arrive at Drake House to pick up keys and am informed by Mrs. Graham that I will be working with her for the remaining few days. No explanation. No Counsellor's Hall. And there's Ronnie, back with the others. And there's Georgie, ready to brush against my body as she did whenever our paths crossed in the corridors of Drake or Collingwood Houses.

The last lunch hour I call Georgie into the little office and close the door.

"Georgie, there's something I've been wanting to do all summer."

"What?" she asks, a smirk on her face, her eyes twinkling with an I-got-to-you-didn't-I awareness.

"Just this," I say, and with all the force I can muster up, I belt her on the upper arm, that muscular, tough-shit arm.

She laughs and reciprocates by belting me back. Damn. That hurt. I laugh and dismiss her from the office. Hurt or not, that felt so good.

"Mrs. Kozak wants to see you in her office. What on earth have you been up to?" Mrs. Graham asks. I just smile and head for "the consequences."

"You know, Miss Perrin, when you accepted this job you signed a statement guaranteeing that you would not in any way physically strike a child. Georgie here says that you hit her. Is that true?"

Georgie smiles at me, all sweetness and innocence, her body language—the defiant slouch, the arms crossed over her chest—indicates quite clearly how much she's enjoying her victory.

"Yes I did." I explain how Georgie has been harassing me all summer. I shuffle, divert my eyes to stare at the stack of files on Mrs. Kozak's desk, clear my throat. I notice three, or was it four, blue sheets, tucked under a round glass paperweight that looks like it could be a lethal weapon in the right hands. Georgie yawns.

The issue's resolved with a reprimand for me and—oh sweet justice—a reprimand for Georgie.

After Georgie's dismissed, I ask Mrs. Kozak, "Will you tell me what Counsellor's Hall was all about and why you discontinued it?"

"Well, with your psychological background we thought that you might be able to connect with those girls. They're very troubled young people and were having a difficult time adjusting in the larger groups."

My psychological background? My introductory course in psychology? My God, if the professor realized what was expected of a student taking this course, he'd probably be afraid to continue offering it without a written and signed disclaimer.

"Yes, I could see that, Mrs. Kozak, but Ronnie? She didn't seem to fit that description. Why was she there?"

"We knew that you and Ronnie had already developed a good relationship and that she liked you. We figured that if the girls attacked you, Ronnie would help you."

Oh, my God!

And it's over. And I've decided. I'm going to be a social worker and work in the correctional field. I know I will have to go on to graduate school, but how am I going to explain that to Mom and Dad, especially Dad, who figured one summer's experience would end this nonsense? And where am I going to get the money?

September 1960, age twenty-two, my graduating year; all I have to do is do it—continue on course, straight ahead, graduate and get that certificate, which is no longer granted by the University of Western Ontario. In this very short time, Waterloo College has been given degree granting privileges and has amalgamated with the Lutheran Seminary to become Waterloo University College under the umbrella of Waterloo Lutheran University.

The pattern continues: the welcoming tea with Betty Lyn, now president; the frosh pinning ceremony with me unexpectedly receiving the first award of the Women's Undergraduate Association, the award that I helped to establish; the track and field meet in London, Ontario; the Purple and Gold Show with me now in charge of makeup; the newspaper column; the sophomore formal dance with Tommy; and the various club activities.

My relationship with Tommy doesn't—continue that is. Tommy and I developed a very serious romance over these months and have alluded to that "m" word. Tommy is ready for marriage, though I'm not sure he is ready for sex. His Catholicism, a deep commitment to a belief system that he and his family embrace wholeheartedly, limits him in experimenting with his sexuality—and mine—before nuptial vows have been enacted. Me? Quite the reverse! The sexual tensions I experience and express no doubt create pressures of a more complex nature for Tommy. The escalation of apparently diametrically opposed beliefs and needs results in the inevitable.

"Tommy," I say, tears creating rivulets of mascara down my flushed cheeks, breathless, heart still pounding. "I can't stand this." "This" Tommy well understands is his reluctance to touch me where I need touching, stroke me where I need stroking, probe where I need probing.

"Not yet, Dale, I can't," he says, disentangling himself, sitting up straight in the front seat of the car, parked in the driveway. I know he can't. I wonder if a whole team of angels "up there" is conspiring to keep me virginal until the day I die, conspiring to have me become an "Auntie Elthea." Alas, I also hear that voice, that voice coming somewhere from deep inside: *You know you're not ready to marry. Who are you kidding?* And I know I can't—marry, that is. And I know Mom will be relieved and probably Dad too. Mom has already expressed her concerns that religious differences can create problems in a marriage. She wants me to marry, but as I experience it for the second time, "not him, dear." I expect that marriage is in the cards, though. Devoting my life to the all-important man and parenting three children seems to be the program, the way to live that gives Mom meaning in her life.

It's Ken who reacts the most intensely to my breakup with Tommy. He becomes less communicative and harbours resentment based on a belief that I am sexually cold and have hurt his good friend. His opinion that the Perrins are passionate and affectionate people extends only to the male side of the family. Increasingly, our relationship becomes strained; the childhood bonds of shared friendship and experiences are not enough to manage the increasing complexity of lives moving in entirely different directions, issues of self-esteem and chauvinism.

In the second term, my focus shifts slightly to include a new possibility, a possibility suggested to me by Dr. Mary Kay Lane, a psychology professor, new to the university this year.

Mary Kay, a brilliant new graduate from the London School of Economics in England, adds an element of excitement and glamour to a very conservative and mature faculty. Along with the addition of Dr. Don Morgenson, another young, enthusiastic professor, new to the faculty and the post of chair of the Psychology Department, seminars explode with challenge and fun, and the courses become alive—I will no longer get a letter from the dean threatening me with the loss of a credit for poor attendance at lectures.

Mary Kay, as good fortune would have it, chooses to live in a small apartment on Gruhn Street, just minutes away from me. Frequently, she drives me to the college in her snazzy little sports car on those days when our schedules mesh.

An avid bridge player, Mary Kay soon becomes a visitor to the Perrin household, where Mom, Dad and Shelley—who's now at the house whenever her schedule permits—match wits, and Shelley and I spend the occasional evening at Mary Kay's apartment, solving the world's problems, which usually takes until sunrise to accomplish. It's on one of these occasions that Mary Kay suggests that I put more energy into my studies and win a scholarship to attend the Graduate School of Social Work at the University of Toronto. What a novel idea! Me? Win an academic award?

A further rush of activities—the winter carnival, the women's sports tournaments in London, the spring tea and fashion show, the awards ceremony in April during which I, or at least, *Mr. Dale Perrin*, receive a special award given to the ten students "who have done outstanding work in College life"—and then, exams.

Four exams done! I think I may have aced at least three of them, and just one more to go. Still cramming in the morning, I make frequent trips into the kitchen to get coffee and complain and crab at Mom, who is attempting to be helpful by keeping fresh coffee brewing.

"You'll do just fine. I know you will."

"I will not. It's my sociology course, all highly theoretical, and I can never remember who said what and why. I'm going to bomb." Mom gives up her attempts at being supportive and pours the fresh coffee.

"We'll be leaving for the wedding before you get back. Is there anything you want me to do for you before we leave?"

The exam over—I know I aced it. I did it! I did it! And I come home to an empty house, the family all in Hamilton attending a cousin's wedding. No one to celebrate with—but a note on the kitchen table, carefully placed under a bottle of Mogen David wine. The note, in Mom's handwriting, reads, "See, I told you. I knew you would do it!"

Another summer experience in Galt, and then on to graduate school, if I can find a way to finance it.

My strategy for success is working. I shouldn't have a problem with graduate school, should I?

ARTEMIS AND ARROWS

What were your early experiences post high school, either with postsecondary education or on-the-job training?

What feelings did you experience as you left the familiar world of high school? Were they "familiar" feelings? Ones you've experienced before when facing new situations?

What thoughts, feelings and behaviours (coping strategies), which you may have developed earlier in life, were helpful? Were hurtful? Can you now identify what are (or were) your most deeply felt beliefs about yourself, others and the world that you carried with you into the "world beyond high school"?

As your romantic relationships with men or women evolve, are you noticing any patterns? Similarities/differences from your parent figures?

Are you having to confront issues, fears, blocks that emerge in expressing your sexuality?

How successful are you in establishing yourself as a mature person in the world separate from parents and the family identity?

BUMPS, BRUISES AND BANDAGES

I do find a way to finance it. I manage to scrape up the dollars to fund a year of study at the Graduate School of Social Work, University of Toronto. Leonard Wilson, Administrator of the Ontario Training School for Girls, suggests I apply to the Department of Reform Institutions for a training fellowship. I do and my application is accepted, thanks to the reference from Leonard. I discover that no scholarships are available so I apply for and receive a U of T General Bursary as well. I'm in!

McLeod Guest Home, 54 Madison Avenue, is a three-story, red-brick, vine-covered, old house in the Spadina-Bloor area, close to the School of Social Work, located on the far side of Varsity Stadium on Bloor. The McLeods, a grey-haired couple, and their Scottish terrier, McTavish, live on the first floor, which also houses a big room for transient guests at the front. The second and third floors accommodate a few single rooms and many doubles, all reserved for female students. My first impression—old: stale air, dark green walls, green bedspreads on single beds, dark furniture. The curtains, heavy, brown, lined with stain-soaked, faded muslin, hide for the most part ugly green pull-down blinds, which must predate the house in style. They serve to muffle the sound of the steam-heated rads just below the windows. A thick carpet mutes the sound of high heels clicking on hardwood floors, floors that give evidence of considerable abuse and layers of polish. Each bedroom has its own pedestal sink. And each floor has two full bathrooms containing big white enamel tubs with squatty cast-iron feet, sinks, mirrors and toilets that, with any luck, will only occasionally overflow.

The basement, with brown patterned linoleum flooring and painted green eight-inch-thick cement walls, was renovated to include a small kitchen and dining area, the centre for nourishment and gossip. The locked-in smells of hundreds of meals brewed over an ancient stove and the noise from a fridge, reminiscent of ice-box days, hardly disguise the fact that this is a basement—dark, dank, mildewed.

"Oh Mom, I can't live here; I just can't."

"It's by far the best we've seen. I think you'll have fun here. Wait until you meet all the other girls. I'm sure you'll have a good time, and it's close to the school," Mom says.

I repeat that statement like a mantra through the early days of school and my placement experience at the Jewish Family and Child Services (JFCS), a thirty-minute walk south to Beverley, just north of Dundas. The course work doesn't frighten me; the massive amount of reading required doesn't daunt me either. Adjusting to living with eleven women ranging in age from early twenties to late forties is a breeze. Mrs. Mildred Bennett, supervisor at the JFCS, assigned to be my field teacher, is a different story—daunting, damningly daunting! I don't recognize this until well into the second term. In early October I'm engrossed in a very different learning experience.

"Harold, you've got to help me. I've got a problem to deal with and I can't do it without some protection. Are you by any chance available this evening?" I say. He's going to think I'm nuts. I've been here just over four weeks and he hardly knows me. Harold Acker and I share an office at JFCS. The other two students are just down the hall. An unlikely couple we are—me, one of the youngest students in the program, and Harold, perhaps the oldest, late forties at least, more likely early fifties.

"It's nothing to do with school. I was walking along Bloor and I heard my name called out and there was this kid, a girl I worked with this summer at the Galt Training School. I could hardly believe it. She told me that Ronnie, a kid I really liked at the school, was turning tricks down at Elizabeth and Dundas, near the bus terminal, and if I wanted to save her I'd better hike on down there before the cops get her. I can't believe that she's doing that—prostitution! She's a bright, pretty, young girl. I've got to do something." I begin pacing in our cramped, windowless office, stepping out the three feet that separate our as-yet-uncluttered desks shoved up against the wall.

"Sit down, Dale, sit down! You're making me dizzy. Sure I'll help you. What do you have in mind?"

"I'd like to go down to the bus station to see if I can find Ronnie. Will you come with me?"

"Okay, sure. I'll pick you up out front of the school at nine o'clock."

Elizabeth and Dundas Streets are located in the part of Toronto known as Chinatown. Flashing neon signs, Chinese symbols, bright red and yellow storefronts decorated with dragons and painted scenes of snow-covered mountains. Some stores with piles of garbage out front, others with outdoor stalls piled with wilted vegetables, naked chickens and rabbits hanging above. Streets full of people milling about, people of all ethnic origins, talking in unfamiliar languages, laughing, pushing and strolling along, all apparently at home with the smells and sounds of this community.

Harold parks the car and we set out on foot to search the bus terminal, the restaurant adjacent to the terminal on Elizabeth and then the hotel bars on both sides of Dundas. Thank God for Harold. I could never do this on my own. In dimly lit, dank, beer-saturated, smoke-filled bars, smelling of sweat and worse, buzzing with muffled conversations, the occasional burst of obscenities and guffaws rising above blaring, tuneless music, we make our way bumping and pushing through the crowds.

Harold and I inspect the horde, the after-hours let's-just-have-a-couple crowd and the regular I'm-just-doing-this-because-I-like-the-taste loners. I don't see Ronnie. Harold points and looks at me inquiringly. I shake my head no. And we exit, much to my relief. After an hour or more, confronting the occasional person with the question, "Do you know a young woman named Ronnie?", Harold suggests we start again at the restaurant on Elizabeth. As we approach, a woman, at least I think it's a woman, dressed in tight-fitting black jeans, a man's black T-shirt and an open, black leather star-studded jacket, with short cropped black hair, exits the restaurant.

"Do you know where I can find Ronnie?" I say.

She looks at me, lips snarled, eyelids half-closed, head tilted, cigarette dangling from her lips, face obscured by smoke, and in a sultry, deep voice, says, "Shit no, sweetheart, but will I do? You're not cops, are you?"

"No, I've got to find Ronnie. I'm a friend. It's important," I say, pushing at Harold to move on. I shiver. *What the hell am I doing here? I must be plumb loco.*

Harold and I enter the restaurant and move to the coffee bar along the north wall of the dimly lit, grungy restaurant. I'm frightened by loud voices coming from behind. I study the oily, peeling, laminated menu, ignoring the escalating voices. Harold turns around to face the drama unfolding behind us. I'm sure he's going to get us killed.

"You fuckers want to get it on?"

I don't move. She can't mean us. A chair is pushed over. I hear scrambling. I peek.

"What yuh looking at, asshole? You fucking pimps think the whole world's shit scared of you, just because you got balls?" yells this mammoth of a woman, dressed in a plaid shirt hanging loosely over men's trousers, chain dangling from the pocket. The man casually lights his cigarette and pushes back his chair just as she lunges for his neck.

"Sit down, Gina!" A woman, similarly attired, minus the chains, grabs at Gina's shirt.

"Yeah, cool it, you old dyke," says the man's dark-skinned companion, his six feet six inches of bulk and muscle slowly rising from the chair. "We don't beat up on broads." The men laugh and exit.

Gina sits down. Harold is all eyes. He now has his back to me and is directly facing the table of six women. Oh my God. She'll kill us.

A couple at the end of the bar is watching us, intensely, glaring, whispering. A man comes in and sits beside me on the bar stool. He brushes against me and smiles. The woman at the end of the bar nods her head and in a voice loud enough for me to hear, proclaims, "Salvation Army." The man beside me rests his hand on my thigh. I nudge Harold—come to think of it, we do look like Salvation Army. I have on a light-coloured, all-weather coat, collar turned up around my ears, just a touch of pink lipstick and moccasins. Walking the

Toronto sidewalks to school in pumps gave me corns on both feet and I took a razor to them—alas, to my regret, so now it's moccasins. And Harold, tall, grey, bushy hair, thick glasses, cleanly shaven, dressed in dark slacks, grey pullover sweater and windbreaker, looks every bit the innocent do-gooder that he is.

"Harold, if you don't start paying attention to me you're going to lose me," I whisper.

"What?" Harold says, loud enough to get the attention of the entire room.

Before I can successfully melt into the floor, Ronnie walks in. "That's her," I yell to Harold and the two of us dash out after Ronnie who, recognizing me, has taken off. Harold catches her and holds her against the wall of the bus terminal until I come up panting.

"Ronnie, Ronnie. Hold on! I just want to talk to you."

"Leave me alone, Miss Perrin. It's too late."

"What are you talking about? Just give me some time to talk. Come on back to my place, please."

Ronnie reluctantly agrees and Harold drives us to my rooming house.

I'm shocked by Ronnie's appearance. This beautiful, young, freckle-faced kid, makeup plastered on her face, green eye shadow, black eyeliner and purple lipstick, clothes tight enough to cause asphyxiation, a short, black leather jacket. How can she? How can she do this?

Ronnie and I talk until after two in the morning. She tells me how her mother threw her out, blamed her for the breakup of her marriage; tells me how one of the other Training School graduates introduced her to this guy and he persuaded her to live with him and earn some money. Where else could she go? And now she wants out but is afraid. She won't tell me why or where she's staying. I tell her all about a friend in Waterloo who knows a bit about her story and that she and her family would be willing to take Ronnie in to help her get started in a new community. She's reluctant, unwilling to say more.

"Just come to the school with me tomorrow. One of my professors is doing a study on prostitution. He's been in the corrections field for years. He'll know what to do. Will you come with me, Ronnie? Please."

"Okay, but I can't stay here any longer. I have an appointment at three and I've got to keep it."

My pleading is to no avail. Ronnie slips out of the residence at two thirty in the morning, promising to meet me at nine in Fran's restaurant, just across from the Graduate School of Social Work. I give her money for cab fare to take her God knows where to do I don't know what.

The restaurant is nearly empty. Newspapers and dirty coffee cups, ashtrays filled with butts, the lingering smell of stale smoke, signs that the breakfast crowd was here as usual. It's now nine thirty and no Ronnie. I knew it. I'm a fool for believing her. And I've missed a class for no reason. Disgusted with myself and the world, I get up to leave the restaurant. And there she is.

"My God, Ronnie, what's happened to you?"

Ronnie has a major shiner on one eye, a puffy, red cheek that is going to discolour badly in a few hours and dark bags under her eyes, adding ten years to a drawn, pasty-white face. No makeup; hair disheveled. She's wearing a pink sweater and matching cardigan and the same tight black skirt she had on when I last saw her. No nylons.

"He beat me up," she says, in a flat, lifeless tone. "He and three other guys were in the other room boozing it up and planning a robbery. I pretended to be asleep on the bed and he came in, accused me of eavesdropping and beat the shit out of me. I had to wait till they all passed out before I could even try to escape. I had to crawl down the stairs on my hands and knees. I could hardly stand up. I'm scared. They're planning a bank job and they have a gun. They'll kill the teller if she makes any false move. I don't know what to do. They'll kill me if I tell. I think I've got to disappear."

"Hold on, Ronnie. Wait! Wait! Let's talk to Professor Spencer first, okay? He'll advise us. Oh Ronnie, I'm so glad you came."

Professor John Spencer, fortunately for me, is at his cluttered desk and agrees to see us. He's in his late fifties, has grey hair that refuses to maintain order, silver-rimmed eyeglasses perched halfway down a straight nose. He peers at us through a haze of pipe smoke.

A soft-spoken man with a slight British accent, nattily dressed in brown corduroys, a blue long-sleeved shirt covered with a not-quite-matching vest, Professor Spencer invites us to sit in the two hard-backed, wooden chairs. I introduce Ronnie and Ronnie tells her story. Professor Spencer listens, nods occasionally, seems very unruffled. I guess this is old hat to him.

"I don't think you should go to the police," he says. "There's a good possibility that they won't follow through if they think you know their plan. But I do believe that you are in danger. And I agree it would be wise for you to disappear for a while. Do you have a place to go?" Ronnie shakes her head no.

Professor Spencer tells us about the Elizabeth Fry Society and Phyllis Haslam, the executive director, and suggests that I take Ronnie there. He will telephone Miss Haslam and let her know we're coming. We agree and, with thanks, exit the tiny, smoke-filled office.

Ronnie tells me that she has to go to the bus terminal to get her things out of a locker. She promises to return and meet me at my residence by three. *Oh God,* I wonder, *is she going to mess this up too?* Sure enough, Ronnie appears shortly after three in the company of a man at least ten years *my* senior. He's going to drive us to the Elizabeth Fry Society. I'm upset. Damn! *She has to screw around one more time and then the john gets to save her?*

Miss Haslam graciously admits us, without a word about the fact that we are several hours later than expected. A heavyset woman, grey hair neatly coiffed, Miss Haslam explains about the residence and the regulations and allows Ronnie time to make her decision. She agrees to stay. Relief! Thank God. This is all a bit much for me. Now that I know that Ronnie is in competent and caring hands, I can get back to my studies and deal with the ever-so-daunting Mrs. Bennett.

The field experience is designed to provide the student with a hands-on opportunity to work with people who have identified a need for service, under the tutelage of an experienced social worker. For two and a half days a week, running concurrently with classes, I'm assigned to work with Mrs. Bennett, a graduate social worker of several years' experience, a recently married, attractive woman, probably in her early thirties. The other three students placed here, all years older than me, are assigned to another supervisor.

I know shortly after I begin working with Mrs. Bennett that I'm very uncomfortable in her presence. She assigns me several cases to deal with: a single mom with three kids, who needs help with parenting skills; an older gentleman, age sixty-one, who is struggling economically and finding it difficult to secure employment; a newly arrived French Moroccan Jewish couple with two children and pregnant with twins, the husband also unable to find work; and shortly thereafter, an ex-prisoner who needs help planning his terminally ill wife's palliative care, plus foster placement for a young teenage daughter. I conduct my interviews, some in the client's home, and write a verbatim report on what transpired. Now that's a challenge— recording "I said, he said" following an hour's conversation. Mrs. Bennett reads my reports and then meets with me weekly in her office.

Sitting in her office, glancing out the window, which gives me a unique view of the top of the building next door, just a suggestion of the Beverley and Dundas Street intersection and a clear view of the grey cloudy sky, ominous with its threat of an early November snowstorm—I might have known something unpleasant was about to happen—Mrs. Bennett informs me that I'm not performing well and not measuring up to expectations.

"I find it very difficult to communicate with you, Dale. You seem distant, reluctant to share your feelings. I've tried several times to get you to open up, to tell me how you feel about the clients you're working with, how you're experiencing the agency, and I get nowhere, nothing but monosyllabic responses. Just what is the problem?"

Instantly I'm anxious, feel close to tears—oh God, don't let me start crying—and completely tongue-tied.

"Uh, umm ... but I really like what I'm doing. I like the people I'm working with. I just don't know what else to say."

I'm unable to say that I experience her as emotionally distant, unfriendly, unsmiling and hypercritical. I'm aware that Mrs. Bennett brings out the very worst in me, creates in me a fear of vulnerability. I'm aware that she epitomizes the essence of what I'd like to be:

attractive, brilliant, professional and married. I don't know how to tell her that this year, unlike all other school years, I have no way of excelling and that the coping strategies I've developed over the years are no longer applicable. I feel transparent and totally unable to explain myself. Can she not see that I'm shy and introverted and need encouragement and support to articulate my feelings?

"Well, I hope you find a way of opening up, Dale," she says and the session goes on as usual, with me responding to specific questions related to the clients and Mrs. Bennett giving me direction as to how to proceed in the following interviews.

Mom and Dad are completely sympathetic. In my weekly letters home and on my occasional weekend visits, I share my heart and soul and receive lots of encouragement. Dad listens, smokes his pipe, periodically offers a suggestion and listens some more. Mom busies herself doing my laundry and making special meals for me and offers the occasional, "She's a bitch." They enjoy my stories of the clients and my attempts to rescue Ronnie and can't understand Mrs. Bennett's assessment of me. I know in my own mind that Mrs. Bennett is not totally to blame for the difficult interaction between us, but it's sure great having someone who's a hundred percent on my side.

On those weeks when I'm too busy to get to Kitchener, Mom and Dad make a special effort to come and visit me and take me out for coffee and a chat at the Varsity Restaurant on the corner of Bloor and Spadina.

Shelley's on my side, too. She's now living with Mary Kay, the professor, while completing her studies at Waterloo, and the two of them keep the parents busy with bridge games and college gossip when I'm not inundating them with my needs.

Later, still early November, Ronnie calls to say that she has left the Elizabeth Fry residence and would like to talk to me about my friend in Waterloo who might be willing to take her in for a few months. She thinks it's time for her to leave Toronto and make a new start in life. And I fall right in with that idea. I call Mom and Dad and tell them that Ronnie and I will be coming for the weekend. I'm delighted at their acceptance—at least they don't say no. I call Judy Lang, the young woman who expressed an interest in Ronnie, and ask if I can drop by on the weekend for a short visit, without explaining that Ronnie will be with me.

"It's late, Ronnie. Are you ready to go to bed?" I say, after Mom and Dad have excused themselves and headed up to their bedroom.

"No," she answers. Clearly something is bugging her.

"Are you getting cold feet?"

"No, I'm just restless. Do you suppose we could go out for a bit, maybe get some fresh air?"

In spite of the hour I get the keys to the car. I take Ronnie on a tour of the city, what's visible with the streetlights and the November harvest moon. A full moon—a clue, is this what's causing the tension in my gut? I drive down King Street, am actually surprised by the amount of activity. People milling about after the movies, walking leisurely along to late-night restaurants, hotels and bars. We end up down at Cedar Street, an old section of Kitchener.

"I heard that a murder was committed at that restaurant," I say, pointing to a seedy-looking all-night truck stop on the corner.

"Would you mind if we stopped and had coffee?"

God, she must be nuts. I'm not going into that dumpy greasy spoon. What the heck's with her anyway?

"Okay, and maybe you can tell me just what's on your mind."

Sleazy! The smell of French fries, greasy hamburgers and cigarette smoke. A man of about forty, wearing a coffee- and grease-stained apron over a sweat-soaked white shirt with the sleeves rolled up that is open at the neck, revealing curly, greying chest hairs, is serving coffee to several men sitting on bar stools at the counter. Ronnie and I sit down in one of the six booths, all unoccupied. The tabletop is sticky; the sugar, salt and pepper shakers, pushed up against a small rack holding a laminated menu, look greasy. The walls haven't been washed in years, I'm willing to bet, and the black Naugahyde bench has two rips. Two middle-European-looking men, casually dressed in work clothes, are at the counter. They look at us, smile, talk to each other in German. They continue to eyeball us after we request two coffees. I can't believe I'm sitting here. They get up, approach us and ask in fractured English if they can join us. I have this sudden inspiration. I'm going to show Ronnie how anyone can sell her body and how ugly it is—how gross it is to do business in the sex trade. I invite the men to sit down. Ronnie doesn't say a word.

Immediately the man beside me, who's at least thirty pounds overweight, places his hand on my thigh. He smiles at me and attempts to make conversation. The man beside Ronnie, who is slightly younger, has a day's growth of beard and is without the extra pounds, begins playing footsie with me, all the time smiling, his brown eyes shining, making friendly gestures. Both of them have very little working knowledge of English, but their message is very clear.

"You, me, go, right?"

Ronnie has previously taught me the language of the streets so here goes.

"Ten and ten," I say.

"No, don't got ten. You, me, go."

"It's going to cost you. No money, no go."

Ronnie excuses herself. The man lets her out. "I'm going out to the car. If you're coming, come now," she says.

The man beside me is not letting me out. "No money. We just go, come on."

Ronnie is gone. I'm stuck here. *Oh my God, what now? Angels, angels, where are you?* I reach into my purse, take out my wallet and flash the men a card that has a big gold star in the middle, with the words Certified Grapho Analyst written in bold black letters.

"I'm an undercover cop. You're both under arrest."

"Done nothing ... not bad ... nice, friendly," and instantly I'm allowed to get off the bench.

"Okay this time. I'll let you off with a warning. If I ever see you in this restaurant again, you'll go to jail. Understand?"

They head to the bar immediately. I exit the restaurant equally as quickly. Ronnie is just on her way in to rescue me, I suppose.

"Damn you," I say, shouting as I storm my way past her, heading for the car. "You bitch! How could you? What a cheap, sleazy, shitty thing to do. See? Anyone can sell their body. God, how can you do this?"

"I'm sorry, Dale. Really I am. I'm ready now to go back. I'm really sorry."

"Well, you should be," I say, still steaming and feeling revulsion. I know my anger has little to do with Ronnie. Rage, humiliation, disgust at myself, at them—all the "thems" in the world that think they can buy my body, anybody's body. How can any woman sell her body? Jesus!

At two o'clock the next afternoon we arrive at Judy's home, a beautiful ranch bungalow in Bridgeport, just outside Waterloo. Judy is home from the University of Guelph, where she is studying home economics. Her parents, out for Sunday brunch, may or may not be back in time to visit with us.

"Hi, Judy," I call out and wave from the car window as we enter the circular driveway. Ronnie is quiet but seems to be in good spirits.

"Judy, I'd like you to meet ..."

"Shelley, right? I've heard so much about you. Dale has told me about your work at the training school. Do come in, and I'll make coffee."

"Thanks."

"And Shelley, you're studying theology, aren't you?"

"Not yet. I'm just finishing my undergraduate work and then I'm off to Toronto for my theology."

"Did you find your work at the training school helpful in crystallizing your goals, Shelley?"

"Yes, I learned a great deal from the young women," Ronnie answers. Looks to me like she's settling in for a long discourse about "her work at the training school." Okay, Ronnie, it's your call.

I excuse myself explaining that I'm out of cigarettes and want to slip out to the restaurant to pick up a pack. Ronnie smiles sweetly and seems ever so content. When I return the two of them are chatting away, Judy explaining about her courses and Ronnie asking all the right questions.

"Can I ask, Dale, whatever happened to young Ronnie, the girl you were so fond of who was considering a new start in life?"

"Oh she's still giving that idea and your offer serious consideration," I answer, looking at Ronnie. "Isn't that so?"

Judy, her blue eyes sparkling in recognition, a blush colouring a tanned face, looks at Ronnie, raises her hand to cover her mouth. "Oh no," she says, "it's you! Oh my goodness; you sure had me fooled. I can't believe it."

I apologize to Judy for the deception. Ronnie apologizes as well, explaining that she appreciated getting to know Judy without being identified.

"I just need a little time now to think about things," Ronnie says, "and then I'll make a decision. I appreciate your offer, Judy. You and your parents are very kind."

We're preparing to leave the residence just as Mr. and Mrs. Lang pull into the driveway. Judy introduces us and off we go, promising to be in touch very soon regarding Ronnie's decision.

I don't hear from Ronnie again until early in the new year. She brings her sister Jody and Jody's boyfriend, fresh out of Guelph Reformatory, over to meet me. She asks to borrow money. No, no more money. No more contact. I explain to Ronnie, "When you pay me the money you already owe me, then I'll know that you're serious about straightening out your life. Then come and see me."

Oh my, I'm getting tough. I know Ronnie is back on the street and I have finally figured out that I'm not going to save her. *What a waste. How sad.* I know I need to recognize when I'm being conned but such a sweet kid. And I don't understand how such a bright, attractive and personable young person can end up a hooker on the streets. Perhaps I'll understand when I'm an honest-to-goodness social worker.

I don't understand what Dr. Albert Rose, my faculty advisor, is telling me either. It's now late February and I'm here to discuss my plans for next semester, presuming there is a next semester. Dr. Rose, balding, precisely dressed in an immaculate white shirt, with a blue-green tie knotted just so, a perfect match to the deep blue of his suit jacket hung carefully over the back of his chair, is explaining to me what Mrs. Bennett has shared with him about my midterm evaluation.

"It appears that you need to vent your hostility through aggression," he says. "You give the impression of having an unhealthy cynicism and are suspicious, critical and hostile."

"I am? I know I'm having difficulty relating to Mrs. Bennett, but not all those things you say. I thought I was doing much better lately," I add, holding back tears, gathering up my clipboard and notes, preparing to exit. I feel betrayed. Dr. Rose is supposed to be my advocate, my advisor, my father confessor. I wonder how he can form such a strong opinion of me when this is the first time I've ever talked to him.

"I'll do my best to work things out," I say and exit before the tears begin to flow.

I carry on, not saying a word. My relationship with Mrs. Bennett seems to be improving. I now have additional cases assigned: one case that I really enjoy—a lovely immigrant Spanish Moroccan Jewish couple in their late fifties who need financial assistance until the man is able to find employment. I'm impressed with their tiny, clean apartment, with its embroidered doilies, little unfamiliar knickknacks. The woman offers me coffee and cakes while we talk, in gentle soft voices, about their needs. She shows me her treasures, lets me touch and hold them.

I move on from here to visit the other couple, now with two babies crying, in their almost bare apartment above a restaurant in Chinatown. It's dark out and I'm not comfortable walking in this area at night. As I enter the apartment I'm overwhelmed with the smell of dirty diapers stuffed in a closet. The two older children sit on the floor against the wall, almost in foetal positions, heads down, like ostriches presuming their invisibility, attempting to stay out of harm's way. The danger: mother crying, near hysteria, the father ballistic, screaming at me about the need for more money for a washer and dryer, gesturing wildly and in very fragmented language attempting to communicate the level of his distress. The smell alone convinces me—he needn't have picked up a knife, raising it over his shoulders and head, as he approaches his wife who is now hiding behind me. Oh my God. Oh my God.

"Now, Mr. Hassida, you don't want to do that," I say, knees shaking, voice trembling, hoping he's too distressed to notice. He drops the knife to the floor and collapses. I tell them I'll do what I can and exit, quickly. Maybe I'm not cut out for this type of work.

Mrs. Bennett thinks that these theatrics are manipulative, that it's time to confront Mr. Hassida—get a job or you're off assistance. We're to conference this case with the neighbouring Jewish Vocational Service, who is assisting the gentleman in his efforts to find employment. Conference? Adrenalin zap—I'm going to have to present something? The instant flooding of anxiety doesn't help me communicate with Mrs. Bennett, who has asked me a question and is waiting for an answer. I ask her to repeat the question. She frowns.

The showdown comes in early April. I'm to be in Mrs. Bennett's office at three. I tell Margaret Stewart, another student at the agency, that I have an uncomfortable feeling in my gut, a sense of impending doom. Margaret and I walk together to and from the agency. I tell Margaret that I might be late, that she may want to go on without me.

"If your work doesn't significantly improve in three weeks I'm going to have to fail you. You seem unable to relate to your clients," Mrs. Bennett informs me. She says a great deal more, but I'm unable to hear it. Fail? Fail? How can I fail? She says something about me being unable to connect to my clients at the emotional level. My head is whirling. I feel a stab of fear, rage, humiliation, bewilderment, a tumbling of emotions like the spinning of a washing machine gone wild. Fail?

It's now after five o'clock and I have endured almost two hours of hearing about my inadequacies, how I could have done this differently, that differently, interrupted only by a phone call that Mrs. Bennett chooses to take. I just can't sit here and take this. I've got to defend myself. Fail?

"Mrs. Bennett," I say, standing up, preparing to exit her office, "how do you expect me to communicate with you? Talking to you is like talking to a blank wall. You are cold, distant and totally critical."

Not much of a victory but I get in the last word and thank God, Margaret is waiting for me. She looks at me and doesn't say a word. She helps me gather up my things and we walk in silence the thirty minutes to the house. In front of the house I say, "Margaret, I'm going to fail if I don't improve in three weeks. Can you help me? Will you read over some of my case records and tell me what I'm doing wrong?" Margaret agrees and we set a time to meet on Sunday to spend the afternoon working together. First thing next morning I'm at Dr. Rose's office.

"Come in by all means," says Dr. Rose. And the tears come. "Ahhh … I'll pretend I'm doing something with my papers and you pretend you're not crying, okay?… She can't fail you. I'm the only one who can do that and I'm not doing that! You wait here. I'm going to get her on the phone right now."

Dr. Rose returns twenty minutes later. "You will not fail. If you improve in the remaining few weeks you will get a C and I will be giving you a C plus." He explains that the problem is not entirely me, that I'm Mrs. Bennett's first student and that she is having difficulties with the teaching relationship. "Do what you can, Dale; you are not going to fail."

Two and a half hours with Margaret over coffee at the Varsity Restaurant and I learn more about interviewing skills and case recording than I have learned all year. Marg informs me that I write like a journalist—just the facts—and have not included the emotional exchanges in the reports.

"You mean that I have to write, 'I smiled,' 'Mr. Smith laughed and winked as he left the office,' that kind of thing?"

"Exactly, you've got it!"

Armed with this amazing new piece of information I rewrite the three interviews I've conducted during the past week, submit them to Mrs. Bennett and I'm informed that I've made significant improvement.

Mom and Dad are upset about the difficulties with Mrs. Bennett but are not in the least surprised to learn that I want to return for the master's year, despite the woman's recommendation to the contrary. I explain about that voice from somewhere within, as unrelenting as any drill sergeant, saying, *Who are you kidding? You don't know enough to go into the world and work with people.*

In late April I contact Frank Potts, Director of Psychology, Department of Reform Institutions, for a summer position, informing him that I will be returning to the school for my master's year. The board that interviews candidates for grant money is scheduled to meet in July and he advises me to attend. He requests that I report to Mr. Barry Sheppard, the social worker at the Ontario Training School for Boys in Cobourg on June 1 to begin summer employment.

A training school? The setting in Cobourg, on acres of prime land a stone's throw from Lake Ontario, consists of renovated estates— huge American summer estates in their earlier life—white stucco walls, stone foundations, tall pillars, second-story wood railings surrounding upper verandahs, lower outside walkways, with gothic arches. The residences each bear the names of British admirals, just like the setting in Galt—Drake, Collingwood, Beatty, Nelson. All have white dormitories with lounge areas, hardwood floors, varnished wood handrails. They're surrounded with carefully manicured lawns and rich, healthy, mature trees magnificently dressed in shades of green.

The setting includes a modest two-story building that houses a gym and auditorium. Behind this building—a recreation area with a ball diamond, a swimming pool, swings and slides and several additional, less formal, functional, one-story, white-sided portables used as classrooms. The counselling offices are housed on the second floor of the administrative building.

I meet Barry Sheppard, the social worker who will be my boss for the summer. Will this man, this tank of a man who could easily be an offensive lineman for the Buffalo Bills, be my guardian angel? Will this man with the baritone voice that booms out arias that can be heard from a considerable distance, that is, when he isn't whistling, be my avenging angel? Or ...?

I wait a couple of weeks, working with the seven young boys Barry has assigned me, submit written process recordings of each session, before I tell Barry about my devastating experience with Mrs. Bennett.

"From what you've read, Barry, do you think I can relate to people?" I say, a slight tremor in my voice, my hands tightly clenched together on my lap.

Barry bellows a right-from-the-depths-of-the-belly guffaw that is infectious. I start to laugh, too.

"No, I'm serious. I need an answer. Do you think I can relate to people?"

"Of course; you're a 'Big Mama,' 'Mother Earth.' The kids love yuh. Why would you ask a question like that?"

I tell Barry about Mrs. Bennett and the trauma of near failure and her recommendation that I not return to the school for the second year. Then I listen as Barry shares a similar story of his first-year supervisory experience and adds, "You're making great strides, Dale. You're learning quickly. If it will help, near the end of the summer I'll write an evaluation of your performance for Frank Potts and send a copy to the school. The school and the department ought to be courting you to make sure you don't slip away." My avenging angel!

Supervision sessions after that—a breeze. The whole summer—a breeze, though not without its unique learning experiences.

"Dale, in my office immediately," Barry says. "And you, Jackie, you'd better come too. And Dale, bring in your recording of the session you had with Geoff."

Oh my God, I must have done something terrible. I rummage through the stack of records and files I have on my desk, find the ten-page report on Geoff and hurry over to Barry's office. Jackie Marshall, the full-time psychologist on staff, a woman several years my senior who is working on her PhD thesis, says, "What's up?"

"Tell you in a moment. I just need to take this report down to George Pollard and have it photocopied for Geoff's record, and then I'll be right back."

George Pollard? Barry wants to give my handwritten process recording to the superintendent of the training school? I've been here less than a month and already I'm in big trouble.

"I don't have time to explain now but wait in my office for me."

I wait, standing at the window, looking over the grounds, Jackie looking at me with a quizzical smile, head erect and chin up.

Barry's booming aria announces his imminent arrival.

"George tells me that you have thirty-three requests for interviews," he says, looking directly at me with his soft, hazy blue eyes. "Every single boy in Geoff's residence has put in a request to be seen by you."

I'm stunned. "I don't understand." I look at Jackie, her mouth wide open, about to say something, something that never gets said.

"Yeah, when Geoff was escorted back to Collingwood after his session with you, he announced to all the guys that you had exposed your breast to him. What really pisses me off is that I had to show George your recording before he was convinced that you didn't actually do that. Can you believe it?"

I couldn't. *George Pollard, the administrator of the school, actually needed proof that I didn't do such a thing? What does that say about the people I'm working with at this school?*

"The staff at Collingwood got wind of this last night and they are all up in arms. They want to send Geoff to solitary, or unofficially beat the shit out of him. They have really overreacted. I had to persuade George to let it be, not to give it any credence, and to let you deal with Geoff. And George, he thinks I should go talk to the staff and explain that Geoff is lying. Can you believe it?" he asks again.

Barry suggests that I call in Geoff later in the day and talk to him about the implications of lying and minimize the content of the lie. And he wants Jackie to be aware in order to ward off questions that may arise from other staff members, most of whom are male supervisory personnel.

As I return to my office, relieved that the issue is such a simple one, Wayne, a fifteen-year-old boy from Collingwood House, is waiting outside the administrative offices. He stares at me, doesn't say a word. He leers, a twisted smile, a smirk that triggers that familiar terror in the pit of my gut, and moves his eyes from my face down the length of my body. It isn't too difficult to imagine what he's thinking. His message is clear. I shudder and continue up the stairs.

Geoff is pushed into my office by the supervisor who escorted him to this session. Reluctantly he stands at the door, reaches into his pocket and brings out a handful of jujubes. "Here, Miss. I brought you something," he says, depositing the treasures on the desk, head down and eyes focused on some imaginary spot on the hardwood floor.

"Well, Geoff, you got yourself into a pocketful of trouble, didn't you?" I say, and the interview progresses from there. I'm learning. Geoff was brought here from the courts having been charged with soliciting on Jarvis Street in Toronto. As a male prostitute selling services to men of varying ages, Geoff was victimized and ridiculed by the other boys in the school. Definitely low status. His claim to fame did bring him attention and significantly improved his status, albeit short-lived, but not as short-lived as I assumed. The boys, and truthfully, many of the staff, I learn, continued to wonder, did I do it? Did I expose myself to Geoff? The lesson is not so much that psychopathic children exist, the lesson that Barry wants me to learn. The lesson is a recognition, a suspicion that not all supervisory staff members are healthy personalities. And I'm not at all sure about professional staff either—especially when one of the senior nurses asks me directly if exposing genitals is a part of a sex education program.

The rest of the summer is uneventful. Barry, his wife Lorraine and the two young children invite Jackie and me and Francia Kalb, a psychology student who has joined us for the summer, to their home for barbeques and fun times. He regales us with stories of the boys and his antics with the staff. He tells of his ongoing battle with the house supervisors about the use of "piss boards," memo boards used in the residences to identify the boys who wet their beds the previous night. Since he is unable to reason with them or persuade them to stop this negative reinforcement and humiliation, he goes into all four houses in the early hours of the morning and steals the boards. They are not replaced.

It is here in Barry's home, in the presence of his wife and family, that another side of Barry's nature is highlighted. Whenever Lorraine, a bright, attractive, gentle, rather reticent woman, attempts to interject a comment or initiate a discussion, Barry slices her to pieces with angry, abusive comments: "Shut up, you stupid woman." "What the hell do you know about anything?" "Keep your goddamn thoughts to yourself. No one cares what you think." And so on. How can this be? How can such a gentle man, tender and caring with the children at the training school, as well as with his own kids, be such a vicious, psychologically abusive person with his wife? Another Frank West, another misogynist?

Jackie, Francia and I spend a great deal of time together in the evenings, just chatting and processing the experiences of the summer. Generally, on weekends, we leave Cobourg. I'm off to Kitchener,

Francia, Toronto and Jackie, Hamilton. In late August, Jackie invites me to go with her to her brother's cottage for part of the long weekend. We spend Friday night at my parents' home, playing bridge, enjoying the banter and teasing that occurs spontaneously when I'm with my parents. Mom insists on calling Jackie "Johnny."

"Oh, Mom," I say, embarrassed by such foolishness. "Her name is Jackie."

"Oh, it's okay, really. You can call me Johnny anytime," Jackie says, laughing and giving my mother a hug. I'm not sure just why but all my friends are attracted to Mom. Clearly Jackie is gobbling up the teasing.

We're interrupted by a phone call. It's Lois, Dad's sister. Obviously something has happened. I can hear Lois screaming on the other end of the line. Dad takes the phone and moves into the other room. Momentarily I hear him slam the phone on the receiver. He rushes out into the living room, stating, "I'm going to kill that son of a bitch. Where's my shotgun?"

I look at Jackie. "Come on, let's get out of here." I grab the car keys, knowing that Dad can't drive if there's no car available, and Jackie and I back out of the driveway and move down the street as quickly as the car will accelerate. I drive for several minutes, going nowhere, feeling anxious and deeply distressed, unable to talk. Jackie breaks the silence, no doubt in the interest of her own safety, as well as mine.

"Do you want to bring your brother in to help?" she says.

"Great idea," I say and head in the direction of Ken's fiancée's house. Ken's not there but I'm directed to Jan's sister's place, where they're both attending a shower.

"Ken, you've got to come. Dad's cracking up. He's going to kill Frank West."

Without hesitation Ken gets into the driver's seat and drives directly home. At this speed he could beat Jacques Villeneuve on any track. We rush in the door, Jackie and I behind Ken. There's Mom, sitting and knitting in her favourite living-room chair, looking perfectly calm, as if to say, "What else is new?"

"Where's Dad?" Ken says.

"He's in the den, reading."

"Is he okay?"

"Of course; he's just relaxing. Everything's fine."

Damn! I'm furious. Jackie and I drive Ken back to his party. I drive around with Jackie and pour out my anger and frustration. I recognize for the first time in my life that Mom is a strong personality. Behind her apparent helplessness and feelings of inadequacy is a very powerful woman. She's fooled me all these years. I thought she needed me to protect her from the world. She'd never stand up to Inez and Eunice; never confront Auntie Elthea directly, just bitch to me about her; she'd get me to talk to Dad about the need to take holidays. Yet when she's faced with Dad acting like a madman, she handles it as if it's a ho-hum event. She's lied to me. Damn her! All these years, letting me think she was defenseless, unable to cope with conflict, with stress. Well, no more. From now on she can handle her own problems!

I do recover from that enlightening experience, though I am shaken. And life goes right on just as if my view of the world hasn't been impacted. A few more pleasant surprises, and the summer is over. Barry writes me an excellent evaluation and shares his perceptions directly with Frank Potts. I learn that I've been accepted for a training grant in return for which I commit to giving the department a full year of service following graduation and that I must write my thesis on a subject relevant to the corrections field. I learn that I'm accepted back at the School of Social Work. The McLeods have a room for me for this school year, which is to be a full twelve-month year. Lynn Quesnell, my roommate this past school term, marries Ron Poth, the only bachelor I know, a good friend of Bayne's whom I introduced to her. I celebrate Shelley's graduation and her acceptance into Covenant College, where she will pursue the designation of "deaconess" in the United Church of Canada. And the family celebrates another wedding: Ken and Janet Harper marry in a moving candlelight ceremony on Friday night, September 7, 1962.

My high-school friends, my college friends and now my brothers—all married and me, still a student. When will it be my turn? Shelley's now in Toronto, living in residence not far from me. On we plod, pursuing the golden grail, the diplomas we need, our rite of passage to the adult world.

The master's academic year is structured very differently than the preceding year: four weeks of intensive classroom study, followed by a block placement in the field, consisting of four days a week of supervised practical work with clients, then a day back at school for work on the thesis requirement. The placement will be terminated at the end of March 1963, to be followed by six more weeks' study, two comprehensive exams and finally completion of the research project.

I approach the Ontario Psychiatric Hospital, 999 Queen Street, with the familiar fist-in-the-gut anxiety. This is the last place I wanted as a field experience. Reluctantly I enter the administration building, an old red-brick structure, one of several located on acres of manicured lawns, separated from the mainstream of life on Queen Street by black wrought-iron fencing. Maybe I shouldn't have come back for the second year. Maybe this is a message to me to get out and revisit the clerk/secretarial pool at the Dominion Tire Factory.

Bob Wan, Robin Duff and Don Lemieux, my fellow students, quite senior in years to me, arrive, and we are ushered into a meeting room with several white-coated members of staff. Bob Lacey, director of the social work department, gives us a brief orientation, explaining how each social worker participates on a team with other professionals in different units of the hospital. I'm to be placed with Sophie Butkevicius, in Unit D, under the leadership of Dr. Cochrane, head psychiatrist. Shortly after, Sophie issues me a white coat, takes me to the office that I will share with Bob Wan and leaves me with a stack of reading material and two patient charts. This is it—baptism by fire; survival of the fittest; make or break; bust or blossom.

I blossom. Who'd have thought that Demeter, the mother goddess who nurtures all and causes harvests to flourish, would twin a soul to work at "999"? Sophie is diametrically opposed to Mrs. Bennett in personality and teaching style. Nurtured by her radiant smile and easy laugh, supported by her focus on my positive achievements and her gentle instructions, I risk vulnerability and share my fears.

I'm to have an interview with the sister of Maxine, a patient diagnosed as schizophrenic, in treatment here for a second time, currently for nine months. I have seen Maxine several times with the intention of learning about possible aftercare plans: where will she go, what will she do when she leaves the hospital? Maxine explains that she is schizophrenic, that she knows she got sick again because she stopped taking her medication. She tells me about her left eye—she used to put purple eye shadow on this eye because it sees evil—and her right eye—she used to put green eye shadow on this eye because it sees good—and is amazed that she could actually have believed that. She knows that was crazy thinking. Her sister Jasmine is her closest friend and her intention is to share an apartment with her when she is discharged from the hospital. Jasmine is coming to see me after work to be consulted about Maxine's plans.

"You have no right to impose on my life," Jasmine begins and proceeds with a tirade of criticisms about this *stupid* hospital, the *stupid* doctors, people who think they can do whatever they want without asking. "If you're so smart, how come you let Maxine get sick again?"

Whoosh! The tirade of anger bombards my senses. Every pore in my body is saturated with a layer of stinging ice pellets. My nose is clogged with the stench of acid rage. I taste dry fear. My stomach threatens to expel the toxins I'm internalizing. Images of mean Frank West and verbally annihilating Barry briefly appear on my internal screen.

"Uh, well, uh ... I'm sorry ... uh ..."

I mutter some innocuous statements that I can't remember and within minutes, Jasmine gets up and walks out the door, leaving me wide-eyed, sweaty and shaky.

I'm at Sophie's office door first thing next morning.

"Sophie, you've got to help me with this one. I really blew it," I say, silently praying for compassion, hoping my inability to deal with anger doesn't get me tossed into the "hopelessly immature" file drawer, right behind the "can't relate to people" file.

I pour out the details of my session-turned-chaotic, watching Sophie's blue-grey eyes for the slightest hint of impatience or annoyance.

"You always get a second chance with people," she says, leaning forward, elbows on the desk, hands folded under her chin, her square face fresh with just the right amount of makeup, every permed, blond hair still in place.

Got it; anger means unhappy. Right, an amazing piece of information! And Jasmine does call back. How did Sophie know that would happen? I keep saying to myself, *anger means unhappy* and guess what? Jasmine is very unhappy—actually frightened—understandably. When her sister is the *crazy one* Jasmine functions quite well in the community. When Maxine is stabilized and functions better in the community, Jasmine starts to crack. Dr. Cochrane calls it *folie a deux*. And I can listen to Jasmine's anger/scare without personalizing it and becoming frightened? Wow—a paradigm shift, a whole new way of perceiving reality.

I also have the opportunity to understand delusional systems in mental illness. Mrs. Berkowski taught me the naiveté of attacking such a system head-on. Mr. Berkowski, a quiet, gentle mid-European man in his late sixties, visits his wife every day during visiting hours. He explains how his wife gradually deteriorated, beginning with hallucinating strange sounds—the humming of some kind of motor—and thinking bizarre thoughts—the next-door neighbour has a machine that is aimed at her stomach and the rays are eating her insides—then becoming increasingly paranoid and deeply depressed. I'm to obtain a social history from him. I visit Mrs. Berkowski in her room and attempt to reassure her in my awkward, I'm-a-very-helpful-person role.

"Mrs. Berkowski, your husband is here every day to visit you. He really does love you."

"If he loves me, why is he trying to kill me?"

Well there you go. Another lesson learned, and this lesson is reinforced in my own residence.

This year the McLeod Guest Home has a very young group of women residents. Are all young women crazy? Or is this just contaminated thinking from my recent 999 experiences?

"Dale, you've got to do something about Gerry. She's hanging over the banister half naked. She's not responding to us when we ask her what's wrong."

Gerry lives on the third floor along with two other young students. Linda Little, a business school student who shares my room on the second floor, along with the women from upstairs, gather in my room to express concern. Gerry, a new graduate librarian, is working at a library opposite a Greek restaurant. Linda informs me that Gerry is in love with the restaurant owner and says she's having an affair. This may not seem all that unusual but Gerry is very dowdy and slow-moving: a "strange" woman, no makeup, thick glasses that magnify blank-staring brown eyes. Her speech is delayed. You're never sure whether she actually hears you.

Earlier in the semester Gerry informed me that she's schizophrenic—which didn't mean anything to me at the time. She related how she had imaginary affairs, most recently with a professor from a graduate school in London, Ontario. She takes medication and now she's fine. Fine maybe, but *strange* definitely! I'm delegated to do something about this. I ask Linda to call the restaurant and talk to the owner—maybe she is having an affair.

"Gerry, Gerry, what's wrong?" I say, gently peeling her off the banister and slowly guiding her to her room.

"I'm going to have to die. I have to die. How could I make such a mistake? I have to die."

That certainly triggers alarm, that all-too-familiar "Oh my God, what do I do now" vice grip in the gut. I manoeuvre Gerry onto her bed and cover her while encouraging her to explain her remark.

"How could I mistake his brother for him, that wonderful Greek god? He is so perfect and kind and his brother is so ordinary. How could I make such a mistake? I can't face him. I'm so humiliated. I have to die."

"Can you not just explain it to him?"

"No, we never talk. We only communicate through our thoughts. He doesn't want others to know we're in love."

"You've never talked? How do you know he loves you?"

"I just know. He is so perfect. He'd never tell anyone. He doesn't want to hurt his wife."

Somehow, somewhere in this conversation, I manage to get Gerry to give me the phone number of her parents. Linda has now talked to the restaurant owner.

"He panicked," Linda says. "He remembers Gerry—'the lady who always orders corned beef on rye, with an extra dill pickle' and he swears he has never even had a conversation with her. He sounds awful, kept saying, 'I've done nothing wrong, nothing wrong. I don't even know her,' and I believe him."

I connect with Gerry's parents and they assure me that they'll call the psychiatrist. Later in the evening, Gerry gets a phone call. Good Lord, how can she sound so normal on the phone when just moments ago she was staring at the ceiling, stark naked? I hear her make an appointment to see the doctor. Relief! Her parents arrive later in the evening and take Gerry back to London.

I'm sitting in the dungeon kitchen with Gerry the following week. She tells me that she is back on medication and will continue seeing her psychiatrist for a while. She acknowledges that she's not well. We're interrupted by Lorraine, in her blue-flowered nightgown and rabbit slippers, pasty looking, hair disheveled.

"I've got to talk to you right away, Dale."

Gerry excuses herself and Lorraine sits down.

"What's wrong, Lorraine? Are you ill?"

"I've just given myself an abortion and I've lost a lot of blood. I think I need to get to the hospital."

"Get some clothes on. I'll go across the street and get one of the men from the frat house to take us to the hospital," I say, going into an act-first-think-later mode of operation. One of the men agrees to help, though highly suspicious of my explanation that one of the girls is having an appendix attack. (Wouldn't you know this had to be a medical fraternity?) He goes for his car; I go for Lorraine, now stepping gingerly out the front door, and we're on our way.

"Your friend is very fortunate," the doctor says. "She's lost a lot of blood. We'll have to keep her in for several days. You'd better notify her parents. She's not out of danger yet."

"Please don't contact my parents," Lorraine pleads. She gives me permission to call her boyfriend but not her parents. I can't believe I actually agree to honour her request. What if? What if?

Linda, with some help, cleans up Lorraine's room and the bathroom, blood everywhere, soiled Kotex pads, shredded, stained foul-smelling Kleenex tissue, a book on anatomy and a coat hanger. Great Caesar's ghost! A coat hanger! She flushes and then plunges the blob of stuff clogging the toilet. Finally, a cleansing swoosh.

Several days of the same excuse: "I'm sorry, I just got in. I don't know where Lorraine is," plus no phone call from their daughter, alerts Lorraine's parents to the fact that something is amiss and thank goodness, they arrive to investigate. Never again! I will never again participate in this kind of deception.

Is it me or is it the fact that I'm a social work student? Several more incidents of recklessness and acting out—the last, our resident judge's daughter is stopped for impaired driving—and again I agree to keep a secret. Am I just a slow learner? Or are the angels trying to tell me something? Am I really cut out for this helping profession?

The McLeods ask to talk with me. Now what? I don't think they are aware of all the shenanigans going on in the house. Or are they?

"We're planning to sell the house this summer or fall," Mr. McLeod says. "Would you be interested in buying it? You seem to have a real way of dealing with people. You would do very well in this business."

Me? Buy a guest home? I don't even have the money to finish this school year. I decline their kind offer, but maybe their perceptiveness is a message to me from the angels. I must be moving in the right direction.

My financial situation is remedied after an unscheduled visit with Mrs. Kirkpatrick, the registrar. I inform her that I only have ten dollars left in my bank account.

"Wait right here," she says and leaves the office. I wait. Within ten minutes she returns with a cheque for two hundred and fifty dollars, contributed by an anonymous donor. And that, with a small loan from Auntie Elthea, ought to get me through until I begin work. *The angels again?*

I'm having amazing experiences: parties, new multicultural experiences with students in the program including ever-charming Bob Wan, my officemate, good marks and dear Sophie. Bob has developed a crush on me and is following me around like a little puppy. At parties he drinks my beer when I put down my glass—ever so concerned that I might drink too much. I only do that on a couple of occasions but Bob sure gets high. I'm bustling about working on an individual research project at my own pace, in my own way, with my very own faculty advisor, Dr. Taduis Grygier, while the others are working in groups, not always harmoniously. My parents continue to bring me food parcels, take me out for coffee and nurture me with gentle caretaking when I'm home for the occasional weekend. Shelley and I support each other with infrequent afternoon or late evening coffee and chats. And I end up with an A minus for my field placement mark.

Just one blip as I head into the comprehensive exams. I'm sick. By the end of my first summer's experience at the Galt Training School, I had developed terrible shakes, couldn't hold the matches to light the girls' cigarettes without one of them steadying my hand. I wondered if this was my body's reaction to the emotional stress of my introduction to social work. It was. My family doctor diagnosed "hyperthyroid," and the medication he prescribed seemed to keep things under control. Until—well, I knew I was way out of whack before the exams. I also knew that if I visited the doctor before exams, he'd take me out of school—which is what he does following the exams.

I'll miss a month on the research project, so I notify Dr. Grygier by phone and he informs me that hyperthyroidism is a psychosomatic disorder. Oh my God. I'm *crazy*. I phone Billie Becker, a social worker at the hospital with whom I have developed a friendship, and ask her to consult Dr. Cochrane. She does and he confirms it— psychosomatic! He also recommends a specialist in internal medicine in the Toronto area. I'm greatly reassured by Vivienne Durden, one of the older students in the program. "Vivienne, I'm crazy," I say, my tears communicating clearly my level of distress.

Vivienne laughs. Yes, just laughs. "If we have to eliminate all the social workers in the field who have psychosomatic disorders of one kind or another, there won't be many social workers left," she says, still laughing.

My month of "healing" is up and not totally wasted, as I have now completed most of the reading for my thesis. I visit my Kitchener family doctor. He recommends surgery to remove a part of the thyroid. No way. I'm not having my throat slit. I ask him to refer me to a Toronto specialist, who then sends me to the Toronto General Hospital, Nuclear Medicine Department. I'm given radioactive iodine from a tube handed to me by remote control arms manipulated by a technician hiding behind a steel door.

I go to the school to give Dr. Grygier the good news: I can now get back to work on my thesis. He insists that I leave all the material in his office and work from there. Impossible! I can't drink five quarts of water a day, as per my instruction from the specialist, and work in Dr. Grygier's office. I wait for him to leave his office, hiding just around the corner. I see him head down the corridor and sneak back into his office. I grab my stack of notes, the early prep work for my thesis, and slink silently away, like a cat burglar in the midnight blackness of a starless night.

At least one good thing happens while I'm sequestered in my bedroom, draped over an old Underwood typewriter, creating a grooved path between my desk and the bathroom. I'm an auntie again. Ken and Jan give birth to a son, Drew. Wow—Ken's a father? I can hardly believe it. And here I am labouring to birth a thesis. I don't know. I wonder if what I'm doing is ultimately of any significance.

I do it. I complete my thesis, a study of the interaction between the male staff and residents of the Ontario Training School for Boys in Guelph, and will submit the final draft in time to graduate with my classmates. That's it. I'm finished. I place my thesis on Dr. Grygier's desk. He's not in. I'm glad. I really don't want to talk with him. I walk down the three levels of stairs, race out to Bloor Street. Yippee, yahoo, hurrah! Never again! If I never set foot in another institute of higher learning it will be too soon.

I can start work now. I do know how to do something. I'm ready for the adult world. I'm to begin my work with the Department of Reform Institutions in Guelph at the beginning of September, at the same setting where I conducted my research for the thesis.

In November 1963 I return to Toronto to attend our graduation party. I can't bring myself to attend the actual ceremony. I don't know why that is. I just wait, along with the only other student who is not at the ceremony, until we get the phone call telling us to head out to the home of the student who is hosting the party. I don't know what I'm feeling or why—just a sadness, a desire to cry that I struggle to suppress, an emptiness. At the party I learn that I'm the recipient of an award—the student whose thesis contributed the most to the field of social work, and Vivienne hands me a cheque for fifty dollars—an unexpected trophy.

Will there be any trophies in the real world? Do I now get an exciting career, the man, the children and live happily forever after?

BUMPS, BRUISES AND BANDAGES

What messages did you get regarding success? Failure? Did you expect to be successful? To fail?

How did you cope with your first "bump"? What thoughts, feelings and behaviours were triggered? Are these thoughts, feelings and behaviours familiar?

Who were your supports?

Did your experiences reinforce your beliefs about yourself, others and the world? Or did those experiences result in confusion, a shifting in your worldview?

THE LOTTERY

Mom has been preparing for this day even longer than I have, at least on a conscious level. My first job—my first very own *home*. On the weekend, Mom and Dad and I load up the car and a borrowed truck with my clothes, my bedroom furniture, odds and ends of furniture Mom collected from relatives and friends, a set of dishes and the RenaWare set of pots and pans I purchased when I worked at the Dominion Tire Factory. We set up my apartment on Gordon Avenue, near the University of Guelph. Seemingly out of nowhere comes an assortment of linens, towels, glasses, sterling silver bowls and other miscellaneous items, all prizes from badminton tournaments I won in my younger years. I think Mom had a "hope chest" in which she secreted these and other items, including pieces of sterling silverware that Gramma and Auntie Elthea started giving me when I was just a child. I don't think that this is what she was hoping for though.

Mom and I are excited about the end result; Dad less so. I hadn't anticipated that his feelings would be hurt. "Can't wait to shake the dust off and get out of here," he says. I wonder if that's why Ken stayed at home until he married. It just didn't cross my mind that Dad would suffer empty-nest syndrome, if that's what is happening. He may not be ready for me to move into the adult world, but I am.

I know this job will be a challenge. I know because I had the opportunity to view the setting and get to know the supervisory personnel, at least on paper, prior to coming here to work. This setting, the Ontario Training School for Boys, in Guelph, a maximum security institution for boys who have committed serious and violent crimes—murder, arson, rape, assault, breaking and entering—or were runaways from open institutions, was the source for the data on which my research was based, the process and results of which were documented in my thesis. Dr. Grygier and I had administered personality inventories and sociometric tests to the supervisory personnel and the residents of the school. So I have insight into the authoritarian personality, the type of personality most prevalent in this setting. I'm ready—or at least I think I am.

"Good morning, Tom," I say as I get into his car this warm September morning, 1964, my first day on the job as a "Professional Social Worker." Tom Bonthron, the head supervisor and second-in-command, and I exchange small talk and pleasantries in the ten minutes it takes to arrive on scene. I'm not about to tell him that, in spite of my previous exposure to this maximum security setting, I'm scared half to death. Well, maybe this fist-in-the-gut tension is really just excitement? Possibly?

I approach the two-story, red-brick rectangular building with determination. I can do this. I know I can. The entrance is dead centre: a set of barred windows on both sides of the building surrounded by two feet of decorative grey angel stone, so characteristic of the city of Guelph. The stone hardly detracts from the cold reality of black steel bars on these and a second set of smaller windows, closer to the main entrance. Tom presses the buzzer and the grey, two-inch-thick, steel door unlocks. We enter a small alcove; to the left, a big window with a small hole that allows people entering to identify themselves and talk to the receptionist in the front office. After the first door bangs closed, the receptionist presses the release for the second door, just to the right, and we enter a yellow, sparsely decorated waiting room. I feel a cold chill of anxiety as the second door clangs shut. No mistaking this feeling.

Don Wilson, the superintendent, a soft-spoken, grey-haired gentleman with a stylish brush cut, is the only person to be dressed in civilian clothes. The other supervisory personnel, including Tom, are dressed in grey slacks, blue blazers, white shirts and ties. Only the ties vary—a slim victory for individuality. Don I estimate to be in his late forties; he greets me and invites me into his office, asking Jane Walker, the receptionist/secretary, to hold his calls. After a brief welcome in his office, with its impressive mahogany executive desk and bookcase, the desk piled high with files, the in-out mahogany tray filled to overflowing, I glance out the small window with its steel bars—*how can anyone work in a place like this, let alone live here?*—and await the arrival of Norm Bamford, the senior supervisor on duty. He's to take me on a tour of the building and help me set up what will be my office, in the basement of the building.

"Let's start with B Section," Norm says. After unlocking the steel door separating the administrative area from the main corridor with a massive brass skeleton key on a chain with several other similar-looking keys, we turn right and meet another steel door. Once through this door we enter a lounge area, with well-used and abused couches, chairs, two long wooden tables with attached benches and a TV set.

"The boys have their meals here," Norm says. "'A' section boys eat at the far table. Both groups can lounge here, play cards, watch TV, or do homework in this area after school and shops are finished for the day. They don't have to go to their *rooms* until bedtime, or unless they're in trouble of some sort."

In the middle of this part of the building, behind a grille with two separate locked gates, is a solid wall of cement containing twenty-four individual cells, twelve facing the north corridor, twelve facing the south corridor. The corridors are wide and devoid of any furnishings or decoration. Each cell contains a cast-iron cot with a thin mattress, pillow, flannelette sheet and grey army blankets, a metallic toilet and a metal locker for the institutional khaki-coloured uniforms that the boys wear and the few personal possessions they're allowed to keep. The cells, with iron bars and individual locks that can only be opened with a different set of keys or an emergency switch in the main office, are open as we walk by. This whole sterile area smells of Javex, Mr. Clean minus the lemons, and other less identifiable cleaning products.

"Would you like to feel what it's like to be locked up in one of these rooms?" Norm says, with a twinkle in his deep blue eyes.

"No, thank you, dawwwwwling," I say, attempting to imitate his British accent and the levity of his mood. Thank goodness he's not privy to the tightness in my gut and the clamminess of my sweaty palms. I can fake it pretty good when I have to. At least I think I can.

The second level of the building contains classrooms, where some of the boys are working on their grade-school and high-school curriculums, each at his own speed and level of achievement. Cecil Reid, the principal of the small school setting, interrupts his work to greet me. Cec is also dressed in the grey slacks/blue blazer uniform of the supervisory personnel.

It's the basement—the hub of this universe—that is most impressive.

"You are privileged, my dear," Norm says. "You will be the first woman in the history of this school to enter the basement area."

He unlocks another steel door and we descend the marbled stairs into a corridor from which four large rooms extend. Bill Smith runs the carpenter shop, the first room behind another, presently locked grille. This room is alive with the buzzing and whirling of saws, the banging of hammers and the scraping of sandpaper. Wood scraps and sawdust cover everything, clouding the visors the boys use to protect their eyes, getting into their noses and mouths. Beyond this room, the sheet-metal shop that Jack Hill supervises is crowded with awkward sheets of metal, blowtorches, welding flamethrowers, cutting machines, pieces of metal piping of various sizes. Jim McKinnon's territory is on the south side of the corridor, a machine shop crammed with a dozen large mounted machines that screech, whine and shriek. The room smells like oil and dirty rags. These men are dressed in casual work clothes more appropriate for the tasks they perform.

Adjacent to Jim's shop, on this side of the grille, is a big office containing two smaller interview offices, each with wooden desks, bookshelves and several wooden chairs—I assume all constructed at some time or another in that woodworking shop. The outer area contains storage closets, a bathroom and a phone mounted on a permanent wooden fixture.

It's Bill, the carpentry shop instructor, who first introduces me to the boys in his class. He whistles a shrill sound, loud enough to stop the buzz and whirl of electric saws and the banging of hammers, and in a voice loud enough, but not commanding or aggressive, instructs the boys to "Stop everything. This is Miss Perrin. She's a social worker and will be working with us over in the small office."

It's then that I notice *him*. Oh God, no. Not *him*. I know immediately that I'm in for trouble. Wayne is that teenage boy from the Cobourg Training School who last summer stood at the administrative office and undressed me with his eyes after that incident with Geoff. My guess is that rumours will begin to fly, and I haven't even completed a day's work yet.

I establish a routine for myself within the first few weeks, interviewing boys who have been referred by Don, the superintendent. In this setting and in my current position, I'm able to read the files that document the reasons for incarceration. Usually court transcripts, social histories and other relevant information are included. Occasionally Tom Loker, the placement officer, has completed a home interview and has outlined possible discharge plans. Less frequently, an assessment by our visiting psychiatrist is included. As much as I can determine, the psychiatrist's role is to place the boys into one of two diagnostic categories: sociopathic or adolescent behaviour disorder. I'm not sure what the significance of this is, but hey, I'm the new kid on the block. And from what I am experiencing thus far, the *only* kid on the block and accountable to no one in this setting. Since Don is not a trained clinical person, technically he is not my "boss." I guess my boss would be Frank Potts, in Toronto. Mr. Potts is responsible for the clinical programs in all Ontario correctional settings.

First thing in the morning I read the daily logbooks, the journals written by the supervisors on shift in the four different sections, and it's here that I become aware of what's transpired during the evening shift. I expect to see recorded in section B's logbook the issue of fistfighting, which has been occurring almost nightly since the first day of my arrival, and ongoing battles, both verbal and physical, between Wayne and Ron. Nothing appears. I know all about these battles, because I've been seeing Ron, one of Don's referrals, on a weekly basis and he has alluded to the problem with Wayne. I'm left wondering why nothing is being recorded: are the supervisors not asking the boys what they're fighting about or are they afraid to share the content of the rumours that are being spread? Perhaps they are protecting me?

After a month of ongoing altercations between these seventeen-year-olds, finally the issue is recorded in the logbook, though nothing is said regarding the reason for them, if indeed the supervisors ever bother to find out. Now that the matter is up front, I can confront Ron with the supervisor's information.

"Ron, you are getting into a mess of trouble fighting every night. What's the problem?"

"I can't talk about it, Miss," he says, averting his eyes.

"Let's have it, Ron. Unless you get this thing resolved, you will continue to get blue slips and may end up losing all your privileges and be restricted to your room."

"Well, Miss, it's not my fault. Wayne's an asshole and he's got a big mouth."

"You have a choice whether or not you're going to fight. Even if you don't like Wayne or what he's saying, you're not solving anything by fighting."

"Yeah, well, Miss, he's saying some stuff about you and it's a lotta bull."

"Do you want to tell me what he's saying?"

"No, Miss, I can't. It's about things you did in Cobourg."

"Do you believe what you're hearing?"

"No, Miss. It's a lotta shit."

"Are you concerned about what you're hearing? Is there anything that is getting in the way of your coming here and dealing with your own problems?"

"No, Miss. It's just that I'm gonna smash him in the mouth if he says anymore."

"Let it go, Ron. Trust your own experience. Let Wayne blow off steam."

A lot of good that did! Words don't have much impact with boys of below-borderline intelligence and limited capability for insight. I'm concerned about Ron and how Wayne's titillating stories might be impacting him. Ron was sexually abused by his mother, who reportedly still bathed him right up until the time he was incarcerated. In turn, Ron sexually abused his sister. He has a solid body structure and well-developed muscles from his work on the farm. And he has the impulse control of a heavy-duty eight-wheeler barreling downhill without brakes, every thought getting translated into physical behaviour. Scary!

Dennis is the first boy to articulate the rumours. Dennis, seventeen, is soon to be discharged from the school and will be placed with a family in a small northern Ontario town, quite distant from his hometown. I don't think he would be welcomed back to the old stomping grounds, not after shooting up the main street like a bad guy in an old John Wayne western. And he definitely needs to develop a few new strategies for getting his emotional needs met. He's a sweet, blue-eyed kid, with curly hair and an appealing "innocence." He's learned to manipulate his way into the beds of older women. This might still work for him, but there are only so many times you can stage an heroic rescue of a drowning buddy, one of this young lad's favourite attention-getting tricks.

"Hey, Miss. Do you know that Wayne is saying stuff about you?"

"Yeah, Dennis, is that a problem for you?"

"No, shit. He's telling everybody that you did it with the guys you saw in the office back in Cobourg. Says you were spotted lots of times coming out of the cottage windows late at night—like, you know, you were doin' it with the staff too."

"And do you believe this?"

"No, shit! Don't think anybody believes him really."

"Well, Dennis, you know what happens in this office. Just trust your own experience."

God, when is this going to end and how? I'm noticing that some of the younger guys look scared half to death when they're ushered into the office. No wonder. Poor Marti, a thirteen-year-old, beautiful, big, brown-eyed kid from Malta, locked up here because he persisted in running away from an open institution, keeps his eye on the closed door and sits on the edge of the chair, practically holding his breath while responding to my questions with very brief comments.

Even though the shop instructors, Cec, the principal, and I are now holding weekly meetings to plan specific interventions with the boys, I don't share with them the escalating drama that is taking place in the sections. I need to wait until they have enough experience with me to trust my version of truth. The supervisory staff and the shop instructors show little interest in developing ongoing meetings with me, Norm informs me. "They don't trust you, Dale. They think you're a soft touch and haven't a clue about these guys."

I soon learn that if I'm going to get any cooperation from the supervisors, I have to use some manipulative strategies myself.

"Hey, John, can I talk to you for a minute?" I say to the supervisor in A section who is giving Brian a rough time.

"Sure, what can I do for you?" he says, continuing to make notes in the logbook. He doesn't even look surprised that I have entered the section, a very rare experience for me.

"It's about Brian. I don't want the other staff to know this so please keep this between you and me." Well, that gets his attention. He puts down the pen and invites me to sit across from him at the boys' lunch table.

"Brian really looks up to you, John. He tells me that you're the best supervisor here, that you understand things better than anyone. He thinks you're really smart and that no one can fool you. Actually, John, the way he talks about you, you'd think you walk on water."

"Oh, I didn't know that. He does, eh?"

"Yeah, and that's why I think you're the guy to help him."

"Well, what can I do?"

"Any compliment coming from you will be a big thing for Brian. You know he suffers from such low self-esteem, has this idea that he can't do anything right, that he's just a dumb jerk. If you could spend a bit of time with him, tell him he looks great or that he's doing a good job or that something he just said was real smart, boy, it would make all the difference in the world."

God forgive me for slightly adapting the truth, but it works. I notice in the logbooks that John is now spending time with Brian and that the relationship between the two is much improved. Brian no longer talks about how he hates John, and he does appear to have a slightly improved self-image.

And still none of the staff have come forward to share with me their concerns about the rampant rumours flying between the guys. I'm sure they must know by now. What is it with these men anyway?

Ron, the defender of my virtue, requests a special session with me.

"Miss, I gotta tell yuh. Wayne says you *do it* with the guys," he says, spitting it out like foul-tasting mouthwash, looking down at his favourite spot on the floor. "And that's not all. The guys are calling him a liar now and Wayne says he's gonna prove it."

"Ron, you know what you've experienced in this office. You gotta trust your own experience." I must admit I don't like what's happening. I don't feel at all safe with Wayne, even with all the staff around. He's a sneaky son of a bitch. I know there is nothing Wayne can do, but ...

Ron, blushing and perspiring, places his hands on the desk in a manner suggesting his intent to leap across the desk and have a go at me. Too late I realize that Ron, like all the boys who come in here, sits between me and the door, and, my God, the telephone is in the outer office. Slowly rising from his chair, Ron chokes, "What are yuh gonna do if someone tries it?"

"Sit down! Such behaviour will not be tolerated! I will report any such nonsense to the superintendent immediately!" I can't believe I've just made such an inane statement. My thumping heart must've bopped my brain.

He obeys! And I terminate the session promptly, with some directive to Ron to "Get on with it." Unfortunately, Ron's sexual excitement is obvious and will cause him some embarrassment when he gets back to the carpentry shop just a few steps across the hall. At this moment, I must admit, I don't care. I'm shaken. I've got to rearrange this office. I can't let myself get cornered like this. Damn, what would I do if ...?

The next day I get a request from Wayne for a counselling session. This is it, I know. Wayne is in a put-up-or-shut-up situation. And me? I know I've got to talk to Don about this. I thought I could handle it alone, but I don't want to take chances. I need to build in some safeguards for this confrontation.

I explain to Don what happened in Cobourg and what has been transpiring here between Wayne and Ron.

"I don't want this to be a big thing and I don't want the supervisory staff to think I'm frightened or unable to handle the situation. I know they're speculating about the rumours and wondering. They can't help but know what's going on. I think this is a make-or-break situation for me in terms of credibility. If I blow this, they'll never trust me."

"Yeah, I think you're right," Don says. "How do you want to handle it?"

"Would it be possible to arrange for Tom to be in the outer office, talking on the phone in his booming voice, during the time Wayne is in my office?" Tom is a big man, six feet five inches tall, with a tough demeanor and a voice that projects like a foghorn. The kids don't mess with him.

I hear Tom's voice outside my office. I'm waiting now for the supervisor to bring Wayne into the office. I hate it when I get scared like this. My stomach is queasy. My heart's beating out a jungle rhythm in my chest. My hands are sweaty and shaking. That's the worst. I can't bluff, can't hide my nervousness with my hands imitating vibrating violin strings. I feel very vulnerable. I've got to hide my hands. I've got to look cool, calm, indifferent. They're coming now.

"Have a seat Wayne. You've asked to see me. What is it you want?" See? I'm cool, real cool.

"I'm having trouble in school, Miss," he says, voice stammering, eyes down, staring at a hangnail that he begins to pick at, an ever-so-slight smirk on his partially hidden face. God, he really is a sleazy guy. I know I shouldn't feel this way but he does give me the creeps. I'm willing to bet he turns out to be a serial rapist.

"That's a matter for you and the teacher to be discussing, Wayne. Is that all you wanted?"

"Well, uh, Miss, uh. Didn't I know you at Cobourg?"

"I don't know, Wayne. I didn't know you. Is that a problem?"

"Uh no, I just thought I knew you."

"Okay, Wayne. Obviously you have no issue to discuss with me. I'll call a supervisor to escort you back to your shop." The session lasts less than five minutes.

I move to the outer office as Wayne and the supervisor move out. Tom is no longer present. I hear laughter coming from the carpentry shop. Bill yells out, "Settle down." Quiet. I listen to the quiet for a few moments. My heart has stopped thumping. My hands are perfectly steady. Wow, I did it. It's over!

The boys seem much more comfortable now when they come into my office. I'm starting to have fun and enjoy the challenge. A few of the boys are very bright and capable of amazing thoughts and awarenesses. I start a conversation group with eight young fellows, who determine the content of the discussion. Sixteen-year-old Shane, serving time for murder, wants to discuss how you know an object exists if you aren't looking at it. Fourteen-year-old Leslie, a boy who loves to play with matches and watch buildings burn, wants to discuss trust, how you know when someone's a liar. Jim, a fifteen-year-old with a real attitude, in for assault and breaking and entering, wants to discuss what to do when you hate somebody.

Eddy sees me on a weekly basis. His mother is coming to visit and he really doesn't want to see her. However, since she's coming from out west, he feels he has to. We spend several sessions uncovering the issues he has with her.

In one session, he asks if he can bring his best buddy, Fred, with him. He's concerned about what will happen when his buddy gets released and tells me Fred has the same problems with his mom. Fred and Eddy come together. Fred remains very quiet, acknowledges that he hates his mom and doesn't want to go back home when he's discharged. He's unable or unwilling to tell me more, even in the two individual sessions we have following the joint one. I pass along this information to Tom Loker, the placement officer. Tom tells me that the arrangements are in place, that Fred is going home to his mother. Three weeks after Fred's discharge, Eddy asks for a special session. They all heard on the news that Fred was arrested for murdering his mother, slitting her throat and stabbing her seventeen times. They're not aware that semen was present all over the corpse. Dear God! Could I have been more forceful in convincing Tom not to place Fred back with his mom? Should I have been? "Could haves," "should haves" haunt me, interrupting hours of sleep.

Work is now going well but my social life is not. I don't have a car, have not developed any friendships with people at work. All the men are married. Jane Walker, the secretary, is a wealthy widowed woman in her mid- to late-fifties. She's invited me to her golf club for the occasional dinner and drinks, but we have little in common. Puzzling, though: the male staff, especially Don, react negatively towards Jane. I don't quite understand why. Jane, always very well dressed and perfectly made up—every bleached-blond hair in place—has a peculiar speech pattern, and occasionally the staff make fun of her. I suspect this has to do with reverse snobbery, but I'm not sure. I know my regard for Don is diminishing. Something very unhealthy is going on. He fires her.

I feel very lonely, isolated. Mom and Dad come and take me out for dinner and coffee and let me borrow the car to go into Kitchener to play badminton at the Granite Club once a week during the winter, but still I feel alone. Shelley's in Toronto. My old friends in the Kitchener area are married. And here I am, still alone and virginal. What's wrong with me?

And wouldn't you know it—Barry Sheppard comes to the rescue.

"Dale," he belts out on the telephone. "Your year at the training school will soon be up. Are you by any chance interested in changing jobs?" Barry left the department over a year ago and is in Winnipeg, Manitoba, the executive director of a group treatment home for disturbed teenage boys.

"Hey, yeah, what's up?"

"Well, I don't have a position here but I was talking with Jack Hawthorne, the administrator at the Knowles School for Boys, and he's looking for an experienced social worker. I told him about you and he said if you were interested he'd pay all your costs for the move. He's offering a good salary. Interested?"

"You bet. Ask him to contact me, Barry, and thanks a lot." Wow, Winnipeg! That'd be like moving to the end of the earth.

He did, and I accepted a position for mid-September 1964.

"Mom, guess what—good news," I say, excitement sparkling along the telephone wire like blips of bubbly Morse code.

"You're getting married," Mom says.

Damn! She sure knows how to rip off the prize from a box of Cracker Jacks.

"No, Mom," I say, deflated and wishing I hadn't bothered to call. "I've accepted a job in Winnipeg. I need to be out there by mid-September, so Dad's going to have to help me buy a car. I want to drive out."

"Well, here's Dad. You can give him the news yourself."

I do, but I'm now flatter than roadkill. No matter what I do, I can't seem to please Mom. Dad does his best to be supportive and excited for me.

"I'll take you out to Al's. We'll pick out a nice Rambler for you, Dale. That's great."

As the end of my employment draws near, something strange is happening to me. Out of nowhere I have these attacks of panic in my gut. My hands shake. My pulse escalates until I'm convinced I'm going to have a heart attack. I start to sweat. I feel absolutely, completely and miserably terrified. I don't know why. Great Caesar's ghost, what's happening to me? I go to the dentist's office, and in the middle of being drilled I have one of these strange attacks. I want to run. The dentist asks me if I'm all right. I can't even answer him.

These attacks increase in frequency, and I gradually become afraid of just experiencing an attack. I'm afraid to reach out to pick up a glass—my hand will shake and surely I'll spill it. Am I cracking up? Why now? I can't tell anyone. Don't want to worry Mom and Dad, and I have no one else to tell.

Mid-August, just two weeks before "the end," I go to Toronto, to Francia's apartment, for a weekend with Francia and Jackie. We haven't seen each other for almost a year now, not since the Cobourg days, and we're meeting to celebrate the acceptance of Jackie's doctoral thesis and my new job. I maintain my cool and say nothing until Francia goes to bed, and then without warning I get another panic attack. Jackie witnesses this, has a concerned, almost alarmed, expression on her face and asks me, "What's happening, Dale?"

"I don't know, Jackie. I think I'm cracking up," I say between gulps of air. "Am I crazy? Am I cracking up?"

"Tell me what's been going on over the past several months—anything different?"

"No—well, I'm feeling a little uncomfortable about the friendship I've been developing with one of the men I work with. Could that be it?"

"What about the 'friendship'? Tell me more. Are you having an affair?"

"No, not really; I've just invited him in for coffee a few times but I certainly am feeling sexual."

"That's all?"

"Well, maybe just a bit of fooling around. Nothing serious," I say defensively, still panicky and sweating.

"And?"

"Well, I'm going to Winnipeg, miles away from my parents and family."

"Is that a scary idea?"

"No, not really, I've been quite independent since the age of fifteen. I don't think that's it." As I respond I feel my heart beat even faster. Oh my God. That must be it. But I don't think I'm afraid to leave my parents. Actually, it will be terrific to be far away, free just to be myself.

"Oh Jackie," I say, tears streaming down my face. "I am nuts, aren't I?"

"Actually, there is a name for what's happening to you. Would you like me to tell you?"

"Oh, please."

"It's called 'separation anxiety' and I think your move away from your parents is triggering these attacks."

In spite of my acute anxiety I have a sudden awareness. Guilt, that's what I'm experiencing—abandonment. I'm abandoning Mom and Dad. I'm leaving Mom alone to manage her own relationship with Dad. She relies heavily on me to support them both when Dad's feeling down. She often asks if they can drop over, "because Dad's depressed and he always feels so much better after he talks to you." She'll ask me to talk to Dad about working too hard or about the need for a holiday, all issues where she feels I can influence Dad to do what she really wants.

"Is this weird or what?" I say, hoping Jackie will tell me that this can't be the reason. Even without a definitive response from Jackie, I begin to calm down. My body relaxes. It's over for now. Thank God. Maybe I'll never have another attack.

In the last week at the training school, still badly shaken inside and still experiencing anxiety attacks, I have to make two decisions. Will I submit the report I've written identifying problem areas in the school, with recommendations for change, to Don, or will I chicken out and just mail it to the Minister of Reform Institutions, with copies to Frank Potts and Don? I know Don isn't going to like it. And do I have the courage to go to the farewell party the administrative staff and shop instructors have planned for me and risk getting all shaky?

The first decision is easy. I don't have the courage to face Don, especially in my present emotional state. So I'm a coward. I'll mail in my report on my last day of work.

The party is great fun. Just a drink or two and I'm relaxed and feeling the excitement of bringing this experience to a close. I have such warm feelings towards these men—the shop men and Cec, the teacher, who have supported me through this introduction into the real world. I'm still glad though to be leaving this field. Enough of severely damaged personalities—the boys, that is—well, I also have some doubts about some of the supervisory personnel—and on to new adventures. Especially after Bill tells me, "Did you know, Dale? You won the lottery."

"What're you talking about? What lottery?"

"Well, the guys all had bets riding on when you were going to get raped. There wasn't a doubt in any of their minds that it was only a matter of time. Guess they owe you the jackpot."

I guess they do!

THE LOTTERY

How did you feel when you started your first job? Did you feel ready to deal with the world as an adult?

If so, what messages were you given that helped to prepare or reassure you that were ready? If not, what messages were you given that undermined your confidence?

After six to twelve months at the job, did you get the support and direction that you needed?

If so, how did these supports reinforce your perceptions of self, others and the world? If not, how did the lack of such support impact your sense of self, others and the world?

Is there a relationship between how you relate to authority figures in the work world and how you related to the authority of one or both parents or parent substitutes as a child?

How did you deal with success on the job? With failure or disappointment? Is this pattern of coping "familiar"?

WHEN ALL ELSE FAILS, FLEE

The trip through northern Ontario in my new green Rambler, purchased through Dad's skillful negotiation—never mind that I don't like green—with Libby Edmison, a social worker who graduated a year before me, is a healing experience. The tranquillizers, baring my soul to Libby, lustily singing Peter, Paul and Mary's hit song "Five Hundred Miles," all help control the anxiety attacks, and with each mile I experience a new sense of freedom. I have a hunch that it's only a matter of time and I'll be *me* again, minus the attacks, though not without the ever-present "Oh God, what's going to happen now" tightness I experience in my gut as I approach new situations. I arrive at the Sheppard residence, 554 Queenston Street, the River Heights section of Winnipeg, September 18, 1964—to begin what? A leap into professional maturity? An exciting romance? Maybe (please, dear God, make it so) I'll lose my virginity?

"They're really waiting for you at Knowles School," Barry says. "And boy, do they need you."

"What's happening? What've I got myself into?"

"The whole place is screwed up. Jack Hawthorne, the administrator, hasn't a clue what he's doing. His background is business. The previous director left under a cloud of smoke and the board asked Jack to take over. And Jim Jones, the second-in-command, he doesn't know which end is up either. He has a group work background but I tell you, Dale, he's not much of a social worker."

"What about the clinical staff?"

"What clinical staff? Stewart Boyce is the only one there, and he's repeating his field placement at Knowles. And besides, he's under the thumb of Bob van der Krabben, his field instructor with the School of Social Work, who is, theoretically, the director of social work. Bob's only there on a part-time basis, and he doesn't know his ass from his elbow. I think they have a consultant psychiatrist but I don't think he's involved in any significant way. I tell you, Dale, you'll be running the place by Christmas."

"Oh my God, it sounds like I've gone from the frying pan into the fire. It can't be that bad, Barry."

I put Barry's doom-and-gloom opinions out of my mind while I apartment hunt with Lorraine. I also take time for fun: dinner and a guided tour with Libby's friends, Ed and Isobel Sokel; ballet and a foreign film with Lorraine; a visit to a nearby badminton club; an evening with Rosemary Bish, her husband and children—Rosemary, a childhood playmate, lives here.

I discover that the Hudson's Bay Company is not a trading post as I had visualized it. Honest to goodness, where do these preconceived notions come from? I stand on the world-famous corner of Broadway and Main and take time to make faces at the monkeys in the zoo. I even manage to sign up for an evening course in music appreciation, a continuing education program at the University of Winnipeg.

Winnipeg is pretty, well-manicured, with white stucco houses and back lanes for hiding garages and garbage. I love it. Lots to do—I'm going to have fun, I just know it.

October 1, a Saturday, is officially the day my employment begins. It's also the day I move into my apartment at 26 Roslyn Road, Suite 17, just a little rectangular box, but my very own sanctuary. I'm fond of Barry's kids, but adjusting to living with a family with two young children—well, I'm glad to be on my own again. I feel very much like Mom. Home is a sacred space; a sanctuary.

October 1 is special for yet another reason: I'm an auntie again. Another nephew, Donald Bayne Stewart Perrin, is born in Germany, Bayne's current posting. Bayne now refers to himself as "Bayne Perrin, the Intermediate," since Dad, Bayne and little Donald all share the same name.

And amazingly enough, judging by the letters from home—and it's a cardinal sin not to write and receive letters once a week— Mom and Dad are surviving nicely without me. Mary Kay Lane is now living with them. "Deaconess" Shelley is in Toronto, working for an "Outreach for Youth" program and manages the occasional weekend with the parents. Dad's now district secretary-treasurer for the Ontario Lawn Bowling Association and he and Mom are enjoying their involvement at the local club. I guess it's okay for me to get on with life.

I journey out Henderson Highway, into North Kildonan and beyond. Surely I've gone too far. I can see an oil refinery off in the distance. Then I see the sign and turn right, into a paved drive. I pass a duplex and round a slight curve into a parking lot. Cement sidewalks lead to a white stucco building on the left and an expanse of joined, townhouse-looking buildings on the far right. A young man directs me to the white building. Here goes. *God, I hope Barry hasn't made me out to be the "second coming." What are they expecting of me? Am I going to measure up? Be still, oh pounding heart.*

As I approach, a short, slender gentleman wearing brown slacks and a simple white shirt open at the neck exits the building.

"Pardon me. Can you direct me to Jack Hawthorne's office, please?"

"I'm Jack Hawthorne and you must be Dale Perrin," he says, smiling warmly, extending his hand. "Come with me and I'll introduce you to the women in the office and we can chat a bit before calling Stewart Boyce."

I detect a slight English accent and a quiet shyness or self-consciousness. He turns immediately and retreats along the sidewalk with me in tow. I'm surprised. It's not that his welcome isn't enthusiastic; it's just that he impresses me as, well, wishy-washy.

We enter the building through two big brown doors leading us into a large foyer. To the right, Jack points out, is a recreation area, housing a pool table, a ping-pong table and other small-group-activity games. To the left, this stucco building houses the administration office, clinical offices and classroom. The basement, I'm told, houses a utility room and a gym. Jack introduces me to the two women in the office.

After a brief welcome, Jack calls Stewart Boyce into the office. Stewart, who will be my colleague and clinical partner, is to do the tour and provide me with whatever I need to get myself ensconced and ready to roll as quickly as possible. I understand what Barry means; I do sense an urgency to have me operational.

"Where do you want to start?" Stewart says, once I have locked up my purse in the desk drawer—I'm told you never leave anything of value lying around.

"First tell me about the kids."

"Well, we have thirty-seven boys in residence and two more are coming in from Saskatchewan on Wednesday. They range in age from seven to fifteen and are placed in cottages according to age. The young kids, the seven- and eight-year-olds, live in cottage two with Mr. and Mrs. Bryant; the nine- to eleven-year-olds in cottage three with Ella Bryant's sister, Nora Robinson, and her husband Ernie. The twelve- and thirteen-year-olds live with the Youngs in cottage four; and the older kids, with Eileen Hunt and her husband Bob, in cottage one. We can house up to forty-eight boys, though I've never known us to be at full capacity."

"Have you determined how we're going to divide up the caseload?"

"Oh no, Bob van der Krabben, the supervisor, isn't in until Friday, so I suppose we should wait for him to make those decisions."

"Why? Can't we determine that ourselves?"

"Well, I guess, but ..." he blushes a noticeable shade of fuchsia.

"Then let's do it right now."

Oh boy. I can see what Barry means. Stewart's a short, stocky fellow, stocky soft, not stocky as in "linebacker for the Winnipeg Blue Bombers football team." His dark-framed glasses magnify clear blue eyes. He's cleanly shaven, freckled, has a pinkish, oval-shaped face and neatly combed dark-blond hair. Neat and tidy—that's Stewart. It doesn't take long for me to recognize that Stewart is soft on kids, too—a gentle care-bear guy.

We have the entire caseload determined before lunch: many of the older boys for me, most of the youngest kids for Stewart; little kids scare me half to death with their dependency and neediness. I'll take the rough-and-tumble teens and preteens. Bob's working with three of the boys, and Claude Dumaine, the part-time caseworker, has two. That's it. And Stewart and I will each take one of the new little fellows coming in on Wednesday. Done!

The dining room/kitchen is housed in an area behind and attached to the four cottages, with windows looking out on a half-acre of beautiful, uncultivated bush separating us from our nearest neighbour. The in-house schoolteachers, house and program staff, as well as the clinical staff, have meals served here. The boys eat in the cottages. As we approach the dining area, Stewart points out that the duplex I passed on the way in houses the Hawthorne and Jones families. We join the staff seated at the tables.

"I'm working with the kids in grades seven and eight, right across the hall from you, Dale. Once you've settled in, perhaps we could talk about the boys we're working with. It's been awhile since we've had any contact with caseworkers," Wilma Essex, the senior teacher, says.

"Great, Wilma. I'd like that."

"And if you need anything, just ask me," says Maurice Quesnel, the school principal, with a smile and a wink. I'm not sure what it is, but something about Maurice sets my teeth on edge.

By the time I meet Bob van der Krabben, I'm oriented to the daily routines and have established a schedule for connecting with *my kids*. I've met many of the house staff, though I have yet to see Jim Jones, the second-in-command. I've become aware that there is no systematic treatment philosophy or program in place, little if any communication between clinical and other staff, no coordinated effort and only limited linkage with the outside agency personnel who place the children here. Each category of staff seems to be operating in isolation. If any of the kids improve emotionally, it isn't the result of a healthy treatment environment. *Ye gods! This is indeed going to be a challenge.*

Stewart and I meet the social workers and the two young boys from Saskatchewan as scheduled. I know immediately that Dennis will be my kid. He looks harmless enough: a physically underdeveloped seven-year-old, a homely little guy with a round face, big brown eyes peering out from behind huge, round glasses. He crawls up onto my desk, sits yoga fashion, looks down at me and explains that he won't be here long. I wonder what that means. The social worker who accompanied him to the treatment centre wishes me good luck and seems very relieved to be discharged of her escort responsibilities.

Bob van der Krabben arrives later that day, after the new little guys are settled in their cottages. I wish I could say that I'm as attracted to him as I am to my new, owlish little charge but, alas, I'd be lying. Bob, a tall, slender fellow with a lovely Dutch accent, reddish complexion and dark, slightly greying, curly hair that sits atop his head like a child's toque, has an air of officiousness about him. He welcomes me and suggests that we, that includes Stewart, meet in his office after he has a brief word with Jack.

"Well, I guess we'd better determine the caseloads," he says.

"Done," I say. "Stewart and I made those determinations immediately so that we could both get sessions underway." I look at Stewart. He's blushing, eyes averted, picking at some imaginary stray hair or dust particle on his yellow cardigan. Damn, he looks positively frightened. *Easy, Dale, don't be so judgmental,* that inner voice tells me. Was I that intimidated by my field instructor? I flash back to the face of Mrs. Bennett frowning and hear her tell me I'd better improve significantly in three weeks or I'll fail. Okay, so I was.

"Oh, well, I guess we'd better decide on supervision then."

"Okay, what do you have in mind, Bob?"

"Well, I can only get in about every two weeks with my schedule at the university and I have to spend some time with the three boys I'm seeing. And Stewart and I need to continue with supervisory sessions to accommodate the requirements of his field placement. I don't know what time I'll have available for you, Dale."

"Why don't we leave it on a 'need-to-consult' basis?" I say, perhaps with more enthusiasm than I ought to be showing. Something about him, I'm not sure what, is really putting my back up; hope it isn't as obvious to him. "Do you have a specialty in working with kids, Bob?"

"Well, no. Most of my work has been with couples and families, not specifically kids. I've just been working with these boys since Stewart was placed here for the MSW field experience."

That's it. Somehow, Bob, I don't think you have much to offer me. For sure you're no Barry Sheppard. I know that's an unfair comparison, but damn!

"Stewart and I have worked out a schedule and a procedure for biweekly treatment planning conferences with Jack, Jim Jones and the teacher who works with the kid being conferenced. We're going to suggest that we link with the cottage personnel and that Jim link with the program staff. Here's an outline of our proposal. I thought you might like to see it before we meet with Jack early next week."

"Thanks, yeah, I'll look through it and get back to you," Bob says, tucking it into his already overloaded briefcase. I look at Stewart, who ventures a quick glance my way.

"And we're working out some procedures and expectations for ongoing contact with outside placement agencies and workers. Perhaps when we're finished you might want to look that over too," Stewart says.

Ah, thank goodness, Stewart's getting into it now. Good to know what side of the struggle he's going to be on. And yes, I've figured out that maybe, just maybe, this issue is mine. I want to win this power struggle. I don't want to be told what to do by some idiot who pops around when he has a moment on his busy schedule. I'll bet we don't hear a word from Bob before our meeting with Jack.

Stewart and I stop off at the Curtis Hotel, just south of Knowles, on Henderson Highway, for a beer and victory party. We're both excited about setting boundaries with Bob.

"Geez, Dale, you really put Bob in his place. I thought he was going to run out of the office," Stewart says, laughing and talking decibels higher than he did in the office. "I'm going to call Carole and get her to come and join us. Let's party!"

"Was I that bad? Do you think he picked up that I'm not too impressed with him?" I say, a little squeamish now that I might have created a problem rather than resolved one.

"*Hardly,*" Stewart laughs, beet-red with excitement, as giggly as any kid who watches the teacher get reamed out by the principal. "It was *hardly* noticeable."

A couple of beers, loads of laughs and Carole, Stewart's wife, also a student in the graduate social work program at the university, drives us home. The tightness in my gut, the familiar anxiety that is threatening to punish me for such arrogance, is squelched. I discover that the Boyces live just down the back alley from me, in an apartment on River Avenue. I recognize that indeed Stewart and I are bonding and will be a team, with the support and encouragement of Carole. And friendships are beginning.

He's gone the next day—Dennis that is. Nora, his housemother, notifies me that Dennis didn't arrive in Wilma's classroom. Before I have the opportunity to report to the police, I get a call. The police have found one strange little kid hiding in the engine of a train, the old steam engine that stands in the CN grounds, a monument to yesterday. Once the police are persuaded that Dennis is not a thief and does not intend to steal the engine, back he comes—for how long, who knows? I think I know now what Dennis means by "not staying long."

The meeting with Jack goes very well. Indeed, I haven't seen or heard from Bob since our original meeting, but I do get to meet the elusive Jim Jones.

"It would be useful to have monthly activity reports submitted for each boy, Jim, just to keep us informed of behavioural changes, attitude improvement, social skills and general interactions. Do you think you can have such reports available for these treatment meetings, Jim?" I say.

"Uh, uh, I don't know," Jim answers. "Uh, you see, uh, uh, a lot of the program counsellors are part-time and some are volunteers, and uh, well, I don't know."

"You could get verbal summaries, Jim, and just make your own report for each kid, could you not?"

I don't understand what Jim Jones is all about. A beautiful, big, athletic-looking, black man, an American by birth, obviously fond of kids. I don't get what his hesitation is all about, nor the stuttering, stammering and inability to make eye contact. "Is he always like this?" I ask Stewart.

"Yeah, though I think he's worse around women."

"Wanna bet we don't see any program reports?"

"Not on your life. Jim is the biggest stumbling block in the whole system, as far as I can determine. You can't nail him down to anything."

My frustration with the system and the lack of any affirmative action regarding communication links and a coordinated effort regarding treatment interventions and behavioural reinforcements, is offset in a large part by the sheer delight I experience in working directly with the boys. They are challenging, sometimes downright frightening, but always lovable.

"Hey, Miss, why are we in this office today?" Johnny says. "How come we're not in your office?"

Johnny, a thirteen-year-old, redheaded, blue-eyed kid, the ideal Norman Rockwell type boy, is a handful to manage. In our previous sessions, he'd pumped his legs frantically when seated, jumped up, moved quickly around the office, playing first with a bunch of plastic soldiers, then moved mid-battle to the half-completed jigsaw puzzle that I had set out on the desk. His hyperactivity and inability to focus on any one object usually escalates after a weekend home visit with his mother and sister. He deeply distrusts women, whom he perceives as weak and rejecting, and engages in power manipulations in a desperate attempt to find some mother figure capable of providing him with firm limits and consistent affection. And frankly, I'm winging it with this kid. I wish I knew what I was doing and had someone to direct me in my work with Johnny, but no such luck.

"Because the last two times in my office, Johnny, you threatened to kill yourself by jumping out of the window and we ended up in a holding match. And I don't want to do that anymore. I like spending time with you and I do want to talk with you, Johnny, and you can help me with this puzzle if you want, but I don't want to do the 'threatening to jump' stuff. If you do that I will leave this office and you will be on your own."

As I speak I turn my attention to the puzzle on the desk. I have my back to Johnny. I hear a rustling of clothing, a zip—uh-oh, I'll bet that's the zipper of his pants being pulled down—an unusual silence.

"Hey Miss, look at me," Johnny demands.

"Nope, I won't. I'm working on the puzzle. If you like, you can help me," I say, hoping my nonchalant manner successfully disguises my escalating anxiety. *Shit, what do I do with this behaviour? Why don't they teach stuff like this in graduate school?*

"No, Miss, just look at me," Johnny insists, raising his voice, almost pleading.

"Nope, kid. I'm waiting for you to sit down here at the desk. No bullshit!"

I'm quite certain that Johnny has exposed himself—his ultimate weapon of power? I wonder where he learned this behaviour and if he's done this with his mom or sister.

I hear a zip—have I won this round?—and Johnny says, "Miss, I'm not staying. But it's okay to go back to your office next time."

"Okay, Johnny you got it," I say. And Johnny leaves the office, heading back to his classroom. Whew, I think we've broken through the impasse.

The weeks speed by faster than jets breaking the sound barrier. Stewart and I are intensely involved in the lives of the little guys, are relating well with the teachers—okay, so I'm having a bit of a problem with Maurice—but gradually we seem to be making inroads in connecting with the houseparents. Jim remains elusive.

Harold, one of my twelve-year-olds, tells me about his problem with Maurice.

"What happened, Harold?"

"Lenny grabbed my shirt and ripped it. I know I'm gonna get shit for it, so I pound him and the shithead screams as if I'm killing him. Mr. Quesnel broke us up and without even asking what happened, he just marches me up front and whacks me with the belt."

I talk to Harold about resolving problems by fighting but really I'm angry at Maurice, our dear principal. He and I have it out, unfortunately in the dining room with other teachers and some houseparents present.

"We've talked about corporal punishment before, about the negative impact this has. Most of these kids have lived with violence—that's what's messed them up in the first place—and you're still doing it. Harold told me you strapped him again, Maurice. What the hell are you doing?"

"The kid has to stop throwing his weight around. He almost beat Lenny to a pulp."

"And you think strapping him isn't the same? Aren't you throwing your weight around? For Christ's sake, Maurice, you're the principal of the school. Surely you have better ways of managing behaviour than to resort to violence," I say.

"Cool it, Dale," Stewart says.

"Well shit, how are we going to role-model loving and responsible behaviour with you whacking kids with a belt?" I say, still agitated. Maurice excuses himself from the table, and I settle down. *Damn, I've got to learn to manage my own feelings, never mind Maurice. I hate it when I lose it like this. Stewart's right. Duplicating the same dumb behaviour with words isn't going to help.*

Back in the office I receive a phone call from Jack. The Mounties have picked up a pint-sized, fast-talking whiz-kid at the airport. Sure enough, we're missing one Dennis the Menace. They report that Dennis was a stowaway. When confronted he said that he was looking for a job on an airplane heading west! God, this little guy is very creative.

Winter comes quickly in Winnipeg. It's November, very cold, and the houseparents have restricted Dennis to pajamas, hoping to keep him from his wild flights of fantasy. It doesn't work. Within days we get a call from an irate neighbour, a mink farmer who is now attempting to round up thousands of dollars worth of mink released from their cages by a pervert in pajamas. Jack has to do some fast talking in order to persuade the neighbour not to lay charges.

And November blows in a possible romance. "'Tis an ill wind that blows no good," and this "no good" is named Geoff Christopher.

Stewart and I stay late this evening to meet with the part-time social worker and the consulting psychologist who has come to test two of the boys, at the requests of Wilma and Maurice. After brief introductions, we proceed to the dining room for an evening meal, a rare occurrence since our workday is usually complete by five o'clock. A nippy evening, dark, cold, clouds blocking the ever-present stars and near-full moon. I'm not looking forward to the dry coldness and I distrust the constant white blanket of crisp snow covering the roads, which, Stewart informs me, will be with us now until late April. I'm convinced that the rutted, packed snow is conspiring with the universal force of extinction to test my winter driving skills, which, admittedly, are not well developed. I'm complaining to Stewart about this grand subterfuge when a tall, dark, handsome, red-nosed fellow, glasses fogged over, enters, shouts "hi" to Stewart and disappears, returning momentarily sans winter coat and boots, his glasses now clear.

"Damn it's cold out there," he says, sitting down next to Stewart, his plate loaded with extra helpings of the cook's evening offering.

Stewart introduces us and explains that Geoff is on the teaching staff. He has returned to university to finish his course work for a special ed certification and does remedial work with some of the boys in the evening in return for free room and board. I feel an immediate zing. Hmm, I haven't felt this for some time now. The hormones become suddenly alert and I'm conscious of flashing my warmest smile and making clear eye contact. He has liquid blue-grey eyes and a smile reminiscent of little Dennis when he talks about his fascination with trains, planes and other inanimate objects.

Geoff shovels in what he can without much awareness of the lushness of smooth, white, mashed potatoes, smothered in dark, thick gravy, the roast beef, rare, steaming with roast onions, decorated with green peas and cooked red cabbage and a dab of horseradish hot enough to clear the highways. He checks his watch every few minutes, explains that he has to see one of his kids. And he's gone.

"I guess Geoff wasn't all that hungry, or did you notice?" Stewart says, with a slight blush and that impish grin he reserves for affectionate teasing.

But I'm cool. Not about to disclose my vulnerability. *Who, me? Interested?*

"Oh sure, the man's on a mission," I say with a casualness I don't really feel. I determine that I'll find an excuse, or maybe two or three, for staying late before the week is out.

And I do, and Geoff joins us for pub time and giggles. The zing is definitely working both ways. Several such events and Geoff, on a chilly Friday evening in December, spontaneously invites me to drive with him to his cottage on Falcon Lake, near the Ontario border. It's already close to eleven at night and we've been drinking at our favourite watering hole near the school.

"But I don't have anything with me," I say.

"Doesn't matter," Geoff says. "I've got a sweatshirt you can wear for sleeping and extra toothbrushes. Come on, let's just go. I've got a six-pack in the car. Let's just do it. It's only a two-hour drive."

And off we go, out of the city, going who knows where. Maybe this is it. *The night.* The night for drinking and driving? Geoff asks me to open a beer for him. I'm very uncomfortable about this, but comply. We've been on the road only thirty minutes when Geoff asks for a second beer.

I can't handle this anymore.

"Geoff, I'm not comfortable with drinking and driving. If you want to drink, how about letting me drive?"

"No way; open a beer," he says, raising his voice just slightly.

"No, if you want to drink, let me drive. If you want to drive, don't drink. This frightens me." *Oh shit! What a way to begin what could be a momentous occasion in my life. Maybe I'm too straight. Perhaps I should lighten up a bit. I wait. What am I going to do if ...?*

"Have it your way," Geoff says after a prolonged silence. He presses down on the accelerator. This is going to be my punishment: a death-defying moonlight ride on a snow-packed highway, heading for a romantic interlude in a cold cottage somewhere next to nowhere in the world.

We arrive—alive—close to two in the morning. It's awesome, the stars like I've never been aware of them before, magnificent, spilled carelessly over a deep, black, India-ink sky. Geoff tackles me and we tumble into a snowbank, laughing and snuggling, the Big Dipper pouring magic to heat our chilled bodies.

Geoff starts a fire in the potbellied iron stove, the only warmth this cottage is prepared to yield. We drink more beer, snuggle on the chesterfield, kissing and touching, ever so tentatively, and then I've gotta go to the bathroom.

"What do you mean 'no indoor plumbing'? You mean I've got to plow my way through snowdrifts and plunk myself onto a block of ice and possibly remain part of the outhouse fixtures until spring thaw?" I say incredulously. How can anyone living in such frigid circumstances not have indoor plumbing?

Son of a bitch and damn! Damn! Damn! My butt's freezing! In total blackness I discover, through touch, that I have my period. Gushing blood—and me totally unprepared. You don't suppose Geoff has a stash of tampons in his kitchen cupboard, do you? No, but he is ever so understanding. We cuddle together, endure the not-so-romantic rest of the night and rise at the first indication of dawn, to return to civilization and drugstores. Crushed! But, God willing, there'll be another opportunity.

And that opportunity comes not long after my return from a Christmas vacation spent in Kitchener with Mom and Dad, Elthea, Shelley, Ken, Jan and little Drew. What fun it is to experience Christmas through the wide eyes of such a little boy. Ken and Jan have taken over Christmas breakfast and I'm impressed with the recycling of emotionally rich childhood traditions.

During the vacation I experience a new awareness, a milestone in my own growth. I meet with Francia and Jackie in Toronto and during our conversations I notice that both Jackie and I use the term "woman" as a self-reference; Francia uses the term "girl." Hey, I've grown up. I'm aware of a new sense of confidence, both professionally and personally. I'm a woman!

After my return, taking my courage in hand, I invite Lorraine, Barry and Geoff for dinner. No big deal for anyone who can cook, but this is the first time I've taken such a risk. I only know one menu— steak, baked potatoes and salad. It's an abysmal failure—burnt steaks that cause near asphyxiation and piercing complaints from a smoke detector; half-baked potatoes; and well, what can go wrong with salad? And here I am, Suzy Homemaker, apron and all, anticipating everyone's needs. "Can I get you a drink? Would you like some wine? Would you prefer Caesar salad dressing?"

"Thanks for the meal, Dale. I've never pictured you in this role before," Barry says, humour threatening to spill from his eyes in giant tears, struggling to refrain from chucking up a gut-rending hee-haw.

Lorraine, always the diplomat, spoke up. "Really, that was a lovely meal, Dale," and turning to Geoff, "I've enjoyed meeting you."

I ask Geoff to stay on, anticipating that this is *the night,* and drink that extra glass or two of wine. He agrees. We sit together on the orange vinyl chesterfield, chatting about the Sheppards, and begin kissing, gently sharing the taste of garlic from the steaks, tentatively exploring with tongues and touches. Geoff pulls me up into a standing embrace; body pressed to body, and urges me into the bedroom. I'm ready. God, am I ready! Does he undress me, passionately ripping away sweater, skirt, bra, panties? No! Does he utter erotic words, driving me to a frenzy of uninhibited abandonment? No. Does he bury his head in my belly, panting short, hot breaths, maneuvering wet tongue over my tingling skin and my already-wet sacred space? No, no, no! He nonchalantly takes off his clothes, expecting me to do the same, and gets into bed; like ho-hum, let's get this over with, no awareness of the crispness and the scent of fresh sheets, the Shalimar-dabbed pillowcases. No attempt to light the candles, the three white tapers on the bedside table.

Fortunately my own well-nurtured fantasies and suppressed desires do for me what Geoff either is incapable of or has no inclination to do.

And it's all over before it really has a chance to flourish—and I'm swinging on the edge of nowhere—no big bang, not even a little sparkling firecracker.

"I'm sorry, Dale. I'm afraid this time I'm the one who's bleeding," he whispers in my ear. I turn away from him, allowing him to spoon against my backside, and the tears come quietly, as silent as cotton snowflakes. Disappointment blankets my passion, covering my body like a frigid funeral shroud.

One more winter visit to the cottage with another couple and Wilma's son, with whom Geoff is very close, and the relationship dwindles to an end. Wilma's teasing is more than Geoff can manage.

"Dale," he announces on the phone, "I'm really sorry but I have to be honest with you. I don't want to get involved in another sexual relationship. That's not what I'm looking for. I've just come out of an intensely sexual affair and what I want now is to find a partner. I'm sorry but I'll not be seeing you anymore."

Jesus, Mary, Joseph! I've been giving off really bizarre messages—sex and no strings attached, because I sensed Geoff was frightened of commitment. What am I doing to myself—and others? Well, screw you, Mr. Geoff, if you can't see through my fear of vulnerability, who needs you? Not me. I don't need anybody!

Thank goodness the kids do. I get back to work and learn that the Mounties are en route from the Minneapolis Airport with little Dennis in tow. He disembarks from Air Canada flight 801 in the company of two nuns, who entertained him on his short flight, fed him and vouched for his good character. At least some things are predictable.

After considerable persuasion, Jack initiates a joint meeting with the entire house, counselling, program staff, Jim Jones and the teachers, and we assemble in the dining room to discuss issues of mutual concern. On this occasion the psychiatrist, Dr. Mick—no one can pronounce Mikelejewski—is facilitating the discussion. The evening is an immense frustration, with the various factions playing "Ain't It Awful," each blaming communication breakdown on one of the other factions. At the breakup of the meeting Dr. Mick takes me aside, our first and only opportunity for individual interaction.

"You know, Dale, you're absolutely right the way you perceive the reality of this community with its specific problems, but you aren't going to be heard."

"What do you mean? Why don't they listen? I just can't understand. The problems are so clear to me and the solutions would be so simple."

"If you want to know, I'll tell you. Do you really want to know?"

"Yes, yes please. Tell me," I say, a knot beginning to chew at my innards. *Oh boy, this is going to be something I don't want to hear.*

"They can't hear what you're saying because they're responding to the intensity of your emotions. Your emotions speak far more eloquently than your words. You are simply too intense. If you want to be heard, you'll have to learn to tone down your feelings."

Holy shit! I had no idea. I'll pay attention to this and see if I can disguise my intensity.

Andy, a native Canadian resident just turning sixteen, is an expert at manipulating through emotional intensity. He's the one boy on my caseload who causes me anxiety. I haven't been able to connect with him at any significant level, as far as I can assess or feel. We play pool in the recreation area and talk about whatever problems surface. But I detect an underlying hostility that I can't quite put my finger on. I just know intuitively that Andy is dangerous.

I respond to a very loud banging on my office door. Andy, now my height, though with a still underdeveloped body, glares at me, comes almost right into my face and says, "I'm not going swimming with the class." His message is clear, though the "you can't make me" is unspoken.

"Andy, you're going swimming with your class."

"No! I am not fucking-well going swimming," he says, moving closer into my personal space, now about six inches from my face, his large, deep, piercing brown eyes blazing with hatred, small beads of sweat on his forehead.

"You are going swimming," I respond quietly, with almost no affect.

"Can't you hear me, you fucking stupid woman? I'm not going swimming!" Andy is now two inches from my face, his fist raised.

"Just go swimming," I say and turn away from him, returning to my seat at the desk. He takes a step into my office, then turning, starts to laugh.

"I've got my bathing suit on already," he says and marches out laughing and hollering after one of his classmates. I'm left trembling, knees weak, my anger starting to break through—okay, so it's fear, not anger. I get up, slam my office door and just sit, sorting out my emotions, my behaviour, attempting to think how I could have handled this differently. Silently cursing the boy; cursing all the penis-people in the world, with their macho testosterone. I may have passed this test, but what about the next one? And where the hell is Bob, the supervisor, with his words of wisdom? Do I always have to figure things out on my own?

And there are some of those men in the outside world as well as in treatment institutions. Carole and Stewart introduce me to one.

"Hey Dale, a friend of Carole's is in town. We're going down to the Viscount to chug beer. Wanna come?" Stewart says.

"No thanks, Stewart, I'm just staying in tonight. I want to watch the football game."

"Come on, Dale. You can't sit around moping about Geoff. You gotta come out and have some fun."

"Buzz off, Stewart. The answer is no."

But he doesn't. Shortly after eleven in the evening, I can hear Carole and Stewart coming down the hall giggling and creating some kind of fuss. They knock at my door. I already know that they're drunk or at least merrily high and I can't help laughing in spite of myself.

"What do you want?" I ask, feigning annoyance but laughing as I see Carole holding a branch of a tree—poor tree, this is not just a little twig. And Stewart, hiding behind an Esso tiger that he's ripped off from some gas station. These silly buggers!

They barge into my apartment and introduce me to their buddy, Danny Jackson, a former classmate of Carole's from her undergraduate days. He's cute, I must admit. The three of them are still in casual working clothes. Me? I'm in my housecoat.

"Put on a dress and let's go out," Danny says.

"No way; I'll get into jeans and join you," I say. *What a strange request. Why would I put on a dress to join a bunch of drunks on some silly escapade?*

We decide to go off to the fountains on Osborne Street opposite the courthouse and listen to the folksingers who congregate there late in the evening and sing until the early hours of the morning. As we walk along, Danny walks beside me, places a firm hand on my backside. I remove it. He does it again. I remove it. Alcohol?

After singing, laughing and drinking coffee at a little coffee bar, we walk back to the apartment, sober and much quieter. Danny holds my hand and we talk. I like him.

"I've just come in from northern Ontario," he says. "I have an engineering contract with a mining company working the area. It's great to be back in Winnipeg. I feel as if I've hibernated all winter. And trading on the stock market's fun but it's not like going out with friends and doing things." I'm fascinated with his interest and activity in the financial world and want him to share more.

We arrive at my apartment building.

"Will you walk down the lane with me over to Carole's? My car's there and then I'll drive you back," Danny says.

"Sure thing," I say, anticipating that he's going to kiss me good night or ask me out. I'd like that.

Danny insists on parking the car and walks with me up the three flights of stairs to my apartment. The door is unlocked and the lights are still on. He walks right in ahead of me. Hmm, he must have been more alert than I thought. I follow him in. Before I can say anything he turns suddenly, grabs me and throws me across the living room. Stunned, I trip and fall onto the orange vinyl couch. At the same time, Danny switches out the light, follows me to the couch and pushes me down. With one hand he yanks the cord to the lamp that isn't connected to the front entrance switch and pins my arms under my body. I struggle but can't free myself. Judas Priest! He must have planned this. He's going to rape me. I'm too stunned to think clearly. I feel absolutely immobilized—and then feel nothing, absolute blanket numbness. He rips open my blouse, pulls at my bra and covers one exposed breast with his wet lips. I wiggle but am still unable to free myself. I say—nothing. Just as suddenly he stops and allows me to sit up and redress. *He's nuts—must be a schizo!* I'm feeling now—terror! *Gotta think; how do I get rid of him?* I remember what I've learned from Jackie about schizophrenic men—dangerous. Do not confront.

"Uh, would you like a coffee before you go?" I say.

"Yes, thank you. Can I help?"

He's nuts. He really is. Maybe he doesn't realize that he's just attacked me.

"It's very late, Danny. I think it's time for you to go."

"Yeah, you're right," he says, setting the mug down on the glass table, which amazingly enough, has survived the pushing and shoving without moving an inch. He gets up, heads for the front door. *Oh, dear God, thank you!*

We get to the front door, me right behind him, and whammo—the same routine. He turns, grabs and pushes me into the little hallway to the bedroom. This time I grab the door frame and resist. *Shit, this jerk is going to rape me.* He's a strong son of a bitch and my resistance is short-lived. I'm hurled onto the bed and he's on top of me just as quickly, ripping the blouse right off and pulling at the bra. *Do I scream? Do I attempt to run out? He'll kill me. He's nuts. "Passivity, that's your only recourse. Go limp,"* says a little voice within me. And I do. In an instant he has my clothes off, his clothes off, and is on the bed beside me, touching and stroking. *"Stay passive. Don't move."* He takes my hand and places it on his genitals. I stay limp—he stays limp. *Aha. He can't maintain an erection if I'm passive.* He has one hand free, free to touch and massage that part of me that ached for Geoff's touch. Minutes, more minutes, an hour? Absolute silence!

I can see myself lying on this bed. I'm dead. Who's going to believe that I didn't invite this? I'm well over twenty-one. They'll think I set this up. What am I resisting for? I'm not a virgin anymore. What difference does it make? Oh, oh; shit, I'm going to orgasm. He'll take this as permission to jump all over me.

"Do you have a condom?"

"Yes," he says and releases me from his grip to get up from the bed.

I start to move, to run. *I'll get out of here. Don't care if I'm naked.*

He grabs me and pushes me back onto the bed. He hurts me. His grip on my arm is painful. I'm sure he thinks I've tricked him. *God, if I could only get him to talk. Maybe if he talks he'll come around. He'll recognize what he's doing. Maybe he won't kill me.*

"You are such an attractive man, Danny; you have such a nice body. I'll bet you could have any woman you wanted," I say, in a deadly flat voice.

"Yes, I could."

Aha, I think I've got him. The arrogant son of a bitch; makes me want to gag!

"Then why are you forcing me?"

"I'm not forcing you."

"I think we could be great lovers, only just not tonight," I say. "I'm too tired to get into this at the moment. Let's wait till another night."

"Okay," he says. "Just let me stay here for another few minutes."

Oh God, he's going to leave. He isn't going to kill me. I just need to be passive; stay limp for another few minutes. The image of my dead body—gone; I'm beginning to feel hope.

Minutes, more minutes, forever minutes—and he moves. He gets up and begins dressing. He's actually going? He walks to the bedroom door. I get up quickly to see him get out—*get out—get out, you fucking bastard!* And he goes, without a word. I lock the door. My body begins to shake. I feel cold, very cold. I get under the bed sheets. I'm so very cold. My teeth chatter. I'm shaking. It's five in the morning. It's seven in the morning. I fall asleep—finally!

After several days I tell Stewart and Carole about Danny. I start to shake. They're shocked.

"But he was such a gentle, quiet guy in university," Carole says. "He was always very polite, kind of shy. I had no idea. I'm so sorry; God, how awful!"

I decide, too, that I don't feel safe living alone anymore. I put an ad in the paper to find a roommate. Patricia Hydak, a home economics professor from the university, responds and together we find a two-bedroom apartment on Stradbrook, quite close to the badminton club. And that's another unique experience. On the upside I gain a new friend, actually two since her boyfriend virtually lives with us, and wonderful, creative meals. On the downside: a boyfriend who virtually lives with us and clutter.

Late spring, and Dennis is picked up along Henderson Highway by a staff member who spots him trotting along with a suitcase; suitcase? Dennis decided to abscond with company this time—a little three-week-old St. Bernard puppy, one of the six that our resident St. Bernard birthed. Can't say I blame him. Little furry creatures love unconditionally.

Willie, one of Dennis's housemates, also has difficulties connecting with people. Stewart and I are walking over to the dining room. I see Willie take off, running frantically into the woods. I take off after him and reach him just after he collapses on the ground and curls up into a foetal position. *Oh God, what's happening to this poor little child?* I sit on the ground beside him, cuddle him into my arms, attempting to reassure him and free him from the demons he's struggling with.

"Willie, Willie, it's okay. You're safe. Willie, come on back. It's me. You're safe."

Willie's grasp on reality is very tenuous. Any conflict or confrontation sends him over the edge, and bringing him back is a sensitive process. Gradually he begins to whimper, and then the tears come. I continue to hold him and soothe with words of comfort. I have no idea what triggered this episode, but at the moment, that's not important. In time I'm able to persuade Willie to stand up. Slowly we make our way back to his house, Willie clinging desperately to me, arms around my waist, face buried in my dress, now smudged with the richness of black soil and green vegetation. Nora sees us coming, swooshes Willie up in enveloping arms and hugs him into the fullness of a very maternal bosom. Willie sobs. Nora carries this very underdeveloped boy up the stairs to the safety of his bedroom.

We approach the end of the school term. At least this term went well with the teaching staff, with Wilma now principal. Thank goodness Maurice decided to leave last June.

Bob van der Krabben, Claude Dubois, the other part-time clinical staff, Stewart and I have a meeting with Dr. Mick to discuss the urgent issues the boys are bringing to our attention. "We've got to take some action," I say. "Julian tells me that he's seen Mrs. Young come in drunk twice this past week. He asks me why he has to stay here when he could be at home with a drunken mom. Bradley tells me that Mrs. Bryant is seeing monsters in the mirror every time she goes up or down the stairs in his cottage. He claims she talks to the monsters and seems very frightened. Most of the boys hate Jim Jones and think he's also crazy. And Jack does nothing. We can't grab Jim long enough to confront him about what's going on with program people. God only knows what they're doing and what the plans are for summer camp. This place is so dysfunctional that the kids' emotional well-being is seriously threatened. We just can't sit here and do nothing."

The others agree. Dr. Mick identifies that the critical problem is at the top—Jack. He has to go.

"I suggest that we passively undermine Jack," he says. "Don't do anything overtly that causes a problem. Just don't cover for him when the community social workers begin asking questions."

"Yeah," Bob agrees. "Jack and Jim both have to go, but we can't be seen to be deliberately sabotaging the program."

That's no problem for Bob. He disappears for the entire summer. Dr. Mick takes off. We see nothing of Claude, Morris, or Jim or Jack. Camp has started and Jim decides to stay there for the duration of the summer, as various groups of boys have their turns at the camp experience. But where is Jack? Decisions have to be made and Jack is nowhere to be found—all summer!

"Stewart, this is intolerable. The kids are really being hurt here. Julian and Bradley are both threatening to run. The agency people are asking questions. Bob's nowhere. The rest of the kids are fighting, squabbling, running away and getting into trouble in the community. I think we should call the agency workers and recommend discharge for a number of the kids, especially the younger ones. What do you think?"

"If you do that, Knowles School will be in a financial crisis. What's that going to mean for all of us?

"Can't be helped; our responsibility is to the client first, then the profession and then the agency. I can't stand the vacuum, the total abdication of responsibility by Jack and Jim, not when I see what's happening to the kids. And where are Bob and Dr. Mick? Nowhere! I'm going to start calling agency workers. Are you with me?"

"Yes, I'll do the same. We'll just have to deal with the repercussions, when and if Jack and Jim ever show up again."

And we do. Together, by the end of August, we discharge twenty-two kids and admit no new residents. We've created a financial crisis of catastrophic proportions! I can definitely read the handwriting on the wall. I'm going to get fired in September: it doesn't take a Mensa genius to figure this out. I start job hunting. I apply for positions in Vancouver, Saginaw, Michigan and to the court system here in Winnipeg. I'm outta here. I have my notice ready.

The Labour Day holiday is finished. They have to come back. I go into the school, and before I can skulk down the corridor Jack appears out of the administrative office. "Dale, I would like to see you in my office at nine thirty."

"Shit, Stewart, this is it. I'm history. I'm about to get fired."

Stewart and I sit in his office with the door closed. I pick up pieces of puzzle on his desk and start fiddling with some child's unfinished play. Bob knocks and walks in.

"I've been talking to Jack," he says, looking flushed, small beads of perspiration on his forehead. "I've got to tell you, Dale, I don't approve of what you've done."

That's it. I snap. "You don't approve. *You* don't approve! Well, whoopee shit! Where have you been all summer? Where were you when difficult decisions had to be made? When kids were crying? Where have you ever been when Stewart and I have needed support? Nowhere, Bob, nowhere! So don't give me shit about approval. I don't approve of your moral cowardice, either! You have no guts. No integrity!" I choke out, so enraged I'm finding it hard to breathe. "I'm going to see Jack now and frankly, what you think is totally irrelevant."

Oh dear God, I must calm down. Why is it that whenever I'm vulnerable Bob jumps all over me?

"Dale," Jack says, "we've got very serious problems here at Knowles School. I need your help. I think you're the one to get us through this. I would like you to take over Bob van der Krabben's job and get us back on track. Will you help? I believe I can secure a significant raise for you."

What? I'm not getting fired? Is this for real? You gotta be kidding! My head's spinning.

"Oh, Jack. I'm so sorry. I've already made my decision. Here's my notice. I'll be gone in two weeks. It's too late for me. I can't take any more. I'm so sorry."

In my last week I provide orientation to Selwyn Watson, the social worker hired to replace me. Bob comes into the office to say good-bye.

"I owe you an apology, Dale. You're right. I am a coward. It's true. Whenever you were vulnerable, I did strike out at you. I've worked it out finally. The problem is that you remind me of my mother. I know it's too late, but I really am sorry for hurting you."

"Spare me, Bob."

Good-bye, Knowles School! Dear God, what's going to happen to the kids who are left? To Stewart? To Dennis? And me? What now? Can I make the transition to working with an adult client group?

The Winnipeg newspaper reports that "downtown Winnipeg shoppers were shocked to see a local bus driving down the street without a driver." You got it—little Dennis. Now if Jack and Jim had the perseverance and courage of one little owl-faced genius disguised as an innocent boy, things might have turned out differently.

That's two very stressful job situations. Must be I'm not cut out for coping with the pain of such damaged and hurting children—or perhaps, children in institutional systems. Things will be much better working with adults, no?

WHEN ALL ELSE FAILS

How did you respond to your first sexual experience? What did you feel? What were your expectations? Did this experience reinforce your "sexual OKness"? Or hurt your "sexual OKness"? If so, in what way?

Have you experienced sexual abuse? If so, how did this (does this) impact your life? What were/are your feelings, thoughts? Did you take action? If so, what did you do? Was this helpful or hurtful?

Have you encountered a work situation in which you were confronted with "ethical" issues? What action (or lack of action) did you take? Did this reinforce your sense of self, others and the world? Or challenge and/or change your sense of self, others and the world?

What messages did you get (and from whom) about what was "right and wrong" behaviour in the situation you identified? How did you deal (or not) with the repercussions of your decision?

WISDOM IN MOTION

What a relief to have a break. Before I start my new job in Winnipeg, I drive to Kitchener to touch base with my family. Dad has recovered from a kidney operation he experienced a few months ago and looks great. Bayne, Bette and the children are visiting. Bayne is now posted to Staff College, Kingston, Ontario. I meet my new nephew, Donald, a mirror image of his father at that age. Shelley is now working with the Christian Resource Centre, helping kids and their families relocate to make way for a new development, referred to as St. Jamestown, and also has time off. We plan a motor trip down east. I discover that I can be bitchy, irritable and downright unpleasant. Shelley, fortunately, accommodates, charitably crediting my ill humour to the rain that dampens most of our holiday. The fog that blankets the beauty of the Cabot trail adds to my irritability. Far be it from me to acknowledge that I'm uptight about the new job, the switch to the adult world.

Winnipeg Family Court administers both juvenile and family services. I assume a position in the family service area, with the understanding that I will, in the near future, be replacing Mrs. Florence Mahaffy, the administrator of the adult court services. In Manitoba individuals can apply to the court to obtain a legal separation, unlike other provinces in Canada. The court processes applications for maintenance orders and orders relating to custody and alimony. Periodically, the social workers in the adult division are asked to provide assessments for the court, home studies regarding the custody of children. Crisis marital counselling is offered and, if successful, referrals are made to family service agencies for ongoing counselling.

Mrs. Mahaffy, a dignified, silver-haired, seventy-year-old woman with a sharp mind and an indomitable spirit, endeavors to orient me to this new service. I sit in the office with her when she interviews clients and trail after her, panting, sprinting the three flights of stairs leading to the stacks of files that cover an expansive area as far as the eye can see. I lag behind like a streamer of exhaust fumes fading from this jet-propelled woman as she enters the area where applications are signed and filed for court action.

"But how do you know this woman must leave her husband? How can you tell her that she must file an application immediately and get out of her marriage? You've only talked with her for thirty minutes," I say, astounded at what I perceive to be arrogance. This direct intervention is diametrically opposed to anything I've ever learned or read at graduate school.

"Her husband lies and is having affairs. It's impossible to maintain a healthy relationship under those conditions," she answers, an amused smile on her face.

"But you don't know the other side. Maybe she's just angry. Maybe they could work out a better relationship. Maybe she's exaggerating. You could be interfering, maybe busting up a family prematurely," I say, upset at Mrs. Mahaffy's insistence on immediate court action.

"Well, you just get to know after a period of time. And let me assure you, Dale, if this is not the right action, you'll know almost immediately," she says.

"But how? You've already set an action in motion."

"If it isn't meant to be, the woman will go home, think it over and either phone to cancel the application or she simply won't show up at the hearing. Believe me, you aren't that powerful. You can't make someone do something they really, at heart, don't want to do. Quite often what they're looking for is confirmation that the spouse's behaviour is as bad as they think and permission to leave a bad relationship. Trust me, Dale. They make the decision and it's usually the right one."

After three days of observing, challenging and being frightened out of my wits by the bang-bang approach of straight-shooting-from-the-hip Mahaffy, my anxiety level is sky-high and I bang-bang into someone's fender. Either I throw out much of what I've learned about nondirective counseling, or chances are I'm gonna make a wreck out of my green machine. Maybe I've made a mistake. Maybe I shouldn't have been so hasty in deciding to take this job.

Actually this wasn't my first choice. I wanted the job at a treatment setting for children in Vancouver, British Columbia, but the director and his board were taking forever to make a decision about my application. I submitted all the information they wanted, flew out to spend a day with them, was interviewed by the psychologist and the psychiatrist, as well as the director, and they were still vacillating. One day after I accept the position with the court, their offer for employment comes through.

And maybe I made a mistake for another reason as well. After several weeks on the job, I realize that Mrs. Mahaffy is unaware that I have been hired to replace her. I don't know what to do about this. I believe that the director of court services was underhanded and manipulative in hiring me without first consulting Mrs. Mahaffy, but is it my responsibility to inform her? God, I hate hidden agendas.

I'm adapting. Just yesterday I raced up the stairs and supported a woman in filling out her application for separation. Now her husband arrives without an appointment and demands to see me. *Damn, I'm gonna get clobbered.* I'm very nervous and doing my best to hide it. I hear that wee small voice inside saying, *Remember, anger means unhappy.*

"Did you tell my wife to leave me?" Mr. Jordan asks, his face flushed, his voice strained, controlled, his eyes piercing, deadlocked on my eyeballs.

"Yes," I say, my heart leaping right into my throat. "She told me that she doesn't feel loved and that she wants out of her marriage."

"But I don't understand. I love my wife. I've worked my butt off to provide her with a beautiful house, a large pool and patio, the best furnishings. She can travel wherever she wants. I've given her everything. How can she not feel loved?" he says, and quite unexpectedly, tears begin to flow.

"Your wife acknowledges that, Mr. Jordan. She says you've given her everything but *you*. She never sees you. You don't travel or holiday with her. You're not available for any of the occasions she feels are important. She says your children hardly know you and she feels like she's living with a stranger."

"Well, it's true. I'm hardly home. But I couldn't be making all this money if I was at home. Do you understand? Please! Understand! I was doing these things *because* I love my wife. God, it looks like I've done it all wrong, but can you understand my motive?"

Mr. Jordan, still crying but very quiet, thanks me for understanding and with shoulders slouched, head down, he leaves the office—at this moment, a very broken spirit.

Whew, I survived that. I go into Mrs. Mahaffy's office. "Tell me, Mrs. Mahaffy, what do you do when a man cries in your office?" I say, shaken by this new experience.

"Well, what do you do when a woman cries?"

"I give her a Kleenex."

"Well, give him a Kleenex," she says, smiling, her eyes twinkling.

"How'd you get so smart?" I say, laughing at my own naiveté.

I continue to see Carole and Stewart and listen to the goings-on at Knowles School for Boys, my heart still back with the boys. I'm invited to dinner to meet Pauline Morris, a friend of Stewart's from his undergraduate days, whom he met when they both worked part-time at the Children's Home on Kenora Street. Pauline has just returned to Canada after working several years in Jamaica, her country of origin. We're friends before the night is over.

Pauline introduces me to a world of spicy foods, rich colour, calypso music and dancing from the soul. Her ebony body glistens as she loses herself in rhythm, her tall, big-hipped body seductively swaying, head held high, eyes closed, her face reflecting a mystery of experience unknown to me. We spend many evenings in her home, clicking with Miriam Makeba, undulating to the beat of Alley Cat and Green Onions, not just because the experience of letting go and releasing tension is so pleasurable, but also to avoid being in my own apartment with my new roommate, Jackie Beechcroft. Jackie, a pencil-thin, uptight, rigid occupational therapist with an irritating, nasally high-pitched voice and an equally irritating naiveté, replaced

Pat Hydak, who left to travel Europe. Avoiding spending time with the intrusive Jackie becomes a high priority in my life.

February 1967 becomes a turning point in my perception of the justice system. I'm asked to do a custody report for the court. A woman in her early thirties, with three young boys ages ten, eight and six, left her husband to move in with a man down the street. She wants her boys to live with her, and her husband is asking for sole custody. I set up individual interviews with the mother and the father in my office and home visits with both. I have lunch with the mom, the boyfriend and the three boys and then have dinner and a visit with the boys at the father's home. I then talk with the boys alone to listen to their perceptions and needs. I record in graphic detail my observations of interactions.

At the mother's house, the little boy starts to rock in his chair. Mom stops him, expressing concern that he will fall. He stops. He gets up and goes over to sit in the boyfriend's lap. The boyfriend ruffles his hair and continues with his meal, not interrupting Mom, who is explaining the kids' favourite activities and what each boy prefers.

At the father's house, the youngest boy rocks in his chair, tilting it back and then forward. Father says nothing. The little one continues to rock, exaggerating his movements. Father says nothing. The chair falls over backwards and the boy cracks his head on the floor and starts crying. The father says nothing. The oldest boy picks up his brother and puts his arms around him. Father, still focused on me, continues to tell me what a tramp his wife is. Does he know the children's favourite foods? No. Can he tell me their favourite activities? No. Their favourite colours? No.

The children tell me they are afraid of Daddy, that he gets mad and hits them. They want to live with Mommy and come down the street to visit Daddy. They ask to be reassured that I won't tell Daddy what they say or he'll get mad.

A twenty-page report, with recommendations that the judge consider granting custody to the mother, is ignored. Boys should be with the father. And so much for "justice"!

"But how can this be?" I say to Mrs. Mahaffy.

"It all depends on the judge," she says. "You win some and you lose some. That's the system."

"But it's not right."

"No, but it's one of the best systems in the world, Dale. This is not a perfect world. You just do the best you can, contribute from a caring heart and make the best of it. I explained that to my grandchildren on the weekend." She leans forward, both elbows on the desk, her chin resting on folded hands. "I took the three of them to the cottage. We were walking through the woods heading to the squirrel's nest that we found on our last hike and we came across one dead squirrel. The poor thing was killed by some larger animal, I presume. Robbie was devastated. It's hard for kids to understand that sometimes bad things happen. That's the way of the world. We had a little burial service for the squirrel and Robbie felt better."

"Do I get to bury the judge?"

Mrs. Mahaffy laughs, "No, but you can bury the experience and just go on."

"Something else isn't right, Mrs. Mahaffy," I say. "I have to talk to you about something that's really troubling me."

"Go ahead; what's on your mind?" she says, tilting her head, a look of concern and compassion registering on her deeply lined and sculpted face.

"I've been hired to replace you. I realize that you're unaware of this and I can't continue the deception. I want you to know the truth. I've also learned enough about your role to know that I can't do your job, nor do I want to. I'll be looking for another job soon and will probably leave the court service no later than June. I'm very sorry."

Mrs. Mahaffy is clearly stunned by this news. "Thank you for telling me, Dale. Let's just think about this for a few days and talk more later."

Strange how things happen; Mom calls me to tell me that she talked to Janet Bain, a social worker who works with Alvis P. Stayt at the Kitchener Family Service Bureau, at a recent stamp club meeting. Janet is excited to learn that I am now a graduate social worker and wonders if I might be interested in a job change. A letter notifies me that Mrs. Stayt will be in Winnipeg in two weeks and would like to meet with me to discuss the possibility of employment at the bureau. The idea of returning to Kitchener, or at least the east, is appealing. I embrace it as my unique centennial project. I meet with Mrs. Stayt and am excited about the opportunity she presents—a senior supervisory position, with the possibility of becoming a field placement supervisor with the Waterloo Lutheran University, School of Social Work. Hey, me, a field instructor with the university.

When I tell Barry Sheppard the news, he breaks into a deep belly guffaw. He's just accepted a position as a professor at the Waterloo Lutheran University, School of Social Work, and will be in charge of the student field placement experience. I'd be working with Barry again.

Whipping around a badminton court chasing birds and slamming them back to your opponent, hopefully not to be returned, is a great way to relieve stress and free up the mind for decision making. It doesn't take me long to decide to accept the contract Mrs. Stayt is offering me. I'm going home. And it doesn't take me long to agree to billet two young women from Quebec, who arrive at the badminton club to participate in the Winnipeg International Badminton Tournament and need a billet. They too bring a new challenge into my life.

I can hear the stereo blaring as I approach my apartment. The young women asked if they could have a party and I did say yes. It's after midnight—I'm just returning from the symphony and an evening with Pauline—and my drab, poorly furnished basement apartment is alive with candles, laughter, a throbbing rhythm, sexual energy and a mob of unfamiliar faces—except for Jackie, that is—all the stuff of romantic novels. I'm introduced to a gorgeous, blue-eyed blond from Norway, who shakes breasts instead of hands, an intoxicated, devil-may-care Scottish gentleman panting behind one of my young guests, and an assortment of other males who disappear soon after my arrival.

"Can you find us some more men?" young Monique says, her disappointment obvious as her friend and the dashing drunk evaporate into the stratosphere along with the other revellers.

"I don't know who I can find at two in the morning. But I'll give it a try," I say.

Selwyn Watson, the social worker who replaced me at Knowles School, doesn't appear to be the least perturbed about receiving such a late phone call. "Sure," he says, "I'll call up some friends and be there in an hour."

I am acutely aware of Hayward Smith, one of Selwyn's friends, from the time he enters the apartment. We dance only once or twice and say very little to each other. I feel an unfamiliar but not uncomfortable tension, a sense of déjà vu. I just know: I know we'll be lovers—me and this tall, solidly built, black-as-in-blue-streaked-anthracite-coal, sensual man, who says little but communicates vibrantly from deep-set dark brown eyes. I sense that he is a gift, a shaman who would bring me through the sexual rejection and trauma of the past few months. It's just something I know.

The party lasts until nine in the morning. The Scotsman, now sober, returns with a frightened, crying young woman who immediately heads for the bedroom to whisper to Monique. Breakfast—the meagre findings extracted from a refrigerator unaccustomed to regurgitating anything but coffee and the odd frozen dinner—heralds the end of the Cinderella-at-the-ball fantasy. Or does it?

The next three months are a whirlwind of dinners, movies, the occasional party and sex, lots of sex, great "I can hardly wait to jump your bones" sex. Finally, I get to unleash suppressed, creative energy with a lover who is comfortable with his own body and very willing to explore mine. Whirlwind? Perhaps that is a slight exaggeration, as Hayward is preparing for exams and graduation from his university program.

I like to consider myself politically and socially aware, aware for instance of the race riots of '64 when Harlem was destroyed by fires, stores owned by whites were broken into and looted and people were killed. I'm conscious of the impact of the assassinations of John F. Kennedy Jr., Bobby Kennedy and Dr. Martin Luther King; of Chicago's Mayor Daley and his Democratic coalition machine set up to protect one group of privileged citizens by the continued victimization of another. I'm disturbed when I read about the squelching of the Mississippi Freedom Democrats by the "liberal" north and the killing of little black girls in a southern church; disturbed by the killing of civil rights workers, deliberately murdered in an ambush. I think I understand what is and has been happening in the world—especially the world south of the border.

Winnipeg doesn't have a black population of Afro-Americans, who brought with them a history of enslavement; who are presently underemployed, undereducated, underpaid and undervalued. Most of the black population in Winnipeg is West Indian, highly educated or becoming that way, a population with a different sense of self, of esteem, of entitlement. And Hayward and I—we're Canadians.

"I forgot the booze," Hayward announces as we get into the car. "We'll have to stop first at the house before we head for the party."

"Won't we be late then?"

Hayward laughs, a deep-from-the-belly laugh. "There's no such thing as 'being late' for a West Indian party. Besides, I'd like you to meet my buddies."

I'm pleased and excited. This is the first experience with Hayward that involves his friends. I acknowledge each introduction with a warm smile, and turning to Hayward standing behind me, I catch a glimpse of—what? Pride? Love? A glow of something that touches my heart.

Sounds of steel drums, a wave of crashing, pulsating rhythm, bombard my senses as we enter the house. Colours and moving bodies—dim lights, a crush of black faces, red/yellow/orange shirts, skirts, scarves moving everywhere—and laughter, unfamiliar smells, bits and pieces of conversation in a dialect unrecognizable to me, flame my excitement. No introductions, just a pull of the hand and I'm up and swinging.

Rice and peas, curried chicken, hundred-proof rum, cigarette smoke and more laughter; a burst of voices shouting out the lyrics of a song played repeatedly throughout the evening, "…the green, green, grass of home."

Only when I drop exhausted into bed do I acknowledge to myself the disquieting sensation still vibrating in the pit of my gut. Hostile glances from the women—not one had spoken to me. I'm going to ask Pauline about this.

"What the hell did you expect?" Pauline says in an angry tone, a frown on her face and a flash of indignation in her eyes. I'm startled; experience a sharp grabbing sensation in my gut. "Why didn't you tell me you were involved with a Jamaican? I wondered why I haven't seen much of you lately. Listen, Dale, I'm frightened for you. You don't know what you're getting into."

"I knew you would say something like that. I know you don't like West Indian men very much. That's why I didn't tell you."

"You idiot; it's not that I don't like West Indian men! Let me tell you the truth. The issue is power, politics and prejudice! These men come up here to get an education, and when they get here they are surrounded with white faces. You have no idea what happens to a Jamaican country boy stepping off that plane for the first time. He's suddenly a minority, frequently a minority of one—he's different! He experiences tremendous insecurity. Frequently he decides that acceptance in the white society means 'getting white.' The issue is sex—sexual politics—screw a white woman and show them! And the black women, the wives, the girlfriends who come later, or the black women who also want to get an education, they come here and the men are 'wearing white.' But, God forbid that a black woman goes out with a white man. Then the whole tightly knit black community goes nuts and the woman is called names and rejected by the men and women alike. And you expect to walk into a black party and be warmly welcomed by black women?"

Pauline's railing at me frightens me half to death. I agree to read Eldridge Cleaver's (Malcolm X's) book *Soul on Ice* and paperbacks by James Baldwin, Stokely Carmichael and Charles Hamilton. *Oh God, what am I getting into?*

"I have something to tell you," Hayward whispers in my ear as we snuggle, legs entwined, after an exhausting, frantic experience of lovemaking—the franticness, I'm sure created in me by the stinging reality of what I'm learning.

"Are you going to hurt me?" I say, having convinced myself that I'm just a white body in a political washing machine.

"No," he says, startled. "I would never do that. Whatever makes you ask a question like that?"

"Well, I've been reading about the issues of black and white."

"Hey come on, this is you and me, Dale. No, I just want to tell you that I will be leaving Winnipeg soon."

"Soon; how soon is soon?"

"In two weeks: I've accepted a teaching position at a correctional setting in Hamilton. I'm going to work for a few years, save some money before I go into a masters program in business."

"I can't believe this. I've accepted a position with the Kitchener-Waterloo Family Service Bureau for mid-June. I was going to tell you this towards the end of May. Amazing how things work," I say, experiencing a cleansing wave of relief. *Relief—how can I be so unfeeling? Hayward's been so good for me, so gentle and healing, so affirming of my desirability as a woman. He's done so much to restore my trust in men—and I'm relieved to have this over?*

"I'll write to you," Hayward says, as he caresses the landscape soon to be yesterday's geography.

"Yes, please do," I say, knowing that it's over. No emotional complications, no dramatic scenes, no hypocritical declarations of undying love and no confronting of complicated, underlying racial issues.

Leaving Mrs. Mahaffy and leaving Pauline involves very different emotions.

On my last day at the court I send Mrs. Mahaffy a bouquet of red roses and a poem I've written entitled "The Silver Birch". I make sure I'm not present when they arrive. I hate getting emotional. How do you thank a mentor for her gift of wisdom?

And Pauline? We drive around the perimeter of the city my last night in Winnipeg and cry. How does one develop such an intense friendship in such a short time? I know what I'm leaving behind. I'm so unsure about what lies ahead. Is it possible to go "back home," to be a recognized professional in the city of one's childhood? Am I ever going to find a lasting love relationship? A "someone" who will journey with me? A life partner like Ken and Bayne have found?

WISDOM IN MOTION

Have you had an experience with our justice system? Even a traffic ticket? If so, how did you respond to that "bump"? What messages did you get about "right" and "wrong," about accepting responsibility for your actions?

How do you react when you become aware of a deception, when you know someone is lying, especially if that someone is in a position of power?

Have you had experiences of saying good-bye to people you love? How did you manage your feelings? Are you noticing any patterns regarding how you deal with conflictual working relationships, with disappointments when people let you down, when "the world" lets you down?

CALLED "OUT" AT HOME PLATE

I'm excited to be back in Kitchener, Ontario—home base—and excited to meet the newest members of the Perrin family. Deanna was born April 19 to Ken and Jan, and since then I've been fantasizing *Auntie Mame* scenes with me and my niece exploring great new horizons, braving daring adventures, conquering male chauvinism, reaching unimaginable heights of feminist glory. Me and Deanna—triumphant! Mind you, now that I can actually hold her, she seems awfully tiny, and when she cries I feel helpless and not at all triumphant. My fantasies may have to wait a year or two.

Coming home has all kinds of implications. I move into the apartment building where Ken and Jan live and Ken is the superintendent. Convenient, but what if Hayward actually comes to visit as he suggested he would do in his unexpected letter that arrived just before I left Winnipeg? Do I want to get into the black-white issue with my family? Do I want to continue in a relationship that I thought was neatly wrapped, ribboned and shelved in my memory treasure box? Do I want such complications in my life? I set boundaries with Mom and Dad—no key to the apartment, no routine attendance at Sunday dinners—prior to arriving back home, but will those boundaries protect my privacy?

My first Sunday home: dinner with the family. Letters from Mom and Dad alerted me to the fact that I have a new "sister," Maggie Mitchell. Shelley gets credit for this "birth."

"How did you and Shelley meet?" I say as we relax in the backyard under the pungent, pink blossoms of the crab-apple trees, looking over the neatly trimmed lower terrace and lawns leading to the back flower beds and cherry trees.

It's a warm, sunny June day and I'm totally sated now, having consumed pot roast of beef, roasted carrots, onions and potatoes and Dutch apple pie—what else would one expect for a Perrin Sunday family meal?

"We met through mutual contacts at the St. Jamestown project. The Central Neighbourhood Centre where I work has a caseload of families from the project. Shelley and I work together with some of the kids in the families. As we got to know each other and became friends, we decided to share accommodations and save money. We found an apartment in an old house on Woodlawn that had been converted into six apartment units. And Shelley just invited me along on her weekend visits with your mom and dad. I hope that's okay with you. I really like your family."

Okay with me? A strange comment! Maggie inhales a deep drag from her cigarette, smacks her lips tightly, threatening to squeeze the life out of the filter. Her freckled face is tight, her sad grey-green eyes—or is that just my imagination?—hidden for the moment behind a mask of spiraling smoke.

"Do you have family?" I say, hoping my curiosity won't be interpreted as an interrogation or "sister interview." Maggie indulges my curiosity, takes no offence and shares information about her family. Shelley joins us shortly thereafter.

"Are you excited about your new job?" Shelley says, now equally shielded behind a thickening blue blanket of smoke and decorated with a few pink blossoms that have fallen from the crab-apple tree. I admit I'm nervous about my new job, which starts tomorrow. I share my anxieties: have I made the right decision? Can I make it as a professional in my own hometown? I ask for reassurances. Both "sisters" reassure me.

I arrive at the K-W Family Service Bureau five minutes early and check my appearance in the car visor mirror. Yup, my makeup is just so. I smooth out my orange flowered dress that slims out my new body—I lost over thirty pounds just before returning to Kitchener—my dark brown, curly, short hair neatly combed to soften the angles of my square face. I blow on my dark-rimmed glasses and shine them with a Kleenex tissue. I'm ready.

Twenty Queen Street, North is in the very heart of the city, an old, two-story, brown, brick building. The entranceway looks grungy, smells mildewed. It wouldn't surprise me to see little black, creepy-crawly things dash out from the threadbare carpet and grab for treasured pieces of my ankles as I study the directory mounted on the faded, apple-green painted wall. The agency is on the second floor.

The office is a rectangular structure with windows on the three outer sides; no decorations or paintings grace the inner wall. Mrs. Stayt, a woman in her fifties, is in the reception area and greets me with a smile and a brisk, "Good morning." She introduces me to Helen Fekete, who is sitting at her desk behind a counter that sections off the secretarial area from the waiting area. A few chrome chairs, with green laminated seats, are pushed against the outer wall, close to a closet with wood veneer sliding doors. Helen, Mrs. Stayt's private secretary, is a dark-haired, slim woman in her late thirties, with dark brown rimmed glasses, dark brown, knowing eyes, tight, serious, strained, thin lips that you just know bite back secrets busting to be told.

Rosemary Summerville, the clerk typist, a shy young blond woman in her early twenties, blushes at the introduction. I'm not sure why. She quickly attends to her typing.

Janet Bein, a Dutch woman in her fifties, has one of the two offices looking out over Queen Street. She smiles warmly from behind streamers of cigarette smoke trailing from a slim, black cigarette holder, which she waves as she greets me. Janet, the only full-time social worker, is strangely reminiscent of the welfare worker from the thirties; oh my God, what does this suggest about the quality of service being delivered?

Ros Adelberg, a woman ten years my senior, works part-time. From behind her desk, she pushes her glasses up onto her head, acknowledges the introduction, smiles and immediately turns her attention back to the open file and papers scattered in front of her, her glasses now settled back on her straight, classic nose.

Formalities complete, Mrs. Stayt ushers me into her office, the biggest space, tucked behind the secretarial area, with a large window overlooking the building next door. She sits behind an executive-styled mahogany desk in the matching reddish-coloured leather chair. A colourful oil painting, reminiscent in style of Canada's famous Group of Seven, graces the wall behind her, a chilling winter scene of Canada's awesome natural woodlands.

And so, my life as a counsellor/supervisor begins—begins in this all-pervasive, don't-approach-me, serious atmosphere, an atmosphere that instantly changes when Mrs. Stayt is not present, I soon experience.

I'm to have supervision with Mrs. Stayt weekly, though not on my clinical work, since Mrs. Stayt is not a trained social worker. I learn that her background is nursing, that she worked as a Red Cross nurse in England during the war years. There is an aura of distance about her, a chill that radiates from a solid body armored with extra padding, not unlike the administrative staff at the Galt Training School for Girls. I learn that she's married to a doctor who lives in Hamilton, yet she shares a house in Kitchener with Janet Bein. As I sit across the desk from her, look directly at the steel-blue eyes peering at me from above the reading glasses, fixed to a black-and-gold cord that allows them to rest on her ample bosom when not in use, now slipped halfway down her pinched, narrow nose, I wonder what she's thinking. Her face—an inscrutable mask, with just the right amount of makeup. It doesn't take me long to recognize that Mrs. Stayt is not a Florence Mahaffy.

Within a few short months I experience that my case recordings are too long, then too short; I'm to supervise a BSW worker, and then no such being appears. I supervise a summer student instead.

By September, Ken Sime, a new graduate social worker from Winnipeg, arrives with his wife Marilyn, also a social worker. Mrs. Stayt asked me to "recruit," and Barry suggested Ken, a student he knew who might be willing to come east. When I called Ken he was delighted and agreed to accept the position. Now I'm assigned to supervise Ken's work—just his clinical work, I learn. Mrs. Stayt will supervise the administrative aspect of his work, whatever that means. Control—I'm beginning to recognize this is all about control!

I share my perceptions and discomforts with Barry Sheppard shortly after Ken and Marilyn arrive.

"Barry, this is not a very spontaneous environment to work in. If it wasn't for Ken, I'd be bored out of my tree. And Mrs. Stayt, I've never been so, so—stifled."

"Yeah," Barry says, "she's not highly regarded in the professional community. She's wanted to have us place students with her since the graduate social work program at Wilfred Laurier began a couple of years ago. However, we don't place students in agencies without staff that have MSW degrees and supervisory experience. You can make a real difference at that agency, Dale. Just do your own thing and don't let her get in the way."

"Yeah, will do; you're sure I can handle students?"

"Not a problem; don't worry about it. You're as competent as anyone else doing field placements for us. And besides, I'll work closely with you. The two first-year students I'm placing with you are both mature students, and they shouldn't have any difficulties handling a caseload and developing the prerequisite skills."

Dear Barry, my guardian angel and mentor, with his big, booming voice still spontaneously belting out arias as easily as needed advice— what would I do without his support and direction? And with Ken Sime here now, hey this will be fun, albeit challenging.

A bigger challenge for me at the moment is what to do about Hayward, who's coming over this evening. So far in his previous visits, we've managed to avoid bumping into Ken or Jan, but I'm uncomfortable. Why didn't he leave things as they were? And why did I welcome moving back into a relationship? This just isn't what I expected; it isn't right. Much too complicated. I haven't seen a black face since my return to Kitchener—not that we've experienced any difficulties when we've gone out, just the occasional sideways glance. I want to stop the relationship. I'm just not up to loving a black man, and Pauline would kill me if she knew I was continuing my relationship with Hayward.

He appears at the door. My resolve disappears and I melt into his arms. Very soon thereafter, we disappear into my darkened bedroom, where the urgencies of the moment soon give way to quiet conversation about my growing discomforts in the work environment.

Next time, I'll do it next time—break up, that is. I don't understand my ambivalence about Hayward and our relationship, but I know I must end it. And I will. I can't seem to do it face-to-face so I'll do it on the telephone.

"Hayward, I'm really sorry but I don't want to see you anymore," I say in our very next telephone conversation. Thank goodness he can't see my hands tremble. And I'm sure he thinks my shaky voice is just the feelings of the moment. *What on earth am I so nervous about?*

"Are you sure? You really want to do this?" he says after a prolonged silence.

"Yes, absolutely," I say in my strong, determined, professional voice. *Oh my God, I'm really doing it.* Another prolonged silence.

"Well, okay. But I'm going to call you every so often just to see how you're doing. If you change your mind you just need to invite me for coffee. I really don't want to say good-bye."

That's it. I'm relieved—I think. The tension in the agency continues to escalate.

"You wouldn't believe what's *she's* done now," I say to Ken, who is sitting across the desk from me. "She gave me a schedule: a timetable for every hour of the day, every day of the week. Can you believe this? I'm to have my first client interview at 9:15 a.m. I'm to return telephone messages from 10:15 to 10:30. At 10:45 I have my second client interview. At 11:45 I dictate my sessions. At 12:00 I may have lunch. And so on. You're scheduled in for Thursdays from 1:15 p.m. to 2:30. And I'm not to talk to you except at lunchtime or in our supervisory sessions."

"Yeah, I know," Ken says. "I got similar instructions. Just ignore the old bitch. Don't let her get to you like this."

Ken's a young man in his late twenties. He's a laid-back, easygoing, caring, gentle guy, blondish hair, neatly shaven round face, with premature smile wrinkles at the corners of his mouth. He's always neatly dressed in a casual suit, coordinated shirt and tie and slightly scuffed shoes. You knew he'd be far more comfortable in jeans and a sweatshirt.

"But you know what she did? I was having a session with my favourite young client, my dowdy, uptight university student who's trying to emancipate herself from a rigid, controlling, fundamentalist mother. Did I tell you she went on a shopping spree with one of her new university friends and bought some stylish, bright-coloured clothes, which, I might add, she doesn't plan to wear when she goes back to visit Mom? And Helen knocks on the door to remind me that I have to be in Mrs. Stayt's office in five minutes for supervision. Poor kid excused herself immediately, apologetic for taking up space in the world. I had to reassure her several times that it was okay for us to finish our discussion. I almost had to hold her down so that she wouldn't just bolt out of the office."

Ken laughs. "She told me that from now on I'll be having supervision with her. Did she tell you, Dale? Guess you blew it, eh?" he says, his eyes twinkling, the ends of his lips curling up ever so slightly.

"No way; she can't do that."

Ten months into my experience I learn that not only can she do that but she can do a lot more. Ken and I attended a conference that focused on a new approach to working with families, called conjoint family therapy. The agency received a copy of the book and I was eager to read it and begin working with these new ideas. Wrong! Mrs. Stayt locks the bookcase and makes it clear that books are not to be taken out overnight. I'm informed that I'm not to attempt this new approach unless we have a video camera and audio equipment to record the sessions. I buy the book on my own and Ken and I read, discuss and begin to work with this model, quietly, behind our closed doors.

Hayward calls.

"Would you like to have coffee?" I say, a note of desperation in my request. My God, it's been such a long, lonely time—at least it feels that way.

"Sure, I'm free now. Would you like me to come over?"

"Yes, by all means. Come right now."

I share with him my discomfort and dissatisfaction with the job situation, my feelings of loneliness and isolation in this, my hometown. All my high-school friends are married, with growing families, and my university friends are off in different parts of the country. The badminton group at the Granite Club, for the most part, is much older and I have little in common with them—with the exception of one of my clients who also plays at the club. Pauline comes to visit for Christmas and is here to help me celebrate my newly decorated apartment, the furnishings and drapery carefully selected with the assistance of an interior decorator. The family is supportive but I don't feel like burdening them with my troubles, especially as Mom socializes with Mrs. Stayt and Janet Bain at the stamp club.

Hayward listens and shakes his head at the goings-on that I report.

"Maybe it's time to get out," he says.

"But I haven't even been here a year yet, and I know Mom and Dad will be so disappointed. Besides, I've just finished decorating my apartment." The very thought of leaving fills me with a sense of foreboding, a horrible sense of failure.

"Well, there's a time to go, and I know that time has arrived for me," he says.

"What? Are you leaving?" More sense of foreboding.

"Yes, but I'm not going far. Just to Brampton to the correctional setting. I prefer to work with young adults. I've had it with young kids. We'll still be close enough to continue a relationship if you want to." *I do; I want to.*

The lovemaking is so comforting. God, how I need him: my shaman, my healer, my lover: this tall, black, handsome man, with the gentle soul and strong, muscular body.

"I have to tell you something," I say to brother Ken, who drops in to see the oil painting the decorator has mounted above the blue chesterfield. The winter storm scene, with a mysterious black figure leaning forward against the formidable winds, captures the blues and greens of my drapes, carpet and furnishings and even has a touch of purple, to incorporate the purple of my velvet-covered wingback chair. Ken often drops by, an opportunity to get away from the noise of two children and a busy wife. He looks carefully around the room, shuffles from one foot to another.

"I guess I'm going to have to dress up to visit you now," he says. This irritates me, a real downer. It seems to me Ken can never celebrate my successes. He just can't be happy for me.

"Come on, Ken. You know that's not so, but forget that. Let me tell you something personal. I have a wonderful man in my life, a man that I met in Winnipeg."

"Oh yeah, how long have you been seeing him? Are we going to get to meet him?" Ken settles in on one of the new blue and green striped chairs, discards his tool belt, the badge of his janitorial duties, and lights up a cigarette. I tell him some background about our relationship and add, "He's black."

"Black; you mean like Pauline?"

"Yes, every bit as black as Pauline."

Ken pauses thoughtfully. "Do you mind if I ask you something personal?"

"Like what? This is all personal and not to be shared with Mom or Dad. I'm only telling you because I'm afraid you will see us together and I don't want you to be shocked."

"Well, you know, uh, is it true that black men have bigger penises? I know that's crazy but I'd really like to know." I can't believe he asked that!

"I don't know, Ken. I haven't measured a random sample of white men or other black men for that matter." Sometimes I really dislike Ken. What happened to the fun kid I played with?

Ken apologizes, looks embarrassed and decides it's time to get back to his apartment.

More tension at work; I arrive, reluctantly, at the scheduled time in Mrs. Stayt's office. What on earth am I going to discuss for supervision? There's nothing that I want or need from this woman.

"I get the feeling that you want my job, Dale," she says, peering at me intensely over the reading glasses, no doubt watching for nonverbal clues to support her out-of-nowhere allegation.

"What? I don't understand. I'm not interested in being an administrator of an agency. Besides, with my stage fright I'd never make it through an Annual General Meeting." I say, smiling tentatively, wondering what kind of test this is. "No, I enjoy what I'm doing."

"Well, whether you know it or not, you are looking at my job; and I must tell you, I don't think you're ready for it."

I certainly can't disagree with that. But what on earth makes her think I want her job? I think I'm in some kind of trouble here. *What is she reacting to? What's this about? I wish Helen wasn't so, so close-mouthed. I'll bet she could tell me what's going on.*

Mrs. Stayt is out of the office. It's now almost four o'clock Friday afternoon and Ken and I have joined Helen and Rosemary to laugh, joke and enjoy the freedom Mrs. Stayt's absence permits. We have a long weekend coming up and I'm looking forward to a break from the oppressiveness of this atmosphere.

"I guess it's too late today for the boss lady to fire me," I say to the group. Helen winces. And just at that moment boss lady opens the outer door and walks briskly towards her office, scowling. Clearly she has surmised that we have sinned grievously in her absence.

"Dale, I want to see you in my office, now," she says, her tone of voice making it clear that this is not negotiable.

I sit in the appointed chair. Mrs. Stayt hands me a letter. I read:

It is with regret that I have to give you notice to terminate your employment with the K-W Family Service Bureau, May 31, 1968, as per the terms in your contract with the agency.

The necessity for this has been brought about by the opportunity that has arisen to secure the services of an experienced supervisor, who would be eligible to eventually succeed Mrs. Stayt as Executive Director.

On behalf of the Board I would like to thank you for such assistance and cooperation as you have given during the year with the agency....

I get it! I'm being fired! I excuse myself and leave her office and go directly back to my own. Soon Mrs. Stayt exits. Gradually so does everyone else except Ken, who is waiting patiently for the opportunity to talk.

"Thank goodness you waited," I say to Ken. My eyes fill up. Damn, I'm not going to cry. "I think I've just been fired!" I hand him the letter.

"Yup, you've been fired," Ken says, looking at me, his clear blue eyes also watery. "And I, for sure, am not sticking around here if you're not going to be here. What do you say we go to my place and fly my kite? I went out and bought a kite—always wanted to do that—and order in pizza? Come on. We'll celebrate the end of a bad situation."

What on earth am I going to tell my family? I've been fired! In my own hometown! Fired!

CALLED "OUT" AT HOME PLATE

Rejection is so painful. Have you had such an experience? Perhaps not the experience of being "fired" but of being rejected by someone, a group or team of people, or an authority figure?

What were your thoughts, feelings, behaviours? Were you able to share your feelings with anyone? What supports or judgments did you receive and from whom?

Are these thoughts, feelings or behaviours familiar? If so, can you recall an experience from your childhood where you first experienced or formulated these thoughts and decided to behave (or not) in this familiar way?

POLITICS, PARANOIA AND
PAINFUL CONFRONTATION

"This looks like such a pretty community," I say to Maggie as we pull into Colonel Sanders, just north of the 401 Highway, for a fast-food fix. "Frank says to be sure and locate north of Bloor Street. Have you found that on the map?"

Maggie, who has volunteered to help me find an apartment, is studying the map held in one hand while she gnaws on a chicken leg held in the other. "Yeah, that makes sense. Oshawa has grown up around Lake Ontario so this is the old section of town. Now here's Bloor," she says, pointing with her half-eaten leg. "So we go straight north, up Simcoe, and we'll be heading for the residential neighbourhoods."

Maggie and I plot out the locations of the apartments for rent from the classified ads, and within a few hours I pay the first and last month's rent on an eleventh-story apartment on Rossland Road, in the north end of town, close to the local airport. The apartment faces south, giving a panoramic view of the city and Lake Ontario. I'm confident that I can move, settle in and be ready for action on June 1, 1968—ready to prove Frank Johnson wrong!

"Why did Barry tell you that you shouldn't take this job?" Maggie says on the return trip to Kitchener.

"Barry supervised Frank as a graduate student from the School of Social Work in Winnipeg. He thinks Frank's a good guy but passive, and he neither likes nor trusts Frank's wife, May. He thinks she's a social climber who manipulates and controls Frank and pushes him into taking on positions that he isn't ready for. He thinks I'll really threaten him."

"How could you do that?"

"Don't know, Maggie. Maybe Frank's just more comfortable with men than women. He told me quite openly at the time he offered me the position of community development worker that he'd prefer to have Ken Sime work for him but Ken didn't want the job."

"He actually told you that?"

"Yeah. I was kind of hurt, but I hope he'll be glad he made the decision once he gets to know me. I think this will be a challenging position and I'm excited about it."

"Just what exactly is a 'community development worker'?"

I laugh. "Don't know yet but I'm sure I'll find out in a big hurry."

And I do!

Millie Stewart, the receptionist, greets me warmly. Ignoring the phone, she gets up, introduces herself, offers me a welcoming handshake and leads me up the staircase, down and around a hallway, to a poorly lit series of small rooms, now functioning as offices in this musty old building, an archive of long-forgotten stories of richness and drama. Frank's office is cramped but has the luxury of a window overlooking the back parking lot. The open window does little to free the confined space of sweet, wood-scented tobacco emanating from a curved pipe clenched between Frank's teeth. Removing the pipe creates streamers of bluish signals that temporarily mask a warm smile. With his very short blond brush cut and liquid pastel-blue eyes, Frank appears much younger than his thirty-some years. A white short-sleeved shirt, pale-blue knit tie and khaki slacks give him an unhealthy, faded appearance, no doubt a result of being confined in these dank quarters.

"Thanks, Millie," he says, indicating by a wave of his hand that I'm to sit in one of the wooden chairs in front of his desk, nearly backed against a faded yellow wall. Millie returns Frank's smile but doesn't move. "Will you shut the door on your way out?" Frank says, waiting for Millie to exit.

"She drives me crazy. May thinks she has a crush on me the way she hovers over me. But come on, Dale, let me introduce you to the team and then we can talk in your office just around the corner."

We pass Art Veroba in the hallway. The introduction is brief and Frank continues on to the end office, just a doorway down from Art.

"Don't bother getting to know Art," Frank says in a whispered voice. "He's on his way out. He just doesn't fit in here." I learn shortly thereafter that Frank is creating an environment that will encourage Art to resign "voluntarily."

Marjorie McKibbon, a matronly, heavyset woman in her late fifties, dressed in a conservative, grey knit dress with a pink rose pinned on the shoulder, her grey hair pulled tightly back from her forehead, reminiscent of Gramma's style, smiles warmly and acknowledges the introduction. Marjorie, the wife of a retired United Church minister, works three days a week and, I learn, we will be sharing an office, at least until we move to the midtown mall just south of Bond Street, a move that is to take place in a matter of weeks.

That's it. Frank, Marjorie and me—we're the team, to be joined in the foreseeable future by graduate students from the Carlton School of Social Work in Ottawa and the School of Social Work, Wilfred Laurier University, in Waterloo.

The Family Counselling Service, I learn, is a unique department within the Durham Region Children's Aid Society (CAS). In 1965 a change in the Child Welfare Act allowed for CAS's to provide preventative services as long as the focus was related to families and children under the age of sixteen. Frank was hired in May 1967 to direct this department under the jurisdiction of Bernard (Barney) Lewis, the executive director of the CAS.

The community, through the Social Planning Council, represented by its chair, Reverend John Morris, and other interested "movers and shakers," had determined that a broader service was needed to provide marriage counselling as well as consultation to and participation in other activities and services already being provided by a variety of organizations. As a result the Community Chest agreed to provide a grant to cover 55 percent of the costs of the new department through "voluntary funds," while the "statutory services" covering 45 percent of the costs were paid for by the provincial government. A group of these folks agreed to act as an "advisory council" to this fledgling service and its new director.

As the "community development worker" I am to devote 70 percent of my time to "community activities" and 30 percent to direct counselling service, including the supervision of students.

Okay, I guess I'd better get out there and find out who is doing what and why and what needs to be done and what on earth I am expected to do about it.

Like the mini squadron of small aircraft housed in the hangars of the nearby airport, I rev up my engine and take off. Within three weeks I meet a significant number of the movers and shakers and discover a richness of personalities with an awesome variety of educational, professional and experiential backgrounds, all contributing in unique ways to the well-being and quality of life in Oshawa. I learn, much to my surprise, that very few of these people know each other. All of them express a deep yearning for connectedness. Aha, when I get my financial situation sorted out, I will do something about this.

Very quickly, in response to the demand for counselling services, my caseload grows. The community has requested our involvement in several Social Planning Council committees, and immediately I'm involved in planning a leadership development program with and for the Parents Without Partners organization and I'm participating in the Youth Task Force, a Social Planning Council committee. And I initiate a major project of my own.

In the early weeks as I went about the city, I noticed a cluster of apartment buildings in one particular area, buildings that are older and less well maintained than the one I am living in. I wondered how living in low, middle and high-rise apartments affected family life; is there a causal relationship between types of buildings and specific social and family problems and needs? I now determine to conduct a study to find out. Frank concurs, and one of the movers and shakers on the advisory board connects me with a research faculty advisor at Durham Community College; the project is underway.

And I have a very personal project to get underway.

I haven't seen Hayward since my move to Oshawa, just long enough to begin to question "what is this/was that all about." The intensity of the romance seems surreal from this distance. Just a dance? A pas de deux in black and white? Karen Cain and Frank Augustyn? Dale and Hayward, creating our own music with no lyrics? I questioned whether or not I really loved Hayward when, during the entire year I lived in Kitchener in the same building as Ken and Jan and only blocks away from my parents, I didn't introduce him to either. How many times I had considered calling the whole relationship off, only to melt into his arms the moment he arrived at the door. Is this "love"? I should break up with Hayward.

And this time is no different. I can't do it. We melt first, talk later.

"I love you, Hayward," I whisper in the glow of sexual warmth, snuggling up to my familiar lover in this still unfamiliar apartment, aware of feeling vulnerable and shy. I can't remember when or if I've ever uttered such a declaration.

"You know what that means," Hayward whispers back.

"Uh, no; does it mean that you love me too?"

"Well, yes; that too."

"What are you talking about then?"

"Marriage; people who love each other get married." *Oh my God, the "m" word!*

"Okay, but let's think about that tomorrow."

How easy for me to pull a Scarlett O'Hara. That is one of her famous lines from the classic movie *Gone with the Wind*. Hayward and I hadn't talked in the past about any of the issues related to our racial and cultural differences, family dynamics, hopes and fears about our relationship and a future together. I'm in no hurry to do that right now. It seems so much more comfortable sharing about our new career challenges. Hayward, too, has made a career change and is now living in Brampton, working as a teacher in a correctional setting for young men.

The distance between Brampton and Oshawa is about the same as the distance between Haggersville (near Hamilton) and Kitchener, all in southern Ontario. Although this poses limits as to the frequency of our time together, Oshawa, a small, one-industry community (General Motors) with a high proportion of blue-collar workers and their families, does provide us with several reality checks as to issues that we will face as a couple.

Two men in white undershirts, beer bottles in hand, are hanging out the window of a second-story room in the hotel as we approach the entrance of the pub. They yell "Hey, nigger-lover," and other derogatory slurs and make obscene gestures. I look at Hayward. "Just ignore it." I did, but I was seething inside. Do we talk about it? No.

On another occasion Hayward and I are just leaving a cocktail lounge where we were dancing, and Hayward stops at the restroom. When he exits the restroom three men approach him. A brief conversation takes place. Although I don't hear the words, the body language is threatening and aggressive. Fear rips into my stomach like wolves on a fallen deer.

"We're leaving, Dale," Hayward announces in a voice that leaves no room for debate. He takes me by the arm and propels me towards the door.

"What happened, Hayward? What's wrong?"

"Nothing—you just have to learn to deal with situations like this. It's no big deal."

Do we talk about it? No. Sequestered in the safety of the bedroom, even the lovemaking with an unfamiliar element of intensity, does not erase the imprint of that encounter. Nonetheless, we decide that the time has come to talk with parents about our intention to marry. I plan to do that just as soon as Shelley, at my request, has time to "accidentally" let the parents know that I'm seeing a "black man." I want to prepare them. Hayward plans to visit his mother in New York in early August.

"I just called to tell you some news, Mom." She answers me just the way she does whenever I want to share anything with them.

"Oh, are you getting married?" I wasn't planning to break the news on the phone. I just wanted to check if they were going to be at home so I could drive to Kitchener for a visit. Now I'm hurt and angry.

"Yes, as a matter of fact I am."

"Not to that black man!"

"Yes, Hayward is black and I'm going to marry him."

"Please come home and discuss this with your father and me," Mom pleads, her voice cracking.

"No, I just called to let you know. You and Father can deal with your own prejudices. I'll talk to you later." And I hang up, shaking. *Oh my God! How can I be so mean?*

Within ten minutes the phone rings and Father asks if I would talk to them if they came right now to my place. That's a two-hour drive and I know this will be an ugly scene. "No, I will drive to Kitchener. I'll see you soon."

An afternoon of tears and accusations: "But we are only interested in your well-being." "But have you thought of the children and how difficult it will be for them?" "He will not be welcomed in this house." "He's not good enough for you." And rebuttals of, "You have never loved me for who I am." "I'm tired of your double messages—'when are you going to marry, but not him, dear.'"

Father insists, "We love you. We only want you to be happy," and excuses himself to go and check my car to make sure the tires are adequately inflated, his fatherly responsibility. Mom and I go down to the basement to attend to some laundry. When we are alone I confront her directly, cleansing my laundry list of childhood grievances about my feeling that I wasn't the daughter she really wanted, that no matter what I did I couldn't please her and as a final shot add, "And I didn't like taking dancing lessons either," in a voice that sounds very pouty and little. *My God! My God! Where is this stuff coming from?*

"But how do you think I felt?" Mom sobs. "You were the daughter I so desperately wanted. I love you so much and I wanted to give you all the things that I never had as a little girl and you didn't want any of it. You wouldn't even let me hug you. My mom never let me do anything around the house, never taught me anything. I wanted to teach you what I had learned and you weren't the least bit interested."

I stop, stunned. I understand! I suddenly understand—a moment of what? Insight, empathy, God?

"Oh Mom; how awful!"

I put my arms around her and together we cry our hurts. Moments later I explain that I have to leave. Father isn't upstairs so I just get in the car and cry my way home. When I arrive home the phone rings. Father, now more upset than before, asks me for a second opportunity to resolve these problems. "We cannot let things stand like this." I agree.

This time we are all more restrained. I explain that I'm not asking their permission, I'm just informing them of my intention to marry Hayward. If they choose not to welcome him, so be it. I also state that I never again want to hear the word "marriage" from either of them.

Father affirms that they both love me and are very proud of me.

And this is the beginning of a new, loving and mutually reciprocal adult relationship. I feel cleansed, almost euphoric, and relieved to be going back to my sanctuary, my home, and the challenges that lie ahead. Father thanks me for being so considerate in driving to Kitchener, not knowing that my motive was entirely selfish. I didn't want discord to contaminate my new environment.

And there are challenges ahead. The plans to move to the mall are complete and the date is set. We will have a separate wing and a separate entrance for the Family Counselling Service. In preparation for the move Frank hires a new secretary, Inge Nugent, to work exclusively with us. This, no doubt, solves Frank's (or May's) discomfort with the "Millie situation" and resolves the problem of space, but the joy of the move is short-lived. I learn that the provincial government has cut off funding for "preventative work," that this unit is in danger of losing its funding base. Frank, Barney Lewis and the advisory board develop strategies to inform the community of the pending crisis and begin negotiations with the city of Oshawa to fund the entire service. And I learn what a community development worker is and does.

"I read your reports, Dale, and what you're doing is 'casework with groups.'"

"What do you mean, Frank? If this isn't "community work," what is?"

"I can't really explain it but it isn't this," Frank says as he hands me back my records with a look of concern or disappointment or disproval—it is difficult for me to read his facial expression or his body language. "Read this; I think it will help," he says—and indeed, it did help. A paradigm shift, another "aha" that permanently alters my comprehension and interventions with systems—all systems:

couple systems, family systems, group, community, political, even national and international, systems. Now I can be strategic in my involvement with the world of Oshawa.

I spend considerable time with Frank and May listening to their experiences with people, the movers and shakers that impact our work, and developing warm relationships with the Johnson family. May and I share "girl talk" and I relish the opportunity to watch her feed and nurture the newest addition to the Johnson family. Inge and I also develop a warm friendship, another opportunity for girl talk that nurtures me.

The politicking begins in earnest. On June 25 an article in the *Oshawa Journal* reads, "Counselling grounded by lack of funds." Frank and I outline the problem, relate the many community activities that have been and are utilizing our services and stress the need for community support. People are encouraged to write letters to the Board of Directors, CAS, to the City Council, to the Social Planning Council and the newspapers. On June 27 the *Journal* reports a response from the Oshawa chapter of Parents Without Partners commending FCS and me, personally, for having responded so quickly to their request for a leadership training program for their volunteer leaders. On July 8 an editorial reads, "Public support to protest cutbacks," reporting that four letters have been received quoting my emotional plea for five hundred such letters. The Social Planning Council is reported to be advocating on our behalf. The article also reports that a plan has been developed for our board to approach the City Council for funds in the fall.

On July 9 the *Journal* writes a two-page spread about my career experiences with the Ministry of Reform Institutions entitled, "She'd fight like the devil to keep a child out of reformatory"—not relevant to the current situation but keeping us visible.

In October, the study I conducted on apartment living and the impact on families is given a full-page report in the *Journal*, highlighting urgent changes that need to be implemented by various levels of government. The Federal Ministry of Housing requests a copy of that report and a copy is presented to our City Council.

And I'm experiencing "fast-track learning" regarding the potency of the media!

I'm now anxious to gather together these individual people I have met, all of whom are contributing to the well-being of the community. Still with limited financial resources, I decide to call this party a "talk-in" so that I won't have to supply food and liquid refreshments, and I schedule it as a midweek experience. Everyone I invite is delighted to come, and what an experience we share: a virtual think tank of movers and shakers, including Reverend Henry Fischer (Lutheran); Reverend Tom Gemmell (Anglican) and his wife Mary (nurse); Father Paul Woodcroft (Roman Catholic priest); Deaconess Barbara Copp, Director, YWCA, who has served as a United Church missionary in Korea for several years; Steve Zubkavitch, a lawyer, and his wife May also a nurse; Joyce Askwith, an archaeologist presently working with the CAS who has lived several years in Japan; Frank and May (another nurse); and Mary Laframboise, a second-year graduate student from the School of Social Work, Wilfred Laurier University, who is now working with us under Frank's supervision.

The evening explodes into "big-picture" visualizations and ideas as to how to change the world, never mind just changing Oshawa. Steve and May leave early, after a pizza fest (I do manage to feed the flock with group donations). Much to my surprise, Steve asks if he can host the next talk-in. This core group, plus add-ons, meets every four to six weeks—each host inviting one or two new participants, including a Buddhist teacher and a town planner with a degree in architectural design from a university in Switzerland, a Coptic Christian from the Middle East.

In addition to meeting a personal hunger that most of us expressed, this group becomes a vital networking resource to support all of us with our many community projects.

From this group and from Ron Dancey, a senior administrator with the Department of Social Services, I learn about the intensity of social problems in the area of town referred to as "the south end." With this information, a map of the city and various coloured pins, I set about to research the locations of our counselling clients with a broad category of social problems. This highlights for me the intensity of individual/couple/family issues concentrated in the south end of town. Observing this data, I have a sense of where and how I might proceed. Aha, I sense a "community development project."

The Ontario Housing Corporation has located five rows of subsidized town housing units in the Phillip Murray-Cedar Street area of the south end, near the General Motors plant. We have several direct service clients who live in this area. One of our clients, Mattie, a single woman with two elementary school-age children, a petite, fun-loving, sensual woman with a delightful sense of humour and a flair for the dramatic, tells me that she is having an affair with the husband of a woman who lives in a house in the opposite row; and she reports that her next-door neighbour is antisocial and doesn't look after her kids. Mattie and other neighbours have made frequent calls to the police to stop her kids from destroying the neighbourhood. As we talk it becomes clear that, in spite of the proximity, or perhaps because of it, no one actually knows their neighbours. I suggest that Mattie might want to invite all the women in her row to have coffee and chat some morning next week and I will be happy to come and facilitate a discussion that might invite closer and supportive relationships. And Mattie does just that.

After introductions, I thank the women for coming together and explain who I am and that I'm interested in knowing what kinds of problems the women and their families are experiencing in this neighbourhood. I ask how the agency and I might be helpful to them. Troubles and feelings gush out like a fire hydrant that has the misfortune to get in the way of a drunk driver. Just one woman, that "next-door neighbour," remains quiet.

"Sara, do you have some thoughts or feelings you would like to express?" Sara, in a very quiet voice, begins to talk, and the room becomes still.

"Last night I sat on my bedroom floor and thought of different ways to kill myself. I have nothing to live for. Bob, my husband, is an alcoholic. He's never here to help me with the kids, and when he is here he just makes things worse by yelling and screaming and frightening the kids and me. He hasn't hit me yet but I'm terrified that he will. The kids are well out of control and don't listen to me at all. Little Bobby is being beaten up by some bullies at school and doesn't want to go anymore. And no one cares. I might as well be dead."

Mattie gets up instantly and wraps her arms around Sara, who begins to weep. Suggestions come pouring forth, offers to look after the kids after school, offers to have an older boy walk to and from school with little Bobby, expressions of sympathy, concern and caring.

Before I leave, someone suggests that she host the next coffee get-together and this becomes an ongoing weekly experience. Before the week is out, I get a phone call from a woman in the opposite row asking if I would come for coffee to talk with the women in her row. Several months later, someone from the third row makes the same request. Individual requests for counselling follow. Months later, I learn that the incidence of police calls to this project has been significantly reduced. And still later, the president of the Tenants Association asks me if I will come to one of their meetings.

Meanwhile I'm keenly aware that August has long since come and gone and no Hayward. Where is he? Why hasn't he called? Did he have a similar experience to mine? Are his mom and his two older sisters and their husbands giving him a difficult time? I've decided not to marry Hayward, but that doesn't ease the sense of foreboding I feel—the gnawing sense of loneliness, of loss, of grief. I have searched my soul and I know that I'm just not cut out to be a politician's wife, someone who entertains and plans gala parties. I don't know whether I could find employment in my field, whether I'd be credible in supporting those who are dealing with problems that I know nothing about. Would I be accepted in this culture, a white woman married to a black man? I don't even know how to cook, let alone Jamaican food—all this without the support of my family, my sisters? But my head doesn't rule my heart! I can't just stop loving.

I share a little with May and Inge, but very little. It's all too painful, too complex. I just motor on, like the community of Oshawa itself, until I hit a sinkhole in the road.

I answer the late evening phone call rather hesitantly. "Hello?" I ask, ready to hang up instantly if this is an unpleasant intrusion.

"Hi, it's Hayward. How are you?"

"Hayward? What's wrong? You don't sound very good." Actually I couldn't tell if I was hearing static on the line or if Hayward had been drinking and was inebriated.

"I just called to tell you I'm getting married."

"Married? Well ... uh, that's nice. I, uh ... wish you well. Thanks for letting me know."

After a long pause Haywood says "Okay ... good-bye then."

I don't understand why I'm so upset. I wasn't going to marry him; I was getting used to the silence. I cry myself to sleep, determined to back up, find my way around this unexpected obstacle on the road and continue to motor on.

And that is just what happens to the Family Counselling Service. On May 1, 1970, we motor on over to City Hall, on Centre Street just south of King, and become a special service of the corporation of the city of Oshawa under the jurisdiction of the Department of Social Services. We settle into one of the vacant floors adjacent to a seldom-used large meeting room. Frank reports to the director, Herb Chesebrough, who in turn reports to Alderman Jim Potticary, the commissioner of the Department of Social Services. We can now focus on thriving as opposed to surviving.

Those of us working with the Social Planning Committee's Youth Task Force are concerned about what challenges bored teenagers, the hippie culture that is evidenced now in our community and the problem of drugs will mean for us this summer. Tom Gemmell, chair of the Downtown Ministerial Association, indicates that this group is interested in developing a youth drop-in centre, picking up on the work of Barbara Copp at the YWCA. Several of us form an ad hoc committee to map out a plan of action to move quickly on this idea. St. George's Anglican Church, under the leadership of Canon Ongley, agrees to put up the funds for us to hire a detached youth worker and provides office space for whoever we hire. The city agrees to "rent" us the old Legion building, just blocks away, for a dollar a year. And the ad hoc committee sets about to hire a person in time for the summer break.

Ian Gamble, a young social worker from London, Ontario, arrives to meet with us and the team of volunteers who are being trained by me to "staff" the centre. Several young workers from the Department of Social Services, a few high school teachers and other interested adults form the core group along with some teenage leaders—and we're ready to rumble.

We didn't expect to "rumble" so literally and so soon. Three nights after the centre opens, two of the core volunteers—Lynda Simpson and John Sauriol—and I are chatting away in my apartment in the early hours of the morning. We're interrupted by a phone call at 1:00 a.m. It's Ian.

"I'm calling from the police station, Dale. Can you get down here? The centre was raided and I've been arrested along with one of the volunteers and some kids."

"Hang in, Ian. One of us will be down as quickly as possible."

I call Henry Fischer, who agrees to go and rescue Ian, and the three of us wait for Ian to arrive with the details. At 3:00 a.m. we get the story. Ian reports that he, along with a few young fellows, was beaten up. That doesn't come as a surprise given that Ian looks very much like a hippie with his long hair, torn jeans and a couple of days' growth of facial hair.

Tom and Henry meet with the police chief the following day. The ad hoc committee meets to discuss possible solutions to the escalating confrontations between the police and young people. We come up with the idea of planning a Police/Youth Forum Day. This takes place the following month. We recruit facilitators from the ad hoc committee, the FCS and the Social Planning Council to help the two conflicting groups talk to each other. And the benefits of our intervention are immediate: no more police raids and, our volunteers report, a less belligerent attitude towards those "fucking cops."

Throughout this period I continue to visit with my parents, spending at least a weekend a month in the family home. Neither parent asks me about Hayward nor do I hear the word "marriage." Our relationships continue to be loving. Mom and I are becoming so much more affectionate with one another. I bring home my laundry on the pretence that I haven't had time to do this myself and Mom is so pleased to help me. I'm learning how to accept love in the way in which she can offer it. Mom enables Father and me to spend time watching football by bringing us lunch on trays and sits quietly while we natter on about this great play or how awful the referees were and how many calls were clearly wrong—when our team was being penalized. Father continues to go out to the driveway and check the tires on the car, makes sure the windshield wipers are working properly and the cleaning fluid is filled up. On one such weekend the stability of the Perrin family life is threatened in a totally unpredictable way.

"Dale, get up! Dad is having a heart attack!"

"What? Don't wait for me to get dressed. Call a cab and get Dad to the hospital and then call Ken."

Near panic, I pull on my jeans and top, rush down the stairs to see a very grey, sweaty father sitting on the chesterfield, unable to talk and in considerable pain. The taxi arrives, and within minutes, so do Ken and Jan. Jan takes over, helps slip a sweater over Father's shoulder and with Ken's support, assists him to the taxi. Mom gets into the front and off they go. We are within five minutes from the K-W Hospital. I'm sure he'll make it; please, God!

Young Mike, Bayne and Bette's son, who is now sixteen and has been living with my parents for several months preparing to go to the local high school to finish his education, waits for me, and together we arrive at the hospital. Mom is crying silently and Ken is pacing. What seems like hours later the emergency doctor comes to inform us that Father has suffered a major coronary heart attack. The next forty-eight hours are critical.

Bayne is called, given compassionate leave from his posting in Germany and arrives home to carry out the "eldest son" role. Father does survive and comes home after weeks—or is it months?—of excellent care, and all of us are on notice. Life is a gift not to be taken for granted.

In September 1970 Frank and I prepare for new students: Frank will work with two students from the Carleton University School of Social Work, in Ottawa, and I will work with two students from the Wilfred Laurier School of Social Work, in Waterloo. It is great to be reconnected with Barry Sheppard and to be working with young, enthusiastic students again. Mary Laframboise, Frank's student from Waterloo, has now graduated and is hired to replace Art Veroba.

Work in the south end continues. I contact the principals of the two public schools closest to the Ontario Housing Project to determine if we can work together to resolve some of the difficulties the children from the project are experiencing in the schools. I'm welcomed by both. This opens up new channels of communication and opportunities for problem-solving. I plan to connect up with some of the churches in the area for the same reason. I learn that South Minster United Church has an A-frame temporary building that is being used for youth projects. I suspect that here, too, connecting the resources and the people in need might be productive.

The Tenants' Association has asked me to help prepare a brief to be submitted to the City Council asking for funds for playground facilities and other recreational and parking resources. Shortly after that brief is presented to the council and Councilwoman Margaret Shaw has visited the premises and met with the association, Peter Munro, the president, asks me, "What on earth have you done to Margaret Shaw?"

"What are you talking about? I've never met the woman."

"Well, she told us that you didn't know what sex you were."

"She what?"

"Yeah, that's what she said."

I assure Peter that I haven't the remotest idea of what Ms. Shaw is talking about but get that "wolf tearing at my gut" sensation. Am I to experience another episode of "did she or didn't she jump on boys and men?" or in this case, "jump on girls"? Ironically, a few days later I get into the elevator and there is "herself," Margaret Shaw. She smiles, nods good morning and I do the same. Clearly, she doesn't know who I am.

The youth drop-in centre continues with the expected problems and unexpected, but hoped for, successes. I learn from the volunteers about various conversations with the young people and hear touching stories of the kids reaching out for an empathic ear and informed guidance. I'm touched by the unselfish hours of time and energy that the core group of volunteers is giving to the project, impacting these young lives. And then I have another "strange" encounter with Margaret Shaw, a telephone call.

"Miss Perrin, this is Margaret Shaw. I will give you until five o'clock this evening to get down to the Legion and clean up *your* toilets. They are disgusting. The whole place is a stinking mess. If they're not cleaned up by five, I will be calling in the Health Department to close your drop-in centre. Am I making myself clear?"

"Yes, perfectly, I will take care of it," I assure her.

I call Lynda Simpson and fortunately she is available and will round up some volunteers to get right over to clean up *my* drop-in centre toilets. Frank can't figure it out either, but since we are both busy with a multitude of community projects, a modified caseload and students, plus for Frank, administrative responsibilities that go along with working for local government, this ceases to be a concern, like yesterday's road repairs. Today's a new day.

I have ceased grieving for Hayward, at least on the conscious level, and am involved in a new whirlwind romance. I signed up for a new computer dating service, a daring adventure—the only way, I rationalized, that I would meet other professional, single men. Talat Zafors walked through my apartment door and hurled me right back into an adolescent dizziness, shades of Paul, my first love. Here is this picture-perfect, five-feet-nine-inches-tall male, with a sensuous, swarthy complexion, black hair and moustache, vibrant, dancing brown/black eyes, an athletic, cared-for body, who could very easily have stepped off the cover of an *Esquire* magazine. Very quickly we move into a "couple" relationship, though I refrain from sharing this news with Frank, May and the others. I cautiously allow them to know that I have a new man in my life but am guarded, perhaps doubting that this could be for real. Or no, the truth is, I have always been very private about anything that is intimate and meaningful to me.

Talat has just recently moved to Toronto from Turkey, leaving behind two young children and an ex-wife, and is employed as an industrial engineer at a plant located near the lakeshore. His brother and his Canadian sister-in-law live close by. During this summer of busyness, I have the opportunity of sharing a couple of weekends with them and some of Talat's brother's friends at their cottage. On one such occasion I have the opportunity to meet Talat's two children, an eleven-year-old son and a ten-year-old daughter, who are just arriving from Turkey accompanied by Talat's closest friend. I am struck by how much the little girl looks like me. I picture a white picket fence, a warm red-brick house with white shutters—Talat, the children and me, the fairy godmother who makes all dreams come true.

My private life develops quietly. Not so with my professional life. The fall of '70 takes off like a marathon runner at the beginning of a 25k race. My agenda is jammed with activity, allowing little time for chatting. The students have arrived and are settling in. Frank, too, is in and out of the office fulfilling his multiple tasks. The vibrant colours of this alive and thriving service match the colours of the season.

The activities and the colours begin to fade as November greyness heralds the onset of a cold, bleak winter. The mood inside the agency inexplicably parallels what is observable just outside the windows. Late afternoon on December 15 the first gust of coldness jars my being and wakes me into action. Inge informs me that May has just called and is unaware of the staff party that is to take place at my home this evening. The date was selected specifically to enable the Johnsons to attend.

"May, what's up? Are you not coming to the party tonight?"

"Frank didn't mention any party to me, Dale. He's out of town," I'm informed in an unfriendly voice.

Frank had alluded to the fact that it may well be time for him to consider a career move but hadn't been specific regarding why, where and when.

"Is Frank out of town on a job interview?"

"Oh no, he's just talking to a man," May says quickly, with an edge of defensiveness.

Frank is not in the office the next day but drops over on the 21 for a brief chat. He apologizes for missing the party but offers no explanation. I don't get it, but then, Frank has always been a bit of a mystery. I'm intuitive but Frank gives very few cues either verbally or nonverbally as to what he thinks and feels. I have learned to rely only on whatever words he shares and frequently even they require interpretation. Nowhere is this more obvious than in the talk-in experiences that Frank and May have recently missed.

The following day, Frank and I are alone in the office and now I have the opportunity to confront Frank about my discomforts.

"Frank, let's talk. I'm experiencing tensions around the office. Little things like inconsistency among staff regarding the matter of recording and the use of the central appointment book and inconsideration regarding use of the coffee equipment seem to be putting people on edge. And you, Frank, seem to be quite disinterested and uninvolved in providing leadership. And I don't understand what is happening between us. You seem so distant."

"If you are having problems, Dale, then I suggest you raise them at the next staff meeting."

"But the students will be here then. That's not a great way to start with a new group of students."

"I guess that's your problem then."

"Frank, what's happening here? What's going on between us?"

"Our relationship has changed, sure. My perception of you has certainly changed, and I'm not prepared to discuss this. I don't want you to fall apart—and I've got things to do."

I learn later this evening from Inge what this is all about. She tells me that during her week off she phoned Frank to ask if she could talk with him. In that conversation he affirmed that we do have problems in the agency and that I have caused them.

"He says that you are a controlling person and have a need to dominate. He says that you constantly controlled the talk-in get-togethers and spoiled the evening for everyone."

I'm shocked. Do I fall apart? No; why on earth would Frank think I would? But I do feel blindsided. What's happening? Why now? How come I didn't have any sense of this before? Thank goodness Christmas is coming and I can get grounded again.

I spend time with my third "sister," Gwyn Griffith, another friend of Shelley's who has been welcomed into the bosom of the Perrin family. The three of us "daughters" (excluding Maggie, the artistic one, who stays back to finish knitting her last gift) and the parents drive through the city singing carols and marvelling at the Christmas lights, an activity that becomes a highly valued tradition.

Fortified with intimate sharing, an assortment of thoughtful gifts, sensually pleasurable food and drink, hugs and kisses and a father who is very much alive and able to deliver his traditional highly emotional speech, I'm ready to face—whatever.

The first week of January 1971: a new year, hopefully a fresh beginning. The new students are a delight. The staff meeting Friday morning is a little strange but leaves me with a sense of optimism.

Frank informs us at the morning meeting that he's seriously considering a position in Kingston, Ontario. He suggests that it would be good for us to use these meetings to plan the future growth of the agency so that it will continue progressing after he leaves. He concludes the meeting by stating that we should begin to examine our relationships—look at ourselves and "put all our cards on the table."

Now I think we are going to engage in a healing process and get our engines revved for takeoff '71. I'm surprised to see Inge sitting at her desk waiting for me at 5:15 PM after a very busy week.

"I need to talk with you, Dale," she says, visibly upset. "When Frank left the office tonight his parting words were, 'I hope you never leave Dale because she's really going to need you.' I really have to tell you what's going on."

And tell me she does. And Frank is right: I do fall apart and cry like I don't remember crying before, but not until I'm safe in my sanctuary, my own sacred space. Inge comes with me and when the door shuts behind us, I dissolve into heavy sobs. Inge is upset and calls Tom Gemmell, hoping that he will know how to support me and help me "come back." Tom arrives by 6:30 PM and I'm still unable to stop sobbing. In due course Inge shares the following story.

At Frank's request, Inge met with him at his home on January 7. He informed Inge that the agency was divided in two: Frank, Mary and Marjorie against Inge and me. He informed Inge that I had ruined the agency; that I had ruined the community (and that Reverend Tom Gemmell and Reverend Henry Fischer shared this view); that I was interested in his job and wanted to control the agency; that I was pushing him to do things that he didn't want to do; that in the event of his leaving the agency (possibly March 31) he would have to arrange for Marjorie to assume the responsibility of acting director; that I was not considering the best interests of my clients and that he had doubts about my activities in relationship to clients; that I was controlling the talk-in groups and ruining these evenings for all concerned; and that I was the cause of Mary's earlier depression. He suggested that Inge reconsider her position and join the three of them against me and that if she did not do so, I would ruin her as well.

Tom is overwhelmed with this diatribe and asks permission to call Henry Fischer. He volunteers that he does not agree with Frank's perceptions of my involvement with the community and that in his perception the talk-in group looked to me for leadership. Henry agrees to meet with Tom, Inge and me Sunday night to help us, and Frank if he is willing, to get through this crisis. Both men agree to confidentiality and I'm soon left alone to suffer through the weekend.

Sunday evening Inge, Tom, Henry and I meet to sort out what's happening and what we can possibly do to fix it. We agree not to involve other staff or the students but to approach Frank as a group; to ask permission to have Tom and Henry act as facilitators, who care about both of us; to enable Frank and me, and Inge, to come to a comfortable place with each other. Tom calls Frank in spite of the lateness of the hour and is invited to go to Frank's home. At 1:30 a.m. he arrives back to inform us that Frank is willing to meet with me alone at his home or on "neutral ground." With persuasion, he consents to having the four of us come to his home.

From 1:45 a.m. until 5:00 a.m. we enter into a one-sided, crazy-making process that leaves me exhausted, shell-shocked and traumatized, with not a hint as to what on earth provoked this crisis. Frank sits, shielded behind cigarette smoke, eyes down, his body rigid, slight tremors as he raises cigarettes to his mouth, never once looking directly at any one of us, and repeats a few "imprinted in concrete" statements: We will only discuss relationship issues at a full staff meeting involving the four students; he intends to arrange for Marjorie McKibbon to assume the acting director role when he leaves the agency and in so doing will inform Herb Chesebrough, Director of the Department of Social Services, and through him, the Social Service Committee of the City Council. As a concession, or at least as a way to get us out of his living room, Frank agrees to meet with me and the two men for a further meeting.

The following week Frank is out of the office or unavailable. On Friday, Mary, Marjorie and the students meet with Frank at the staff meeting that I'm unable to attend since I presumed the meeting was to be cancelled and arranged for a home visit. Following this Mary and Marjorie do not make eye contact with me nor speak with me and only talk with Inge when it relates to work. One of my students inquires about "the problems at the agency" and I inform him that

I prefer that the students not get involved and that their learning experiences not be impacted.

I learn later that at eight thirty that morning Inge telephoned Frank to relate that she was going to take the day off, as compensation for accumulated overtime, to prepare for her daughter's wedding. Frank tells her to get to the agency immediately or "don't bother coming back at all."

The rest of the month Frank's "strategy" to force me and Inge to resign "voluntarily" becomes clear, shades of his manipulation of Art Veroba. The isolation and hostile atmosphere escalates; now Mary shrinks, attempting to melt into the wall, if she is unfortunate enough to be caught walking in the corridor when I'm coming or going. Frank pulls rank and informs me that I will appear in his office every Monday morning for "supervision," a far cry from the "horizontal structure versus vertical structure," the "professional system" he professes to practice. During those sessions Frank does not respond to pleasantries or make eye contact. Fortunately, to endure "long silences," I learned in my work in the treatment centre with boys how to stare at a spot just above the eyes and appear to be open for dialogue. I could estimate within minutes when the hour was up by the number of cigarettes Frank smoked—a wee, small victory, but then, it is impossible to out-passive a passive person. Inge points out that Frank placed in my inbox most of the referrals that came in during the month.

I know that sooner or later I will buckle under this pressure. I set about to get consultation from legal, medical and collegial resources. Barry Sheppard, ever the mentor and wise man, tells me, "I told you so"; the executive director of the Professional Association of Social Workers tells me that they don't like to get involved in these matters unless it is absolutely necessary; the lawyer tells me to "document" and suggests a "strategy."

The drama continues to escalate through the month of February. I do cave in to a flu bug and miss a week of work; I return to find five more new referrals waiting for me. Frank informs me that I will need to get a medical certificate, and I receive a phone call from Herb Chesebrough requesting "a coffee."

Herb is a somewhat disheveled gentleman with a weather-beaten face more characteristic of fishermen than civil servants. He begins our casual, designed to be nonthreatening session with, "Frank has been sharing with me that a conflict exists between him and both you and Inge Nugent. He is concerned and totally unaware as to why these difficulties exist. Can you enlighten me?"

Thank you, Steve (the lawyer)! "Well, I have prepared a documentation of what has been happening and I'll be happy to elaborate," I say, handing Herb my typed report. *Do you think maybe we are about to introduce some sanity into this "locked ward experience"?*

Herb puts down the report and says, "You know, Dale, that if I was to ask ten people in Oshawa who runs the Family Counselling Service, nine out of ten would say Dale Perrin."

"I can't help that, Herb. I have been hired to work in the community so it follows that I will be visible." No response. *Crash, bang! I'm still in the locked ward!*

I do inform Herb of the steps I have taken to get professional advice and indicate a strong desire to resolve these difficulties and continue with my present job, expressing that this has been the most creative and productive social work experience I have encountered.

Just a week later I arrive at work after lunch, begin supervision with one of the students and am interrupted by a call from Frank informing me that I'm to be in Herb's office at two o'clock for a meeting.

I'm greeted by three men: Frank, Herb and Jim Potticary, chairman of the Social Service Committee of the City Council. Jim is the epitome of the seasoned politician: tall and dressed in the latest-style suit with matching everything. I'm informed that *we* have three months to resolve our differences. If we fail to do so, further action will be taken. Frank is to meet with Herb or Ron Dancey, the second-in-command, on a weekly basis.

Frank suggests that we should discuss relationship issues at a full staff meeting, implying that the students would be present; again I refuse. I explain to the other men that Frank has had several discussions with staff and students and I have not. I ask permission to talk with other staff and am graciously allowed to do so.

"And," I venture to say, "I would appreciate if you, Frank, would be willing to share with this group and me just what relationship issues we are talking about and what it is that I've done to upset you?"

Herb interrupts. "It is not important to go into these matters now. You may return to your office now. Ask Inge to come down here immediately."

In a rage, I approach Marjorie and request an appointment. She agrees, but not now. Mary is nowhere to be found.

Later that evening my male student arrives at my apartment and with Inge present informs me that Frank's female student, who shares accommodations with my female student, has become a good friend with May Johnson. She informed my students that based on ethical considerations she is siding with Frank in "this conflict." May has told her that I relate better to men than to women, that I spent too much time with Frank after the agency had gotten off the ground and that I had interfered with the Johnsons' marriage.

Oh Barry, how smart you are! I now understand why May asked me if I related differently to men than to women. Time to revisit Barry and Steve, the lawyer, but not before I get yet another surprise.

"Hello," I reluctantly answer in response to the persistent ringing of the telephone. *How much more can I handle today?*

"Hi," responds a familiar, sensuous voice. "It's Hayward."

Oh my God, my shaman has arrived to heal my wounded soul? Or to break me even further?

"Would you be agreeable to a cup of coffee?"

"But, but … your wife?" *Why is my heart drumming out "the green, green grass of home"?*

"It's over. We are in the process of separating: coffee, please? I'll understand if you say no, but I really want to see you."

"Yes, oh yes, if you're really sure *it's* over."

We agree to meet the next night in the cocktail lounge of the hotel we used to frequent. I don't dare invite him to my home. I'm afraid of the "melting phenomenon."

A very long dinner, an even longer discussion and not a word about what happened to us. I'm in trouble. I so want him back in my life; now what do I do with two loves?

Fortunately I don't have to make that decision this moment—my Scarlett O'Hara rationalization is pulled out of mothballs. I'll think about it tomorrow. As it happens, "tomorrow" I have a more pressing issue to deal with. I'm informed that I *will* attend a staff meeting at nine o'clock, with Herb Chesebrough and the permanent staff—no students. The onslaught begins. Frank sits back quietly, an ever-so-thinly-disguised smile of satisfaction flickers across an otherwise blank face. He lets the women go at me since they all agree that I have a problem.

"You are the one who went to the Johnsons' house in the middle of the night. What do you expect from a relationship with Frank? Are you not asking for something inappropriate? Why should Frank be more intimate with you than he is with us? What right do you have upsetting the Johnson family like this when Frank and May have been so good to you when you came here?"

"Just what have I done to the Johnson family?"

"Well, when it gets to the point when the family gets threats ..."

I interrupt, "What threats?"

"It really doesn't matter," Frank says. "We don't have to get into this."

Mary picks up the hot potato. "Well, you had no reason to involve Tom and Henry. You should have brought up your problems during a staff meeting, or at least talked to Marjorie and me first."

My attempts to explain why I chose not to involve the other staff, why I chose to ask for confidential professional intervention, are not heard—they are passed over without comment in a manner I might expect from an audience of the hearing and visually impaired, the same righteous indifference that I experienced just a few minutes ago when I shared my written documentation.

Herb does speak to the "bringing in outsiders" issue. "We must be aware that we are City Hall employees and that problems should be dealt with internally."

Before the meeting is adjourned Marjorie expresses concern for my well-being. "Your report should be read by a psychiatrist, Dale. It is such a nightmare. I am really concerned about you."

I manage to mumble out one concern, that I was receiving a disproportionate number of intakes, and am told that if I'm having trouble organizing my time that I will have to learn to prioritize. I just don't know when to quit. I'm totally incapable of pulling out of my right brain a flamboyant Scarlett O'Hara "knock them on their butts" exit line.

Stumbling out of the meeting, beaten and abandoned as road kill, I make a foolish attempt to talk with Marjorie. She dismisses me quickly with the comment that perhaps I am "too dependent" on Frank. Mary also dismisses me, with the comment, "It's too late."

Do I know enough to roll over and play dead? No, I call Tom and Henry to come and meet with me two days later. I haven't seen or heard from them since our midnight madness. We have a brief meeting and I thank them for their effort to help me and tell them that I will be dusting off my resume and beginning a job search. I share very little about recent events.

Nine AM sharp, an emergency staff meeting. Herb confronts me with, "Have I not been *very clear* that we are not to discuss agency problems with anyone outside of the agency?"

All eyes turn to me. I mumble in the affirmative.

"Then why have you gone against this? You have, haven't you?"

"If you mean did I speak with Tom and Henry, yes. Did I discuss 'city business'? No."

"I regret to do this but I must ask for your resignation today or I will take other action. You have been insubordinate."

I get up, leave the office and City Hall and head straight to Steve's place.

Steve advises me that he cannot take on my case; that this is a "political hot potato" and that I will need a lawyer outside of the area. He articled with Nell Starr, the Perry Mason of the slander world and head of a prestigious law firm in Toronto, and he contacts him on my behalf to see if he would represent me against the city of Oshawa. He agrees, and an appointment is set. I return to the office and am informed by Frank that Mr. Terrance Stevens, the personnel director, wants to see me.

Mr. Stevens sits at a well-organized desk. He gets up from his leather chair and introduces himself. He indicates that I'm to be seated. I'm informed that neither Frank nor Herb has the authority to fire me; that privilege is his alone and he intends to do his own investigation. When I hand him a copy of my report, he says that he does not want to read my documentation—the investigation, I conclude, is to hear what "they" have to say, not me. His concern is City Hall. He appears reluctant to accept my statement that I did not share city business with outsiders.

I inform Mr. Stevens that I consulted a lawyer, have an appointment scheduled for March 12 and am considering three litigations: illegal dismissal against the corporation of the city of Oshawa; a slander suit against Frank Johnson; and a breach of professional ethics suit against Frank Johnson. At least I get his attention.

I'm told to take the afternoon off as "sick leave" and to report on Monday as usual and I'm to maintain confidentiality about this conversation.

I take what is left of me over to the Midtown Mall, the Country Hearth restaurant, to meet a male friend for lunch—and who walks in but Frank, Tom and Henry? I feast on the irony but can't digest food.

Monday morning I stop at Mr. Stevens's office and inform him of Frank's "violation," presuming that Frank will have to be fired, no? I report that on the weekend I learned that Frank's student shared with a colleague at the Addiction Research Foundation that I had been fired. I presume Frank violated confidentiality, no?

Thirty minutes later I'm called back to Mr. Stevens' office. I have misunderstood his directive. I'm to go home immediately and stay there until he calls me. He has already met with the mayor and his investigation will soon be complete.

"Soon" is the next day. Mr. Stevens and Herb Chesebrough inform me that I'm to resign immediately or be dismissed. When I ask for the grounds for dismissal, I'm informed that the decision is based on information Mr. Stevens received during his investigation. I request that I be allowed to keep my appointment with the lawyer on March 12 before making a decision. I'm given until March 10. Mr. Stevens will be meeting with the Board of Control that morning and he wants "the matter" all over before then. If I oblige he will recommend that I be given "grievance pay" up until May 31, though he can't guarantee the decision of the board. I do get to see my Perry Mason in his downtown Bay Street office, an office bigger than my entire apartment. Nell Starr is a striking man. I can't believe he is as soft-spoken and gentle in the courtroom as he is as he talks with me this evening.

"I have reviewed all your material very carefully, Miss Perrin. I can tell you this. You will win an illegal dismissal suit. You will win a slander suit. It will take two years. You will be awarded three months compensation pay *and* you will be unemployable. The decision is up to you."

"But that's not fair. That isn't right."

"True, but it is the reality of the situation. No employer will risk hiring you. Do you think you can get a job?"

"Yes, I think so."

"Well, I advise you to resign. I will instruct you as to the 'conditions regarding a reference' and suggest you go ahead and find another job."

"Yes, you're absolutely right. But it's not fair."

"No, it isn't."

On March 10 I resign and on March 16, one day after my thirty-third birthday, I receive my "Registered, Personal and Confidential" notification.

Compensation pay? No.

I take time to recuperate. Before I heal enough to invest serious energy in finding new employment, I learn from Lynda Simpson, the social service worker employed in the Department of Social Services and volunteer at the youth drop-in centre, that Ron Dancey (the second–in-command to Herb Chesebrough) related that Herb had information about me that "nobody knows" and that is why I got fired. Other staff in that department inform Lynda that I told Herb to "fuck off" and that was the reason for my dismissal. Indirectly, through Henry Fischer, I learn that Inge Nugent and I have been seen holding hands in the Family Counselling office and that was the reason for dismissal. And a former teenage client of mine comes to my apartment one evening and informs me that one of her buddies, a ward of Jim Potticary's, the Commissioner of Social Services, is telling this story: Jim and his wife are entertaining another councilman and his wife for dinner. Jim shares the news that I got fired for sleeping with my clients, male and female.

And then Ross Gibson, the third most powerful member of the council, telephones me requesting information about my resignation. He senses that an injustice has been committed and he has an appointment with the mayor, at which time he intends to request that my case be reopened. He requests a copy of my curriculum vitae and any documentation I might have. After a quick call to the lawyer I'm instructed to give Mr. Gibson my documented material with no editorial comments so that he may draw his own conclusions. Mr. Gibson drops by after four, invites himself in for a drink (he just happens to have a bottle of scotch with him) and proceeds to get very inebriated. A quick call to Inge for help and she comes to witness my knight in shining armor attempting to corner me in my bathroom. I guess he is determined to find out firsthand just what my sexual preference is. Undeterred and showing not the least inclination to leave my apartment, dear Ross Gibson determines to wow us with his interpretation of what is behind the British-Arab conflict in the Suez crisis, a crisis resulting from the fact the British women prefer Arab men as lovers because of their superior endowments. A quiet plea to Inge results in a commitment to stay with me until Talat arrives at 7:00.

I quickly whisk Talat into the kitchen, explain the situation and silently pray that Mr. Gibson is too drunk to notice the swarthy complexion of my sweet Talat and make some inappropriate remark.

I explain to Mr. Gibson that Talat and I are going out to dinner and offer to drive him home. In spite of our protests, he is convinced that he can drive himself; and since we decline his offer to go to dinner with us, he rides down the elevator with us, staring intently at Talat with a puzzled look on his face, and reluctantly heads for the door. I mumble something to the effect that I have forgotten my keys and we turn and ride the elevator back up.

Now secure again in my cleansed sanctuary, I collapse into Talat's arms and dissolve into tears of despair, my last hope swimming in a cesspool of alcoholism.

A few days later, I receive a call from Mr. Gibson requesting that I meet with him at the golf club. He would like to report on his interview with the mayor. I learn that the mayor has received a letter from the Tenant's Association demanding that I be hired back and assigned exclusively to work with their project. I learn that the mayor refuses to "open up that can of worms again." I thank him for his efforts on my behalf and make a quick exit.

I learn that the kids at the drop-in centre are preparing a petition demanding that I get my job back and continue working with them. I receive a phone call from Lloyd Weiderick, principal of Canon Public School, offering sympathy. He is willing to give me a reference if I need one.

In all this drama I ask myself, where is the heart and soul, the integrity, in the helping professions? Where is God, love, in the profession of the ministry? Where is integrity in the political system? Where is justice in the justice system?

I conclude that heart, soul, integrity and justice do exist—in ordinary, everyday good people, the Inges in the world. Thank God for ordinary good people, for Inge who goes on to suffer way beyond my departure from Oshawa.

And where am I? How can it be that I get fired from not one but two jobs? I haven't met any other social worker who has been fired once, let alone twice. Will I ever get to work again in the field of my choice?

POLITICS, PARANOIA AND PAINFUL CONFRONTATIONS

The issues here parallel those identified in the last chapter.

Rejection is so painful. Have you had such an experience? Perhaps not the experience of being "fired" but of being rejected by someone, a group or team of people, or an authority figure?

What were your thoughts, feelings, behaviours? Were you able to share your feelings with anyone? What supports or judgments did you receive and from whom?

Are these thoughts, feelings or behaviours familiar? If so, can you recall an experience from your childhood where you first experienced or formulated these thoughts and decided to behave (or not) in this familiar way?

Have you experienced an interaction with an important person that seemed to you to be "crazy"? If so, how did that impact your self-esteem? Your core belief about others, the world and what you can expect "out there"?

What did you do with your feelings? Did you cope with this trauma the same way you have handled situations and feelings in the past, or have you changed?

THE APOCALYPSE

I am at peace now as I experience the waves of Lake Ontario lap ever so gently against the sandy shores of Darlington Park. The nuclear plant that provides energy for over a hundred thousand homes in the world around Oshawa/Toronto is just over there, but I'm not concerned about the potential for catastrophic events happening. I'm healing from the one I've just experienced.

I look. I watch the seagulls cutting an uncoordinated pattern of movements against the backdrop of a perfectly cloudless, faded blue sky, squawking out of harmony with the hypnotic music of the waves. I watch the sandpipers, at least a hundred of them, scurrying back and forth to the water's edge. As the waves come in and cover the sandy shore, the sandpipers pit-a-pat farther inland. As the waves recede, they go again venturing out to chase the waves—never allowing themselves to get wet. How like Frank, Marjorie and Mary—never moving beyond their comfort zone, never risking finding out the truth lest it disturb the ground of their being.

And dear Talat, I wonder what is disturbing the ground of his being. How can such a vibrant, passionate, loving man, a man who describes his world and his dreams in exotic blues and greens, who describes sunsets bathing his Istanbul in hues of oranges, peaches and shades of purple, suddenly become a morose, quiet, lethargic father? What has happened to the man who just recently sat naked in front of me, lotuslike, in the middle of the living-room floor, drinking wine, his love-saturated eyes bathing my body as his words lulled me into a healing comfort zone? I rarely see him now that he is fathering his beautiful kids. I could help him if he let me; but will he?

And Leonard Wengle, will he let me? Does he have the courage to hire me and let me contribute to the community, the clients, the agency?

He does; at least he hires me. After a second interview I'm hired to begin my new position as senior social worker responsible for a caseload of direct service clients, supervision of some of the junior staff and supervision of graduate students from the University of Toronto, School of Social Work. I will be able to develop a community-focused service as the agency grows. I begin July 1; well, actually July 5.

"Dear God, Maggie, it's been almost four months," I say in one of our lengthy phone conversations. "If I don't make it in this setting, I'm finished as a social worker."

"I hope you aren't going to start this new position with a defeatist attitude, Dale. That's a sure way to set yourself up for another bad experience."

"No, no, I won't. It's just, well, the way I've been turned down by the four positions I've applied for, something is going on; the handwriting is on the wall. The executive director of the Family Services Agency in Ajax told me that he wasn't even prepared to give me a second interview. He said that he had heard about the problems in Oshawa. Rumour spreads quickly in the social work world and I'm labeled 'trouble,' just as Nell Starr, my Bay Street lawyer, predicted. And all the gossip stuff."

"Yeah, you've been a Rorschach for the whole community of Oshawa. You certainly did get weird projections. But tell me about this new job. What's the new executive director like?"

"Leonard Wengle is about my age, a senior professional social worker, probably with the same length of experience as me. He's about five feet eight, has thick, dark, slightly wavy black hair very conservatively cut, average weight, though he obviously isn't into working out. He has sparkling brown eyes hidden behind thick glasses, again conservatively styled. And he has a soft, fresh, cleanly-shaven, almost boyish-looking face. If his clothes are an indication of what I can expect—well, he's not a fashion statement. He's excited about Peel Family Services and the potential for growth. It only opened up on May 24, with Leonard, two new graduate social workers and one full-time secretary. I have a hunch this is his first executive director position, and it wouldn't surprise me to learn that he's aspiring to make this agency as progressive and renowned as the Jewish Family and Children's Services in Toronto."

"I take it he's Jewish."

"Yeah, and one of the young workers is Jewish as well; it takes me back to my student days. I didn't like my supervisor back then but I loved the agency and its progressive philosophy and programming. I'm really looking forward to this experience, a chance to help build a service from the ground level up. Leonard seemed genuinely interested in my background as a community development worker. So hopefully I'll be up and running in no time."

"Do I detect a 'but' in your tone of voice?"

"No, not really; but I do wonder why he hired me. I know he talked to Frank Johnson after our first interview and despite the warning my lawyer issued to the city of Oshawa threatening a lawsuit if they interfered with me getting another job, I don't trust Frank to not do an 'off-the-record' hatchet job."

Setting aside all niggling doubts, doubts that I'm hardly in a position to entertain, I find myself an apartment at 2440 Hurontario Street, on the main highway that extends from Lake Ontario to the south and then north to the upper regions of Peel County. The apartment is located just two blocks south of Dundas Street, the main east-west highway. The office is located at 93 Dundas Street East, on the second floor of a very old, two-story, long-since-outdated strip plaza that houses a Consumers Distributing outlet and a gym on the ground level. The two bright aspects of this location: it is only a hop-step to work and the Peel Social Planning Council is housed in the same building, adjacent to our offices. I won't have far to travel to 'move out' into the world of the movers and shakers here in the county.

Peel County encompasses a large territory of land that includes several villages and territories: Port Credit, the oldest section of development that has grown up around the lakefront; Cooksville, where the agency is located; and Streetsville, an even smaller community to the northeast of Cooksville. I learn that in the foreseeable future these three communities and Malton, a small village northwest of

Cooksville, where the Toronto International Airport is located, are to be amalgamated into a new corporate body to be known as the city of Mississauga. This too excites me—lots of potential to grow and innovate. Peel Family Services has a mandate to provide services to the entire county.

On July 5 I'm warmly welcomed by Noreen Lachapelle, the receptionist/secretary/intake worker, a slim, trim, five-feet-three, blond-haired woman in her early thirties. Leonard greets me with a warm handshake and ushers me into his office for a brief discussion before he introduces me to the counselling staff. And I experience my first "bump." In the orientation session I comment, "I'm delighted to see that the Peel Social Planning Council is right next door. Perhaps I'll drop over sometime this week and introduce myself to the executive director and see what's happening in the county."

"No, that's premature, Dale. Our first priority is to get the waiting list issue resolved. We've been inundated with requests for service, and I'm in the process of looking for another family counsellor to meet the demand. At this point, we need to establish our direct service program. *I* will represent the agency in any community-related functions."

I learn that I will be supervising Linda Williamson and the new person when that position is filled. Leonard will continue supervising Lily Shainfarber, plus the student from the University of Toronto, School of Social Work, who will be joining us in September. And off we go to meet and greet.

Lily has the first office, directly opposite Noreen's reception desk. All the offices stretching along the west wall are the same in size and décor: ten by twelve feet, walls paneled with off-white, fabric-like sections separated by black metal strips, a desk the same as Noreen's, two chairs in front of the desk, one or two extra chairs, a comfortable high-back black leather chair on casters behind the desk and a standard black phone. Unlike the outside of the strip mall, Peel Family Services (PFS) is welcoming, still alive with that "new-carpet" perfume and quietly buzzing with phones ringing and people moving about in an orderly, purposeful manner. Lily too greets me with a handshake and words of welcome as she prepares to greet the couple who have just entered the reception area.

I'm introduced to Linda—another warm welcoming handshake. My office is next to hers. On the desk Leonard has placed the PFS manuals that I'm to read before proceeding with phone calls to new clients. Once alone I decide that the office needs warmth and I determine to hit the art galleries on the weekend to see if I can find a painting to personalize my new surroundings and take "ownership." If I'm going to live in this space eight hours a day, five days a week, and one evening until nine I learn, I'd better stamp it as mine.

Hayward is delighted that I'm settled again in a new apartment.

"I've got another change coming too," he says.

"Uh-oh, what now?" I feel that familiar scare, that gripping, sinking, horrible anxiety accompanied with its now companion sense of foreboding. Hayward has been my strongest support during this arid period. He's my shaman-healer-lover who always seems to come into my life at times of crisis and our relationship has been fun and blossoming. He can't ... he can't ...

"I've registered at Carleton University to take my master's year in political science and public administration. It's only a year and then I plan to come back to Toronto."

Instant relief! "Great! Bayne and Bette are in Ottawa. Will I be able to visit you?"

"Sure, I'll be staying in residence, but I'm sure I'll be able to sneak you in through a backdoor," he says as he wraps himself around me. Enough talking—as if we ever really talked! Neither of us has approached the "whatever happened to our plan to marry?" issue; enough that he is here now, at least until mid-August.

The summer and fall months fade into winter with nothing to break the sheer monotony of doing what I did years ago except for the delight of working with Linda and one particularly salty, crusty woman, usually dressed in a blue baseball jacket, faded men's blue jeans and worn-out runners with grayish-white socks that occasionally match. Hilda, who belches louder than any eight-year-old boy I'd ever heard, arrives every week to regale me with stories of the two boys she is raising, one belonging to her unmarried daughter, though he doesn't know it, and the other from a man she needed "about as much as she needed a dose of Epsom salts." The heart and soul of this woman, the wisdom that her life of poverty and abuse has illuminated, enrich my life far more than I am able to enrich hers.

Linda, full of energy and the enthusiasm of the young professional eager to learn and grow and make a difference, ready to try something new, fuels my own passion for teaching, nurturing and creative thinking. Linda and Mike Provencher, the young male psychologist whom Leonard hired shortly after I'd started, agree to develop a ten-session group counselling experience for married couples, a weekly program that starts in October and is to end before Christmas—which at its conclusion is a very successful experience, largely through Linda's facilitation skills, her warmth and willingness to risk. Linda, too, is excited about the possibility of developing a generic social work experience, one that includes community development work.

My relationship with Talat also fades, loses its rich colours and is tucked away into my heart's treasure box of memory in sympathy with the season. No more wine and cheese picnics on riverbanks, surrounded by a world dressed in October colours, sailboats moving ever so slowly through the Trent Canal. No more equally intoxicating fantasies of "the house with the white picket fence" and two beautiful, dark-skinned, brown-eyed beauties running about shouting for attention. Talat sinks into a deeper depression and seems unwilling to do anything about it. My heart tells me to let go with love, and I do; it's enough to deal with the oppressiveness of my work world.

"Bayne, you've got to help me," I say in a brief telephone conversation. "I knew after two weeks that I'm in trouble again. How do I survive a boss who has an ego the size of the Goodyear blimp? His need to control and to be the only one who knows anything about everything is absolutely killing me! You must have met these types of authority personalities in your career. What do I do? How am I going to survive?"

"Oh yes, I know exactly what you mean. What I learned to do was to make sure that everything I wanted to initiate came out of his head, that I needed his 'wisdom and experience' to blow my nose. And I made sure he knew that I was applauding him in public. I never expressed a negative thought or implied any criticism about him to anyone in my command."

"But that's so isolating and so phony. I don't know how long I can do that."

"I think of it as 'strategy' and 'survival,' Dale. In the military you can't choose your boss."

I spend hours and hours with Leonard talking about generic social work, about the place of community development in the profession and how this agency could be instrumental in developing services across the county. Leonard nods knowingly and encourages me to think about how we can educate the entire staff so that as a group we can decide how we might want to approach this. He is concerned that we take the time to have the staff, as well as the board, buy into the idea. All this takes time and he doesn't want me to move on this before the direct service program is well-established.

I make it through to Christmas and am nurtured and refueled by my family. I register in the fall for a night course at Erindale College, an affiliate of the University of Toronto; it's an undergraduate course in philosophy and literature and this refuels my need for challenge and learning. At least my grey cells are being stimulated by considering such weighty matters as, "Is a stone the same as a person?" and hopefully this will carry me through until March 1972.

In early January, at Leonard's request, I prepare a twelve-page self-assessment of my performance for the mandatory probation evaluation; I submit it to him prior to our evaluation interview. In this session Leonard essentially agrees with my self-evaluation. I'm encouraged; this seems to be the time to introduce the two sensitive issues that I hope we can work out together: I experience Leonard as somewhat controlling and rigid administratively, somewhat compulsive about detail, and I feel patronized. His attitude towards me makes me feel like a new graduate.

I feel relieved when Leonard is open to discussing these sensitivities and appreciate that he "may have been influenced by what Frank Johnson said to me over the phone and felt an unconscious need to keep you under careful control—although I don't think so," and that "I have never worked with anyone as competent as you before and I don't quite know how to relate to you." I'm optimistic.

I never do see the evaluation that Leonard prepares "for the file" but I do get a formal letter later in the month affirming that I successfully completed the probationary period, just a few days after Catherine Ford of the *Daily Times* writes a lengthy article about me in her column called "People and Events," along with a photo of me sitting at my desk in my "office ... with its large abstract relief ... designed to give the visitor a feeling of quiet escape from pressure and tension." The article is entitled "Counselling in Group for Married Couples Successful Peel Family Services Venture." In it I applaud the success of Linda Williamson and Michael Provencher in conducting their ten-session couples group and give anecdotal descriptions of what marriage counselling is all about.

Unfortunately Mike does not get such applause when he experiences his probationary evaluation. Michael's academic program did not prepare him for the kind of work that traditional family counselling entails, and as a result, he is encouraged to seek work more suited to his programming and personality. Leonard replaces him with Bruce Whitney, an MSW with a few years' experience, whom Leonard himself will supervise.

In March, Leonard hires Bill Adams to be our full-time budget counsellor. Bill, a gentleman in his mid-fifties, fits the stereotype of "wise banker." Shirley Lance, a woman in her early thirties, is hired to work full-time as Bill's secretary. Shirley is the third woman bustling about in the reception area, joining Rita Clark, an experienced secretary/clerical worker who was teamed with Noreen several months ago. We are growing quickly and the demand for service still far exceeds our ability to respond immediately to requests for service.

When winter finally yields and submits to the inevitability of letting me back on the road, I'm off to Ottawa in my sexy red Datsun 200SX, the first car I bought without Father's help, much to his displeasure, to encounter a new experience in my relationship with Hayward: finally I'm willing to introduce him to my family—at least to Bayne and Bette.

We have a lovely animated dinner, animated in a way that does not amuse me.

"You are a chauvinist!" I say as we drive back to Hayward's residence. "You and Bayne talked up a storm and excluded me the whole evening," shades of all the Sunday family dinners when Father and his sons get to talk and Dale and her mom get to serve and be quiet.

"We did not! I was just enjoying Bayne. He's an interesting guy and we have some things in common. I just wanted to get to know him."

"Yeah, and you totally excluded me."

"Hey, come on. You were enjoying yourself. I saw the look on your face, the smiles, the knowing glances between you and Bette."

"Well, maybe a little, but you could have invited my opinion. I hate it when men presume that women don't have any political sophistication or any sense of the economic world. And I'll bet I know a hell of a lot more about hockey, baseball and football than either you or Bayne."

My bruised ego is assuaged by the giggling and gyrating on the narrow dormitory bed. I make a hasty dash for the safety of my sexy sports car after kissing Hayward good-bye at the front door of the residence in the wee hours of the morning and cherish a delightful sense of being bad and violating rules as I make my way back to Bayne and Bette's home in the suburbs on an eerily quiet predawn highway.

I sense tensions again, that tightening-in-my-gut signal, when I'm told that I missed an interesting staff meeting in late May. Leonard presented a paper entitled "Peel Family Services: Statement re Services and Programmes." During the discussion, Stan Benner (the student) suggested that we plan a day's workshop to look into the issues related to community, community practice and our agency's attitude towards preventative services, and the staff all supported this idea. My momentary excitement—wow, finally we might be getting somewhere with a staff-initiated suggestion—is instantly replaced by that familiar vice-grip scare. This news is followed by the comment that after the meeting Leonard called Stan aside and suggested that he is being biased by me.

What a strange comment! My only interactions with Stan, Lily and Bruce, all of Leonard's supervisees, are over lunch at Sam's Greasy Hamburger Joint, the tiny restaurant just across the side street from us, and an occasional beer night at the local pub just east on Dundas. And with this group, conversations are light, often silly joking and tension-releasing kibitzing (at least for me), but I file this away as a "red flag." During the days that follow, nothing further is mentioned.

At the June meeting the issue of a day's workshop is again raised by staff, and I volunteer to prepare a working paper for discussion. Linda volunteers to work with me to develop relevant questions that we might want to explore, and the other staff agrees to assume other responsibilities—all for a meeting that will occur following Leonard's holidays.

After this meeting Leonard comes into my office, sits across from me, leans forward and with an intense look on his face and in his most official voice says, "I am formally handing over the decision-making responsibilities regarding our service program to you for the duration of my time away. All the staff will be notified that they must consult with you." I assume he is putting me on, so respond with equal "sincerity," "Thank you for your confidence," to which he replies, "You're welcome," and exits the office. He's serious.

At Linda's request, supported by Lily and Bruce, the three weekly staff meetings that will occur in Leonard's absence will focus on the issue of sexuality. Linda and Bruce are both married and Lily is in a committed partnership, still considering marriage; but nowhere in the graduate training in social work is the issue of sexuality addressed. These young workers are beginning to hear things that they are unprepared to deal with. We have very enlightening sessions and the three staff and Stan are pleased to draw on the collective wisdom and readings from all participants.

As a dutiful second-in-command I share with Leonard what transpired in his absence, including an anecdotal story of an interaction with Lily at which time we jokingly suggested that Leonard is "prudish." Shortly thereafter, I learn from Lily that Leonard has confronted her with his suspicions that I'm putting ideas into her head. Lily denies this—and I have another red flag for my "watch your back" file. Then I hear that Leonard is bringing in a psychiatrist to give us a three-hour professional development training program on neo-Freudian psychosexual development. This person is going to help us understand what "healthy sexuality" is and what it is not. I wonder how the current Ford executives would feel if Henry himself came in to explain the dynamics of the automobile.

My July evaluation to determine if I merit an increment in salary again invites a rehashing of the relationship tensions. Leonard encourages open and free discussion of ideas and differences both in staff meetings and in our evaluation sessions, and I continue to take him at his word. I learn now that he's upset that I question the need for the quantity and quality of forms that we are asked to fill out, which I frequently tend to let slip by. "If I can't trust you to follow my administrative procedures, I can't appoint you as branch director when we open up in the north." Though I don't get to read my evaluation, I do get a formal letter stating that my merit increment is "well earned" and "I (Leonard) would like to express the pleasure I have had in working with you this past year and to express my appreciation for your contribution towards the development of this agency and its services."

I've made it through one year. *Dear God, how will I ever survive a second? If I don't—what then?* I soon learn how challenging this next year will be.

Before Leonard leaves for a second holiday period, we have a further staff meeting devoted to community development—to the "talking about," that is. The paper that I prepare, which Leonard reads in advance and supports, opens up a lively and productive discussion. We're making progress. We might actually do something. Well, not quite. I'm reprimanded and told that my "interventions were not helpful" and that I'm to be less directly involved in future discussions.

I sit alone at my desk. It's well past five o'clock. And I know, I *know* I can't continue this way, taking the "high road" or as Bayne calls it, the "strategic" road; keeping my thoughts and perceptions to myself; attempting to deal with Leonard on a one-to-one basis and only talking agency issues at staff meetings. Father has an expression, "lower than a snake's belly." I'm there now. I certainly can't feel any lower than this: caught in the desperate grip of a double bind—damned if I do, damned if I don't; quit and be unemployable, stay and get fired and/or be soul-destroyed. I'm immobilized.

Lily comes into my office, my lovely, comfortable "prison," my purgatory.

"You've been awfully quiet these last few days, Dale. Are you okay?"

That does it. I dissolve into tears. When I find my voice, I begin to share my discomfort with Leonard and my perceptions. "He's rigid, controlling and compulsive. God, I'm so unhappy here. I'm so afraid to share anything with you, Lily, because Leonard already thinks I'm contaminating your thinking."

"I assure you, Dale, I'm quite capable of forming my own perceptions of Leonard and you. Actually, Linda and I have been saying this for months now." And that opens the floodgates. Blessed relief! I have a similar discussion with Linda the next day. I'm not alone.

Leonard joins us at Sam's for lunch the day of his return from holidays. Lily, Linda and I share a booth and listen dutifully to stories of his holiday experience.

"And guess where we went?" Leonard says with a boyish grin, delighted that he has a captive audience.

"I give up. Where?" says Linda.

"To L.A.—and guess where we stayed?"

"I give up. Where?" I say.

"At *the* Palace Pier—and guess who comes into the dining room when we're eating?"

"I give up. Who?" says Lily.

"Johnny Carson!"

"Did he recognize you?" says Lily, and the three of us break up.

"No," says Leonard and carries on with his story.

September brings temporary relief. Gail Selley joins the staff to give us some additional support with the ever-oppressive waiting list. Potential clients need to wait up to three months to see a counsellor and we have no plan in place to do crisis intervention during the waiting period. And I welcome two very bright first-year students from the University of Toronto, School of Social Work.

For the rest of the year, we continue to struggle with expansion plans both in terms of locating a branch office in the north and moving ever so slowly into the world of community involvement, the preventative aspect of service.

One of our three-hour meetings focuses attention on the idea of locating on a map where our clients are coming from to see if any significant patterns emerge. We spend most of the time discussing who will get the pins and what colours will be used to differentiate presenting problems, such as budget, marital, family, individual. I look around the table and recognize that all the staff are "involved" and animated, all of them quite content to be spending this time, effort and dollars in this way. An epiphany—it *is* me! I'm the one who doesn't fit. I remain quiet, glancing out the window, imagining a field of beautiful, fully blossoming yellow daisies and in their midst, a rugged purple thistle. The thistle will have to be removed.

Several meetings later, Leonard presents his paper outlining what he determines will be the program for 1973. He didn't change a word since his presentation back in May. Little, if any, staff thoughts or discussions are included in this paper. Listening to his plans, I hold little hope of ever being released from the confines of my office and even less hope of stretching my job here at PFS for a complete two-year, let alone three-year, term. What he gives with one hand he takes back with the other. I'm asked to assume the position of coordinator of community programs, draw up a new job description on the one hand, and then I'm confronted privately in my office with a very different message.

"I need to discuss with you what I perceive as a potentially serious problem; I want to nip it in the bud," Leonard says, pulling up the chair across the desk from me, leaning forward, face tight, eyes narrowed, holding me in a fierce grip.

"Good Lord, what is it? What's up?" My oh-so-familiar anxiety response prepares me for "fight or flight."

"I'm beginning to experience from others feelings of uneasiness. I'm getting expressions of complaints, opposition in some of the staff meetings and perhaps undercurrents of discontent that could lead to serious problems. I sense what is happening here might be the same thing that happened in Oshawa. You are a very influential person, Dale, and if you feel that I'm 'rigid, compulsive, arbitrary or undemocratic,' you might be influencing the others in that direction." The fight response wins out.

"Yes, I shared my perceptions with others and they have reciprocated. Leonard, I can assure you that all your professional counsellors are mature, independent thinkers, perfectly capable of forming their own conclusions about you, me and where and how the agency needs to grow. I will not accept responsibility for putting ideas into other people's heads."

"But you have, Dale. You convinced Lily that I'm a prude."

We talk and talk and seem to come to a comfortable place, but I know this is only temporary.

To show his authority, Leonard calls in another professor from the School of Social Work to take us through a three-session introduction into the process of generic social work. He's only temporarily set back when Dr. Jim Albert greets me with a warm handshake and says, "I didn't know that you were here, Dale. How great. How's our buddy Barry doing these days?" I don't get time to answer as Leonard, coming up behind me, says, "Hi, I'm Leonard Wengle," and off we go for our orientation session.

I now am eagerly waiting for the Christmas break and some holiday time. Before the break I'm approached by Leonard regarding a request from a reporter at the *Mississauga News*. Frank Florio, an editor and writer of a column called "Newsmakers," has requested an interview with a counsellor. I'm to be that person. My intuitive self tells me "no, no" but I'm not in a position to say no. Sure enough! A full-page write-up entitled "Is Your Marriage Worth Saving," with more statistics and anecdotes and five facial shots of me strategically placed throughout the article; and to make matters worse, a shot of me behind my desk with a couple in front of the desk, with their backs to the camera. I can hear it now: "If you ask ten people on the street who runs PFS, the answer will be Dale Perrin."

Thank God for family, for sisters, for drives through the city on a snowy Christmas Eve singing Christmas carols, for shelled nuts to crack, a big jigsaw puzzle that invites group participation, for the Queen's speech, the turkey dinner, the toasts and Father's speech—a place to be loved and nurtured.

Because 1973 can only just get worse!

Leonard decides to implement one of Jim Albert's suggestions and forms a board/staff planning committee to develop plans for community outreach and arbitrarily appoints Bruce and me to be the staff representatives. In the following staff meeting Linda voices a concern that I have been hearing for some time from various staff, "What do we have to do to be heard?" and I know that I will get credit for sabotage.

I prepare a working paper for this new committee at the request of Tom Dwyer, chair of the board, outlining the staff's position on this, plus solutions to the waiting list problems, staffing and a branch office. I'm again confronted both at a staff meeting and in private: my behaviour is problematic and unhelpful, even childish. I'm accused of exercising poor judgment. And so it goes, double-binded: damned if I do, damned if I don't until my body and soul scream out, "Stop—enough!"

On April 12 I arrive at the bottom of this Olympic ski jump at an escalated speed that propels me right into the emergency ward of the Mississauga Hospital, my heartbeat attempting valiantly to keep up with the soaring leap into what has to be a catastrophic outcome.

I'm not alone in suffering "stress-related" problems. The following week Noreen arrives at my home in a state of "shock and upset." This is the third time Noreen has asked for my support in dealing with issues that relate to her family situation and her distress with Leonard. She tells me that her psychiatrist credits "carrying home problems from the office" for most of the problems she is experiencing at home and she has been advised to resign. Rita, too, has notified Leonard that she plans to resign in June, that she finds her job "boring and lacking in any challenge and responsibility." This follows Leonard's arbitrary decision to turn over the responsibility for the agency's bookkeeping to Shirley, whom he has also promoted to be Bill's assistant.

I'm aware that Linda, too, is talking about "getting out" this summer. Lily is discontent and she and her partner are thinking of moving to Montreal. Gail shares that she is "fed up." All of these women express in private that they resent being discredited as professionals, that they are being accused, privately, in long one- to four-hour discussions initiated by Leonard, of being contaminated by me. The four of us and the two students can only share our excitement about our clinical sessions or "potential" community projects (Linda is the only one who actually gets permission to participate in a community group planning a "trailer project," a project designed to take services to one of our more remote areas) behind closed doors. And I become aware that the tests my own doctor prescribed have indicated that I do indeed have a thyroid problem—a condition that has been medically stabilized over these past twelve years.

I'm not well and I know I have to move out of my passivity, out of this state of immobilization, and do something that might result in problem-solving. On May 10, I telephone Tom O'Dwyer, chair of the board, and Earl MacDonald, chair of the personnel committee, and ask for consultation. Mr. MacDonald suggests that I let Leonard know of the meeting we have tentatively scheduled. I agree to do so.

On May 11, I arrive at the office and greet my client and her five children in the waiting area. Before I can invite them into my room, Leonard appears and says he must talk to me about an urgent matter.

"I'm about to talk with Mrs. Smith, Leonard."

Gesturing that I'm to move into my office immediately, Leonard says, in a voice easily heard by Shirley, Mrs. Smith and the five children, "I am the executive director of this agency and when I want to talk with you I will talk with you."

He begins before I can take off my coat and sit down.

"I have to talk to you immediately about a matter that came up in yesterday's staff meeting, which you missed."

"Leonard, please. I'm not well and I'm simply not up to your harassment today."

"If you are sick, then you should see a doctor."

"I have."

"Well, then, you should be under medical care."

"I am."

"Well, if you can't cope with what I have to say, then obviously you can't cope with the job either."

"I can cope with the job just fine, Leonard. It's you I can't cope with." I now have my coat off and am sitting behind the desk. I know

I'm not handling this well. My stomach is again signaling distress and I feel myself shaking. I sense a wellspring of rage threatening to overwhelm me, and that frightens me more than Leonard's aggressive tone and body language. "Okay, now will you please shut the door and tell me what it is that is so important that you have to address it now."

"No, I want you to come to my office. I have my notes there."

I listen to a bombardment of questions to which I'm to answer yes or no and then accusations of "poor judgment," to which I finally say, "Leonard, enough! I'm not going to talk with you further until I've met with Earl MacDonald and Art Morgan two evenings from now. As of this moment I'm on sick leave," and I get up, apologize to Mrs. Smith on my way past her, explaining that I will call her to rebook, get my coat, notify Noreen that I'm ill and go home.

I suppose I shouldn't have been surprised to get a phone call from Earl MacDonald the following day to inform me that he and Tom would not be meeting with me as scheduled on the fifteenth. Instead, I'm to appear before a committee of the board at Reverend Art Morgan's church Thursday evening, May 17, at 7:30 p.m. Leonard will be present. Anything I have to say can be said then. I'm to bring a medical certificate. *Oh great! I'm to be crucified in a church.* This time I *am* going to have lots to say. This time I'm going to fight—I'm not going quietly. I have more at stake than just this job.

I recruit Noreen's help and in the next few days we manage to prepare a twenty-page report with twenty pages of appendices to validate every claim I make. The report's entitled "Peel Family Services: Evaluation and Personal Statement." The table of contents identifies six sections, three of which have six to eight subsections. I prepare three copies, all neatly bound, and I'm ready. So help me, God.

"Oh Maggie, I'm scared to death." I really didn't need to say this. Maggie, a keen observer of behaviour, couldn't help noticing me pacing back and forth. Dear Maggie, here to hold my hand and pick up the pieces after the kangaroo court, reassures me. "I'm sure they'll understand about your stage fright. Don't hesitate to ask one of them to read your report for you. You'll be just fine. Your report says it all. What you have trouble 'speaking,' you sure pack a punch with your 'writing.'"

"You're not just saying this because you're my sister?"

"No, really Dale, who knows, maybe they'll hear you. Maybe they won't, but the picture is clear. I'll be right here when you get back."

I take an extra Librium just to be sure I look calm. I'm much too high on adrenaline to appear doped up—I'm assuming. I pack up my volumes in a grocery store bag, my very clever disguise, and off I go—to church.

The church looks very much like the church of my childhood—the steeple beaming out the love and justice of God, the foyer awash in cream-painted walls and warm, greyish-blue carpeting. A welcoming table with appropriate literature greets me. Somehow that doesn't make me feel welcomed. I'm met immediately by Earl MacDonald and ushered into a small lounge furnished with soft couches and matching chairs and a few coffee tables with church magazines and literature on display. The windows on the far wall are covered with a sheer white drape, clear enough for me to observe the parking lot—and there's Leonard's car. He obviously has arrived ahead of me. I'm told to wait here until they are ready to call me. The setting invites me to put in a little prayer for—what? Justice? Sympathy? Solutions? Now that would be nice.

Earl comes, leads me to the room where six men and one woman stand to be introduced. Leonard, at one end of the long boardroom-like table, is smoking a cigarette, looking anxious and every bit as jumpy as I feel. The woman, whom I have never seen before, is introduced but I'm unable to catch her name. She has been seconded from the Peel Social Planning Council. I'm informed that she is to take notes of this meeting. She is seated at the other end of the table kitty-corner from the vacant chair I'm directed to occupy. I dutifully sit, discreetly placing my package under my chair. The other participants are board members.

Now that I'm here and this is real, this is "happening," I'm surprisingly calm, thanks perhaps to the Librium, but maybe, maybe not.

Art Morgan begins. "We understand, Dale, that you have something you want to say to us, so we will ask you to speak first."

"Okay," I say, reaching beneath me to pull out my three bound volumes. "I only had time to prepare three booklets, so perhaps you could share two of them while I read the third."

The room becomes eerily silent. I take pleasure in the fact that I have stunned them, judging by the looks on their faces. "As some of you are aware, I suffer from stage fright. Reading out loud is especially difficult for me. So I'm asking you, Earl, as chair of personnel, if you would be so kind as to read out loud for me."

Earl agrees and begins reading.

I allow Earl to read three pages and am so uncomfortable with his lack of reading skills (he reads at about a grade eight level and is putting the emphasis in all the wrong places) that I interrupt. "Thanks Earl, I will take over now." And I read it all—every single word—minus the appendices! At the end of the reading, with a flair for the dramatic that I didn't know I had in me, I turn over the back cover and announce, "Now, that is all I have to say. I have no intention of entering into a debate."

"I agree," says Art. "There will be no debate. Leonard, you and Dale are excused now and can wait in the other room until we call you back."

Earl leads us back to the room I was previously waiting in. Leonard and I are alone. We make a few comments about meaningless things. I take delight in the fact that he is extremely uncomfortable, obviously agitated. I'm still absolutely calm, not even a tremor in my hands or voice. *What's happening to me?* I can feel a sense of exhilaration blowing up inside me that I know I've got to contain.

In twenty minutes or so Earl returns to the room. "Dale, you may come back now," he says.

"We would like to know how you are feeling, Dale, and did you bring a medical certificate with you?" Art says.

"I'm really fine now," I say, handing over my doctor's letter, which I have in my purse. "My thyroid is stabilized and I have now changed my medication, but I'm really okay. My health is not a problem."

"We're glad to hear this, Dale. We were concerned for you. We have decided that you can leave now. We will be meeting with

Leonard for a short period. You will learn our decision from him. Before you go, though, would you be willing to sign one copy of your report for us please?"

I sign the book, thank the board for their willingness to hear me and take my leave.

"Maggie, I did it!" I explode; the exhilaration that has filled up my insides erupts like Mount Etna and I pour out my story. I'm flooded with the euphoria that comes from conquering a demon that's haunted me most of my life. Do I take delight in one-upping Leonard? Not really. I have no desire to hurt him—well, maybe just a tinge of "gotcha." But *I read in front of people. I read out loud!*

Maggie is thrilled for me too. "Do you think it worked? Do you think you have saved your job?"

"No, I doubt it. But who knows?"

I don't have to wait long. Shirley phones me and instructs me to meet with Leonard in his office Monday at 1:00 p.m.

I arrive a few minutes early and head for my office. I sit at my desk, open my desk drawer and discover—no files. Noreen hustles in and instructs me to go to Leonard's office immediately.

As I enter the waiting area, the staff are straggling in from their lunch hour and are headed off by Noreen and instructed to go immediately to the boardroom. I catch Gail and whisper, "Can you give me Joel's phone number right away, please?" She hurries back to her office and then on the run passes me a note as she heads for the meeting. Joel, Gail's husband, is a lawyer and I'm quite sure he's aware of the goings-on at the agency and I'm equally sure I will need legal advice very quickly.

Helen Desroche is sitting in Leonard's office. She's a board member and social worker with the Board of Education, with whom I have had contact in relationship to several troubled young children. A woman in her early fifties, moderately dressed as befits a "truant officer" and sitting appropriately with legs crossed at the ankles, she says not a word.

Leonard reads from a prepared letter, which he then hands me. He deeply regrets that he will have to fire me. I must leave the building immediately as my presence poses a threat to the well-being of the agency. He makes it clear that he is willing to give me his evaluation of me, but the offer extends only until this Friday.

I decline his offer and leave his office to return to mine.

Noreen has brought me two boxes to load up my personal possessions. Before I can do so, Helen approaches and asks permission to come in.

"And what exactly is your role here?" I say.

"I'm here just in case you want to talk, Dale. I know you must be upset."

I decline her offer to talk and give her permission to watch me pack up if she wishes. She does.

On the way out of the office I say to Noreen, "As of this moment I'm in private practice, Noreen. I would appreciate that all calls for me are directed to my home."

That's it. May 22, 1973, at the age of thirty-five, fired for the third time. I'm finished! The end of my world! The apocalypse!

THE APOCALYPSE

I was certainly aware of feeling stuck and not being able to see alternatives. Have you experienced such feelings? When? What were the circumstances? What allowed or forced you to move out of this position? And what feelings did you experience when you moved?

I'm beginning to recognize a familiar pattern of thoughts, feelings and behaviours. Can you identify patterns that you can now trace back to childhood responses? For example, look at your most recent experience of rejection, betrayal or disappointment in relationship to a significant person and identify what you felt, thought and concluded. Then, go back five or ten years and see if you can identify an experience where your feelings, thoughts and behaviours were similar. Then go back another five or ten years—and then go back to the earliest experience you can recall. As you go back in time, the feelings are less sophisticated but close enough to see parallels.

Now ask yourself, "Am I bringing the same thoughts, feelings and behaviours of the little girl/boy I was into today's events?"

And if so, are they really "true" for today's reality? Are they helpful or hurtful in helping me move forward?

Do I need to change my thoughts, feelings or specific behaviours?

BOOK TWO

BOOK TWO

OUT OF THE ASHES

And that's what happens when you live "in script." "Reoccurring dramas" is one of the indicators of script. When something happens twice, three times, four times, when someone carries a set of beliefs, feelings and learned behaviours into new situations, it follows that the same results are inevitable. That doesn't mean that those inevitable consequences hurt any less with repetition. Quite often the pain gets stored in a special memory box and is used to reinforce the very set of beliefs, feelings and learned behaviours that gave rise to the painful outcome in the first place.

Some people live their entire lives in such pain, not infrequently with catastrophic results. Others may not have catastrophic outcomes, but living in script results in living a life of banality, of not quite maturing into the radiant beings that are their genetic and spiritual predisposition. It seems to me that the healthiest option, assuming that we want a different outcome, is to change something, maybe a whole lot of somethings.

And I've got a lot of "somethings" to change.

"Joel, can you help me? I've just been fired," I say, after setting my two boxes of books on the kitchen table.

"Oh Dale, I'm not surprised from what Gail has told me. I can't represent you but I know an excellent firm in Toronto where you can get the advice you may need. Let me look up their number."

After a brief pause, Joel gives me the name of McCarthy & McCarthy and the number and address of the Toronto firm and offers to phone and set up an appointment for me.

"Thanks a lot, Joel," I say before the tears start to flow, a torrent of pain busting through the now-crumbling defensive posture. I barely get the floodgates back in place and the doorbell rings. *Oh, God. Now what?*

"Do you need a friend? May I come up?" says a very familiar voice.

In comes my favourite client: same old baseball jacket, same faded men's blue jeans and same salty attitude, bearing her gift of authentic caring.

"I called the agency twice this past week and they told me you were on sick leave. Then when I called this afternoon they told me you no longer work there. I kinda assumed you were fired. You were, weren't you?"

"That I was, Hilda, my friend. That I was." I make coffee and the two of us chat, just two people who don't quite fit the stereotypes of … what? Normal? After a surreal hour we agree that Hilda will continue to see me once a week for the same fee she was paying at the agency, zero dollars, for as long as she feels the sessions are helpful—a small price to pay for the affirmation that "people are essentially good."

And then the grief? No, not yet. The next day, the next few days, actually the next month, I'm propelled by an unstoppable hurricanelike energy, energy long suppressed, that hurls me into productive, creative activity. I'm free! I'm going "out there"! I'm going to be me, be visible, do it my way.

Brother Ken, like Hayward, my shaman healer, is there for me when I'm in "crisis mode." He agrees to design professional letterhead and calling cards. I prepare to send an introductory letter, a business card with a wedding-invitation-like card (also designed by Ken) announcing the opening of my private practice as of July 3, to an extensive list of lawyers and medical doctors in family practice and other health and social service agencies. Ken also tells me that he is willing to cover my rent if I'm in need. He can be such a sweetie.

Armed with the "Red Book" (the directory of health and social services in the Peel region) I telephone the executive directors of all significant services, including Dorothy Ross, the executive director of the Social Planning Council. I set up appointments to introduce myself and my new service. In these meetings I begin to experience the heartbeat of the community, the vibrant forces of change, and I'm invited to participate. Many of the agencies are planning their annual general meetings and I'm encouraged to attend and let my name stand for board positions.

Before the summer ends I'm on the boards and/or committees of the Canadian Mental Health Association, Big Brothers, the Social Planning Council Youth Task Force, the Police-Community Relations Committee and several others. I make significant contacts with the Addiction Research Foundation (ARF) personnel and a special project involving the ARF and Juvenile Court Services. Judge Warren Durham, newly appointed to the bench, invites me to his "inauguration ceremony." And Rochelle Saunders, the executive director of Rapport House, a drop-in counselling centre for youth between the ages of eighteen and twenty-five, invites me to do an evaluation of the administrative structure of this relatively new project, funded by the United Way—a paying contract!

I send my information to the schools of social work for which I have been a field instructor and to the community colleges in Hamilton, Oakville and Toronto, announcing that I'm available to do seminar teaching. Jim Robertson, coordinator of the social services program at Sheridan College, Oakville, calls and asks to come and see me. After an hour and a half of discussion, Jim offers me a part-time position as coordinator of the field placements for his program to begin mid-August. Do I know how to do this? No, but I'm sure I can learn in a big hurry. Wow—that's seven hours a week income, enough money to pay my rent.

One more former client from Peel Family Services calls. Now two clients, and one who actually pays. Maybe, just maybe, I'm going to survive.

During this frenetic period I attend a weekend conference on transactional analysis (TA) sponsored by two professionals connected with Queens University and the hospital in Kingston, Ontario. Presenters from the United States as well as Canada, several of whom have written articles for the TA journal and newsletter, conduct a variety of workshops. My student Rob McFadden introduced me to the book *I'm OK, You're OK* by Tom Harris and I was instantly hooked on transactional analysis. I signed up for this conference several months earlier, and in spite of dwindling financial resources,

I'm determined to attend. This experience is the beginning of "the rest of my life," the beginning of "healing into success."

Although I don't entirely grasp the significance or magnitude of this experience, I intuitively know that I have been directed to the guru who can show me the way. This is the beginning of what I sense will develop into a long association with Vince Gilpin, Registered Social Worker, Certified Transactional Analyst, "guru." Will I sign up immediately for training in TA? Maybe not right away, but soon, I promise myself.

My optimism, fed by the adrenaline of "freedom" and the theory of TA, is tempered with the gnawing anxiety of "what if?": What if I can't make it in private practice? What do I do if I can no longer stay in this field? Haunting questions that create dreams with catastrophic images.

The lawyer recommends that I sue the agency for illegal dismissal. He believes I have an excellent chance of collecting a healthy settlement package. I don't have the courage to ask how much but I do hope it will be enough to get me a year or two of postgraduate education. The only other career choice that interests me is writing—journalism or something to do with the publishing business.

Jessie Matheson, my other student, a bright, ambitious "mature student," married and with two children, feeds me information regarding what is happening at Peel Family Services, both in the office and at the board level. Coincidently, Jessie is good friends with her neighbor, who just happens to be on the board. Knowing that Jessie is a student of the agency, he is quite willing to let a few tidbits of confidential information slip. Jessie informs me that the board is preparing for a lawsuit. They are well aware that I have grounds. They have set up a subcommittee to plan a defensive strategy. She also informs me that Leonard notified all the staff that they are not to be in communication with me. "If you see her on the street, you are to cross the street."

I consult with the Canadian Association of Social Workers for information regarding other private practitioners in the field and learn the names of six people in Ontario who are operating private practices, three of whom are in the Toronto area. There are only eleven such practitioners in all of Canada. I learn that private practice is a controversial "grey area" in social work and I get the impression that "only losers" go this route. *Oh my God! I'm one of them?* Phone calls and a personal interview with one woman who is offering counselling on a private basis support that impression. *What am I doing? What am I doing?*

Dressed in this heavy coat of pessimism, I make an appointment with Professor R. W. Van Fossen, head of the English department at the Erindale College campus in Mississauga (University of Toronto). Professor Van Fossen, a man about my age, graciously agrees to read my collection of poetry and assess if I have any literary skills. He explains what courses I would need to complete an MA in literature. A week later he informs me, "Well Dale, your poetry is very nineteenth-century. Dorothy Livesey is here at the college and is going to read from her recently published collection of poetry. If you want to know how poets express themselves now, I suggest you stay and attend."

I do, and that is the end of my poetry-writing career.

"Oh Maggie, what am I going to do? How am I going to survive?" I say to my ever-patient "sister" as we make coffee and sit at my tiny white kitchen table in my equally tiny white apartment kitchen.

"You can always get a job, Dale," she says, puffing at her cigarette while stirring coffee with her other hand. I still have ashtrays handy in spite of the fact that I quit smoking back in 1971.

"But I'm unemployable, Maggie. Where am I going to get a job?"

"Get any old job; you'll survive."

"You're not getting it! I am unemployable! No one is going to hire me."

"Dale, you can get a job!"

Before I erupt—no doubt Maggie is keenly aware of my frustration level and the underlying despair—she adds, "A job, Dale, like at Eaton's, in the lingerie department."

"Oh, you mean a job-job! I've never thought of that. You have a point." Actually with this revelation comes instant relief. It's true, I could actually survive. I could get a job-job. I will be able to maintain my independence.

A further incident injects a sense of hope—hope, that is, in my basic assumption about the inherent goodness of people. In late June,

Linda Williamson telephones to say that she would like to drop by and say hello. *My God! Linda is risking breaking Leonard's injunction.*

"I just want to say good-bye, Dale, and thank you for all your support and encouragement. I'm pregnant and have resigned my position at the agency—not, I might add, for that reason though. No one at the agency knows that I'm pregnant. I brought a copy of my letter of resignation. Would you like to read it?"

"Sure, please," I say, just barely restraining myself from jumping up and screaming yippeeeeee!

The first letter (there were two) gave two principle reasons. Though she recognized the need to let me go, she did not support the way it was handled: that I was instructed to leave immediately and not given the opportunity to resign. And secondly, that I was "let go" prior to an investigation of the problems identified in my report to the board (the kangaroo court).

The second letter was in response to Leonard's request following a lengthy interview after he received the first letter. Linda was insistent that the board be notified of the reasons for her resignation. She added that she had additional concerns about the reasons stated for my dismissal: that, in her experience, the atmosphere and the problems in the agency were not conducive to inspire good work. She felt the agency made a regressive move by immediately cutting out the community development program.

What a gift: another professional social worker willing to confront an injustice, willing to make a statement through the act of resignation. First Ken Sime, now Linda Williamson—blessed be!

The relief is short-lived. It is July now and I've done it all. I have nothing to do but wait; wait for one of the seeds I've sown to grow and produce. Wait! And wait some more! Thank goodness for the Senate Watergate hearings, which are being televised every day. I'm addicted to Watergate Hearings and American news channels and American politics. I soon have very clear ideas as to who the bad guys are and what needs to be done, but alas, no one is willing to pay me for my keen observations.

Hayward drives with me to Kitchener to pick up the letterheads and cards that Ken has ready for me. Finally I'm willing to risk introducing Hayward to Ken and take my chances that he will be graciously received. And he is. Actually, Hayward quite likes Ken. Who knows, possibly we might just have family blessings for our growing relationship.

I needn't have worried about that. When we are back in my apartment Hayward tells me. "I took it," he says. "This job offers me the opportunity to do what I've always wanted to do. And besides, I haven't received any other offers. I'll be leaving for Jamaica in three days. I have a lot to do, so I won't have another opportunity to see you before I leave."

Oh my God, my God. He's leaving. I know how unhappy he's been these last several months, struggling to find a job in the field of public administration and economics and living in Toronto with his sister and her partner. But it hadn't occurred to me that a job would take him back to the country of his origin. *My shaman, my healer, my love—this is it?*

"I'm really happy for you. I know that this is what you've always wanted. That's terrific," I say, too stunned to know what was happening deep within me. I begin to cry; slowly, unexpectedly the tears flow. Sobs erupt, releasing a torrent of emotion, surprising both of us. Hours of lovemaking, each orgasmic experience releasing an emotional explosion of equal intensity; no need for words. Flashes of memory, fragments of the relationship revisited, intrude as we act out our good-byes. And then he's gone. He's gone! And I'm here, just waiting.

The first call comes late July from a doctor in Etobicoke—a referral for counselling. And then another.

With time on my hands when the Watergate hearings end for the day, I busy myself reading all the books I can find relating to the theory and practice of transactional analysis. I become a regular member of the International Transactional Analysis Association and receive newsletters, the journal and information about upcoming training groups and conferences. I go through the application process and am accepted into the American Association of Marriage and Family Counsellors. I'm still a member of the Ontario and Canadian Associations of Professional Social Workers. I now have impressive credentials to include in calling cards and brochures.

I get the necessary business and legal insurance protections and then secure the services of Lynne Meredith, a new and budding financial wizard (who's been in business for almost six months already), an "angel" I'm convinced who is to manage my few dollars and secure me a pension should I live that long.

And with the "lettuce" that my mother leaves in my fridge every time she and my father come to visit and take me out to dinner, I manage to ease my way into August and into my contract at Sheridan College in Oakville.

I now sense that I just might make it and think that to pursue legal action against Peel Family Services might just drain funds and possibly hurt my reputation in the long run. I decide to stop the legal action—a good thing since my McCarthy & McCarthy lawyer informs me that he has to "drop my case," that one of the partners is representing Hazel McCallion, the mayor of Streetsville, who sits on the board.

Jim Robertson is standing just inside the front entrance of the Oakville Sheridan College campus and greets me with an outstretched hand and a warm smile. He's an attractive man, with a healthy head of soft, fine, chestnut-brown hair that shows no sign of receding. With an equally soft, gentle voice, he says, "Welcome, Dale. I've just been gathering up the material I have on the field placements we used last term, but I thought I'd show you around the college before we settle down to talk." It's a good thing he did. The college is a two-story, sprawling warren of different coloured corridors going in every which direction, and since few teachers or students are wandering around just yet, I never would have located Jim's office. No one was visible in the outer office area, though the untidiness of the reception desk indicates that Jim isn't the only one working this warm August day.

The field practicum of Jim's program, not unlike the programs of the graduate students, provides the college students with valuable "in field" experiences and helps reinforce practical skills in developing relationships, making assessments and providing crisis intervention when necessary. Within the two-year academic program, students complete six hundred hours of supervised hands-on work. In order to do that, they need to have supervisors/instructors in social or health-related services.

"Here is a list of the agencies we used last term. We will need several more to accommodate the twenty-two first-year students, assuming they all actually arrive in September, and we need them up and ready for the fifteenth of the month. We'll probably need eighteen more placements for second-year students, beginning in the January term. The students are responsible for their own transportation, so you can send them anywhere in Oakville, Burlington, Hamilton or Mississauga. Do you think you can find field instructors and get them up and running that quickly?"

"I'm on it, Jim," I say, and armed with the directories for the Oakville, Burlington and Hamilton areas, I hop, skip and do cartwheels back to my car. I'm going to make it. I know I am. I know I can.

I thought I could! Now here I am, mid-September, standing in front of a classroom of eager young men and women and a handful of "mature students" (women over thirty who are returning to an academic setting), and I'm wondering, "What on earth am I doing here?" Jim introduces me and leaves the room. They are smiling, looking at me expectantly, with pen in hand. Oh my God, they are expecting me to say something worth writing down! I freeze—for a very long moment—and then ask them to "Please just put your pens down and let me chat with you about the opportunities we have available for you."

Obediently they do so and I tell the scared little kid inside of me that I'm not really "teaching," I'm only chatting, and away I go. I did it! I *can* do this!

The semester flies by. Two doctors have now "discovered" me and the referrals for counselling are starting to come. By Christmas, just three months later, I really don't *need* the "lettuce" Mom continues to leave in the fridge, but every little bit helps. I now have an accountant, a former client from my Kitchener days, who sets up my books. The tax man will now know me as Dale Perrin and Associates.

I'm visible. I'm doing it my way. No more *Miss Perrin*; no more hiding behind a desk with clients on the other side. No more "sterile" office environment, but rather a warm, inviting home environment decorated in gentle blues and purples, beautiful oil paintings, fresh coffee ready. I'm no longer going to be the "healthy, all-knowing one" and the client, "the sick one." Now the client and I can work as a team, both of us okay and both of us learning, growing and recognizing new and rich possibilities. I'm so looking forward to Christmas with my family and sharing with my "sisters" that I did and will continue to survive.

I move into 1974 with a sense of excitement that I haven't experienced for several years. I'm ready to bust out, to grow the business, to steep myself in transactional analysis. I continue to ingest the monthly journal articles, read all the new books as fast as they hit the market and incorporate this new learning into my work with the new clients that slowly but surely find their way to my door. The medical referrals continue. I now have several doctors who are using my services. To quote Dr. David Clarkson, "I don't know what you're doing with my patients, but it's working. So here's another one for you."

It is former friends and acquaintances from my Oshawa days who insist that I take the next step in my professional development and begin group therapy. Several of the volunteers from the youth drop-in centre have decided that they want to work together as a group. "Get us a couple more people, Dale, and we'll be your first group." I do—in fear and trepidation. It's the "fear and trepidation" thing that distresses me. Why do I always approach new experiences with fear and trepidation? The group experience works out very well. I learn as I experience. I begin a second group several months later. And still—fear and trepidation!

And now I'm back in the newspapers, this time without the fear and trepidation that public exposure will get me fired. Anne Redfearn, a tall, thin, peppy young reporter who freelances for the Brampton *Guardian* and the *Mississauga News,* whom I have met through my community work, asks to interview me for a feature article. On May 9, 1974, the *Guardian* has a lengthy feature entitled, "Her study condemned high-rises," in which Anne manages to give my entire resume.

Ironically the *Guardian* also has a column entitled "You asked," a column of advice on community and family problems. This column is shared by Marianne Farkas, a community consultant with the Addiction Research Foundation in Mississauga, and Reverend Gordon Williams, with the Contact Centre in Peel Region. I have been invited to be the third contributor. My first contribution—two "letters" from readers identifying marital or family-related problems that I make up and then answer—appears in the same issue. Several months later, the *Mississauga News* picks up the idea and introduces a column entitled "Can I Help," with the same three contributors. I'm encouraged to continue these articles indefinitely. My Ann Landers "voice" blossoms.

As my practice, my knowledge and skill base grow, I too am confronted with the need to grow. I have now been exposed to the theory of scripts. Eric Berne, the founder of transactional analysis theory and the International Transactional Analysis Association, published a book entitled *What Do You Say After You Say Hello*; and Claude Steiner, one of his protégés, followed with a book entitled *Scripts People Live.* Armed with this new learning and a "script questionnaire" developed by Robert Goulding, another core member of the San Francisco professionals who are developing and expanding Berne's work, I proceed to do script analysis with twenty or so clients. What an amazing tool for uncovering and explaining early life messages that determine an entire life script. And so, I did it. I did my own script.

I cry as I recognize that my life pattern, my "play," could be entitled *The Woman Behind the Man*, the gentle nurturer behind the scenes, just like my mother! Only the setting is the professional stage, not the family home, and the children are not my own children, but the clients. Oh my God! Oh my God! Then why didn't those three "bosses" appreciate all the things I was doing to promote their well-being and the well-being of the agencies and the clients? It worked for my mother. That's the way it was supposed to be. And they fired me! I don't get it.

And I don't "get it" when months later I experience a major anxiety attack following my Tuesday night group. The business has been growing steadily; I now have two evening groups, individual clients and my Sheridan College work with twice the number of hours from the first contract.

"Billy," I say in a cracking, little girl's voice, "I'm having an anxiety attack. Can you help me? My heart's racing; I'm hot and sweaty. What's happening to me?"

Billy, one of my Oshawa friends, says, "Easy, Dale, easy! Go ahead and cry. Let it out. I'll wait."

I do. I sob for ten minutes without any sense of what I'm crying about.

"What's happening, Dale? When did you start feeling this way?"

"I was fine when I went out for dinner. I came back and listened to my messages and then got the coffee ready for group. I noticed as the group was coming to the end that I began to get this gripping sensation in my gut. I managed to hang on until I hugged the last person and she left, and then my heart started racing."

"Anything in the group dynamics that threatened you?"

"No, one fellow did some work on a kinky sexual thing, but I don't think that was troublesome for me."

"Well, back up a bit. You came in from dinner. You listened to your messages and made coffee. Anything in the messages?"

"Oh no, just a message from the bank saying that my mortgage application was approved." And the sobs erupt. "Oh my God—it's the mortgage. When a bank says that you are eligible for a mortgage, then the whole world will know that you are successful. You are out there onstage—visible! Everyone will know," I say in my little scared voice.

That's when I begin to appreciate the potency of the early life messages: "women are behind the scenes" and there is a price to pay if I break that rule. Several months prior to this experience, Edie Wilson, a client in my Tuesday night group and a successful real estate agent, talked to me about buying a townhouse. Together we worked out how I could buy a new car, which I had determined to do, and also buy a condo. She found me a perfect location, a beautiful end unit in a new development in a lovely residential neighbourhood. I put in an offer conditional on being accepted for a mortgage and now I'm accepted. And everyone will know I'm successful!

I also learn that just "knowing something" doesn't make my anxiety go away. Berne and Steiner both talk about how breaking key script injunctions results in three or four weeks of gradually decreasing anxiety, and they were right. It takes me that long before I'm able to convert the scare to excitement. Wow, in less than six months now, I will move into my very own home!

September 1975, I now live and work from my very own residence: a five-level townhouse that allows me to have an interview room and a separate room set up as an office on the upper level, along with my bedroom, the only room in the entire house that is actually "private." The kitchen area becomes "the business centre," the living room functions as a waiting room and a small, finished room in the basement with a fireplace becomes the group therapy room. Soon, very soon, I may just be able to hire a part-time secretary and free myself from the financial record keeping and other secretarial responsibilities.

Before the year ends I have an opportunity to do my first "formal" training with Vince Gilpin in Ottawa, and I discover that I'm "all work and no play"—another "aha" that leads me to the realization that it is time for me to get some assistance with my practice. And who better to have as an "associate" but Jim Robertson. Jim is willing to take on a few clients in the evenings, thus reducing the pressure I've been feeling to say yes to everyone who calls. Now I can offer an alternative to a "waiting list." Jim is now sold on TA and has signed up with Vince to enter into a year of training, which I'm still too scared to do.

To take care of the fun part I decide to explore the world of cats. I'm going to decorate my new purple and blue house with furry creatures, something I have wanted to do for some time. Why haven't I done it? I discover I have my father's voice recorded in my head, a stern voice that says, "You don't want to do that. Cats are impractical and a nuisance." January 1976 offers me an opportunity to attend a cat show. I discover American shorthair classic silver tabby cats (the ones with the bull's-eye on their sides and necklaces around their throat, neck and legs and cute, little round faces) and meet Myrna Ford, a breeder who lives in Lewiston, New York, just south of the Canadian border. A weekend visit in Lewiston and I come home with two silver tabby kittens, Sanford and Samantha, and one smoke tabby kitten, named Shroeder, and a new friend (well, she doesn't actually come home with me) to play with.

Myrna is a powerhouse of a woman, brilliant, assertive, highly skilled as an educator and women's rights advocate—a five-feet-five, "don't mess with me or those I love" Texan woman, who can be as playful as the kittens she breeds. I determine to draft her as a new associate and she willingly agrees to develop a six-week (consecutive Saturdays) assertiveness training program to offer my clients—and "show me" how to play. The program is an instant success. Myrna, too, becomes interested in transactional analysis and agrees to enter a TA 101 course being offered in Toronto.

It is Myrna who pushes me out of my comfort zone and insists I begin offering workshops, which I manage to resist doing for at least another year. Did I mention that I approach new situations with fear and trepidation and did I mention I have stage fright?

More columns in the *Guardian*, more columns in the *Mississauga News* and a feature article entitled "Marriage Counselling: helping people separate is sometimes part of the job" continue to keep me visible in the community. Tina Ivory, another freelance writer, quotes me as an authority in a major *Mississauga News* piece on "Marriage and Divorce: new solutions to old problems" and in an article in the *Canadian Living Magazine* entitled "Divorce!" But, I discover, it may not be the public exposure that attracts new business. Approximately 85 percent of the new referrals come from clients who have already experienced positive results working together with me individually or in one of the now three ongoing evening groups.

I now have a secretary, Penny Moore, my neighbour who is living kitty-corner from me in the townhouse complex, the mother of three young children. Penny starts working four evenings a week and as the demand increases, begins working afternoons as well as evenings. What a thrill. I now have someone to talk to, someone I can share my daily struggles and successes with. Private practice can be an isolating experience.

Penny, a dark-haired woman with a shy smile, is a major source of information as to what's going on in this townhouse community.

She is a welcoming presence for people coming and going from the office and proves to be a reliable and steadfast confidant.

And now Dale Perrin & Associates soars, propelled by a momentum of collective energy that brings Carol Morris, a perky, questioning, bright, insightful woman who has been in training with Vince Gilpin for several years, into my world. Like Jim, Carol is willing to give me some hours, day and evening, to assist with the ever-growing waiting list. Carol, just beginning to develop her own counselling practice in Toronto, is open to sharing her knowledge and experience and is the first person with a TA background who is geographically close enough to me who can help me integrate theory and my actual practice.

"Oh Carol, I just had a really neat session," I say as we both meet in the kitchen following our sessions.

"So tell me; what happened?"

"I just walked a young woman through a dialogue with her five different ego states (her Critical Parent, Nurturing Parent, Adult, Free Child and Adapted Child ego states—all with their own thoughts, feelings and behaviours), and she recognized that her Critical Parent was telling her that 'it's not nice to disappoint people.' She always said 'yes, okay' when she really wants to say no. She learned as a child that it displeased her mother when she didn't comply to a request. Her little Adapted Child automatically says yes. She decided that she really didn't have to say yes *all the time*, that in the particular situation that she was struggling with, she could say no and still be valued. Then she did a dress rehearsal with her friend (imagined to be sitting in the chair across from her), said no and explained, and her friend said okay and that was that. She laughed when she recognized how simple it was and how she was really doing all this stuff in her head."

"Ah, you just helped her break a third-degree impasse."

"Oh, that's what you call this work?"

"Yes, way to go, Dale."

How sweet it is to be able to talk jargon with someone who knows. When am I going to get the courage to do my own formal training?

I don't have to deal with this sticky problem at the moment because no sooner have I integrated Carol into my practice and yet another new associate, Stephanie Tonin, one of Carol's contacts from her training group, when another business opportunity presents itself.

"Hi Dale, this is Albert Powell from the Oakville Association for the Mentally Retarded. Do you have a moment?"

"Sure do, Albert. How are you?"

Albert, a short, sweet, Jamaican "country boy" as he loves to say, with his soft, stuttering, lilting voice, is one of the field instructors for Sheridan College students.

"Just great; actually, I'm quite excited. I'm about to have a dream come true. And I'm hoping you will help me."

"I will if I can, Albert. What's the dream?"

"It's called Marcus Garvey Homes. I've always wanted to set up a group home for kids of West Indian origin. A bunch of us are meeting in Toronto on Saturday to discuss how we might do this, and I'd like it if you would join us. I have a psychiatrist and a dentist who both specialize in work with kids; a woman with a doctorate in special education, who works in the North York Board of Education; a very successful Christian businessman; and about six other men and women from the Jamaican-Canadian Association who are interested. Would you be willing to come, Dale? You will hear all about it at the meeting."

"You bet, Albert. I'd be pleased to participate," I say, wondering why Albert chose to invite me. He is totally unaware of my personal relationships but we've talked a lot about the problems facing the West Indian immigrant integrating into this complex, big-city, money-driven "white" community.

The meeting results in the development of a whole new business adventure: an exposure to corporate partnerships and share ownership; a new opportunity to be involved with children with special needs; staff training with folks who have as much to teach me as I can share with them; and brilliant colleagues who operate "the Jamaican way." Since I'm a minority of one on this board, it is I who needs to make the most significant adjustments.

Within months, we open up the first group home for kids of West Indian origin who, for a variety of reasons, must live separate from the parent(s) who have brought them to Toronto. I'm exposed to a whole new world of consultation, crisis intervention with the police, racial injustices and prejudices and staff-child conflicts, the likes of which I haven't experienced since my days at the treatment centre in Winnipeg. It is exciting, challenging and sometimes exhausting.

The Region of Peel Social Service Department challenges me with another "growing edge" opportunity. I'm asked by Paul Vezina, assistant to Jim Crozier, the commissioner of social services, to conduct a training session with the staff, an advanced training workshop related to developing interviewing skills. Oh boy, something new—that familiar gut reaction is triggered immediately—and *I accept anyway.* I tell that scared little kid in me, "It's okay; this is only 'training.' It isn't 'teaching,' and I don't have to make any speeches."

By the end of 1977 I'm gliding through my days like a totally committed California surfer, thrilled by each wave of newness and growth, no longer concerned about being crashed by an unexpected superwave, not even concerned about snowstorms forcing me to cancel "group night" and losing needed income. I have moved from surviving to thriving. It can only get bigger and better, no?

OUT OF THE ASHES

Transactional analysis theory provided me with the tools that I needed to begin to unravel the mysteries in my life—not the least of which was the question, "Why does this keep happening to me?" I'm not intending to "teach" you the theory or explain the model in any depth, but the concept of "script" may help you examine certain phenomena in your life. I will include a list of books that are available if you wish to learn more about theory. And I will include the relevant information regarding how to locate a TA therapist. But for now, let me ask you these questions:

Have you experienced troublesome work relationships (or personal relationships) that ended unpleasantly? And then find yourself repeating the same conflictual pattern in other relationships?

Have you asked yourself, "Why does this always happen to me?"

Can you recognize the characteristics or behaviours in the "other" that trigger for you "conflict"?

And can you recognize in yourself why it is or where in your personality you are vulnerable to this type of person or behaviour?

When you examine the significant caretakers in your family of origin, do you see any parallels, any patterns of personality or behaviour that are similar to those people who presently create difficulties for you?

Are you responding to today's difficulties the same way you responded to those significant people in your childhood?

Do you recognize any thoughts, feelings or behaviours that you could now change in order to deal with today's situations differently? Are you willing to commit to changing those thoughts, feelings and/ or behaviours?

When you've encountered a significant "bump" in life, a rejection, a "failure" of some kind, how did you respond? Did you "give up" and sink into depression? Just pout and feel sorry for yourself? Or did you "come up swinging," determined to show them? Did you seek consultation from friends, associates, professional counsellors and determine to move forward?

Have you experienced an interaction with an important person that seemed to you to be "crazy"? If so, how did that impact your self-esteem? Your core belief about others, the world and what you can expect "out there"?

What did you do with your feelings? Did you cope with this trauma the same way you have handled situations and feelings in the past, or have you changed?

Is this "response" a pattern? Have your responses been helpful or hurtful? Do you recognize any thought, feeling or behaviour that you now want to change?

Are you catching on to this truth: something "out there" happens and you see, hear, touch, smell, that is, you experience that something through your senses?

An example: my partner enters the room and he/she is scowling, huffing and puffing and turns and looks right at me. When I see this, I then have a thought: "Uh-oh, now what have I done wrong?" based on a familiar pattern. And then I have a feeling in response to that thought: I'm scared that he/she is going to yell at me and put me down.

Based on that feeling, I behave in a certain way: I say, defensively, "What have I done this time?" and your partner says, "What? Would you believe some idiot driver, talking on his cell phone, almost smashed into me as I turned into the driveway? I could have been killed!" Now I was scared and defensive—for what? And do I *always* want to/have to respond this way?

I NEVER PROMISED YOU
A ROSE GARDEN

"Well, are you ready to tell me the truth?" Myrna says as we sit down at the dining-room table. The last person in my very special Thursday-night group gave me another big hug and quickly joined the others now exiting the front door. The table is cleaned up; the kitchen tidied. The last of the birthday cake is sitting on the kitchen table. We have just celebrated my fortieth birthday on this March 15, 1978.

Instead of words, I respond with tears, then sobs. I cry for ten minutes or more before I can choke out any words. Myrna, bless her soul, waits patiently.

"There's something terribly wrong with me," I manage to say. "She doesn't know what it is but when I asked if it was MS she said no, that it couldn't be that."

The "she" I am referring to is the orthopedic surgeon, a friend of Carol Morris, my associate, who graciously agreed to see me and assess what is happening in my lower spine. Several months earlier, when accompanying my father on his routine two-mile walk, I experienced a strange sensation in my right leg, a grabbing of sorts that caused me to start limping. Father and I had aborted the walk and returned home. By the time I rested and had a cup of coffee, my leg was fine and off I went, thinking nothing of it. Several days later, I noticed that in the late evenings when I finished my last session, usually around nine fifteen or shortly after ten, I would be limping as I headed up the stairs to the bedroom level. Carol commented last week that I was deteriorating, that I was now using both hands on the railing to pull myself up those stairs. She suggested that I seek medical advice. My first response was to dismiss the need for consultation.

In my Oshawa days I was diagnosed with a degenerating disk in the lumbar region of the spine and told that I would just have to live with it. I presumed this was just the disk problem and that I was "just living with it." Carol insisted that I seek another opinion and said that over the last few months she had noticed considerable deterioration. She offered to contact her friend and set up an appointment. The surgeon friend examined me this morning.

I don't know why I asked her if I had MS (multiple sclerosis). I have never known anyone with this disease, nor do I have any information about it other than an awareness of the fact that the disease usually is diagnosed in young people between the ages of twenty and forty. This is the second time I have raised the MS issue. The week before, I arrived early for the board meeting at Marcus Garvey Homes and was on the floor stretching my legs when Dr. Granville da Costa walked in. In response to his question as to what on earth I was doing on the floor, I explained about the leg problem. He wondered why I didn't have it checked out. My response: because I don't want to find out that I have MS. He told me that I couldn't have MS; didn't have the right symptoms. So where on earth is this idea coming from?

"She said that the problem was certainly not a disk problem, that I have something seriously wrong happening in my spine and that I need to be seen by a neurologist."

"And just when might this take place?" Myrna says, a look of concern and compassion on her face.

"I wasn't sure when I left her office. She said that her friend at Women's College Hospital was away on a holiday for two weeks, but this couldn't wait for two weeks. She personally would contact another neurologist and get me an appointment at the earliest possible time and would let me know as soon as the appointment was in place." Another outbreak of sobs: *My God, I can't even wait two weeks? Am I dying? I'm only experiencing a bit of a limp. Can it be that bad?*

"And early this afternoon she called to say I have an appointment to see Dr. Allan Gordon at Mount Sinai Hospital in Toronto on Monday afternoon. My God, Myrna, what am I going to do about this weekend?"

I explain that the family is gathering at Bayne and Bette's home in Ottawa on Saturday morning to celebrate my fortieth birthday, a tradition in the Perrin family. I don't think I can deal with my own scares about "what if," let alone have to take care of Mom and Father and their scares.

"I just can't face them, Myrna. What am I going to do?"

"Call Bayne and tell him!" Easy for her to say!

At 11:30 at night, I do place the call and Bayne is very caring.

"Not a problem, Dale. We'll postpone the party. The food can be frozen. Not to worry. Just take care of yourself, sweetie," he says, the last words barely audible.

Ken was less understanding, possibly because I woke him up.

"But the plans are all in place. People are coming from all over. You can't just call off the whole thing. What about Mom and Dad?"

"I would like you and Jan to drive to Kitchener tomorrow and explain things to them. I don't want to talk to them personally and I don't want them to hear it on the telephone. Will you do that?"

"Yes, sure; I'm really sorry, Dale. I hope everything will be okay. When will you be talking to them? I know they'll ask."

"I'll talk to them when I know what's happening. I'm going to Lewiston with Myrna for the weekend. Thanks, Ken."

Thank God Myrna is here for the TA course being held in Toronto. She will keep me grounded and help me prepare for—whatever.

Just one thing to do before I run away: I must tell Jim Robertson. I'm scheduled for a class and, well, maybe I can bluff my way through it, but I do want Jim to know.

I can't bluff my way through; I start crying the minute Jim greets me. He sends me home, with love and a big hug, and tearfully he heads for the classroom. I wonder if he can make it without crying.

Monday morning we arrive back at my residence to find Mom and Father waiting. "We just want to take you for lunch," Father says, and off we go to my favourite, the VIP Restaurant, for lunch and a "casual" visit. Both parents are very careful not to probe. They just let me tell the story in my nonemotional way. I really am glad to see them and they do seem to be handling the situation well.

After lunch Jan, my sister-in-law, comes to accompany me to Dr. Gordon's office. I'm sure she—an emergency room nurse—will understand what the neurologist tells me; I'm not sure I will be able to take it in. She does—and when I'm back home, Jan and Penny, who is now at the kitchen table/desk, both hug me as I (we) cry and let the feelings flow.

"He said that Dale could have one of five possible problems and he won't know what the diagnosis will be until he can conduct extensive testing," Jan explains to Penny (and me). Amongst those five: a brain tumor, a spinal tumor, a blood blockage of some sort, MS and ... (I still couldn't take in number five option). "Dale is to prepare for hospitalization in the next day or two."

The call comes later that afternoon: I'm to be admitted to Mount Sinai Hospital in Toronto on Wednesday. The next two days are busy. Myrna will come in from Lewiston and drive me to the hospital and attend to the business aspect of my practice by phone and a visit every few days. Carol Morris agrees to take two evening groups and Jim Robertson will do the third. Penny will be over every day to look after the cats, the phone calls, the coffee for the groups and just about everything else. I'm blessed with compassionate and competent friends.

Late Tuesday afternoon Myrna arrives and drives me to Oshawa to see the two sisters who form the nucleus of the Wednesday night group to explain my absence. Both these young women were traumatized by early life abandonment issues and other forms of abuse, and I'm most concerned about possible additional trauma with my sudden "indefinite" hospitalization. Myrna assures them that she will keep them informed and gives them permission to contact her whenever they need to do so.

As we exit my townhouse door, I hesitate for just a moment. Will I ever return to my home again? Will I come back here on my feet? Questions with no answers threaten to overwhelm me. We drive to Toronto in silence. And I'm admitted. I go through a week of testing; I am "held" by the good wishes of so many people—over a hundred cards, a dozen bouquets of flowers, phone calls (Bayne calls every morning at eight o'clock and Shelley calls every couple of days), visits (when I'm ready) and then—the results.

Dr. Gordon, a troop of interns and several nurses enter, filling up what little space exists in this small room that I share at the moment with an empty bed. Dr. Gordon, who stands as far from me as he can get, starts talking. He rambles on about the protein count in the spinal fluid being inconclusive, in the "high normal" range. But—and on he goes. I don't understand what he is trying to tell me and, at this moment, all I want is for this group of onlookers to disappear so I can cry, not about what the good doctor is saying because I don't get it. I have just now come back to my room from a very unpleasant experience and I need to cry.

As they exit, finally, one nurse stays behind, notices that I have turned over on my side and am starting to cry. She says, in a gentle, compassion-filled voice, "Forget whatever you have heard about MS, Dale. I have to go on rounds but I will come back and talk to you later. There are lots of reasons to feel optimistic about what is happening with MS research."

"It isn't that. I'll explain when you come back," I say, choking on my words as the sobs begin. Now I feel intense frustration, helplessness and relief, relief that I *only* have MS. Of the five possibilities, that was the least threatening to me, possibly because I don't know what that really means. What is upsetting me is the way I have been abused by a totally insensitive, callous lab technician. For some reason I was scheduled for a last set of X-rays—X-rays that required me to hold my head in an awkward position while this woman pointed the equipment down my gaping open mouth. I was subjected to a spinal tap the day before and told that it was critical to keep the head still and level for twenty-four hours, otherwise I would experience a "grand-mal" headache. I am now experiencing that headache! And this woman couldn't care less. It was her job to get the X-rays and get the X-rays she did, even if it meant forcing my head to twist just so. The searing pain didn't allow me to say much other than, "Stop, you're hurting me," to which she responded, "This will only take a minute." *Why is it that when I am most vulnerable someone always wants to hurt me?* a little voice within me says.

For the next two weeks I am given a heavy dose of steroids and a great deal of advice. The occupational therapist tells me to remove any scatter rugs I may have. The physiotherapist and the physiatrist show me a set of stretching exercising I must do for my legs, as well as instructions as to icing the right thigh muscles twice a day for twenty minutes. The nurse advises me to stay away from any organization with support groups related to MS because other people's stories may frighten me. She also advises me to let go of the idea of having hot baths or showers. The urologist gives me a huge bottle of red pills I am to pop, just like I would an aspirin, at the first sign of bladder infections. *My God, I just have a gimpy leg—or did.* Right now I'm euphoric and have no sign of any gimp. I could run a marathon, I'm sure. I don't understand what all the fuss is about. To me, MS means I limp when I'm fatigued and I intend to live with that reality until my body tells me otherwise. I do love my hot showers!

Finally I'm allowed to go home—to my very own home! I begin to cry as Myrna turns into the driveway of the townhouse complex. I'm home. *Is there life after MS?*

I NEVER PROMISED YOU A ROSE GARDEN

Have you experienced a catastrophic illness or accident or event in your life? If so, how did you cope? What thoughts, feelings and/or behaviours surfaced, and were these helpful or hurtful?

What were the responses of the significant persons in your life? Helpful? Hurtful?

Did you gain any new awareness about yourself? Did the trauma reinforce old patterns or did you have to develop new coping skills and/or life skills?

FROM DOUBTS TO DREAMS

I manage quite successfully to push this nagging question out of my awareness. I'm much too busy to worry about "what-if's." Before my hospitalization I was introduced to Larry Cash, MSc, who developed a private practice focusing on career assessment and counselling. Larry agreed to be identified as an associate in my practice and provide career counselling to those of my clientele requiring that service. I use this opportunity to develop a new brochure and do another major mailing to the lawyers and family doctors in the area (the profession prohibits advertising.)

Myrna persuades me to design a weekend workshop that she will cofacilitate (in order to assuage my "scared" little kid) and this opens up a whole new world to me. I'm on my way—moving through my comfort zone to new, previously unimaginable, successes. I know now that I can do workshops on my own.

Carol adds to my growing sense of competency.

"I have never experienced a TA group like yours, Dale."

Oh my goodness, what if I've been doing it all wrong? What if I've misunderstood the journal articles and books I've been reading and set up my groups—well, backwards. Am I going to hear "I can't explain it to you but it isn't group therapy," echoes of Frank Johnson?

"All your clients are 'little therapists.' I've never experienced a group with clients who are so sophisticated and knowledgeable about TA theory. And I've never experienced such loving and compassion."

"What do you mean, Carol?"

"Well, I finished a piece of work with Barb and was about to continue on with another group member when John stopped me and said, 'Wait a minute. We haven't given our strokes yet.' [Strokes are compliments and/or other comments or behaviours that acknowledge and recognize the person being addressed.] He proceeded to tell Barb that she had done a brave and beautiful piece of work. And then he got up and hugged her. And then the other group members gave strokes and hugs. I was so surprised. At the end of the evening, they gave me strokes and hugs, too."

"Is that unusual?"

"Yes, actually I was very touched."

I'm surprised by this. Carol has been attending international conferences and has witnessed many therapists "doing therapy," teaching core concepts and giving and receiving hugs and other forms of strokes. What does this say about me?

I'm not sure of my own potency as a TA therapist as compared to others, but I am sure of the potency of this particular model identified as transactional analysis. I know these concepts help me, and others, understand ourselves and indicate ways in which we can grow and change. And I'm beginning to recognize the potency of loving: how people expressing authentic caring and compassion for each other nurtures growth and enables both the one who strokes and those who receive strokes, to risk vulnerability, which facilitates the healing process. And it isn't just the "client," the "group member," who begins to blossom and grow. It's me too.

What is becoming so clear to me now? Ego states! What I now understand is that I (we) am (are) like a three-drawer filing system. In the top drawer, labeled Parent Ego State, I stored the thoughts (attitudes), feelings and behaviours of my mother, father, and even my grandmother and aunt at various impactful moments. For example, I stored "Anything worth doing is worth doing well," a familiar theme of my father's. I stored my mother's behaviours, her "random acts of kindness" towards my relatives, even towards "the sisters" who were unkind to her. She didn't say the words, "Be kind to others," but her behaviour spoke volumes. And I recorded gestures and behaviours of both parents. Bette, my sister-in-law, will tease me with comments like, "Boy, I see your mom in you."

The second drawer is labeled Adult Ego State. In this ego state I filed away lots of life skills that I learned and experienced as useful in dealing with the world today. For example, my dear field instructor in graduate school explained to me that "anger" means "unhappy." I now deal with anger very differently than I did before I had that piece of wisdom. To elaborate, instead of getting scared and wanting to defend myself, I now ask the angry person to tell me more, to help me understand what I did or said that was hurtful; and I listen to the explanation. I can then relate to the person's perception and the lens through which they viewed my words or behaviours or the situation and sympathize. I then ask if they are willing to hear what I *intended* and clarify my thoughts and feelings. It is truly amazing what a difference it makes to the angry person to know that they are heard. Poof—there goes the anger.

The bottom drawer is labeled the Child Ego State. In this drawer I carry with me the little kid I was "back then" and the decisions I made when I was experiencing various significant events. For example, that time when I dashed into the kitchen and asked my father to help me—Bayne was stuffing snow down Ken's throat and I needed my father to intervene. My father accused me of being a tattletale and proceeded to collapse, literally sliding down the fridge to the floor. I remember thinking that "my needs are overwhelming" and promising God (or the powers that be) that I would never ask anything from anyone again. And I have lived with that decision for a very long time—*without being aware of it.*

I visualize these ego states as repositories where "energy" is stored. And you, the observer, can't see what is in my filing system—because I have covered the cabinet up with my outward appearance, disguised as "me." What you can see, hear, feel, experience, is my words, my behaviours, the look on my face and other gestures. You can begin to surmise what is stored away when I *act*. The Parent Ego State contains two sections, one referred to as the Critical Parent, the other as the Nurturing Parent, each with hundreds of little files, also called parent ego states. When I'm acting from the Critical Parent ego state, I'm being critical, judgmental, prejudiced, and I frequently use the terms "should," "shouldn't," "right" and "wrong," and/or I'm frowning, being patronizing or righteous. For example, "You shouldn't dress like that to go to a party" or "That was a stupid thing to do. What on earth were you thinking?"

When I'm acting from my Nurturing Parent, I'm being supportive and caring. What I learned from Carol is that I modeled and encouraged "nurturing" in my groups, a behaviour that is second nature to me. My Adult ego state lets me know when such nurturing is appropriate and useful; when it is healthy for me to give myself or others permissions to do or be; and how to protect myself when I'm vulnerable, how to "be me" safely and how to create a safe environment where others can risk being vulnerable.

The Child Ego State also has two major sections, labeled Free Child and Adapted Child. Oh my, what a treasure house of material these ego states contain. The free child is the natural, beautiful, spontaneous, creative, imaginative being that I am spiritually and genetically meant to be. Here is the little girl that loved to cuddle little animals, that loved adventure, that loved Gramma's cookies, that loved learning new things. And then we meet the Adapted Child, that little girl who decided she had to be strong and figure things out on her own, who learned that it wasn't safe to be vulnerable, who learned that men are onstage centre front and women are gentle people behind the scenes. Oh my, what pain she carries/carried.

As I learn and understand all this, I provide others who are willing to explore what is stored in their ego states, opportunities to grow from their awarenesses. And script patterns emerge. What is now in my awareness I can change, sometimes overnight, sometimes it takes longer.

I really appreciate now that "script" involves several components. What my parents did and said, the stuff stashed away in the Parent Ego State drawer, has a set of files that tell me what they believe is the way to success (or failure), their prescriptions. That is fairly easy to identify. I know, for example, that working hard, doing my best and being kind to others are helpful messages. If my parents had said things like, "You're just like your (drunken, lazy, good-for-nothing) dad," the message might suggest the path to failure.

The tricky aspect of script is to identify what messages I'm getting from the Child ego state of my parents, especially the Adapted Child ego state: those thoughts, feelings and behaviours that are out of our awareness. What I'm understanding is that my mother never said to me that I was not okay, not the daughter that she wanted. But from her "disappointments" in my lack of interest in domestic and craft activities, I "concluded" that being the me I am is not okay, and I interpreted it to be a "don't be you" injunction (a nonverbal message that the child experiences as a prohibition). And my father never said, "Don't be a child," but I "concluded" that having needs like feeling scared, wanting to be cuddled, expressing anger, or being silly, giggly and noisy, was not okay. He was clearly disappointed when I behaved in those ways, and my mother made it very clear that I was not to upset my father.

How powerful, how amazing to uncover these mysteries! Now I'm in the process of changing, of letting go of the behaviours that have held me back. I'm growing, my practice is growing and my clients are growing, as they too become increasingly aware of script patterns and conclusions and behaviours that they want to change.

As my practice mushrooms and I move into activities that previously I was "too scared" to even consider, I'm beginning to recognize the need for me to do some planning, to take charge of the growth of this business. I sign up for a crash course being offered at Sheridan Community College, the first of a series of business management courses. Finally I'm going to find out "how to start a business," the basics of "business law" and "how to manage the financial aspects of business." As I begin the first course, I'm presented with a wonderful opportunity that I experience in a dream.

A dream—no, I don't mean a goal. I literally have a dream, a nighttime-early-in-the-morning-just-before-you-wake-up dream. And I wake up seeing the words "Perrin, Patterson, Farkas and Associates." I'm so excited. I can hardly wait to call Terry Patterson and tell him what I've "dreamed" and the plan I have for *his* life!

It is now early 1979 and the housing market is bottoming. The economy is in recession or depression—I'm not sure just what the difference is—and people are being forced out of their homes. Unit 19, the end unit tucked in behind my row of houses, is being offered for sale at a reduced price. I decide to purchase it—it's perfect! I can run my business tucked away at the end of this complex, with parking spots between the two units, and have room to invite Terry and Marianne Farkas to set up business with me. We can deliver a range of services operating out of these two units without bothering anyone. That's what I'm going to present to Terry.

Now Marianne is a different story. Marianne is the community consultant with the Addiction Research Foundation. She is the woman who introduced me to court programs and invited me to participate in the newspaper columns. We are developing a lovely friendship when she informs me that she is leaving for Boston to earn her doctoral degree. I doubt if she plans to return to this area, but hey, I neglected to tell my dream world about that fact.

Terry laughs on the telephone when I tell him about Perrin, Patterson, Farkas and Associates, but is willing to meet me at the VIP Restaurant for lunch and hear about this "dream." Terry, a man of average height and weight, with a warm smile and a gentle manner, is the community consultant and director of the Addiction Research Foundation in Mississauga. I'm sitting at my usual table in this busy family-owned restaurant (Tina and Nick now consider me "family" since I eat most of my meals here—I never did learn to cook) when Terry arrives. After exchanging pleasantries and placing our orders, I share my "dream-dream."

"Actually Dale, I am planning to move into private practice but not until I complete my doctorate. That's about two years down the road."

"That's great, Terry. I will rent out Unit 19 for two years and then we have an office," I say, attempting to mask my growing excitement. I explain my current setup, the present associates and my move into providing a wider range of services. Terry doesn't make any commitments, but in my heart I'm nurturing the dream in its modified form—Perrin, Patterson and Associates, Enrichment and Growth Resource Centre.

By the fall I'm in a position to act on another dream—or perhaps "fantasy" better describes it. I'm going to "investigate the Watergate scandal"! I have now read the published memoirs of all the leading (and secondary) characters in the Watergate drama, the drama that captured my interest back in my "lean, mean" days. I make reservations for accommodations at the Howard Johnson Motel, opposite the Watergate Hotel, in Washington DC, the same motel where Howard Hunt and his "burglar team" stayed to execute their scheme. And I'm going to explore the Watergate Hotel itself, to see if I can find any bugs, or at least an exquisite meal. I'm going to "do" Capitol Hill and the White House, and I'm going to eat at the same restaurant where the president frequently dines. And, to accommodate my mother's fears, I agree to get myself a cane—a cane! A visible sign that I have a problem! *Oh my God! Everyone will know I'm vulnerable.*

Not only am I vulnerable, but when I arrive at the Howard Johnson, I realize that I will have difficulty standing in lines of tourists awaiting entrance to these historic places. I notice a brochure on the desk that describes babysitting services, so I call the number and ask if it is possible to "hire a babysitter" to take me through these particular sites. The woman who responds to my inquiry is delighted. She will place a few calls and see if she can find someone to accommodate me for a day of touring. I know that public buildings have wheelchairs available, and my plan is to drive as close as possible to the sites and have this person go into the building and get a chair for me. In five minutes I have a call back. A young university student will meet with me the next morning. I will have my one and only (I hope) experience in a wheelchair—which is okay. Nobody knows me. I'm not ready to acknowledge that such a need may exist in the very distant future, maybe. I am now learning about "reaching out" for help, a very new experience.

And I have another reason to dream: this one, a daytime hope, a possibility that touches my heart at a different level.

The phone rings just as I'm about to exit the front door. Mom and Father are waiting for me to go out for dinner. "Hello," I say, rather irritated at this interruption.

"Hi, this is Hayward."

Oh my God—it's been five-plus years. I'm stunned.

"Are you there?"

"Oh yes, yes. How are you, Hayward?"

"I'm fine, Dale. Actually I have some news for you. I'm going to be in Toronto in a couple of weeks and I'd really like to see you. Would you be willing to see me?"

"For sure, yes, yes. Is this a business trip?"

"In a way, yes, I'm going to look for a job and if I can find one, I will be coming back to live." Now my heart is jumping and I can feel my face flush. I can't believe I'm this excited.

"I'll explain it all in a letter, Dale; I just wanted to know if we could get together. I'm really looking forward to seeing you. Will you give me your address?"

I do that and we end the conversation. He's coming back! I guess I shouldn't be surprised. He is my shaman healer, my lover, the one who helps me through all my traumas. How does he know?

Hayward explains in his letter that his wife (*oh dear, he married again*) left the marriage after just two months. She couldn't take the political turmoil and the physical danger, the upheaval that threatened the stability of the government and those associated with it, and decided to move to New York. Hayward feels committed to work towards stabilizing his country, has a deep sense of love, a passion for his country of origin and wasn't willing to leave—until now, now that his life has been threatened.

In my letter to Hayward I explain that I have "changed," that I have learned a lot about myself and am so looking forward to exploring new possibilities with him.

A friend drives Hayward in from Toronto and then leaves. I have carefully hidden my cane—now's not the time to tell him. Not yet. We talk, we hug, we head for the stairs—and I need my cane.

I tell him. Tears begin to roll down his cheeks. "My God, my God, how could this happen to you? You're so good, so beautiful! Bad things are not supposed to happen to good people."

"I'm okay, I'm okay; really I am. Hayward, Hayward, just hold me, just love me and let's not talk about it anymore." I'm not ready to go there yet, to grieve the loss, the health issue that threatens my well-being. What I most want this moment is to experience myself enveloped in unconditional love—to affirm my womaness, my desirability, my wholeness.

The following week we have dinner in the Forest Room, my favourite dining room, in the Ramada Hotel. And then we talk.

Sitting across from Hayward, only slightly aware of the guitarist pouring his soul into romantic ballads, totally unaware of the obsequious waiters hovering about noting every mouthful of food being consumed, I ask the question that has been on my mind for years.

"Why didn't we marry, Hayward?"

"You don't remember?"

"Remember what?"

"You told me that you needed time to do some thinking. You were very clear that you would contact me when you were ready to move ahead with our marriage plans."

"I did?"

"Yes, and you never did."

"What, I never called? But ... I was waiting for you to call and tell me about your visit with your mom and her reaction to the news."

"No, no, you were very clear—'don't call me. I'll call you.'"

"But why didn't you call me, Hayward? How could you just let me drift away like that? I felt abandoned, unloved. I began to question my perceptions of you, me, us. I began to think the whole relationship was fraudulent, a rationalization for sex, nothing more."

"I did! My God, what a selective memory you have! I called you, remember? I just had a car accident."

"Yeah, but that was five months later. You sounded drunk. I couldn't figure out what that call was about."

"I was calling to hear you say that you loved me and wanted to marry me!"

"Well, you didn't ask me. I was waiting for you to explain your sudden disappearance. I was hoping you would say, 'I love you, Dale, and I can't live another moment without you.' Not only did you *not* say that, but three months later you call and inform me that you are married. Now you're married, divorced, remarried and separated— more or less. Where does that leave you and me? And when do I get to hear, 'I love you, Dale, and I insist you marry me.'"

Such craziness—I realize now. Hayward explains how "inscrutable" I have been, how he never knew when he called whether I was pleased that he called, whether I missed him during those long weeks and sometimes months when we were geographically unable to see each other very often. Even when we made love—he never knew what was pleasurable, what was in my heart.

Never again, Hayward, never again! I explain what I have been learning about me and promise him that he will never have to guess what I'm thinking or feeling again, that I will tell him. How could I have been so closed, so defended?

The restaurant is empty. Only one waiter remains. We're both surprised when he informs us of the time and politely requests that we pay the bill and leave.

The lovemaking is intense, passionate—no more words, just the release of unfettered energy, no holding back. As our relationship grows I'm now willing to introduce Hayward to the world, starting with Pauline, who has arrived for a long weekend visit.

"I'm so nervous," I admit to Pauline as we drive to Toronto. "After so many years you are finally going to meet Hayward. If you make a scene or give him a rough time, I swear I'll leave you stranded at the restaurant."

We're seated at our reserved table at the Hungarian Restaurant, one of Hayward's favourite dining places, and have ordered our wine when he walks in. I'm tense, expecting Pauline to make a comment about Hayward operating on "Jamaican time." She doesn't. I make the introductions and comment on the quaint décor, the sensual appeal of the restaurant. I needn't have bothered. Pauline and Hayward connect immediately when Hayward comments that he is a friend of so-and-so, a dear friend of Pauline's, and they are off and running.

Stories of "back home," anecdotes about their shared friends and acquaintances, laughter about similar educational experiences, occasional lapses into the familiar patois of the Jamaican marketplace, discussions about the legal system and the role of women in Jamaican society, are consumed with more obvious delight than the culinary offerings placed before us.

"My God, it's late," I say, yawning conspicuously, thoroughly sated with spicy, meaty goulash and dumplings, several glasses of dry red wine and conversation that to a large extent excluded me. "We really have to go."

The uneasiness I'm experiencing for reasons I don't really understand quickly dissipates on the drive home.

"Well, what do you think?"

"He's great—not at all your typical Jamaican male."

One hurdle crossed, fueling the possibilities that just maybe this time we'll get it right.

As our relationship matures, so too does another creative idea, another dream. This one is called CALM, an acronym for Caring and Loving Myself. After I ventured out to do a "day workshop" for women volunteers who work for an organization known as the Peel Lunch and After School Program (PLASP) (another breakthrough in tackling the stage-fright issue), a workshop based entirely on the concept of self-nurturing, I sensed that I could design a kit, a do-it-yourself therapy kit, that would give women (or anyone, for that matter) an opportunity to get the same information in the comfort of their own homes. I'm so aware that my programming, my script, is so stereotypically the cultural norm for many North American white middle-class women. I, like so many women, am highly tuned to anticipate the needs of others. I'm the gentle caretaker in the background, like my mother, *the woman behind the man.* Other women I'm working with (and most of the women attending this workshop) reflect other familiar "women" patterns, most of which do not encourage women to take care of their own needs as well as the needs of others.

Throughout the past year I have been writing, editing, recording on my Sony ghetto blaster, a program that evolved into four cassette tapes and a workbook. In six weeks the program walks the listener through a change process based on learning all about the potency and necessity for positive strokes and then, how to get these strokes in a healthy way. The need for recognition, for acknowledgement, for validation, to know we are loved and appreciated, is so basic, so critical to our emotional and spiritual well-being—every bit as critical as our need for food, water, sleep. I'm convinced that such a program, if marketed the right way, could reach out and touch the lives of many women, right in their own homes. By the summer of '81, I have the program ready to be produced. Now the challenge is to incorporate a company to produce the kit, find investors willing to fund the project, someone to produce and package it and someone to put together a marketing and promotional program to sell it—and, oh yes, someone to store and then mail out the kits. Do I know how to do any of this? No, but I do know how to find people with expertise and I do just that.

Each step in the process is a challenge. I keep pushing up against my script issues. I have to reach out to others and "ask." I must be willing to trust—to trust that someone would actually want me to succeed and be willing to give time and energy to support me—and money. And I must be willing to be "out front," to be onstage centre front, to be important and be successful.

With the help of Margaret Black, a delightful pint-sized lawyer with a powerful presence and persuasive voice, and her accountant, who has graciously agreed to support the business proposal that has been prepared by Debbie Larson, a former client, I call together a group of folks who have indicated an interest in investing in the project and becoming shareholders in this new company. My brothers and a nephew are willing to do this. Other friends and acquaintances I have met over the years also agree. By the end of the evening all that remains to be done is for Margaret to prepare the paperwork.

September '81, SAGE KITS, Inc. comes into being. SAGE is an acronym for Self-Administered Growth Experience—the CALM (Caring and Loving Myself) KIT being only the first of five that I have in my mind. It's a go! *Dear God—don't let me blow it!*

Drake Norman, another former client, owns a printing company. This lovely man is excited about the project and is willing to design the kit that will contain the tapes and workbook, print the workbook and package the materials. He asks his graphic designer to listen to my "practice tapes" and design an image that will cover the kit and workbook. Voilà—a stylistic sketch of the "new woman."

Then I need to find a recording studio and someone willing to walk me through hours and hours of talking into a mike. I do find such a studio and talk and talk I do, following the directions of the "professionals." And then I'm confronted with another bit of reality. After six hours of recording and a few days of waiting for the master tapes, I get to listen to me, to preview the results—and I cry. Oh my God, I sound like a loud, fast-talking salesman pushing a new, improved vacuum cleaner. Since the tape includes several guided meditations and is meant to be quiet, reflective and supportive of self-nurturing, this is an absolute disaster. Now I have to trust my own wisdom and tell the professionals that the tapes that they think turned out to be "terrific" now have to be scrapped and we have to do it all over again, *my way.* I know this will cost me money but will it cost me "cooperation"? Am I going to bruise some egos and be sent on my way? No, they are willing to go through the process again, for half the original cost—and I am pleased with the results.

The business plan outlines the primary marketing strategy: the placement of two ads, one in the *Homemakers* magazine and another in *Chatelaine.* The secondary strategy is a direct mail program to women's centers, libraries and other services promoting the well-being of women. I'm given the name of an ad agency that is willing to work with new ideas and fledgling companies, and now I bump into another problem. The creative ad people want me to use language antithetical to what I believe is healthy and nurturing. They insist I use "you should" and "you must"—words coming from the Critical Parent ego state. They insist that if I use the words that are more comfortable for me, I will get zero response. Dear Drake agrees with me and fixes the ad they have prepared with my wording. I go with "my words"—and the ad company will place the revised ads for me, but that will end our relationship. *Dear God, dear God—what have I done? And what if ...?*

The next challenge threatens to do me in completely! I will have to *conquer* the stage-fright issue. Ann McRoberts, a tall, attractive British woman with years of experience in working with the media, agrees to develop a media kit and set up a cross-country tour of all the major cities except in the province of Quebec—I don't speak French. The material attracts a great deal of attention—a whopping success in Ann's eyes—and I'm invited to appear on major TV programs and newscasts and a variety of different radio programs. I'm scheduled to be interviewed by newspapers and some magazine reporters from across the country. Now the thought of one on one interviews with newspaper and magazine reporters doesn't frighten me anymore. We are to start with the Toronto media and then Ann has a two-week schedule for me to travel from St. John's, Newfoundland to Vancouver, B.C.

I started to break through my stage-fright issue in March by accepting an invitation to present a ten-minute paper at a day conference for women sponsored by the Peel Social Planning Council, a conference looking at women's issues for the eighties. Just a ten-minute paper—I thought I could bluff my way through this, though I did prepare by attending a six-week program in Toronto that was advertised for those who suffer stage fright. I actually have a dress rehearsal with a small group of participants who report that I don't look the least bit nervous. But TV—lights, camera, action?

To help me prepare for TV, Ann arranges for private tutoring with Margo Lane, who anchors a popular noon-hour program for one of the Toronto stations. After two sessions Margo reports to Ann that I really don't need any more coaching, that I will do just fine—perhaps it looks that way to her since we are working one-on-one, with the TV cameras and lights blazing, mind you.

And then, the big one! Ann drives me to the studio in Barrie, Ontario, in late December and with the help of a gallon of cold water, I talk my way through a ten- to twelve-minute interview—and I don't collapse, I don't go blank, I don't pee my pants. Ann tells me I did just fine and I want so much to believe her, but I'm not convinced. Maybe by the time this is all over I'll get used to it. Please, dear God.

The last piece is in place. I find a small direct-mail company run by two delightful women who are willing to store the kits and handle the packaging and mailing. December 1 the ads appear in the magazines—I'm ready for anything.

I'm sailing into '82. Perrin, Patterson and Associates is up and running with new associates. Jim, Carol and Myrna have moved on their own career paths, and Sonja Tran and Stephanie Tonin are presently providing therapy sessions for me. The "association" with Larry Cash doesn't work out. I really don't have a sufficient number of clients that need this service. We continue to work together by referring clients to each other when the need arises. Marcus Garvey Homes is surviving and presently experiencing only one or two major catastrophes a week. SAGE KITS, Inc. is operational, and I'm embarking on my own path of script-busting. My relationship with Hayward is flourishing. And yes, I have MS, but that only means I'm walking with a little gimp and I have a cane.

What else could I possibly want?

FROM DOUBTS TO DREAMS

Understanding ego states and recognizing the thoughts, feelings and behaviours associated with each functional ego state is very useful for developing self-awareness and identifying decisions, behaviours and feelings that we now may want to change. How I began this process of understanding was by doing a very simple exercise. I encourage you to experience it too.

First, identify something that you presently need or want. For me, what I most wanted was "leisure time" (I was working ten hours a day).

Then draw five stacked circles (as in a really big snowperson), representing the five functional ego states. Label the top circle as Critical Parent, the one below as Nurturing Parent, the next as Adult, the second to last as Free Child and the bottom circle as Adapted Child.

Now place the "want" beside the Free Child and fill in the "voices" in your head.

My loudest voice was, "You have to work hard if you are going to succeed!" Aha, the Critical Parent voice!

The next voice I heard: "If I say 'no' to someone who wants to come in right away, I won't please them and they'll be mad and go away." Aha, the Adapted Child voice.

The next voice I heard: "You could ask someone to come in as an associate and help you and then you'll have time to play." Aha, the Nurturing Parent voice.

And finally, with a giggle (my little Free Child), my Adult voice kicks in: "Yes, I'm my own boss. I can arrange my own schedule *and* I can look for an associate!"

Bingo! I talked with my friend Jim Robertson at Sheridan College the following week.

Now you: what awareness do you have? Do you have dreams? Goals you want to reach? Is there anything holding you back from achieving these dreams? If so, can you identify the "what-if's," the scares that block you from moving forward?

Are you willing to change the thoughts, feelings or behaviours that are getting in your way?

THE LAW'S THE LAW

It's a bust! I'm devastated! Not one response to the ads. The ad professionals were right. And the ad company feels that their integrity has been violated and they sure don't want me to come back. Now I've blown half of the investors' loans. They're going to hate me.

They don't—bless them. I'm encouraged to move on to Plan B and initiate the direct-mail program. Over the next several years I initiate several targeted mailings across both Canada and the northern states, more specifically, New York. This succeeds in moving many kits and allows me to stay in my one-person business (with the help of the dear women distributors, who agree to store the remaining inventory free of charge) for a few more years. And in addition, I now volunteer to do "CALM workshops" for one particular MS support group and many churchwomen's groups. With each presentation I donate kits for their personal use.

Why did the program bomb? That's a question that puzzles me and the investors. The responses I receive from several folks (and services) who purchased the kit are all positive. We conclude that I'm years ahead of the market. Only one American company has produced audiotapes of a self-help or self-improvement nature. The majority of people (and our culture) are visual as opposed to auditory in learning style. And "therapy" or "personal growth" is still a matter to be kept in the closet. Perhaps this is the explanation. We'll never know. What I am sure of, though, is that risking moving a dream to its end is never a failure. What an amazing learning and growing experience—and how affirming to know that others are willing to support me, even to risk financially and lose, without a word of reprisal, without rejection.

And I experience another "bust."

"Is she back?" I say as the sobs break through, refusing to be suppressed another minute. We are in the kitchen of Hayward's new townhouse. I knew that his estranged wife had contacted him now that he had fled Jamaica, but I didn't know that she had moved in. The evidence was hanging in his bedroom closet.

"I'm so confused, so confused," Hayward says, choking back his own tears. "She hasn't moved back in yet; she's just visiting."

"But sweetheart, you are here now. I am here now. I love you and I know you love me. Can you honestly say that you love her, that you want to make a life here with her?"

"No, no, I can't. I don't know. I don't really know who she is anymore. But I made a commitment. I don't want to experience another marriage breakdown. I feel like such a failure! I have a moral responsibility. I have to give myself, and her, the opportunity to find out if we love each other and can make a life together. Right now I can't make a decision. I have nothing to offer anyone."

The depth of Hayward's despair doesn't ease the pain in my heart, nor can I hold back my own tears. "I told you that night in the Forest Room, Hayward, that I would tell you my truth from now on, that I wouldn't leave you guessing. I know what I want, and I'm not going to make it easy for you this time. I'm not going to walk away. I love you. You decide what you want. I'm not walking away whether you're in or out of your marriage. It's your decision."

I leave Hayward's house, and Toronto, in tears, unable to come to grips with what is happening, unable to even think about the implications of what I have just said—just acutely aware that I'm experiencing a big rip in my heart, the possibility of losing what has taken me years to recognize—the love of my life.

And then the "tax man" calls. We are in another recession/ depression—I still don't know the difference—and this government is particularly mean-spirited. I have nothing to worry about though; I'm so straight that I squeak. For two years now several of my business clients, especially those who have their own small businesses, tell me I'm foolish to "give receipts" when someone pays in cash. I'm glad now that I am so honest. That is until these two men, who have spent two days reviewing my relatively few records (this is not a six-figure operation) and drinking my coffee, give me the results of their audit.

"Is this the painting you rented and then purchased for your business?" the senior auditor asks, his face totally expressionless, his dark eyes piercing even behind thick rimmed glasses.

"No, it's that one," I say, pointing to the large painting hanging in the stairwell.

"You can't deduct that. It isn't in your interview room." And then I realize this is not going to be an easy process. By the time these gentlemen are ready to leave, I learn that I owe the government some $20,000—a pronouncement that leaves me speechless and staggering. I'm to let them know within seven days how I intend to pay the amount owing. Seven days!

It doesn't take me seven days to talk to my accountant and another Bay Street lawyer, a specialist in tax matters. He advises me to hold the payment (I have a choice?) and he will do the negotiating with the government. While this negotiating is going on over several months, I get a phone call from the tax man every two or three weeks to pay now—and possibly be reimbursed with interest when the matter is resolved. I continue to stall. Edie Wilson, my friendly real estate agent, is in the process of finding me a condo to sublet to allow me to sell my home, Unit 20, and pay the tax man. Terry and I can both work from Unit 19.

During this stressful time Terry, and I are faced with a new threat. We come back from lunch to discover a business card under the door of Unit 19—the bylaw enforcement officer has been by for a visit. I dutifully respond to his request for a phone call. He is back within the hour to inform me that we must "cease and desist" from operating our business immediately or apply to the Committee of Adjustments to request a hearing to vary the bylaw. An anonymous person has complained to the city. I will need special permission to operate a business from a "high-density residential"-zoned location.

Terry, Penny's husband Colin Moore (who is also the president of the condominium corporation) and I arrive for the scheduled hearing this warm fall afternoon in late '82. The room looks very much like a courtroom, with two tables and chairs at the front of the room for applicants, complainants and their lawyers. The panel of judges sits on a raised platform about twenty feet in front of the tables. Three gentlemen will be adjudicating this application. Two men arrive and sit down at the complainants' table. I don't recognize either one.

The chairman of the adjudicating panel confirms that I am the applicant. All the information is written and is presented to the other panel members by the chair. Colin reads a statement of support that the condo board has prepared. The complainant is introduced. George Norman, a retired senior citizen who lives immediately adjacent to the condo property, separated only by a fence, is the person who initiated the complaint.

"I'm out in my backyard working in my flower beds and I've noticed people coming and going from Unit 19. Sometimes they stop and say stupid things to me."

"Like what, Mr. Norman?"

"Like 'your garden is lovely' or 'what kind of flowers are those?' and once I saw two people come out and they talked for a while in the parking area and kissed and then got into separate cars and drove away. And I figured they were running a business in there. And, well, the law's the law. They shouldn't be doing that."

"And you?"

"I'm John Sagar. I live in the unit opposite where the cars park. I happen to know that there have been complaints about the parking problems she is creating, even if Mr. Moore isn't reporting it."

The chairman thanks the complainants and informs us that the application is denied. I have thirty days to appeal to the Ontario Municipal Board if I so choose. And that's that!

Terry and I return and begin discussions regarding a move. I have already moved into a sublet condo on the northwest corner of Bloor and Dixie. Clearly I must now find a new place big enough for me to live in and the two of us to work from—and in an area that permits such an operation. Not an easy task. I'm enraged that a "citizen" who is not a resident of the condo and a resident who has a reputation (I learn) for being an obstreperous alcoholic can turn my life upside down like this.

Now, a whole lot wiser, I seek consultation from a planning consultant by the name of John Rogers. John suggests that if I find a single-family dwelling in a "mixed use" zoning area I have a good chance of having an application to vary the bylaw accepted. The regulation (used by chiropractors and similar businesses) is to have a business sign within the specific dimensions prescribed and to avoid any outdoor storage that detracts from the aesthetics of the house—not a problem since I do not intend to post any visible sign that indicates I (we) are in business. He then suggests that when we have located a house, we introduce ourselves to the neighbours and solicit their support. No neighbour complaints, no bylaw problems.

Hurontario Street south of the Queen Elizabeth Way (QEW) offers the best possibility. Although not officially designated as a "mixed use" residential area, several houses along the east side of the street have business signs out front. John believes that it is only a matter of time before the west side of the street will also be used for business purposes. After an extensive search, Edie finds a home on the west side that might serve the purpose. It is an old bungalow that will need extensive work, but, Edie informs me, there is no place in town that will allow me to live and work from my own home. Preliminary inquiries indicate resistance. The possibility of this location working out quickly evaporates.

Edie locates what she believes will be "the perfect" house, a huge back split that has sufficient room to have separate living space, several interview rooms and office space for both Terry and me, plus a group therapy room and a large living-dining room that could host larger workshops. To make it even more perfect, the basement is completely finished and offers a separate place from which to run the SAGE KITS business. The house is located right next to a medical office (on the corner of Bloor and Grand Forks) and backs onto a ravine, in a quiet older residential neighbourhood. The driveway is big enough for six cars—how perfect can it get? Terry and I agree—and I put in the offer and the contract is set. Now all I have to do is find a buyer for Unit 19 and hope I can have all the sales coordinate.

The tax man phones—I assure him I will have the money "very soon." He insists I get a line of credit and pay now. I explain to him that my line of credit is maxed out and that the bank manager is asking for a debt payment plan—or else! The difficulty we are experiencing financially is this. My clients pay as they go so my cash flow is stable. Terry's income comes, for the most part, from government-sponsored programs that he is contracted to provide. With this economy and this government, many "service-related" programs have been cancelled, severely limiting Terry's present income-earning potential. We hoped that we could hang on until the economy changed, but we can't. Terry informs me that he will not be able to continue the partnership. I'm on my own.

Now I'm close to panic-stricken. My anxiety level is sky-high. The money I was going to use to pay the tax man must now be applied to the purchase of this new house. And I have yet to solve the financial crisis at the bank.

I prepare all the financial papers and Terry and I approach the accounts manager with the news of the dissolution of the partnership and the plan for repayment of the line of credit. In fear and trepidation I hand him the statements. Terry explains that I will be taking all the partnership assets and he will assume full responsibility for the repayment of the line of credit. I'm immensely grateful for Terry's integrity and his full support. We are both startled by the manager's offer to Terry of a line of credit equal to the amount that is presently owed, "in order for him to set up business on his own." Terry graciously declines and I comment that I will return in a week to arrange for my own line of credit—so far, so good. I return a week later and learn that I will not be given a line of credit since I do not have "accounts receivable" and I'm unwilling to have my retired father cosign an agreement. My protests fall on deaf ears. Humbly I return to the bank manager I worked with prior to the partnership and *she* is willing to grant me a line of credit. She assures me that she will cover the tax man's demands when the crunch comes—blessed be!

Meanwhile John Rogers, the planning consultant, has submitted my application prior to my actual move for a variance of the bylaw to permit me to live and work in this new residence. When he arrives at the hearing on March 17 he discovers that thirty neighbours turn out to oppose the application. He asks for a deferral until a public meeting with the neighbours can be held, and when this request is turned down, he withdraws the application until a new application can be prepared for a future meeting.

By some mysterious work of God (at least my prayers are heard!) and the formidable workings of one awesome real estate agent, the two houses and the new residence on Grand Forks all have the same closing date, Friday, April 29, 1983, and movers are in place to collect belongings from the two residences to get me plopped into the new house by early afternoon. A team of volunteer friends and clients are there to get me set up and operational for the following Monday.

The tax man calls just ten days later and is furious that I have sold the properties without his permission. "If I had known what you were up to, I would have slapped a lien against Unit 20 and your move never would have taken place." I was within ten days of total ruin. Thank you, God! I plead innocence and apologize to the tax man. Somehow my apology lacks a ring of sincerity, but there is nothing Mr. Tax Man can do about it now. My Bay Street lawyer is still in negotiations to get this matter resolved.

I know now that I must use an entirely different strategy and a different "consultant" if I'm to have any chance at gaining the approval of the Committee of Adjustments to work from my new home—and work from my home I must. I no longer experience working from my home as a "logical choice" because of the nature of the business. I experience it as a "necessity" to limit stress and fatigue, both of which have exacerbated my mobility and balance problem.

I credit Donna Chevrier, a dear friend and my "wardrobe consultant," for coming up with a plan. Donna, who makes shopping a pleasure and minimizes the physical stress involved in doing this necessary task, is a vivacious, entrepreneurial, creative wiz with a flair for reaching out to a network of resources for whatever she needs. She suggests that she contact John Stewart, a staff writer at the *Mississauga News*, prior to any of my actual moves and I agree; media attention—that's worked for me before.

John Stewart has a gentle, unassuming manner. His gentleness and attentiveness is disarmingly calming and I pour out my story. What unfolds on March 23 is a major story in the *Mississauga News* with a caption "Horror story" and a lengthy column entitled "A year of upheaval for psychotherapist," detailing my tax man story and the anonymous complainant who precipitated a Committee of Adjustment hearing and the steps I've taken since then—an article with detail I hardly anticipated and a photo of me. This unassuming, gentle guy "listens"—and writes a potent, factual report. I suspect I have an advocate!

The editorial in that same edition entitled "Troublemaker" shocks me even more. It begins with "There is nothing so spineless as a worm and nothing so disgusting as the human equivalent of that creature. Our case in point this time around is the faceless entity who has turned a Mississauga woman's life upside down" and ends with "We firmly believe this person and those of a similar nature form a minority, a very small minority in our society. It is our misfortune that they are also not mute." I'm totally surprised and a bit unnerved by this intensity of support.

Empowered now, I decide to follow up on John's suggestion that I approach Mayor Hazel McCallion and ask for her support. I hope the mayor doesn't associate my name with the legal issue I created for the board of directors at Peel Family Services (she was on the board at the time)—but that was a few years ago.

The mayor's reception is politely distant—perhaps a little hostile? Or is that just my own shyness about asking for help? Mayor McCallion, perhaps in her early sixties, speaks with a strong, distinctive voice, the voice of one who knows how to intimidate. She reminds me of Miss Godfrey, my grade four teacher, who so relished my discomfort. Mayor McCallion's two most memorable comments: "You made it look as if Mississauga is picking on disabled people," and "If you don't like the law, perhaps you ought to change it." I don't think I will be getting much support from this source. I think the mayor and Mississauga are one and the same to Her Honour.

The following Wednesday John Stewart writes a follow-up column entitled, "The law must be upheld says bylaw informer," in which John gives quotes from the two men who appeared at the hearing—and he includes their names. He quotes George Norman, the senior citizen's line, "the law's the law." Two weeks later, the "letters to the editor" section of the paper includes two letters from clients of mine who have volunteered to support me.

I have tons of things to do before I request a new hearing since I am now forewarned about the opposition I will be facing. My first action is to involve Margaret Black, a young lawyer who is familiar with Her Honour, to represent me and present my case. Margaret and

I strategize as to the material I will need to support my application, and I proceed to organize a political campaign—that is political with a small p.

Several clients and friends will be writing letters to the editor of the *Mississauga News* to appear in as many of the weekly publications as possible. I design a petition in support of my application that includes 625 signatures (with addresses and phone numbers for purposes of verification) by the time the hearing takes place. I contact Jim Crozier, commissioner of social services for the Region of Peel, Ron Luciano, executive director of the Peel Region Children's Aid Society, and Leslie Hannel, executive director of the Social Planning Council, all of whom have used my services at various times and all of whom write letters of support. Six medical doctors from the region in written statements attest to the quality of my services and the need for such services. My personal physician, who is located in the medical building adjacent to my residence, writes a detailed medical report that will be read at the hearing. The report supports the need for me to avoid stress, limit physical activity and have access to convenient handicapped washroom facilities.

I contact the Provincial Multiple Sclerosis Society and meet a delightful woman, a passionate advocate for individuals and families coping with this disease. Bluebell Plank agrees to act as a witness and educate the committee members about the issue of MS and why, amongst other reasons, it is in the financial interest of the city to do everything possible to enable me to continue to support myself. Her statistics shock me—hopefully they will be a potent persuader of the need for the committee to support my application, as she suggests. And Michael Stein, a lawyer from the Advocacy Resource Centre for the Handicapped (ARCH), has agreed to testify about the rights of the handicapped under the Charter of Rights. He has many examples of how other communities have granted variances to bylaws to enable the disabled to work from their own homes.

Margaret arranges for an independent traffic consultant to do a study for us regarding the traffic issue. As well, I document where every client car parks from the time of my application for variance, July 3, to the time of the scheduled hearing on August 11.

The last piece of the strategy, knowing that the neighbours will be out in numbers, is to organize fifty supporters (clients, friends, associates) to arrive a half-hour early to fill the seats closest to the front of the Committee of Adjustment auditorium; all of them will be wearing little name tags identifying them as "Dale Perrin Supporters."

We're ready! Except for one glitch—a police raid!

After an evening group experience I receive three frantic phone calls from clients who were in to see me earlier in the week. All three of them report that a uniformed police officer came to their homes asking questions about me and about the service I was providing. The clients felt intimidated—violated by the breach to their confidentiality and upset about having to respond to intimate questions regarding why they were at my office and what was discussed. I too feel intimidated and violated and can offer no explanations for police involvement, only my deepest regrets and a commitment to get to the bottom of this.

I arrive at Margaret's office early the next morning for a scheduled appointment with a whole new agenda—after a sleepless and tearful night and a fourth phone call from another client in the early morning.

"I wonder if the police think you are operating a 'house of ill-repute,'" Margaret says as she picks up the phone to talk to the detective in charge of the Vice and Morality Bureau. After a brief conversation, she reports, "Well, that's a relief. You're not being investigated by the Morality Bureau. I'll have to make further inquiries and get back to you."

And then the day comes. I'm as ready as I can be. I have arranged for a party back at my house after the evening hearing—win or lose—to thank these wonderful people who have supported me through this. I just so appreciate Penny, my secretary and friend, Fern Gue, the associate who came to work with Terry and me earlier this year after a year or more of gentle persuasion, and Edie Wilson, the indefatigable Energizer Bunny who is working so diligently above and beyond what I have any right to expect.

Margaret, her associate Barbara Armstrong and I sit at the applicant's table. Don Shep, representing the surrounding neighbours who overwhelmingly oppose the application, and Chad Murray, president of the Applewood Hills Homeowner's Association, along with Rudy Skjarum, Councillor for Ward Three, sit at the complainant's table. Prior to my actual entry into this "theatre," I notice Mayor McCallion chatting with a group of neighbours. It's no secret which side of the issue she is supporting. Margaret has our witnesses seated close behind us. The committee members appear and take their seats on the raised platform. The eighty to a hundred people in the auditorium become eerily quiet. I'm sure my thumping heart can be heard at the very back of the room. Am I nervous? On the inside I'm fighting to keep myself from crying and losing my composure. These four men are going to decide if I can or cannot legally do what I know I must do to protect my physical well-being. On the outside I'm consciously sitting in a relaxed position, hoping to convey confidence and a sense of dignity—dressed in my gold power-flowing outfit.

Rick Mortensen, committee chairman, raps his gavel. We are underway.

Margaret submits copies of our brief, a neatly bound, one-inch-thick volume of statements, supporting evidence, the traffic survey results and the petition, and proceeds with her introduction. Before she has completed her remarks, it starts—a cacophony of hisses and boos the likes of which I have only heard in the cowboy movies of my childhood. Startled, I glance behind me and notice the animated hostile faces of the back four, four and a half, five rows. The neighbours, like the lynch mobs of the old Westerns, are making their feelings known. Those in the front rows are sitting quietly, listening intently.

The chairman calls for order. Margaret proceeds. Bluebell Plank and Michael Stein give their statements. The boos and hisses continue at a slightly lower volume. Bluebell Plank gives a detailed description of the disease process and the necessity for me to be given every support possible. Michael identifies the rights of the disabled and gives several examples of considerations granted by every other application for a variance that ARCH has been invited to address. Margaret reads a report prepared by my personal physician, who was unable to attend the hearing. This is the only time the neighbours are quiet. And then the traffic report—and the hisses and boos again escalate in volume. Our report indicates that the increase in traffic flow in this immediate area is equal to that which would be caused by a homeowner with two teenage drivers.

The neighbours are then invited to state their concerns. Don Shep, a gentleman in his mid- to late-fifties, presents a brief that he personally has prepared, which includes the signatures of all but one person on this and the closest neighbouring streets, 126 in all (I silently thank the one holdout), and proceeds to talk about the horrendous parking problems my clients have created and the danger that poses for pedestrians.

Chad Murray, a gentleman of similar age, speaks of the need to protect the character and quality of life of those who have invested in this well-established, quiet neighbourhood.

Both gentlemen have concerns about allowing a business enterprise to exist in the neighbourhood—a slippery slope to deteriorating quality of life and property values.

And then the bombshell! Rudy Skjarum, Councillor for Ward Three, gets up and in a dramatic fashion, waves a sheaf of papers that, he proudly pronounces, is a list of 126 license plates from cars parked in my driveway and on the street, license plates that do not belong to anyone in the neighbourhood. He also objects to the petition I have submitted, as several names are from people who do not live in this neighbourhood or Mississauga. He also objects to the fact that I started my business without first asking permission from the city, even though "she knew she was violating municipal bylaws."

The chairman invites anyone else to speak if they so choose. A woman, Natalie Ostapchuk, an eighteen-year-resident of Grand Forks Road, speaks to the traffic congestion that has occurred in the past three months. When asked by the chairman if that is all, she responds, "No, one more thing. The other day I walked past her house and she was standing on the verandah and she looked right at me."

"That's it?"

"That's it."

And that is it. Margaret questions various statements, but there is nothing further to be said. It is time for the adjudicators to adjudicate.

I experience a heavy sense of foreboding and tense up for what I sense will not be a decision in my favour.

Chairman Mortensen invites the panel members to render their decisions. Allan Randals is the first to speak. He picks up the brief in his right hand, waves it to the assembled crowd and says, "This is a successful business. We can't have businesses like this operating in residential neighbourhoods." He expresses concern about the traffic problems.

William Karda agrees with Mr. Randals, noting that those most affected are against the idea. "I feel it's an inappropriate location for this type of business."

William Lindsey responds with a remark that makes absolutely no sense to me. He is interrupted by Mr. Mortensen, "Mr. Lindsey, that was the last application."

"Oh," says Mr. Lindsey, a senior gentleman who has obviously "drifted off" during the hearing. "Well, I oppose."

Mr. Mortensen states the obvious. "The application for a variance is denied," and the back of the room erupts with excitement as the crowd begins to disperse.

The party back at the house is subdued. Most of us are too stunned to debrief. Lots of hugs, commitments to continue to support in whatever way is necessary, and I'm left alone with Edie and Fern, to let down and cry. My "persona," my "never let them know" Adapted Child posture, once an automatic response but now a "chosen" response, was useful; but now I'm safe, I'm with loving people. Now I can cry and express my greatest fear.

"Oh God, God! I'm going to lose my legs! I won't be able to cope with the stress," I say and dissolve into tears.

Both dear people hold me. "Dale, Dale, the essence of who you are is not in your legs. You'll make it just fine," says Fern. In my heart I know she's right. I will find a way. This is just another obstacle, right?

THE LAW'S THE LAW

Have you bumped up against a "law" or "regulation" that blocked you from reaching a goal? If so, what thoughts and feelings were triggered? And how did you behave?

Did your behaviour help resolve the problem? Or did you succeed in making it worse? Who and where were your supports? Your advisors/counsellors? Were they helpful? If so, in what way?

Have you had experience(s) with the media regarding a personal matter? Did you find that helpful or hurtful? How did the experience impact on your life? What feelings, thoughts, or behaviours were triggered? Were these "familiar" feelings, thoughts, behaviours?

Has this (these) experience(s) altered your perception of yourself, others, the world?

YOU CAN'T BEAT CITY
HALL, CAN YOU?

As expected, John Stewart has a detailed report on the committee process in the next edition of the *Mississauga News* entitled "Household therapy business rejected," with a two-column-wide photo of me and Barbara Armstrong; me looking oh so cool and Barbara looking oh so lawyerly. An additional article appears on the editorial page, "Therapist fight to continue." "Perrin will appeal to the Ontario Municipal Board," comments the editor. He duly notes that "Mayor McCallion is among those who have told her she should be able to find a home in an area that would allow her business to operate. But Perrin says she and her real estate agent went to great lengths to try to find such accommodation and were unsuccessful."

And in the same paper there is another letter to the editor entitled "Ashamed," beautifully written by Donna Chevrier. Since I have every intention to fight the good fight, I'm pleased to utilize the supports offered by friends, clients and associates. What I don't anticipate is the political fallout precipitated by Rudy Skjarum and his police raid. In the next edition of the *Mississauga News* John Stewart, who also covers the city and regional council beats, in an article with the caption "Clients terrified" and entitled "Abuse of power charges made in bylaw case" written in big bold letters, reports, "Ward 3 city councillor Rudy Skjarum called in Peel Regional Police to investigate a bylaw infraction in his ward last month, a move one fellow councillor says is 'an act of overkill and possible harassment.'" I learn that Rudy Skjarum is a member of the Peel Police Commission and in that capacity he initiated an investigation. I also learn that one of my clients refused to sign a witness statement and wrote a letter of complaint to the police chief Douglas Burrows. Way to go, lady! The lengthy report ends with a quote from Councillor Larry Taylor, "I think Councillor Skjarum owes Dale Perrin a public apology."

The following week another lengthy John Stewart feature column appears, entitled "Special Needs." It ends with a most encouraging paragraph: "The Ontario Municipal Board may very well reverse the local decision, but it would have been oh-so-much nicer if our own community had recognized Perrin's right to live and work here in an appropriate location." The editorial page includes a column entitled "Harassment," which concludes with similar sentiments. "We are optimistic the OMB will overturn the City's decision; we pray Perrin's opponents and city officials learn something about compassion from this incident so other sensitive, courageous individuals do not have to endure this sort of harassment."

Two more letters to the editor appear in the same edition, both unsolicited by me: one written by my medical doctor and one lengthy, articulate account of the proceedings and unanswered questions written by someone unknown by me. That letter concludes with the question, "Why did it take so little time to resolve a 'very involved case' (a comment made by the chairman prior to asking the adjudicators for their decisions)? Dare I suggest, along with many other observers, that the case was decided before the meeting began?" I confess, that thought had crossed my mind.

I have some time now to collect my thoughts, recuperate my energies and strategize for the Ontario Municipal Board appeal, which is scheduled to be on November 16. Margaret and I suspect that the neighbours will show up in even greater numbers for the appeal hearing, and we decide to accentuate my vulnerability by having no one present, not even Bluebell Plank, the spokesperson for the Ontario MS Association, and Michael Stein, the lawyer from the Advocacy Resource Centre for the Handicapped (ARCH), since they have already testified. I will relate my own medical concerns and needs. Surely this time, common sense will win out. I'm optimistic; I feel so supported by the news media and my friends, clients and associates.

This "story," though, has a life of its own and does not want to wait quietly for the hearing to take place. My most recent "knight in shining armor," Larry Taylor, Councillor for Ward Four, insists on raising the issue of possible abuse of power by his colleague, Rudy Skjarum, in council and with the police, suggesting that the delay in responding to his questions regarding how the investigation began were "symptomatic of a cover-up," according to John Stewart's next report, October 26. Deputy Police Chief William Teggart insists that the investigation into my "infraction of a bylaw" was properly handled by the police and in his letter to Councillor Taylor he vehemently denied insinuations of a cover-up.

Superintendent Joe Terdik states in his letter to Councillor Taylor that the police cannot answer his questions because the issue is before the Ontario Municipal Board and could be the subject of civil suits. Now there's a thought that hasn't entered my mind! But Councillor Taylor, ever the pit bull terrier, plans to take up the issue at Regional Council and involve the Regional Chairman, Frank Bean.

John Stewart, equally tenacious, in his opinion column on October 26, reflects that, "Sometimes a side issue in a public controversy ends up getting more attention than the real issue," and proceeds to document the allegations made by Councillor Taylor and the police replies. He reports that, "Mayor Hazel McCallion, miffed that something had actually happened in Mississauga in which she was not directly involved, accused Taylor of playing for headlines." He concludes his column with the following statements, "But all of this is truly secondary to the real issue: the fact that a handicapped person may be denied the right to earn her living. Dale Perrin will have to put her case again to the OMB on Nov. 16."

I'm enjoying Stewart's comments until I read in a separate article the following information:

"Early yesterday morning, Mississauga Council, in a 6-4 recorded vote, approved Skjarum's motion to send a lawyer to the OMB to support the Committee of Adjustment decision. Dale Perrin will once again have to fight city hall. Maybe she'll finally prove you can beat them, no matter how powerful their friends are."

The fact that Mayor McCallion is "miffed" is abundantly clear in John Stewart's report in the November 2 edition of the *Mississauga News*. The mayor takes it upon herself to answer the question Councillor Taylor asks at the Regional Council Meeting since the police repeat their position that they would not answer because of their legal advice. What follows is an angry, long and ultimately frustrating debate for everyone involved. Chairman Frank Bean was kept busy answering a succession of points of order and privilege as the councillors traded accusations."

Still before I get to the OMB, the matter is moved to an even broader public audience. Paul Burton, a staff writer for the *Toronto Star*, pays me a visit and the story is repeated, along with another two-column photo of me holding one of my cats, my cane visible for the world to see.

I do appreciate the publicity, the support I'm getting from the media, and it is "strategic" to be identified as "a victim of MS" and be presented as a "poor little handicapped woman," but I do not like it! I do not feel like a victim. At one level, I deeply resent being perceived as "helpless." I'm hurt by such labels and find them patronizing—strategic, yes, but patronizing. I express my frustration in a poem that I submit to a "select newsletter" and readership—the *MS Ontario Newsletter*, a poem entitled, "I AM!"

Victim!... she has MS you know ...
victim!...It's not fair ... it's not
right ... her of all people ... I'm furious ... victim ... MS
I am not your Rorschach.
Don't inkblot me with
Your projections.
Don't blur the edges of
my being with your
sense of helplessness.
I have never been more powerful!
My energy touches newspapers.
My anger moves political blocks.
My scare mobilizes supporters.
My love nurtures, eases pain.
My strength supports risk-taking.
My joy impacts on those around me.
My sensuality invites pleasures.
Remove your distortions.

See beyond my rigid limbs
and come, work and play
and experience with me.
I am!

Mind you, I'm not feeling powerful as I sit with Margaret Black in this eighth-floor Ontario Municipal Board hearing room, 180 Dundas Street, in downtown Toronto. The room still looks like a court to me and I still feel "accused" of doing a dastardly deed. The neighbours have turned out—about forty of them—and, I suspect, are surprised to see just the very few of us. The contrast is quite significant.

Margaret begins her opening remarks and the hissing and booing starts. Mr. D. S. Colbourne, chairman of the two-man adjudication board, raps his gavel and says, "Be quiet. You will have an opportunity to state your case later," in a manner that leaves no doubt as to his authority. The room becomes silent.

"Without being overly dramatic, I want to say to you that if you refuse this appeal, you will be ending the livelihood of a woman who is forty-five years old." She goes on to explain the circumstances of MS and the need for me to work from my home and the results of the traffic survey conducted by the traffic engineer, Christopher Middlebro, who has concluded that my business generates no more than an additional 2 percent increase in traffic flow, no more than a family with two teenage drivers.

I'm invited to testify. Margaret walks me through the details of my deteriorating health and the need for me to work from home. I'm surprisingly calm throughout this process. I feel that I'm presenting myself well, another personal victory against my own personal demon—stage fright.

Virginia MacLean, the lawyer representing the city of Mississauga, is invited to cross-examine me and so she does. She has me state that "Yes, I was aware that I was operating my business for six and a half years illegally, knowing that I was violating the bylaw." She then makes it clear that "If Ms. Perrin doesn't like the law, she should change it." This is the second time I'm hearing this statement—I know where it is coming from. And this time I'm hearing this as a direct challenge, a challenge that I decide this very moment that I will pick up if—for any reason—I do not succeed in winning this appeal.

Ron Miller, of the city's planning department, says in response to Ms. MacLean's inquiry, "It's my understanding that the official plan has very few policies regarding the design of buildings for the handicapped, outside of provisions for parking spaces." In response to Margaret's question, he says, "There is no provision for home-occupation uses in the city's official plan. Only doctors, dentists and drugless practitioners are allowed to practice in homes in which they live, as long as they are located 800 meters from one another."

The neighbours are invited to testify. Don Shep, the organizing neighbour, shows the board members the results of a survey taken by three families on the street over a twenty-five-day period last spring; a survey that was conducted in the evening. He says, "There is an average of 7.3 cars parked outside Perrin's home as a result of her business and often as many as twelve cars. There is a very serious congestion problem there and sometimes it is impossible to pass. Several neighbours are adamant that the operation be closed because of the increased traffic and street parking it generates." He reports that they are afraid that allowing one business to operate on the street will set a dangerous precedent.

A second neighbour, James Harrower, says, "What concerns me is that if we allow this one, what will happen to the quiet residential area that I moved into years ago? I take pride in the street and my home."

Shirley Campbell, past president of the Applewood Hills Homeowners Association, tells the board, "I canvassed 1,200 members and determined that they are overwhelmingly opposed."

In her concluding remarks, Margaret suggests that the OMB would not be setting a precedent because very, very few cases where a disabled person wants to operate such a low-key business will ever be heard. She likens my business to that of a medical doctor, who would be allowed to live and practice in a home to provide marital and family counselling. She points out that the only difference is that I have a master's degree in social work rather than a medical degree, an argument that to me seems abundantly logical.

Margaret concludes her remarks by reiterating an appeal to the humanity of the adjudicators. "This is a very special case," she says and reiterates the fact that there is no area in Mississauga where Perrin can work and live in the same building. "If you refuse this application, then you will be jeopardizing her livelihood."

Ms. MacLean concludes that while "everyone is sympathetic to the position of the applicant, the decision should not be based on sympathy for her 'plight.'"

And it's over. Mr. Colbourne states that he and Mr. H. W. Kelly will issue a written decision "shortly." I'm disappointed. I didn't realize that the decision would take time, but I suppose that allows for logic to prevail. Perhaps this will be in my best interest.

Shortly after the hearing I receive support from an anonymous source. In my mailbox is a plain white envelope with just my name on it. I open it with a sense of foreboding, that terror-grip-to-the-gut response of the scared little kid in me. Am I now going to get hate mail? What a delight to discover a list of six names and specific addresses of businesses being operated from homes on this very street. Just a short note to explain that the sender thought I might like to know this. Bless you, Mr. (?) Anonymous, who I presume is the person who delivers the mail, a person I have never actually seen. I believe the information is ironic if not explosive. Excited by this good fortune, I do a study of the Mississauga Yellow Pages Directory and discover seventeen businesses operating in this Applewood Hills neighbourhood and ninety-one in Ward Three.

I'm on the phone shortly after these remarkable discoveries to report this information to John Stewart. Sure enough, another front-page article, this one entitled "Home-run therapy business not alone in bylaw violation," appears in the November 30 edition of the *Mississauga News*. Four of the six people contacted state that their business is different and proceed to explain those differences. One of the other two doesn't have time to talk with the reporter because she is "too busy." Will this information help? Perhaps I won't even need more data to support my passionate desire/need to work from my own home.

When John asks me how I felt about the OMB hearing, the fighting me, still rankled by Ms. MacLean's challenge, lets go, perhaps indiscriminately, with my intention to do exactly what Ms. McLean suggested—to change the bylaw. I share with him that I'm prepared to work with local groups such as the Social Planning Council, the local chapter of the MS Association and the March of Dimes, if need be. This, too, is duly reported, along with a head shot of me, in an article entitled "Therapist vows to change bylaws."

I have the Christmas period to nurture my body and soul in the bosom of my family. Although I don't share with my parents the drama that is unfolding (it is important not to upset my father), I'm blessed to have a place where I feel loved and valued. I'm quite ready now to get on with my life—please, OMB!

The news breaks late February 1984. The OMB supports the Committee of Adjustment decision. I'm not allowed to operate my business from this residence. And that's it!

I'm devastated. I really thought the OMB would come through for me. The *Mississauga News* duly reports the decision: a big headline "MS victim loses city hall battle" and an editorial entitled "Handicapped options." The *Toronto Star* follows suit with an article in the March 6 paper entitled "Disabled woman loses bid to work in home" and includes a double-column picture of me, my cat and my cane—poor me.

Only after I let John Stewart know that I will honour the OMB decision and move my practice into a commercial area do I learn from Michael Stein, the lawyer from the Advocacy Resource Centre for the Handicapped, that they would have funded an appeal to the Supreme Court of Canada. I had told John that I was emotionally exhausted and physically stressed and did not have the financial resources to continue "fighting."

Edie Wilson, my indomitable real estate agent and friend, sets out to find me an appropriate space and a new condo residence. I so hope that this home is "a keeper." I certainly did not anticipate another move. Edie, in what I thought was a spontaneous gesture of warmth and empathy, made the remark, prior to my moving into this Grand Forks residence, that if I was forced to move again, this move would be "free." I forgot this remark but Edie reminds me and, true to this spontaneous generosity, insists on following through. How fortunate I am to have such caring people in my life.

The story will not die. The April 25 paper duly reports "MS therapist forced to relocate" and notes that my new premises are located on ground level and that "her new landlord has provided her with a reserved handicapped parking space only six feet from her office door." Another editorial—"Perrin fights on"—in the same paper reports, "Multiple Sclerosis sufferer Dale Perrin will officially open the new location of her therapy business next month, and that opening will, in part, serve as a testament to the lady's indomitable will. Perrin may have been defeated in her bid to continue operating at her current location but she was not destroyed by the loss." It concludes, "From her new location Perrin can continue to fight the ignorance and inhumanity exhibited by those 'Archie Bunkers' responsible for forcing her to move. And she can continue that battle from a neighbourhood where the air is a little cleaner."

Two more unsolicited letters to the editor provide support from a whole different segment of society. One gentleman, who asks that his name be withheld, states that he too was operating illegally for the same reasons I chose to do so in the first place—convenience and economic necessity. He suggests that all the other unnamed illegals form a coalition to fight city hall, pointing out that if the city wasn't moved to allow Dale Perrin to operate from her home, what chance would he have to get a variance to operate legally? Another brave soul, in a letter to the editor of the *Toronto Star*, talks about the problem of social priorities and refers to the belief that "the cottage industry wave of the future will never be more than a ripple."

I'm delighted by the support and anxious to get out of this neighbourhood. I'm also fatigued—enough of being a "poster child" for the disabled population. I never intended to be a political advocate. I just want to go about my business: do what I dearly love doing—working with people who want to make changes in their lives—and protect my own health. But to do that, I still have to find a way to change the bylaw. I'm not finished yet.

In late May my friends help me set up business at my new location at 2022 Dundas Street East, near the Etobicoke/Mississauga border. Penny, Colin (her husband), Edie and I, along with several clients who work with me in small groups, set about making this new setting look as homey as possible. The same lovely couches and love seats, coffee tables, lamps and artwork that furnished the second townhouse now decorate the new large teaching area. This new setting, with my office furnishings, now presents like a well-furnished office instead of a crowded kitchen masquerading as an office. Even the bathroom is decorated with ink prints and guest towels. The reception area and interview rooms look comfortable and cozy—just more like an office rather than a home, but at least a sensually pleasing office. And my own interview room/office houses my wooden bookshelves, with my precious books, my black contemplative Buddha and Chinese lamp.

We plan to have an open-house celebration from 4:00 to 8:00 p.m., with ceremonies at 5:00, a celebration combining the opening of my new offices and my ten-year anniversary of providing service in this region. Invitations go out to both current and former clients, to friends, associates, my former partner Terry, Councillors Larry Taylor and Ted Southhorn, Frank Bean, the Regional Chairman, and dear John Stewart. And what a time we have. One lovely young woman brings balloons. Several bouquets of flowers are scattered throughout; the wine flows, the goodies are consumed and we have speeches. Terry and Fern say a few words. Councillor Taylor reads a letter of commendation from Frank Bean, already laminated and ready to be hung in the reception area. Councillors Southhorn and Taylor hold the ribbon that I get to cut, and I get kisses from my two advocates.

As the celebration unfolds, Hayward arrives. When all the tidying up is complete and the last person leaves I have the opportunity to debrief, let down and "feel," wrapped in the safety of his protective arms.

The next edition of the *Mississauga News* reports, "Forced out by neighbours, family counsel therapist celebrates new location," and an editorial entitled "Happy endings" starts with, "It's a real pleasure for us to report stories that have happy endings" and ends with this paragraph: "Perrin's case may have reached a conclusion but the larger story of educating some Mississauga residents and councillors, as well as bringing some City bylaws in line with reality is continuing. And that is a story desperately in need of a happy ending."

And it is my intention to see that story written in the *Mississauga News*!

Ten more days—just ten more—and I will be moving my residence to my new condo on Mill Road. This uniquely structured building with its zigzag design is just east of the Twelve Mile Creek, which separates Etobicoke (a community/suburb just west of the city of Toronto) from Mississauga. It tickles me to know that I'm still connected emotionally, and through my private practice, to Mississauga, but do not have to give Mayor McCallion and the city a penny of taxes.

Ingrid, a young woman client of mine, is staying with me for the rest of my time here in order to "have some space" from a very tense home situation. Together we work our way through packing boxes and furnishings stuffed in various sections of rooms through this big house. Ingrid is sleeping on a mattress in a room adjacent to the family room—my "former" office/group therapy room—while I continue to use the upper-level master bedroom. At 4:00 a.m. I'm awakened by the sound of a bloodcurdling scream, the kind of scream I have only experienced in a movie theatre. The scream continues, followed by Ingrid bounding up the stairs yelling, "There's a man in the house! There's a man in the house!"

"Are you sure?" I say, in my befuddled not-quite-in-this-world state.

"He's still here!" she screams.

That brings me quickly into the here and now. "Get out the front door and run to the neighbours. Get the police; run, run!"

Ingrid does just that, first grabbing onto the wrought-iron three-pronged candlestick holder that was temporarily parked at the curve of the stairs. *My God, if she hits him with that she'll crush his skull.* "Go, go! Don't wait for me!"

I struggle with my balance as I make my way down the hallway without my cane, which remains up in my bedroom. I just want to get out—anyway I can. As I make my way up my driveway, I hear Ingrid yelling at the top of her voice, "Call the police!" to the equally startled neighbor, who is obviously unsure about letting this ranting, raving young woman, clutching a deadly weapon, into his house. Finally I see the door open, and then I yell to Ingrid to come back and get me as I can no longer move. By the time Ingrid and I make it to the neighbour's door, Mrs. Switzer has joined her husband and is coming forward, along with Ingrid, to help me. We are ushered into the living room. Mrs. Switzer, fortunately, brings two large sweaters for us to cover ourselves, both of us being very exposed, me in a flimsy black nightgown. Mr. Switzer dials the police and Ingrid is given the phone. In a voice close to hysteria, this terrified eighteen-year-old woman attempts to give the 911 operator the address and respond to questions. Within minutes we hear the sirens and know that help is near at hand.

Two police officers enter the home and proceed, very gently, to get the story from Ingrid. As she tells her story, I become increasingly anxious. Around 3:00 a.m. Ingrid wakes, sensing more than hearing unfamiliar sounds. She doesn't move. Someone approaches the bedroom door and quietly stands there. Without moving a muscle, Ingrid can recognize that whoever is there is wearing running shoes. She dismisses her first thought, that perhaps I have brought someone home with me—I wouldn't likely be bringing someone home who wore running shoes. She doesn't move. She hears the person move away and retreat up the hallway. She hears him going up the stairs to my room. No sounds. She considers making a run for the patio door in the therapy room or a side door an equal distance away and decides not to risk it. She remains motionless. He returns, stands at the door and then comes and stands over her. Ingrid remains still, ready to jump, kick and scream if he touches her. He is breathing rapidly—not sexually, she says, more like a nervous boy. He retreats and goes away. She wonders if he has killed me and should she risk attempting to run. Not enough time—he returns. He retreats a third time and she can hear him quietly roaming through other rooms. He returns, stands beside her and then kneels down beside her. He is breathing rapidly. He gently pokes her—as a child might do to wake a mother, and when she doesn't respond, he reaches towards her mouth. She sees that he has something in his hand. And then she screams bloody murder and jumps up kicking. He runs into the therapy room and she heads for the stairs.

By this time I'm beginning to shake all over. My dear, sweet Ingrid has been living this nightmare for an hour *before* the scream. *My God, how did she keep her cool?* She explains to the officer that she was getting angrier and angrier as the time progressed. Me? I would have been immobilized by fear. Thank goodness her defensive system prepares her to "fight" instead of "flight"—a much healthier response in this situation.

Two other police officers enter the house to report that my residence has been searched and no one is there. It is now safe for Ingrid and me to return. One of the interviewing officers accompanies us back to make sure we are okay. Every light in the house is turned on.

We both go through the rooms turning off lights and searching for my three cats. We find two hidden away under one bed; the other one is nowhere to be found. I pray that she hasn't gotten out the wide-open door. The police officer reports that when the house was searched, they found the patio door open. The intruder must have left the door open as a quick escape. They also found Ingrid's keys in the front door.

It is now 6:00 a.m. Neither Ingrid nor I feel safe. I call Edie, who lives just a block away, and ask her if she will come and stay with us for a few hours. She is there in ten minutes. Only then is Ingrid secure enough to take a shower and dress. Packed and ready, she decides that she will now go back to her parents' home, and Edie and I are left alone. As we set about to replace the therapy room furniture, we discover a red bandana with white polka dots and a transparent tooth guard. I phone the police officer, who has now gone off duty. I'm instructed by another officer to place the evidence in an envelope and put it into my mailbox. And now Edie waits while I shower and get ready for work. *Thank God for friends!*

By ten in the morning I return home to pick up some work I forgot and decide that I will return Mrs. Switzer's sweaters to her later. As I start up my car, Mrs. Switzer exits her home and is heading over to me. She asks to talk with me. We settle in the kitchen and I explain what we found. She asks to see the bandana and mouth guard. When I show them to her, she says, "I think I know who your intruder is," and goes on to explain that the mouth guard and bandana belong to her sixteen-year-old son, Eric. She tells me about the history of his "disturbed behaviour" and the conflict between her husband and Eric.

"Where is Eric now?"

"He's upstairs in his bedroom sleeping."

"Mrs. Switzer, I have to call the police. Would you be willing to let Eric sleep until the police arrive?"

Mrs. Switzer is now crying quietly. "I have to. We have to do something before something even worse happens."

I sympathize with the poor woman and call the police. Someone will be by later in the day to talk with Eric.

For the next nine days, one or two clients accompany me home—just to be sure I'm safe, they tell me. I sleep with several lights on in the house and my cordless phone under my pillow, along with a bat that I found in the basement walkway. I will be one happy soul to get out of this neighbourhood.

My A-team of friends and clients help me settle into my new residence and by mid-June I'm ready to resume the mayor's challenge to change the bylaw. I set up interviews with Councillor Ted Southhorn and Regional Chairman Frank Bean to ask for mentoring and support for getting the bylaw changed. Both men are very supportive. Ted gives me instructions as to how to begin the process. I'm told by one that, unfortunately, if Mayor McCallion doesn't like you, you will not get what you want—that she has enough support on council to have her own way. I check this out with the other and he affirms that this is so. I find this to be shocking—but over this past year or two, I'm letting go of a lot of illusions about power and political systems. I do not intend to let this deter me—I'll learn how to circumvent such obstacles.

Over the next many months I write to seventeen communities (incorporated cities and villages) in Ontario and receive copies or other documentation regarding their home occupation bylaws. I learn that only five of the seventeen do not have a bylaw in place: Mississauga and four of the Toronto boroughs. I document my findings and Councillor Southhorn and I meet with the head of the planning department to determine how to proceed from here. We are advised now to approach the March of Dimes to solicit their support and let them proceed with interventions at the council level. The planning department will work with Councillor Ted Southhorn to do their own studies to support a request to introduce new legislation. And we agree that the name Dale Perrin will not be raised in any way.

As time passes, everything moves according to a political rhythm that maximizes the chances for a successful outcome. I already have the support of four of the nine councillors. It is critical to sway the mayor, or at least one of her supporters, in order to pass a motion to introduce a new bylaw. Ted does his work. But financially, time is running out for me.

After Councillor Southhorn informs me that the issue is before council and that it is only a matter of time (perhaps months) before the proposed new bylaw is voted on in council, I decide that I cannot wait any longer. Financially the extra burden of carrying a sizable mortgage and a high monthly rental fee is threatening to ruin me. I'm going to look for a new home in Councillor Taylor's ward and move myself back into a single-family residence. Thanks to Edie's genius, on June 29, 1986, I move into what surely will be a permanent home on a small crescent just north of Square One, a three-bedroom bungalow with a finished basement designed to accommodate a very large group room and two interview/office/group therapy rooms—absolutely perfect for my needs.

On October 17, the *Mississauga News* reports that "Home-based businesses reconsidered" and Councillor David Culham is given credit for bringing this issue forward. The article concludes with the comment, "Had the new provisions been in place a few years ago, the celebrated battle of Mississauga psychotherapist Dale Perrin, who suffers from multiple sclerosis, might have had a different outcome. After a long battle to try to operate her practice from her home, Perrin moved to a commercial area." An editorial entitled "Opening doors" quotes Councillor Steve Mahoney as saying, "Our treatment of the handicapped is coming out of the closet" and adds, "as well it should."

Is this it? Well, no. Not until August 21, 1987, does the *Mississauga News* report, "New bylaw to allow physically disabled to do home business." The article, written by—who else?—John Stewart, ends with the statement, "Perrin says she is delighted by council's decision, which she termed 'very progressive.'" And the editorial "Progressive move deserves applause" again mentions my name. Nowhere does it mention that Dale Perrin was reached at her residence in Mississauga where she has been operating illegally for over a year, and nowhere does it say, "Yes, you can beat city hall!"

YOU CAN'T BEAT CITY HALL, CAN YOU?

This story raises the same kind of questions as the previous story. Does it evoke different questions for you? If so, just record your questions and answers.

Have you bumped up against a "law" or "regulation" that blocked you from reaching a goal? If so, what thoughts and feelings were triggered? And how did you behave?

Did your behaviour help resolve the problem? Or did you succeed in making it worse? Who and where were your supports? Your advisors/counsellors? Were they helpful? If so, in what way?

Have you had experience(s) with the media regarding a personal matter? Did you find that helpful or hurtful? How did the experience impact on your life? What feelings, thoughts, or behaviours were triggered? Were these "familiar" feelings, thoughts, behaviours?

Has this (these) experience(s) altered your perception of yourself, others, the world?

SCRIPT BUSTING ... WITH TEARS AND CELEBRATIONS

Exciting things are happening during this *forever* law-busting time. I can't just sit and wait for "justice"—I need to close some doors to free my energy to open new ones. Fortunately I win a healthy compromise with the tax man. One door closed.

I'm invited by Ruth Chambers, a woman just a few years younger than me, to provide therapeutic services to some of the very young girls in her care. Ruth is codirector/cofounder of a specialized residential group home for girls from seven to sixteen—not just any girls, but specifically young girls who have been incestuously/sexually, emotionally and/or physically abused by parents or parent substitutes. These children do not fit into a regular foster-care environment but require highly skilled and sensitive, compassionate treatment.

Louise Judge, her partner, is uniquely suited to work in this demanding environment. She has a nursing degree and culinary skills to meet the essential nutritional needs of kids, staff and consultants. She, too, has experience in working with very needful kids.

Working with children, or even adults, who have experienced the trauma of incest is new to me. Prior to my visiting Cricket Hollow, their residence located on an acre of land in the country near Hillsbourg, Ontario, Ruth brings a little slip of a young girl to my townhouse office. I listen, totally unprepared to bear witness to the horrendous pain this child is sharing with me in a monotone voice. I can only respond in a choked voice with, "How awful; how painful; I'm so sad that you've experienced such hurtful behaviour," or words to that effect, as the tears well up in my eyes and silently slip down my cheeks.

"Ruth, what is it you want from me?" I say in private, disturbed that I offered no words of wisdom or brilliant interventions.

"I can't really tell you, Dale. You're actually giving just what I believe Chris needs."

"Like what?"

"Well, like an authentic response to the pain she's expressing. You can see that she's totally blocked off from the horror of the abuse. That's how she survived. Gradually we hope that Chris will risk trusting some of us and begin to own her feelings. Then the healing is underway."

I'm not at all convinced that I can handle listening to eight children with equally horrendous stories, but Ruth convinces me to work with her, Louise and their staff. I agree to visit the residence and become familiar with their program. As I continue with this awesome group of women and children in their rural setting for the next many years, I open myself to a whole new reality, enrich my knowledge base, develop new skills and explore new feelings. I continue to believe in the innate goodness of "ordinary people," but I have dipped my spiritual toe into a whole new level of awareness of the horrendous harm we humans are capable of inflicting on the most vulnerable in our society. I open myself to an enriched awareness of my own vulnerabilities, to wisdom—the intimate knowledge of good and evil. I have a whole new appreciation for the parenting I received as a child. A new door of need, of opportunity and professional practice, has opened.

In a rage, I push open another door, a door that has long been closed in silence—the door of patriarchy and chauvinism. Okay, it isn't pushed wide open, but I do keep my foot in the opening to keep it from slamming shut, never to be addressed again. September 9, 1983, my parents are celebrating their fiftieth wedding anniversary. Bayne and Ken are busy planning the event, which is to take place over a weekend: Saturday evening for a cocktail party with the extended family, including Elthea and Father's siblings, and Sunday afternoon in a reserved room at the Walper Hotel in Kitchener, with our extended family. It is on that occasion that we are to have speeches and presentations. The problem is I'm not included in the planning process. I don't want to participate in a "family event" that includes Father's sisters, *"the sisters."*

"Well, that's just fine. I won't participate at the cocktail party, but I will attend the Walper for the dinner," I say, choking back tears. I'm so angry I'm trembling all over.

"You have to," Ken says. "You don't have a choice. It's mandatory."

"I do have a choice. You can exclude me from the planning but you can't force me to attend—and I will not attend. I will be busy that night."

"You have to come. You will be hurting Mom and Dad," Ken says, raising his voice, clearly angry at what I'm sure he perceives as my obstinacy.

I know this is true and I know I will attend for that very reason, but I'm stuck in my rage and won't let go of the churning and surging adrenaline that is creating havoc in my whole body. I haven't had a blowout like this since my confrontation with Mother when I was thirty.

"I'll let you explain that to them since the two of you chose to exclude me from any decision-making in the family".

Bayne moves us forward into a discussion regarding the presentations for Sunday's events. I remain silent, only occasionally nodding yes when he goes through the agenda. Before our meeting is over, I do recant.

"I will attend the cocktail party but not because you say so. Don't you *ever* again make plans that include me without consulting with me!"

A small victory but a beginning; the door is partially open.

I'm invited by Carol Morris, one of my former associates, to participate on the fledging CATA (Canadian Association for Transactional Analysis) board, an organization about five years old that attempts to link those of us across the nation who are utilizing in some way this remarkable theoretical model. Now this is a challenge— to participate with others, some of whom are certified transactional analysts, a few certified as teaching and supervising transactional analysts. The certification process is an arduous one of meeting specific criteria developed by the International Transactional Analysis

Association, whose head office is in San Francisco, California. The challenge: my vulnerability! Am I going to find out that I'm not okay, that I'm doing it all wrong?

The board people are gracious in welcoming me to this new experience in this beautiful setting in Vancouver, and I "move in," exercising my familiar pattern in approaching new situations—my oh-so-familiar churning stomach and lots of questions. By the end of two days of meetings I'm still unsure of my acceptance in this group, still cautious, but excited and eager to participate. I'm "moving out" professionally.

During a social evening following our business meeting, I have the opportunity to chat with Vince Gilpin, the current president of CATA and a certified teacher/supervisor whom I met years ago when I first began private practice. I decide that it is time for me to plunge in—enough sitting at the edge of the pool with my feet in the water—jump I do. I ask Vince if he has room for me in his next training program. I'm going to do it—go through the process of becoming a certified transactional analyst. Vince suggests an alternative to me joining his current training program in Ottawa. He suggests that I gather together ten to fifteen people who would like formal instruction, with or without the intention to continue through to certification, and he will come to Mississauga to provide training. A year's training involves five weekends of sixteen classroom hours and two five-day residential experiences, one in the spring and one in the late fall. The residential experiences take place in what Vince refers to as "the Barn"—a fully furnished, winterized "cottage" that sleeps twenty people, in eastern Ontario, just north of Gananoque, on the shores of Lake Ontario.

I accept the challenge and once I'm settled in my new office location, we begin training. I'm now embarked on a fast-track to script-busting and a slow track to certification as a transactional analyst.

How does script-busting occur? During the classroom time we study the basic concepts involved in the theory of transactional analysis: ego states, strokes (words and behaviours that recognize the self and others, both positive and negative), games (unhealthy ways of manipulating to gain recognition and/or get what we want), scripts (those life patterns that propel us towards self-limiting, predictable outcomes), transactions or patterns of communication with others. The reading material, the lecture or presentation of information, is just a part of the formal training. What makes the concepts and words come alive? Makes me stand up and take notice? The exercises we do to apply these concepts in our own lives! And then, the opportunity to work with a colleague and/or Vince in a "therapy-client" experience, to develop skills both in working with these tools and in working out our own "stuff."

And then I begin to connect the dots, connect my present feelings, insecurities, defensive behaviours, to those early life scenes. I begin, or perhaps continue, my journey from the performance of roles to authenticity. I begin to understand and to change my behaviour—one little step at a time.

One such step—one such understanding—is the "why" and the "so what now" regarding the scare that grips my gut when I face new situations, especially situations that put me onstage centre front. I'm astounded to learn that some people actually face new situations with a sense of adventure, a sense of excitement and an openness for whatever emerges. Some people even enjoy performing and being onstage—imagine that! On one occasion Vince asks me to read from notes I prepared regarding a concept we were studying. I begin reading—and I feel that familiar anxiety grip my gut and I begin to "fog out." I'm aware of an inner voice saying, *Everyone is looking at me.* The words on the page become blurry and begin to spin—I'm being dragged into a funnel of chaos, caught in a cyclone of incomprehensible feeling. I hear another voice: *This is stupid.* And then I hear Vince's voice, "Dale, Dale! What's happening? Where are you?"

I'm cold, shaking; breathing in quick, short breaths. I can scarcely respond. In a little child's voice I answer, "I'm scared."

Vince is now right in front of me. "Look at me." I look. I see a concerned, very familiar, bearded face with big brown eyes that emit warm rays that bathe me and begin to soothe the cold shakes. "Tell me what is frightening you."

"They're all looking at me," I say, in a wee small voice. "They think I'm bad—stupid."

"Are you bad or stupid?"

"No," I say and begin to cry. I can't help it. It just happens.

"Where are you?"

"I'm on the stage."

"What's happening?"

"I'm peeing."

"And now what?"

"The lady is coming. She takes me to the bathroom."

"And then?"

"That's stupid. She's stupid. I already peed. I'm going home."

"Yes?"

"Daddy is coming towards me. He has the camera around his neck. He asks me to come back to the Sunday School room with him 'cause he wants to take my picture. I don't want to go but I go. He hands me a piece of paper rolled up with a blue ribbon on it. I'm supposed to hold it in my hand in front of this little gate and smile."

"And what are you feeling?"

"I feel bad. I don't really want to smile."

"And then?"

"I don't know. I guess we go home."

"What are you thinking?"

"I guess peeing my pants is *soooo* bad Daddy doesn't want to talk about it."

"Do you ask him?"

"No, he'll get mad."

"What d'yuh say we invite him to come in right now and you can ask him? I'll be right here with you."

"Okay."

"Daddy, are you mad at me for peeing my pants?"

"And what does he answer?"

"No, no, sweetie. That just happens sometimes. Your mom and I are proud of you. You can go to the big children's Sunday School now."

"You're not mad?"

"No, no. Your mom and I are *very* proud of you."

"Okay."

After a long pause, Vince asks, "And what do you feel now?"

"Better."… Actually, I'm feeling quite calm, quite present. Very much like me!

Vince invites me to look around the room. "And what do you see on the faces of your colleagues?"

I laugh. "They look so concerned. I think they're going to cry."

The group laughs—relief I'm sure that I'm back to being me again—and just maybe, just maybe I have put this stage fright to rest. *Please, God!* I'm ready to continue reading my answer.

By the end of my first year of training, I decide to "fast track" the script-busting even more. I seek out a female therapist who is familiar with the TA model of therapy and enter into an intensive therapy experience. I now know that I'm stuck with a deep-seated belief that "I'm not okay, you're okay" and I want to move into the only healthy position, "I'm okay and you're okay, too." I want to face new situations with excitement. I want to let go of needing to please others, often at my own expense; to let go of thinking I have to be strong and never expose any vulnerability. And I want to be me—visible and onstage centre front *comfortably,* to free myself from my role of "the woman behind." And, like most people I have worked with, I want it all to be fixed *now.*

Will I change if I don't seek out a therapist, if I don't do this intensive training? Possibly, but most likely I will be constantly responding to these deeply imbedded conclusions and suffering the same bad feelings throughout my lifetime. And that's "crazy"; doing the same things over and over expecting a different result—well, that's just plain crazy!

The more I learn about me—and move forward with my own changes, the more effective I am in working with others. The more skilled I become in understanding and developing the "change tools" that this theoretical model has developed, the more quickly I can facilitate those who are asking me to help them in their journeys.

As I work with others, individually and especially in groups, I become aware of a new door opening, ever so slightly. I become increasingly aware of the potency of loving: a healing presence that I feel in the group and within myself that frequently manifests as "coincidences," as interventions that just happen. I don't quite know why and how they come about. Sometimes, for example, one of the group members will ask to work with a situation that occurred the past week, and as the story unfolds, I suggest we do a certain type of work with that material. It could be a track-back, five-chair work, redecision work, dream work, game analysis work, or a variety of the other tools available to assist the person to go deeper and touch new awarenesses. I initiate a process and suddenly the individual finds himself or herself touching a very deep early-life pain experience, a moment at which he or she made a decision that has resulted in ongoing pain. He or she then moves through the intense pain, frequently with deep sobs, into a new decision, a life-changing decision that opens him or her to new possibilities.

When we (me and the group member who has just completed his/ her work) pause and invite responses from the other group members who have witnessed this experience, the outpouring of love, the hugs, the healing words exchanged, touch my soul—and I feel I'm a participant in a much larger mystery that in my own mind I call God. Occasionally a group member will ask, "Why did you choose to go in that direction?" and I really don't know. Or, "How come you decided to do that work tonight, Al?" and he responds, "I really don't know." What is becoming so clear for me is the potency of loving: the healing power of "friends" bearing witness to another's pain and affirming the lovability and inherent value of that person.

My clinical practice offers me so many opportunities to celebrate—and I learn another powerful "psychological/spiritual" truth. How healing and freeing it is to "celebrate." When each person enters into a working relationship with me, we form a "contract to change," a written statement, signed by both of us, that identifies as clearly as possible how they want to be different from the way they are this moment. We articulate a goal (or two or three) and then specific measurements as to how we will know when they reach that goal. For example, they might say, "I will be joyful, happy and feel alive." And then the measurements they identify might be: "I will accept positive strokes and reject negative strokes; I will hear what others are needing and wanting or asking without redefining it as a negative stroke; I will fill up and use time in ways and activities that are fun and healthy—instead of addictive behaviours such as overeating and unhealthy sex."

Then, after a period of time, which could be anywhere from one to three years, when they have accomplished what they wanted to accomplish, we plan a process of termination—a way to celebrate and bring the therapy process to an end. When someone has worked in one of the groups, this process involves several weeks. This gives the individual and the group time to adjust to the change and what it means to the individual and to those continuing in group. The person then goes through their contract in detail and shares how they have changed. And the group members affirm the changes they have observed and tell anecdotes regarding specific work experiences that the person did. And they give buckets of positive strokes, including how important that person has been in their own healing process. These are the times that for me are very personally rewarding and for others, sometimes their first experience of letting go, of saying good-bye or putting closure to a relationship, in a healthy way.

On the final evening, that person gets to "celebrate" in whatever way is most meaningful. Usually that involves having coffee/wine and cheese after group in my living room, or adjourning to the favourite after-group hangout (the Ramada Hotel restaurant up the street). And those of us who are continuing on and preparing to welcome a new member to the group, usually the following week, get to share both the sadness and the joy of "change."

As I settle into this new office setting and then, two years later, in June 1986, into my new home, my energy is freed up and I take more risks in sharing my knowledge and experience with others. I accept an invitation to conduct a workshop for the Ontario Association of Marriage and Family Therapists, of which I'm a member. I'm asked to repeat this workshop entitled "The Business of Private Practice" on a few occasions and again for the Ontario Association for Professional Social Workers. The changing economy has made the field of private practice much more appealing for social workers and other helping professions. And a new door, an opening into an expanded professional world, opens for me.

I now have the courage (and financial resources) to move further into that world by attending an international conference sponsored by the International Transactional Analysis Association (ITAA) in Orlando, Florida, the first of many powerful learning experiences.

Do I go in fear and trepidation, with just a little stage fright? Well yes, a little, but this time I'm aware of a sense of excitement. Now the "authentic little kid" in me is kicking in and my "scared kid" isn't nearly as powerful as she has been in the past—that's change. I'm sitting alone in the hotel dining room the first morning when the workshops begin feeling giddy and powerful, congratulating myself for taking new risks.

At this conference I meet Lucy Freedman, a woman with a presence that radiates confidence, competence and caring, and another door is opening up. Lucy invites me to become actively involved in ITAA through participation in a task group known as the transition team. The group, consisting of a variety of folks from different countries in the world, plus various board members, is exploring new directions for the growth of the international association. I accept and commit to attending the next preconference meeting, which is scheduled for Chicago the year that Lucy becomes the president of ITAA.

Not only am I moving out into the world but I now bring the world into my environment. Lucy agrees to come to Mississauga and lead a two-day workshop for me, which enables me to provide a new experience for clients of my practice.

There is still one door that challenges me—do I open it wide? Do I close it? Or do I just keep it ever so gently open slightly: my relationship with my sweet Hayward—who is, indeed, married.

I do continue to see Hayward, less frequently than before his wife returned, but the frequency is irrelevant. After three years of questions—Do you love her? Are you happy? Are you getting what you want?—and getting vague answers, I'm not uncomfortable; I have no complaints. I do get cultural understanding and there is social approval: we live our own lives; we coexist—I stop asking. The answers really are expressed through hours of passionate lovemaking, a deep connectedness that only comes with years of familiarity and physical communication, I know.

To continue this relationship means breaking cultural/social script messages. Do I follow my heart? Can I do so and maintain my own integrity, my own value of being a compassionate, caring person who does not deliberately hurt anyone? To do so means to accept definite limits on what I can ask for and expect from Hayward and even what

I can freely give to him. Am I willing to live responsibly within these limits? We have very few public experiences now: an occasional evening out, birthday parties, office Christmas parties—just with intimate friends and associates. The answer—yes, for now. I don't know about tomorrow.

SCRIPT-BUSTING ... WITH TEARS AND CELEBRATIONS

Are you becoming aware of early life decisions (those decisions you made and feel you have lived with ever since you can remember) that have been blocking you from moving forward in life?

If so, are you beginning to connect the dots? Are you recognizing that the old decisions, beliefs, thoughts, feelings aren't appropriate today? Are you consciously attempting to change those thoughts, decisions, beliefs?

Are you getting support from an outside professional, mentor, friend, or are you going it alone?

There are several books available that may assist you in your change process, and I will identify just a few of them in the resource list that follows. Frequently librarians or bookstore personnel can direct you to self-help books that can assist you with the changes you want to make.

And remember to celebrate every little success you experience: every time you say "no" instead of saying an automatic "yes"; every time you resist that urge to smoke, to drink, to gamble, to eat that extra serving of potatoes; every time you risk doing something that is scary for you.

AM I THERE YET?

When I move into my new home on Bismark Crescent, June 29, 1986, I feel like I've "arrived." Am I *there* yet? Not sure, but I know that I am *here now* and sense that I am "at home" and free to let my spirit expand into the universe; let the me that emerged ever so gently into the world forty-eight years ago manifest the possibilities that are opening for me.

Niola Del Maestro, my tall, blond receptionist/bookkeeper, works with me now since Penny Moore, my long-time receptionist and friend, was forced to retire for health reasons a year ago. Niola's flashy yellow Nissan 380ZX sports car adds brilliance to my driveway—a sharp contrast with my snazzy little red Nissan 280SX sports car, which frequently takes up space on the same driveway. Niola takes up space in the kitchen, which has become the business centre, the "chatting and entertainment while waiting for the therapist centre" and the "help yourself to coffee" place.

The sexy red sports car houses my disassembled candy-apple-red scooter, which now serves to transport me from car to shopping mall, to the theatre, to the Toronto Blue Jays baseball games at the O'Keefe Centre in Toronto and anywhere else I choose to go. I discovered that I was unable to walk with my canes across the underground parking area at my Mill Street condo. I purchased a little scooter to make that long trek. The inconvenience of having to take the scooter apart and load it in the hatchback proved to be the lesser of two stressors—and an awesome convenience for many other reasons.

Shortly after settling into my Bismark home/office I add a student associate, Irma Franks, to assist me in offering service to the occasional person who is unable to afford fees but has heard about us and wants to work with us. Irma, a beautiful, brilliant, young woman who was diagnosed with MS a year earlier, worked with me to resolve her own childhood traumas and is now midway through her second year of training with Vince Gilpin, the guru. She is now ready for supervised experiences. When I suggested to Irma that she enter the TA (transactional analysis) training program, the intent was for her to have an opportunity to reorient herself, assess her strengths and limitations now that she is living with an active disease process that claims space in her body and determine how and where to move back into the world. It didn't occur to me that this gentle soul was a gifted healer. This soon became apparent and within the next several years, Irma becomes a full-fledged associate attracting her own clients, which greatly enhances my business and my personal sense of well-being.

Ron Abbott, a young elementary schoolteacher, also in training with Vince, becomes a second student associate and for a short period joins us to work with one or two selected people. The two of them decide to share accommodations in a century-old home that backs onto a ravine, just inside the Etobicoke boundary.

I'm up and thriving: supervising students, carrying a heavy load of individual clients, conducting two ongoing weekly therapy groups, still involved with Marcus Garvey Homes, still struggling with the SAGE KITS business and selling my CALM kits, now attending CATA Institutes and an ITAA conference. I'm writing a satirical column for the CATA-LOG (the newsletter for the Canadian Association for Transactional Analysis) and having the time of my life—amazing how the creative energy flows when I'm allowed to freely follow my passion. I'm happy! And a new opportunity arises.

My CATA board experiences provide constant challenges to exercise my script-busting resolve. I soon learn that board members are required to facilitate workshops for the community that hosts the institute and social events. Now I will have to *perform* in front of my colleagues. Gadzooks! Can I do this without being overwhelmed by the old insecurities—that is, the insecurities I would like to believe are old? I'm excited about a new piece of theory I've developed that, I decide, I will offer at the Alberta Winter Institute, in the form of a three-hour workshop entitled "The Liberated Parent." I describe this workshop as follows: The ability to nurture ourselves, give ourselves permission to be, to love, to risk, to experience and to protect ourselves as we move onward through life is essential if our journey is to be rewarding. How do we develop this ability if our parent role models were limited? Muriel James (my personal favourite TA therapist/ teacher/writer/role model) talks about "Self-Reparenting," Laura Boyd (another favourite, highly skilled TA therapist/teacher/writer) talks about "Restructuring the Parent Ego State," and I will introduce the participants to a model I call "Liberating the Nurturing Parent by working with Child Ego States."

I tested this out by presenting it to my training group in an earlier barn experience (one of Vince's five-day residential experiences) and received lots of applause and encouragement, but now I'm taking the show on the road. Do I suffer stage fright? Okay, I do have the old "flight of the butterflies" in the stomach from the night before until five minutes into the presentation, and then my excitement takes over. Once I have a volunteer person to demonstrate my new theory, who is actually putting his emotional life in my hands, I'm 100 percent present and with him throughout the process. He is thrilled with the outcome. The others at the workshop are enthusiastic in their responses; and me, I'm relieved and then soar with the angels— hallelujah, I'm busting on!

Not quite so hallelujah when I hit San Diego for a preconference transition team meeting and the ITAA annual conference. The conference theme is women's heroism and I'm excited about this, quiet and gentle feminist that I am. The first workshop that I attend is facilitated by two lovely women, both of whom are new to me. The intent of the workshop is to help us acknowledge and emotionally touch the heroism of our own ancestors. We are invited to close our eyes and go back in time through our mothers, our grandmothers and our great-grandmothers. After a few minutes we are invited to open our eyes and introduce ourselves by our great-grandmothers' names and briefly tell our stories.

As we begin to speak, the room becomes charged with an awesome, respectful, transformative energy—"I am so-and-so, a Romanian princess," "I am so-and-so, a slave worker, and I can outwork any man here," "I am so-and-so ..." I feel the tears welling deep in my belly and moving up to my throat, threatening to overwhelm me and render me speechless. I begin to tremble. When it is my turn, I say, "I am Pauline. I am a German immigrant. I work hard and I never complain." I manage to hold the tears a few more moments as the next woman begins to speak. And then the tears start to roll quietly down my cheeks. As the remaining four or five women speak, the tension within accelerates and I'm close to erupting into sobs. I make it through the remaining fifteen minutes, I don't know how. And as the facilitators close the experience, I burst into sobs!

Two Canadian women whom I know from my CATA experiences, also participants in this workshop, come to nurture and support me. I'm totally unable to talk. One of the facilitators approaches and asks if there is anything she can do. I shake my head no. She asks if I would be willing to approach her at some point throughout the remainder of the conference and share with her what is happening; I nod yes. My two Canadian associates accompany me from the room.

What I dearly want to do is to go back to my hotel room and withdraw. I'm feeling very vulnerable, overwhelmed with the "aha" experience and need to regroup, get my "be strong" defenses up and running. What I do takes a lot more courage. I acknowledge to the caring friends that I will proceed to the "process group" that is scheduled to begin in fifteen minutes. All the international conferences have small groups available on a daily basis for participants to share their experiences and learnings and to get support if needed. These groups are facilitated by some of the world's top TA therapists. John McNeil, a minister and certified clinical transactional analyst and trainer, is leading this group.

One of the women helps me (I'm still sobbing and unable to speak) disassemble my scooter. Various group participants arrive and agree to carry pieces of scooter up the stairs to the second-story conference room. I'm still sobbing. Very quickly the room fills with a dozen people, some of the top TA people around the world, another Canadian woman, a past-president of CATA who has worked with *the* Eric Berne, founder of the TA model, and another of Eric Berne's protégés, along with a psychologist from South Africa who epitomizes for me true woman's heroism. I'm still sobbing.

John enters the room. Dead silence except for my sobs. It's abundantly clear who will be "working" with the facilitator this session. I timidly put up my hand, indicating that I would like to take the floor—so to speak. John invites me—sitting in my reassembled scooter—to take my time and share what is happening.

I gradually gulp out that in the previous workshop I had an "aha" that is causing me such pain. Eventually I am able to share that I'm a duplicate of my grandmother. I don't ever complain—and I really need to. I tell the story of how vulnerable I am and feel, getting off the airplane in a foreign country, knowing no one, having to depend on total strangers to bring me my scooter, assemble it and help me get to a cab to bring me to the hotel. I then have to reassemble the scooter, go and register and be directed to my room, again on the second level. I take the scooter apart, get assistance to get up the stairs, to the dining room—on the main floor—the assigned transition team meeting room, in an adjacent building, again on the second floor—and so on. Every time I must ask for assistance to get my scooter up and down while I tentatively negotiate the stairs with my two canes. At the last meeting prior to the opening ceremonies, which are to take place later in the evening, one of the transition team members asks if it is really necessary for me to take the scooter apart, suggesting that I could just leave it sitting at the bottom of the stairs. I am hurt and angry. The scooter has no locking device. Several times at airports when I left my scooter unattended while I used the bathroom facilities, I found it standing in a different place. On one occasion I discovered a forty- to forty-five-year-old man riding it. All I can mumble is, "Do you leave your legs behind when you go up to the second level?"

As I'm telling my story, I'm acutely aware of the silence in the room. My sobs and my choppy words echo back at me. My sobs are dissipating and I'm just crying now.

"Put your grandmother out in the chair," John says, indicating an empty chair close to me. "What would you like to say to her?"

"I need to complain, Gramma. This is too hard."

"Are you a duplicate of Gramma?"

"No."

"Well, tell her."

"I am not you, Gramma. I need to complain."

"Tell her again."

"I am not you, Gramma. I need to complain." The truth of this is landing in my soul as smoothly as a space shuttle returning to planet earth. I'm feeling much calmer now. The tears are subsiding.

"So, how do you plan to complain?"

"Well, I could write a letter to the editor of *The Script* (the ITAA newsletter) explaining my experience and requesting that conference sites be fully accessible."

"Yes, and that every workshop room be accessible?"

"Yes."

"Anything else?"

"Yes, I could approach the president of the board before the conference ends and make this request. Yes, I'll do both."

I'm calm now and venture a quick glance around the room, wishing someone else would venture out onstage front and give me some relief. Instead, gradually all but the person beside me quietly get up and come over and hug me, some commenting, "I'm so sorry." "Thank you for sharing. I really had no idea." One woman says that she is the conference site person and she will guarantee me that this will never happen again. She will raise this herself with the board at their meeting. The gentleman beside me says, "Thank you for sharing this side of you. I've seen you at other conferences and you always seem so strong," to which I respond, "Yes, I am that, too."

The comment that touches me the deepest comes from the white South African psychologist who, I believe, puts her life on the line almost daily. "Dale, you are a true hero."

Another script-busting experience—the potency of vulnerability. I'm aware that I touched the lives of the participants in this group in a way that just words written in a book cannot. I'm humbled.

And no, I'm not there yet. Not all experiences at script-busting result in permanent, immediate change, but I'm on my way to just being and not having to mask my vulnerability.

I have two experiences that highlight the gains that I've made before I'm confronted with yet another challenge. Lucy Freedman arrives in Mississauga to do a two-day workshop entitled Women and Power for fifteen of my women clients. This workshop focuses on enabling women to understand, identify and own their own personal power, both in the workplace and in the home. Through her skilled exercises I affirm how far I've progressed and moved out of script.

I affirm this again by hosting the 1987 CATA Winter Institute and ITAA board meeting here in Mississauga. With the help of a committee of skilled people, including my associates, I'm able to offer clients in my practice and others from across the province and Canada at large a wonderful opportunity to experience some of the best TA therapists I'm privileged to know. And I do this with very little anxiety.

Shortly thereafter I attend the ITAA conference in Chicago and experience a Jean Houston workshop. This brilliant spiritual leader encourages us to touch that God-self within us; to touch a power that I have only begun to sense. And in this workshop I encounter Muriel James, the woman who has been for me my personal guru (through her writings). I'm soaring with an expanded sense of self.

Sure enough, shortly thereafter I'm given another opportunity to be onstage centre front, with my family as "audience," the very family that helped me work out the details of the script!

Early in the new year, I get a phone call from my dear niece, Deanna.

"Hi, Auntie Dale" … and after our usual warm greetings … "I have a favour to ask. Gary and I are getting married in June and we'd like you to be the mistress of ceremonies at the reception." Dead silence! "I'll understand if you say no, but I really want you to do it, if you're willing. Mom and Dad thought I should ask Uncle Bayne, but you are my first choice."

I'm still struck dumb … "Uh, Deanna … uh, you know I have a little stage-fright thing. I don't know if I could really do a great job for you. You sure you don't want to ask Bayne?"

"I'm sure, and Gary wants you too."

"Will you give me twenty-four hours to think it over? I'd really like to do this for you. I just need a little time to get used to the idea. How about I'll call you tomorrow?"

What a very brave thing this young, attractive woman is doing! Brother Ken is every bit as chauvinistic and programmed as Father. I've watched her script develop from the time Deanna was quite young. In this family, Drew, the firstborn son, is the "onstage centre front" personality. And now Deanna is asking me to take over Bayne's role in the family dynamic?

I agree. How could I not? If Deanna can script-bust at her young age, I just can't let her down. June 18, 1988, at the mature age of fifty, sitting up at the table closest to the head table, with my entire family beside me, Father and Mom to my right, I pick up the mike and take charge of the next hour and a half. And I'm having fun! Deanna is a beautiful bride; the wedding party, including the men, looks gorgeous; and I, sitting in my reliable scooter, am glowing. If you can "be," move out of role/script in the context of the family of origin—well then, you've pretty well made it to the other side—to authenticity.

It isn't over—this business of moving congruently with the heart and the intuitive wisdom of the soul.

Another phone call: "Dale, I can't move ... I can't move!"

Oh my God. "Irma, what's wrong?"

"I woke up this morning and tried to get out of bed and I'm unable to move my legs. I can't use my arms either."

"I'll be right over."

A phone call to her doctor, a phone call to Ron, followed shortly thereafter with a phone call for an ambulance, and Irma is whisked away to Toronto Western Hospital.

How can this be? Just last evening Irma, Ron and I had a very lovely Thanksgiving dinner and I was struck by how fond I am of this awe-inspiring young woman. The experience felt like "family" and I was aware of how blessed I am to have her in my life and in my private practice. This past March, to celebrate my fiftieth birthday, Irma wanted to give me a special birthday experience. One of her childhood fantasies was to prepare a big celebration for her mother, and since this was not to be, she asked if she could do this for me.

And special it was! Irma sent out handwritten invitations to a very few select friends to attend a dinner celebration at the Top of Toronto Revolving Restaurant in the C.N. Tower on Front Street. On a blisteringly stormy winter night, Pauline and I (Pauline flew in from Winnipeg to be with me that evening) braved the elements and joined the guests at a table specially decorated for me, with beautiful bouquets of white flowers arranged "just so," candles that are "just so," and a special birthday cake that is very "just so." Hayward joined us to make the evening entirely magical—so Irma. And now here she is—totally incapacitated.

Two mornings later I arrive at the hospital around ten in the morning. I inquire at the reception desk where Irma is located only to be informed that she is not allowed visitors. "Not even her mother?" I say in all innocence—*my God, is she that ill?*

The receptionist, assuming that I am "mother," phones up to the floor and is told that I may visit. I arrive to witness the doctor finishing his examination.

"Will you step outside so that we might have a word together?"

Oh boy, he is assuming that I *am* "mother."

"I want you to know that Irma is very ill. We can't determine yet what the problem is, but we're treating her with powerful steroids. We think she has a kidney infection that could be … very serious. We think that triggered the MS exacerbation. She will be here for a period of time. We won't know about the kidney situation for several more days. We thought you ought to know."

Oh my God, oh my God, please don't let her die. I enter the room after a brief cry and Irma is awake. We talk gently. We'll have lots of time to talk "reality" when we know what "reality" is. And we do—three long months of hospitalization!

While Irma is hospitalized, I bring a new associate on board. Laura McKenzie, just a few years younger than Irma, is a graduate from a university in Florida, with an MScEd degree and a major in marriage and family therapy. I have accepted associates from a broad background of education and have discovered that what works best for me is not the background education but familiarity with the transactional analysis model of psychotherapy. I'm reluctant to take on someone so young and unfamiliar with TA, but I'm persuaded by Irma to give the young woman a chance. Laura accepts a trial experience and indicates a willingness to join Vince Gilpin's training program. And, as it turns out, with supervision and a clearly defined contract, Laura adds new life and energy to the practice.

Irma's hospitalization comes to an end when Irma, after confronting the entire staff with the systemic negativity that breeds dependency and undermines emotional as well as physical healing, discharges herself—another powerful example of the potency of vulnerability and God-inspired courage. She's to come home with a wheelchair that she can negotiate with her arms until the deluxe motorized model is delivered—home to an awkwardly structured, steep-staircased century-old two-story house. And this is to occur when I'm in Fredericton, New Brunswick, at another CATA board meeting and conference. Here I'm planning to deliver a comprehensive paper to the CATA board and facilitate a discussion. I also plan to offer my Liberated Parent workshop a second time. I find it very stressful and difficult to concentrate, knowing what will be happening for Irma in my absence. Bits and pieces of our history together intrude throughout the weekend.

I had no idea four years ago when she walked into my office that this beautiful, young, gentle, delicate-looking, thirty-year-old woman would permanently alter the carefully sculpted structure of my existence.

"I'm here to make changes in my life," Irma said in response to my opening question. And change she did. During the next fourteen months she courageously opened her Pandora's box of childhood traumas and embarked on her healing journey.

And then the phone call, the MS exacerbation—how could this battered young woman manage another trauma, one that I knew from my own experience could shatter an individual's sense of self like few other life crises? And now, just as she is moving back into the world, another catastrophic event?

The interaction at the board level is stressful and for me unpleasant. I'm hurt by some insensitive remarks and I'm feeling unsafe. When I leave the experience the next afternoon, I discover that I will be on the same plane with one of the folks who has been "insensitive." I really want some space just to let down and free myself from the woundedness I'm experiencing, but for two and a half hours I make small talk, resorting to familiar defenses while my mind is really focused on what I may experience when I see Irma. Ron is to meet me at the airport and take me directly over to the house. Okay, so I'm not wholly *there yet.*

When the plane lands Ron is waiting. We end up waiting together for another hour for my luggage to arrive on the next plane. Not surprising—when one thing upsets my equilibrium, the universe is willing to play along with me. I indicate to Ron that I don't want to talk just yet and he complies, stating that Irma has a surprise for me when we reach their residence.

I burst into tears the minute Ron packs me and my scooter into the car. How good to be in a safe place again. I attempt to get control of my tears before I enter the house. I don't want to add to Irma's distress. I enter the residence with trepidation. What will I confront?

And Irma is *descending the steep stairs* just supporting herself on the handrails! Another outpouring of tears; I'm witnessing a miracle!

By Christmas, Dale Perrin and Associates is thriving. Irma, Laura, Niola and I, plus a third student and another associate who works on a "need for special assistance" basis, have crystallized into a productive and harmonious team.

The year provides yet another "aha" experience—a special pre-Christmas dinner party in Irma's home, with me and Hayward, this elusive lover of twenty years that she's known about for a few years now and only met at my fiftieth birthday party.

"You will come, won't you? And you will invite Hayward to stay overnight, won't you?"

I admit to feeling a bit nervous, like a blushing young woman taking her first lover home to meet Mom; but I say, "Yes, I will, I will."

"I promise I won't make a scene, honestly," Irma says, only slightly masking her amusement. "He is going to stay overnight with us, isn't he? I do want an opportunity to get to know him after the party."

"I expect so, sweetie. We'll see."

The home is beautifully decorated with Christmas lights everywhere, a perfectly coordinated pink Christmas tree, matching pink wrapped gifts displayed underneath, the big oak dining-room table perfectly set for four, with exquisite dinnerware and crystal goblets. The fireplace is lit, the glow of the flames perfectly highlighting the flower arrangements on the mantle. As the evening progresses I observe how comfortable Hayward is with Irma. The meal is perfect, the conversation very pleasant, and I experience a soft pink/purple serenity, like the day gently yielding to the evening stillness. An "aha"—this is *family*.

As Irma and Ron tidy up, I whisper to Hayward that Irma wants us to stay over in the guest bedroom.

"I can't go to bed with you here," Hayward says. "She's like a daughter."

"For heaven's sake, Hayward, she's an adult woman. I want you to stay with me. You can't just leave. I need you. I want you. She wants us to experience her new home, to bless the house with our unique loving energy. Really she does."

"But what kind of role modeling would we be doing for her?"

"My God, I can't believe you. She's known about us for years. If you leave I swear I'll never speak to you again!"

He does, around three in the morning; just slips out without my knowing it, my sweet, ever-so-concerned Hayward, still my shaman healer.

March 1998 school break; Ron and Irma leave for Mexico.

I don't know when the idea began to germinate in my conscious mind. Actually, it never really did. Like Athena, the idea pops out of my head fully grown, surprising me as much as Irma.

"Welcome back, Irma," I say, reaching out to give her a big hug. "I can't believe how much I missed you. Did you and Ron have a good time in Mexico?"

"We had a wonderful time, Dale—lots of sun, excellent food, beautiful people. And you were on my mind, too. We talked a lot about you and how important you are to both of us."

When Ron leaves the room I look at Irma, feel an overwhelming bursting in my heart and say, "I have a proposition for you to consider. How would you like to be my adopted daughter?"

There it is!

Irma immediately moves to the chesterfield where I'm curled up, sits facing me, tears streaming down her cheeks, unable to speak.

"Does that mean yes?" I hardly notice that I'm holding my breath.

"Yes, my God, yes! Do you really mean I can be your daughter officially? You've been my 'mom' in my heart for years now. You really want to adopt an adult daughter?"

"Not any daughter, sweetie; you!"

With the help of a lovely lawyer, Jill McLeod, we have a court date: ten o'clock on a warm, sunny July 7 morning. The judge's chambers—not at all intimidating, just a rather large room with His Honour's desk up front and a table with a few chairs for the petitioners and their representatives. Jill's expected baby decides to be born prior to July 7, so we have a young woman associate with us. In less than an hour, Irma *Perrin* and I leave the chambers for a special dinner at Oliver's in Oakville, a lovely restaurant that becomes our sacred place for special celebrations.

Announcements and an invitation to celebrate our new mother-daughter relationship at a summer garden party to be held Saturday, July 15, at 18 Riverdale Drive, Etobicoke, Ontario, are sent to very special friends. Under a huge pink tent, with beautiful flowers and exquisite decorations, with a catered meal befitting the splendour of the occasion, with a few speeches and blessings from a minister friend, we begin to live the miracle of "birth." Like the biblical heroines Sarah and Elizabeth, God has gifted me with a daughter at the mature age of fifty-one. Unlike Sarah and Elizabeth, my "child" is thirty-five.

My extended family gathers together at Irma's home just before Christmas to have a private family celebration dinner. Irma is graciously received and welcomed.

Am I there yet? Am I out of script? Yes, I am living my truth, living from my authentic self—not perfectly, but surely most of the time.

AM I THERE YET?

Do you recognize personality traits, thoughts, feelings, or behaviours that are just like your mother's, father's, or grandparent(s)'s? If so, are these helpful or hurtful? If hurtful, are you willing to "let go" and behave from your authentic self?

Have you identified any thoughts, feelings or behaviours that you have begun to change since you started reading this book?

Are you doing or planning anything to celebrate how much you've grown over the past few years? If not, will you do so now?

A TIME TO WEEP AND A TIME TO LAUGH; A TIME TO MOURN AND A TIME TO DANCE

And now what? With a sad heart, I give up my investment in the Marcus Garvey Homes business and put my SAGE KITS business to rest. After a kickoff, an exciting weekend experience with Lucy Freedman, CTM, ITAA (that powerhouse of a woman from California), entitled "Women's Stories: Women in the Workplace" in early February 1990, it's time to concentrate on achieving what I once assumed to be a totally unachievable goal—certification as a clinical transactional analyst. I have special permission to write my clinical exams right here in Mississauga. This three-hour exam will be proctored by Judith Ryan, in her home. Judith is a dear friend and regular member of the ITAA (International Transactional Analysis Association) as well as a fellow CATA (Canadian Association for Transactional Analysis) board member. Judith and I traveled to several conferences together and share a passion for this model of therapy. She appreciates the effort, the intensity and commitment I have to succeed in this endeavour.

"Are you ready?"

"I am," I say, the microphone in my now sweaty hand, three tapes stacked beside me ready for action. Because of my MS and arthritic fingers, I have special permission to tape my answers and have them transcribed immediately for submission to the board of certification. I just finish talking when Judith arrives to let me know that the three hours are up. That's it! Off I go to another dear friend, Dawn Anne Chisholm, who agreed to transcribe.

The word comes several weeks later. I have successfully completed part one of the examination process and I'm now eligible to sit oral exams in a year, pending a review of the other requirements. And now I'm giggling—relief that I've succeeded and just a bit of anticipatory anxiety regarding appearing before a panel of four examiners in a wee short year.

The drive to St. Louis, Missouri, in early November 1990, is surreal. The trees are dressed in their finest reds, rusts, yellows and greens. They sway elegantly to the mysterious rhythms of nature's wind instruments. Not a cloud in a pure azure sky. Just a very few cars. I'm alone, quiet, just absorbing the peace and serenity of the moment; there will be time enough to rev up my internal engine.

Vince Gilpin knocks on my door the evening before the scheduled exam. He worked with me intensely throughout this past year, reviewing my taped interviews, helping me with presentations (I have three taped sessions: one with a client I have been working with for three years, most of those years within the context of a group experience; a segment of one session with a second client to illustrate another type of intervention; and a segment of a group process), and reassures me that I know my stuff and am as ready to sit this exam as any student he has ever had. He gives me a reassuring hug and leaves me to be still and mobilize my inner resources.

It is *now* and I'm calm; well no, I'm actually excited. I do know my stuff. After an amazingly quick hour I'm invited to sit in with the panel of examiners and listen as they evaluate my performance according to set criteria. My excitement escalates as the discussion and marking process affirms that I do, indeed, know my stuff! I sail out of the room, drifting on a magical carpet of accolades and affirmations and scooter up to my room in high speed to phone my office.

And then it hits me—a heavy, almost overwhelming, all-pervasive, thick, suffocating blanket of depression. I want to cry. I want to pack up and go home. I call Niola and speak to Irma, who is anxiously awaiting word.

"I did it. I aced it."

"Then what's wrong? You sound awful!"

"I don't know. I guess it's that response both Vince and Suzanne (his associate) warned me about—the flatness that often descends after a mountaintop achievement. I thought I would be dancing—I'm not. I want to come home and I have three more days to put in here at the conference."

"Well, hang in there, Mom. Perhaps in a day or so you'll feel like celebrating. At any rate, we'll celebrate when you get home. I'm proud of you. I knew you would do well."

The success settles in and rests comfortably in my soul as I continue on to new challenges. Once again, Mississauga is to host the ITAA spring board and committee meetings, which means that once again, I (and my associates) am privileged to offer the client group and other interested persons across Canada an opportunity to experience the brightest, most exciting and committed TA therapists and teacher/trainers from around the world. In addition to CATA and ITAA board meetings, preconference workshops, examinations of candidates for certification and a postconference workshop, the two-and–a-half-day conference, entitled "When Walls Crumble ... Rebirth," provides intensive workshops and experiences that offer opportunities for healing at different levels.

Our beautiful guru and friend Vince Gilpin sets the stage, the emotional/spiritual tone of the conference, in his keynote address Friday night. He says, "The abusive use of power constitutes oppression. Oppression is humiliating, demeaning, restrictive and leads to the demise of creativity. When our creativity is stultified, we experience a kind of death. There is a great deal of focus these days on the effects of oppression and abuse on the human spirit. Practitioners in the field are endeavouring to discover more and more creative ways of facilitating recovery from abuse. We believe that when the walls of oppression and abuse, be they political, social or familial, are removed, it gives rise to the rebirth of the spontaneous, creative potential in everyone and a resurgence of healthy lifestyles and prosperity in the community."

And I experience this profoundly at the "Saturday Night Live Celebration of Life." The lights are dimmed; the participants are joined hand-to-hand in a circle around the periphery of the room, each holding a candle. After a moving introduction, one participant's candle is lit from a candle held by Vince, and that participant proceeds to light the candle of the person beside him/her until the room is shimmering. Music begins and Irma appears, dressed in a black cat suit, and proceeds to perform a creative contemporary jazz dance—a celebration of life, a victory over the oppressiveness of MS. The tears flow silently down my cheeks. Vince, too, wipes tears from his eyes—and the three of us gather in the centre of the room to hug, to blow out the candles and to invite the participants to join us in dancing and playing.

I do "dance"—not quite like the others, but with two people holding me up by the hand. I do get to shake my butt and undulate to the music, both to the recorded music that fills the large hotel conference room and the spirit music that fills my soul.

I get to preside at the closing brunch on Sunday and speak to and thank the participants and our guests from ITAA—onstage centre front with my international peers. Another script-busting moment!

I move into 1992 with optimism, riding on successes and experiencing an inner peace and comfort. My clinical practice continues to offer me rich experiences and new opportunities. I decide to initiate a third "ongoing" group, a "survivors group" for women who have experienced incest and/or sexual abuse as children. I've never attempted to bring together women who are working through such deep trauma and have no idea just how successful this will be for the five women who agree, in fear and trepidation, to risk such vulnerability. *Please, God, may this be a healing experience!*

For the next three to five years this group, with only one or two changes in participants, provides the women and me with unbelievably rich healing experiences. I witness again the potency of the healing power of loving: the genuine, deeply felt empathy that wounded souls have for each other. I'm moved by the healing presence of a power far greater than the individual or collective interactions of the group members, or me. I'm asked to bear witness to indescribable pain, to listen empathically and nonjudgementally to what harm adults, acting out of their own woundedness, can do to vulnerable children. I'm asked to witness in court, to prepare and role-play woman-to-father confrontations, sister–to–brother confrontations.

And I, like the women in the group, grow immensely through these shared experiences.

I'm asked to bear witness to another suffering experience.

"I think I'm going to crack," Hayward says, choking on his words, scarcely holding in the tears swimming in his deeply sad brown eyes. "I made the wrong decision ten years ago."

"I know, Hayward, I know," I say as I move to put my arms around him.

What follows is an explosion of hurts and rage, a litany of wrongs, of invasions of boundaries and violations of agreements that Hayward has experienced over these past ten years of marital discord. I listen in shock. Hayward never shared any of these grievances with me— believing that to do so would somehow diminish him and do an injustice to his wife.

I listen in silence, tears streaming down my cheeks.

As the intensity subsides, Hayward, still teary, says, "A man my age should be settled, should be esteemed in his own home, should have acquired a lot of material benefits to enable him to retire in comfort. Unlike you, Dale, I have never fulfilled my career aspirations. I will never be the man I had hoped to be. I will never be able to retire to the country home, to be the 'gentleman farmer.' You know I always wanted to retire to a farm, to have horses, chickens, even pigs. I wanted to roam around the gardens, groom the horses and go off riding. I'll never have that now."

I'm overwhelmed with sadness. Hayward never shared his hopes, his dreams. We could have had this. We could have lived out our retirement years graciously, with dignity, with respect—the gentleman farmer and the therapist/writer wife.

The passion of the moment, the depth of sadness and despair, dissipates in lovemaking. When Hayward leaves my bed, I'm alone with the disquieting sadness of "what could have been." If only I could have moved out of script sooner; if only Hayward could have moved out of his script; if only …

In January '94 I face another of life's truths. To everything there is a season, and it is now "time to mourn." How hard it is to witness the parents I love so dearly moving so quickly to the end of their journeys, having completed what I believe they were meant to complete—healing their own wounded souls through the power of loving. Through nurturing and ongoing support, they witnessed their ever-expanding family of creation grow into responsible, loving, caring and contributing members of society, a dream they both shared.

On September 9, 1993, the three of us (Ken, Bayne and I) plan to help Mom and Father celebrate their sixtieth wedding anniversary, a goal long cherished and articulated by Father. Father has been hospitalized with an assortment of complaints for several weeks, leaving Mom in the home alone, with the support of homecare services, a situation that we knew had to be short-term. Her health has deteriorated over the years, leaving her stooped, unbalanced and very fragile. Father took over all the domestic responsibilities, something he cherished doing for his Weesa, something that had the unfortunate consequence of contributing to Mom's emotional deterioration and incapacitation.

We arrange with the hospital staff to provide us with a room large enough to bring in a prepared lunch and set up special decorations. Bayne and Ken have secured certificates of congratulations from Her Majesty Queen Elizabeth; the Right Honourable Kim Campbell, Prime Minister; Jean Chrétien, leader of the opposition; the Governor General R. J. Hnatyshyn; the Honourable Bob Rae, premier of Ontario; Walter McLean, MP for Waterloo; and Will Ferguson, MPP for Kitchener.

Jan and Bette arrange the decorations in the room and bring the special Perrin wine and the decorated sixtieth anniversary cake. And a celebration we have—Mom and Father both decked out in their finest track suits, proudly displaying white corsages, sitting humbly in wheelchairs, surrounded by the extended family. Each of us presents a different certificate and our own thoughts and feelings. After the lunch, the cake, the photos, Ken takes Father back to his room and Bayne and Bette leave with Mom. I dissolve into tears just as Ken returns, and he holds me. I'm so grateful to have the opportunity to witness this milestone in the lives of my parents. The tears—I don't quite know, perhaps my soul weeping with a "knowing" I'm not quite ready to face.

The next day we meet to make decisions, to face the realities of aging and infirm parents, and I agree to do the research into nursing home facilities. Mom is moved to a very homey country residence in Cambridge, Ontario, a community just a few miles from Kitchener, on Thanksgiving weekend. Father joins her a few short weeks after. On January 2 I receive *the* phone call.

"Dale, its Tracey from the nursing home. We're sending your mom to the Cambridge Hospital. We're just waiting now for the ambulance. She doesn't look well and is not responding. We think you may want to meet her there."

Gwen Snow, a friend who is visiting with me, volunteers to drive me to the hospital, a trip that takes forty minutes and seems like forever. I'm there and in my scooter as the ambulance pulls up.

"Mom, Mom, I'm here. I'm right here with you."

No response, but Mom looks at me. I'm not sure she recognizes me. I'm overwhelmed with sadness and some trepidation. *My God, is this it? Is she leaving us now?*

When Mom is examined by a physician, taken for X-rays and finally settled into a ward, I ask Gwen to call Bayne and Bette. Ken and Jan are in Ottawa to share the New Year's festivities. I don't want to leave Mom's side for a moment. Just moments later I'm paged and do need to leave Mom's bedside.

"How serious is it, Dale? Do we need to come right away?" Jan asks.

"I don't know, Jan. I've never been in this kind of situation before. I just know that I would want to be here now."

"Okay, *Sister*, we'll pack up and leave as quickly as we can. Just hang in there. We'll call just as soon as we're close." The tears come. "We'll face this together."

I know I'm in for a long wait. The trip from Ottawa is at least six hours, and it will be another hour if they first head for Woodstock. I alert Irma. Gwen will drive my van back, and Irma will come to get me when I have more information.

I reassure Mom that I will be right here with her. She acknowledges me with a slight nod but doesn't speak. I stroke her hair, hold her hand, oblivious of the fact that two other women are patients in this ward, though the bed immediately adjacent to Mom's bed is empty.

The sterility of the room, the hospital smells, the monotone droning of calls coming from the PA system are meaningless to me. I am totally present with Mom.

Thank God I resolved my issues with her so many years ago. We have so enjoyed our relationship. I have spent every Christmas of my life with Mom and Father (have I mentioned that I started calling Father "Father" as a special term of endearment from my days in Winnipeg?) and have taken them both on long holiday weekends to a variety of places since the days of Father's heart attack, and especially since his retirement. Father shared with me that he was frightened to take Mom away on his own lest something happen to him. He didn't feel Mom would cope well with the situation, a view I too shared.

The Perrin family has met together to celebrate many special occasions. We began celebrating fortieth birthdays when Bayne turned forty, fiftieth birthdays when he turned fifty, then celebrations for Ken, Bette, me, Jan, Shelley, Maggie, Gwyn when possible … and so on. We celebrated the parents' special birthdays and anniversaries, Elthea's seventy-fifth and eightieth birthdays, marriages of my brothers' children—any occasion we could find to be together. We have not come together to "celebrate" end-of-life experiences—until now.

Bayne, Bette, Ken and Jan arrive in the early evening hours. They greet Mom with a kiss and let her know they are present. Mom has not spoken since her arrival but is able to acknowledge each person with a look. After several quiet discussions, I'm persuaded to "go home" for the night. Irma comes with the van, and I leave Mom in Bette's care. The others go back to Woodstock.

I arrive in midmorning to relieve Bette and remain alone with Mom until the others are rested and ready to return. At three in the afternoon as I sit at Mom's bedside, holding her hand, gazing out the window, I sense a "presence." I look in the corner of the room—heatlike waves.

"Oh Mom, Gramma is here," I say, looking at her so vulnerable, fragile, beautiful old face.

"She's in a coma," the nurse informs me when I call out to her. Assured of her comfort, I go out to make a phone call to Woodstock.

I suggest they may want to come right away. I call Irma, who is attending to business in my absence and is "standing by."

The family arrives around 4:30 in the afternoon. Ken sets out to get Father from the nursing home and Bayne stays with me and with Mom.

"Oh Mom, can you just wait until Father gets here? I know he wants to say good-bye," I say, stroking her face.

And she does. Fifteen minutes after Father arrives, with Father holding her hand and telling her, "I love you, Weesa," and choking on tears, with Ken and Jan, Bayne and Bette holding each other, and Father and I, knee-to-knee in scooter and wheelchair, both touching her, blanketed and comforted with love, Mom takes her leave.

Jan takes her pulse, calls a nurse and gently closes her eyes. We adjourn to spend time in the chapel as Ken goes to Kitchener to get Elthea to join us for a quiet, reflective time. Irma and Laura, her friend and our associate, arrive together and provide gentle, caring support for me.

We all adjourn to the nursing home and are nurtured by the caring staff, who prepare a late snack for us. Ken and Bayne both hug me and tell me how grateful they are for the way in which I eased all of us through this experience. I wasn't aware that I did that, but this acknowledgement of my gifts is, for me, a healing moment. I feel a dramatic shifting in my relationship with Ken, and I'm able to express my gratitude for the energy he has spent in attending to the physical needs of both parents throughout this very stressful time.

The funeral takes place on a bitterly cold, stormy, winter morning. Shelley arrives from Halifax in time to help with the planning process and the visitations. She conducts the service and articulates our love and appreciations. I thank God for the life and gift of this mother—this beautiful, unique soul that I have come to love, to know and to value so much in my adult years.

How will Father cope without his Weesa? Not well! For the next two years, I spend every Friday and occasional days on the weekends visiting with Father, listening to his grief and loneliness, attempting to ease the brokenness of his heart and the aching in his soul. It isn't possible.

But there is an event to celebrate. My heart bursts with joy as I prepare to listen to Irma and Jon Fitzsimons exchange personally prepared marital vows. They have chosen to marry in the now beautifully decorated living room of her friend Laura's apartment, conveniently located in the same building where Irma lives. The grey/black/cream modern luxury apartment is transformed into a magical, mystical world, white tulle carefully draped from the ceiling. Beautiful bouquets of white and pink flowers fill the space with a gentle fragrance. Specially selected music complements the décor and adds to the aura that Irma and her friends have created.

Jon's two little girls tiptoe into the room, dressed in matching pink dresses with splashes of green and fancy white collars. Irma and Jon follow behind—Irma dressed in a cream pantsuit, with a high-neck lace cream blouse and a single strand of pearls and matching earrings. Jon, two inches taller than Irma, looks *Esquire*-magazine-like handsome with his short, neatly trimmed black hair and stylish black moustache, wearing a sharp black suit, white shirt and stylish rust-coloured tie. A handful of valued friends are with us. The ceremony begins and my heart and soul dance, though tears insist on spilling down my cheeks in spite of my best attempts to suppress them. I'm so happy that Irma has found a partner with whom she can share her journey. My "family of creation" is expanding.

In the midst of these emotional highs and lows, the economy is again slipping into a recession, only this time the major cutbacks occur with the executives and management people, as well as the independent small business folks—all of whom are suffering. As a result, I too am impacted. I now need to downsize my business and minimize my expenses. On the positive side, I do get to free up the time to be with Father. On the negative side—as it turns out, this too is a positive—I move to a condo apartment on Marine Drive, in Oakville, in October 1994. Oakville is a beautiful, culturally sophisticated, artistic community, ideally situated on the north shore of Lake Ontario. This condo, on the tenth floor of an attractive, well-maintained brownish-pink brick building, creatively landscaped, allows me a view of the expansive, mood-changing waters of Lake Ontario from every room.

With the downsizing, I no longer require the services of a full-time secretary and additional associates. I part company with Niola Del Maestro, who has now been with me for ten years, and Laura McKenzie, who has been with me since 1987: more sadness—necessary losses, with celebrations and appreciations.

In late April 1996, it is apparent that Father is preparing to leave us and be reunited with Mom. On the first day of May, as I sit with Father who is clearly very ill, though not in pain, I know that I cannot leave him. I determine that I will spend the night with him. Ken and Jan are on standby. Bayne and Bette are prepared to come, though choosing to delay as long as possible since Bayne is performing as a member of a barbershop quartet in a theatre production now performing in Ottawa. Irma and Father's favourite registered nursing assistant, Dorene Woodland, are equally determined to stay with me throughout this night.

The home is quiet. The country night blankets us with comforting darkness, a brilliant moon and very visible stars. No incessant announcements from the PA system. No nurses or staff intrude to do routine checks. Even the crickets and tree frogs have silenced. Dim lighting from the hallway casts a mystical aura into this large single room, reflecting a bluish glow over the east wall lined with shelves of Father's favourite books and treasured family photos.

We talk quietly, sharing our stories, our thoughts and feelings for this wise and loving soul looking so peaceful, his gaunt face now relaxed. Suddenly, at four in the morning, Father sits bolt upright, opens his eyes, though not seeing us, and just as suddenly lays back down again. Irma lights the candle she has brought with her and talks gently to him. I let the tears flow, though suppress the sounds, not wanting to intrude on this moment. Dorene, also with tears, sits quietly and reaches for my hand.

In the morning Father is still with us, though uncommunicative. Ken and Jan arrive and we congregate in the hallway, near a nursing station. Bayne and Bette, Mike and Vicki (Bayne and Bette's son and daughter-in-law) are called and arrive later in the afternoon. Shelley is called and is preparing to come from Halifax. It is Father's wish to remain in the home. We've known this for some time now. I'm finally persuaded to leave Father, as Bette will stay this night. She reassures me that she will call the minute she has news.

The call comes at 1:30 a.m. May 3. Once again, Shelley takes us through the funeral experience. She and Father talked together following Mom's funeral, and she is intimately aware of what Father wants. And once more, I weep for this beautiful soul whom I was privileged to call "Father."

Later this month, the family meets at Elthea's retirement home to celebrate her ninetieth birthday. Elthea and I planned this event to invite the community to come and celebrate the life of this remarkable woman. I prepared a two-volume album with photos, graphics and other mementos as a gift to Elthea, to acknowledge her many contributions to others in her community, her extended family, people and causes throughout the world. We entertain over two hundred and fifty well-wishers. Both Elthea and I are overwhelmed with the turnout, both admitting that we hadn't anticipated such a crowd.

How very fortunate that we have this awesome experience together. The following month Elthea falls, breaks her hip and is hospitalized for a prolonged period of time. Ken and I and a young woman whom Elthea has "emotionally adopted" (this seems to be a characteristic of this family) are the primary caretakers. As Elthea deteriorates, it becomes clear that she will no longer be able to return to the familiar retirement home and it is I who must break this news to her.

The hospital forces us to make another decision that breaks our hearts. We are asked to move Elthea into a long-term care facility, a move that is going to take her out of the Kitchener area where she has lived all ninety years of her life. Clearly this fragile, old woman is dying, and yet we must force her to relocate, by ambulance, to a small community near Woodstock where Ken and Jan live. She is distressed when I give her the news. We both cry.

The next day Bayne and Bette come to visit shortly after I arrive to go through the steps with Elthea. She has lapsed into a regressed state and, in a child voice, reenacts a trauma that must have occurred very early in her childhood. The dear woman has lived with a dark secret all these years and is only now able to free herself from its pain. As we bear witness to this most intimate experience, Bayne and I grasp its significance, and the mysteries that we have lived with all our lives are now clear: the reason for Mom's competitiveness with Elthea, her only sibling, now clear. I'm grateful to be privy to this healing experience. Both Bayne and I are able to affirm and reassure Elthea that she is and has been truly loved and is and always has been lovable.

Elthea is moved to the new residence the following day, early August 1996. I arrive early the next afternoon to discover that Elthea died, sitting in a granny chair, just an hour before. I sit with her for thirty minutes to express my love and appreciation for all of us, for the contributions she has made in the life of us Perrins. God bless! Gwyn, my other minister sister, in conjunction with a brethren elder from Elthea's church, facilitates the funeral. Elthea is put to rest near Gramma's gravesite. Later in the fall, Mom and Father, forever together in one urn, are buried at the foot of Gramma's grave. The immediate family gathers with Gwyn to bear witness and bring closure to the lives of these valued parents—a blessed farewell to the loving elders who helped nurture, direct and support me and my siblings in our own unique journeys, who helped colour and design and weave the fabric of my (our) tapestries.

In the midst of these intensely emotionally exhausting experiences, I'm confronted with another intense and exhausting drama. In June 1995, I receive notification from ITAA (the International Transactional Analysis Association), San Francisco, USA, of a complaint received from a former client, whom I will identify as "Madeleine, or Maddy," alleging that I'm directly and indirectly responsible for the breakup of her marriage. Along with this is a list of whatever professional ethics charges she can manipulate from the code of ethics given her by the association.

Before I'm able to clarify what this is all about and what procedures are in place for me to "defend" myself, I receive a package of material from the American Association for Marriage and Family Therapy (Washington DC) with the complete allegations from Maddy and the investigative procedures I must follow to respond to the charges. I learn that the allegations are based primarily on the "testimony" of another former client, "Dorothy," who has given Maddy a series of stories to fuel Maddy's hurting and raging soul. Dorothy, too, holds me responsible for the breakdown of her marriage, aiding and abetting her spouse to leave her. The two of them, formerly friends by the association of their partners, now form an alliance of convenience. Dorothy, by far the more manipulative and devious, also a suffering and deeply wounded soul, unable to accept responsibility for her own issues, defends her fragile sense of self by projecting blame onto the "others" in the world. I get to be "it" this time in her life.

The charges are deeply distressing to me and to Irma, my daughter and associate, who walks with me through this tirade of abuse, of assaults against my name and my practice. Dorothy initiates her own complaints, including the College of Certified Social Workers here in Toronto (which somehow Maddy had missed), later in '96.

With Irma's support and with legal counsel, I begin what turns out to be a five- to six-year process of writing briefs, five in all, to the three professional associations of which I'm a clinical member. I'm subjected to an intensive investigation by an ITAA Ethics Committee member, who comes to Toronto to personally interview the complainants and me, plus all the witnesses who have agreed to respond to specific allegations made by the two women. Shortly thereafter, I'm notified that the charges have been dismissed as "having no merit."

Not so with the other two associations. The College of Certified Social Workers continues to add new material collected from ongoing phone contacts with Dorothy, and I continue to write new briefs. My lawyer is told by the college lawyer that even though they are aware that Dorothy is "crazy," nonetheless, the college must protect the client. This position is made explicit when my lawyer and I appear before the complaints committee of the college. They announce that they intend to move the process on to the next level of authority.

After the interment ceremony in September 1996, my body and my soul are demanding peace. I have been using a walker now since my move to Marine Drive. The economy is beginning to improve, but my enthusiasm for expanding my practice isn't. I recognize, in fleeting moments, that I'm very rapidly approaching sixty, and perhaps it is time to think about retirement. While this idea is germinating in the dim recess of my subconscious mind, I receive a real estate flyer in my mailbox regarding new condos that are being constructed in Burlington, a smaller community bordering Oakville.

By a strange coincidence, this condo is just blocks away from where Irma and Jon reside. And the condo is much smaller and would allow me to be mortgage-free. Would this work? On a cold winter day, Jon and I decide to "just look" while Irma is resting. Before the day is over I call Edie Wilson, my super real estate genius. It's a go. I move at the end of February 1997 into a cozy, new two-bedroom condo, hopefully the last move I will make for a good many years. Instantly I feel at home.

And I have another of my "aha" half-asleep-half-awake awarenesses. It's that "three-times" message, that "How many times do I have to tell you?" message. It *is* time to retire! It *is* time to move into a whole new phase of life, a new and exciting unknown. My soul cries out "yes"; my body, "about time"; and my daughter, "That's perfect! Yes, yes."

I inform the college and the American Association for Marriage and Family Therapy that I will no longer continue this process. I'm informed that to do so will be to invite censure and notification of same in the professional newsletters. And it doesn't matter. I feel an immense sense of freedom and empowerment.

Irma and I plan a retirement party, a party to which we invite all of the people who have been significant throughout my professional life (those who are within traveling distance). Irma rents the space; the balloons, the flowers, the decorations—all are just perfect and festive, a typical Irma gala event. Pauline, my dear friend from Winnipeg, and Hayward, just recently home from a prolonged period of hospitalization, are present to share this moment with me. Wonderful speeches, lots of hugs. My parting gift to all who attend—a three-act play (without dialogue) describing the scenes and the players throughout my twenty-five-year professional career, all nicely rolled and ribboned. March 31, 1998, I dance my way into tomorrow.

A TIME TO WEEP AND A TIME TO LAUGH;
A TIME TO MOURN AND A TIME TO DANCE

Have you experienced the death of a significant parent, parent substitute, sibling, loved one? If so, did you have the experience of resolving early life issues prior to the death, either within yourself or together with the significant person?

If yes, were you able to "let go" in a way that brought closure and allowed you to keep the warm memories of your experiences in the treasure box in your heart? If not, would you be willing to "let go" and get relief from those unresolved issues through sharing with a friend or counsellor/psychotherapist?

Are you in a position now to celebrate the successes you have achieved? If yes, how do you celebrate? If no, what are you willing to do to "move out of script" and into owning successes? And when?

BOOK THREE

BOOK THREE

EPILOGUE: BEYOND SCRIPT

As I look back and scan the narrative of my life, written from the heart and mind, highlighting my most challenging moments of learning and growing, I recognize a pattern that certainly wasn't obvious to me during the *then and there* experiences. I recognize that offstage a "director" is and was choreographing the whole dance, the whole drama, setting up the opportunities and experiences I needed to mature (or not) into a self that lives *beyond script*.

I have various names for the director, but most frequently, I call that unnameable, indefinable force, that spirit or energy, or source of all coincidences, "love" or "God." And in the ten years post retirement, I have had many opportunities to focus my learning and growing in pursuit of greater connectedness with that source. I entered an online master of theological studies program offered through schools of divinity associated with universities in Alberta and Saskatchewan and briefly attended one particular course being offered at McMaster University in Hamilton, Ontario. I read and continue to read and learn from several spiritual teachers. My focus of attention has shifted from "me" and my immediate "others," my particular preference for theological grounding, to "creation" and "the well-being of all."

I participate in the life, the studies and activities, of a relatively "progressive" mainline church community where I, too, am nurtured and supported.

I am now seventy years old, confined to a motorized wheelchair, experiencing the sundry aches and pains of aging, dependent on the daily support of others to maintain my independence in the condo that has been home since 1997. I am, for the most part, serene and contented and thrilled to be. Just to be! What a blessing it is to greet each morning with a cat purring in my ear, knowing that for the most part, I can choose what I will do and experience this day.

I continue to see a few clients throughout these years. In spite of my many moves, people still manage to find me and ask if I will see a friend or relative and I'm pleased to do so. I've contributed volunteer time to several causes and organizations that have touched my heart, especially organizations that deal with the concerns of seniors. My involvement with my parents and long-term care facilities encouraged me to commit energy to doing something to address the issue of the scarcity of resources in this area, as well as the shortcomings in services being offered.

I have also been given the opportunity to mentor and support several women who are developing their own businesses or are engaged in leadership roles in various organizational systems.

I'm especially fortunate in being able to work with and support Irma in her growing consulting and professional development work with movers and shakers and their teams in the corporate world.

What lies ahead? More challenges! The world has opened for me ongoing opportunities for fun and developing and maintaining loving relationships, challenges for new learning and the mastery of new skills. The limitations of my physical body are overshadowed by the limitless opportunities offered for exploration and connection through cyberspace.

And I rest with the confidence that the director will continue to provide what I need until the last scene is complete and the curtain closes.

EPILOGUE: BEYOND SCRIPT

Thank you for reading and witnessing my life story, the weavings in and out as I created my unique tapestry. If in so doing you have come to understand and appreciate the beauty of your own life process, I'm delighted. If you have glimpsed some information that might help you untangle fragments of knots or glitches from unresolved issues that block you from being authentically and comfortably you today, I'm even more delighted.

Wherever you are in your journey today, I encourage you to keep your heart and your intention focused on authenticity, on being the best of who you are and recognizing the beauty and "OKness" of others. And may you arrive at your journey's end in peace and comfort.

ABOUT THE
AUTHOR

Dale Perrin, MSW, Certified Transactional Analyst

Courage, compassion and resiliency are the prerequisites for a pioneering soul who finds herself constantly bumping up against stereotypical roles and expectations. And to find such characteristics in a vulnerable, passionate woman who intended only to be helpful and facilitate positive change—well, surprising.

When Dale Perrin graduated with her MSW (Master of Social Work) degree in November 1963 from the School of Social Work, University of Toronto, she expected to work in a traditional family service agency. After three attempts at working in such settings, Perrin discovered that "systems" didn't appreciate independent and energetic souls who didn't want to be the "onstage centre front" administrative/political director but preferred to continue working quietly with individuals, couples, or family systems.

"I was pushed and shoved into success," says Perrin. "I didn't go willingly."

Private practice was virtually unknown to the profession of social workers in the early '70s. Only "losers" and those rejected from traditional practice for one reason or another attempted to "go it alone." But somehow Perrin thrived! "I felt liberated, exhilarated and oh yes, scared." And she never turned back. She credits a student who introduced her to transactional analysis by suggesting a book for pointing her on the path to success. The books, the workshops that followed and eventually formal training in transactional analysis and certification as a transactional analyst in 1991 enabled Perrin to constantly develop her skills as a psychotherapist. Her private practice mushroomed accordingly.

At age forty, Perrin was confronted with another challenge—multiple sclerosis. That didn't stop her from thriving—and opposition from neighbours and the bylaws of local and provincial governments also didn't deter her from her passion. "I just want to make a difference, to help men and women be the person(s) they were meant to be—healthy, contented, contributing members of society."

As her practice developed, Perrin provided consultation and mentoring to other professionals and students and achieved recognition on a national and international stage. She developed a do-it-yourself therapy kit called CALM (an acronym for Caring and Loving Myself), containing four cassette tapes and a workbook that encouraged women to change and grow emotionally in the comfort of their own homes.

Perrin retired from full-time clinical practice at the age of sixty, though she continued for several more years on a part-time basis. At the age of seventy-one, she moved from her condo into a long-term care residence where she presently resides. She continues her outreach to others through this autobiographical self-help book.

APPENDIX

BOOKS AND OTHER RESOURCES

James, Muriel, Dorothy Jongeward. *Born to Win: transactional analysis with Gestalt experiments.* Cambridge, Massachusetts: Addison-Wesley Pub., 1996, 1971.

James, Muriel. *Breaking Free: Self-Reparenting for a New Life.* Cambridge, Massachusetts: Addison-Wesley Pub., 1988.

James, Muriel. *It's Never Too Late to be Happy: Reparenting Yourself for Happiness.* Bantam Books 1974: Quill Drive Press, 2002.

Steiner, Claude. *Scripts People Live: Transactional Analysis of Life Scripts.* Grove Press Inc, New York, NY, 1974.

Stewart, Ian, and Vann Joines. *TA Today: A New Introduction to Transactional Analysis.* Chapel Hill, N.C: Lifespace Publishing, 1987.

These references are specific to transactional analysis. Most bookstores have a section devoted entirely to self-help books, which cover a wide range of issues that many of us encounter in our journeys. Check with store personnel or online Web sites for references that may help you confront specific issues.

For information about transactional analysis and/or for information about locating a certified transactional analyst/psychotherapist near you, contact: The International Transactional Association, 2186 Rheem Drive #B-1, Pleasanton, CA 94588, Phone: 1-925-600-8110.